Instruments of Land Policy

In dealing with scarce land, planners often need to interact with, and sometimes confront, property right-holders to address complex property rights situations. To reinforce their position in situations of rivalrous land uses, planners can strategically use and combine different policy instruments in addition to standard land use plans. Effectively steering spatial development requires a keen understanding of these instruments of land policy.

This book not only presents how such instruments function, it additionally examines how public authorities strategically manage the scarcity of land, either increasing or decreasing it, to promote a more sparing use of resources. It presents 13 instruments of land policy in specific national contexts and discusses them from the perspectives of other countries. Through the use of concrete examples, the book reveals how instruments of land policy are used strategically in different policy contexts.

Jean-David Gerber is Associate Professor at the University of Bern. He graduated from Swiss Federal Institute of Technology (ETHZ) with a degree in Environmental Sciences (2001) and holds a postgraduate degree in Urban Development, Resources Management and Governance (2004) from the University of Lausanne. Subsequently he attained his PhD in Public Administration (2005) at the Swiss Graduate School of Public Administration (IDHEAP). After a postdoctoral position at the University of California, Berkeley, he took a position at the University of Bern where he teaches urban and regional planning courses in the Institute of Geography. His long-term research interests focus on the interaction between property rights and public policies, and on the resulting regulation of natural resource uses.

Thomas Hartmann is Associate Professor at Wageningen University & Research, Environmental Sciences, Land Use Planning Group, and also at the Czech J. E. Purkyne University (UJEP) in Ústí nad Labem, Faculty of Social and Economic Studies. He is also visiting professor at the University of Vienna, Department of Geography and Regional Research. He holds an engineering degree in spatial planning and a policy science-oriented PhD from TU Dortmund University. He is involved in various academic activities relating to land policy, planning, and property rights. Thomas Hartmann is a founding member and vice-president of the International Academic Association of Planning, Law, and Property Rights (PLPR) and he organized a PLPR conference in 2010, and an AESOP congress in 2014. He is an expert for the Dutch cadastre on land readjustment, and he is involved in the OECD water governance initiative.

Andreas Hengstermann is a PhD student at the Institute of Geography, Research Unit Urban and Regional Planning, University of Bern. He is educated in spatial planning (TU Dortmund University) and local and rural development (Universidad de Huelva). In his PhD project, he compares the effectiveness of land use planning in Switzerland and the Netherlands by analyzing the cases of food discount stores. He has been a member of PLPR since 2010 and is part of the Local Organizing Committee of PLPR 2016 in Bern.

Urban Planning and Environment

Series Editors: Donald Miller and Nicole Gurran

For a full list of titles in this series, please visit www.routledge.com/Urban-Planning-and-Environment/book-series/UPE

Maintaining and enhancing living conditions in cities through a combination of physical planning and environmental management is a newly emerging focus of governments around the world. For example, local governments seek to insulate sensitive land uses such as residential areas from environmentally intrusive activities such as major transport facilities and manufacturing. Regional governments protect water quality and natural habitat by enforcing pollution controls and regulating the location of growth. Some national governments fund acquisition of strategically important sites, facilitate the renewal of brown fields, and even develop integrated environmental quality plans. The aim of this series is to share information on experiments and best practices of governments at several levels. These empirically based studies present and critically assess a variety of initiatives to improve environmental quality. Although institutional and cultural contexts vary, lessons from one commonly can provide useful ideas to other communities. Each of the contributions are independently peer reviewed, and are intended to be helpful to professional planners and environmental managers, elected officials, representatives of NGOs, and researchers seeking improved ways to resolve environmental problems in urban areas and to foster sustainable urban development.

Titles in the Series

Nordic Experiences of Sustainable Planning
Policy and Practice
Edited by Sigridur Kristjandottir

Governing for Resilience in Vulnerable Places
Edited by Elen-Maarja Trell, Britta Restemeyer, Melanie M. Bakema, Bettina van Hoven

Bicycle Urbanism
Reimagining Bicycle Friendly Cities
Edited by Rachel Berney

Instruments of Land Policy
Dealing with Scarcity of Land
Edited by Jean-David Gerber, Thomas Hartmann, Andreas Hengstermann

Instruments of Land Policy

Dealing with Scarcity of Land

Edited by
Jean-David Gerber,
Thomas Hartmann, and
Andreas Hengstermann

Routledge
Taylor & Francis Group
LONDON AND NEW YORK

First published 2018
by Routledge

4 Park Square, Milton Park, Abingdon, Oxon OX14 4RN
605 Third Avenue, New York, NY 10017

First issued in paperback 2022

Routledge is an imprint of the Taylor & Francis Group, an informa business

British Library Cataloguing-in-Publication Data
A catalogue record for this book is available from the British Library

Library of Congress Cataloging-in-Publication Data
Names: Gerber, Jean-David, author. | Hartmann, Thomas, 1979– author. | Hengstermann, Andreas, author.
Title: Instruments of land policy : dealing with scarcity of land / Jean-David Gerber, Thomas Hartmann, Andreas Hengstermann.
Description: 1 Edition. | New York : Routledge, 2018. | Series: Urban planning and environment | Includes bibliographical references and index.
Identifiers: LCCN 2017049033 | ISBN 9781138201514 (hardback) | ISBN 9781315511658 (ebook)
Subjects: LCSH: Land use, Urban. | City planning. | Right of property. | Land use—Law and legislation. | City planning and redevelopment law.
Classification: LCC HD1391 .G47 2018 | DDC 333.77—dc23
LC record available at https://lccn.loc.gov/2017049033

Typeset in Sabon
by Apex CoVantage, LLC

ISBN 13: 978-0-367-40413-0 (pbk)
ISBN 13: 978-1-138-20151-4 (hbk)
ISBN 13: 978-1-315-51165-8 (ebk)

DOI: 10.4324/9781315511658

Contents

Foreword

Land scarcity is a perennial challenge facing urban and regional planners anywhere. With that theme as its backbone, this book offers a fresh and much-needed perspective on one set of instruments that planners in many countries use to resolve competition among land uses – instruments grounded in property rights and land use regulations.

To an untrained observer, planning laws and development controls in every country seem to offer similar sets of instruments for achieving planning policies. In fact, however, what may seem as minor nuances can make or break a particular instrument's effectiveness. All too often, planning policies fail in the implementation arena. Paradoxically, although there is a shared quest for more effective instruments, cross-national exchange of knowledge is still inhibited by the localized character of land-related laws and policies.

This book is a welcome contribution towards dissolving the boundaries and promoting cross-national learning. The editors have compiled a set of chapters from authors of several countries, which discuss a variety of land policy instruments. The discursive format, enriched with commentaries on each chapter, illustrates that even in countries with similar sociocultural and physical characteristics, where the legal framework offers ostensibly similar instruments of land policy, the specific contexts of policies and politics lead to differing degrees of success or outcomes.

To me, this book grants a special type of satisfaction. The editors tell me that their awareness of the merits of cross-national analysis of land policy instruments evolved from their active participation in the International Academic Association on Planning, Law, and Property Rights. I initiated this association in 2007 with the mission to bring together planning researchers interested in law and legal scholars interested in planning, as represented by the contributing authors to this volume.

This volume is an appetizer to continue and expand the international exchange of knowledge on how planners and policymakers may design more effective land policy instruments and at the same time achieve more socially just, economically viable, and environmentally sustainable cities and regions.

Rachelle Alterman
Faculty of Architecture and Town Planning, Technion, Haifa, Israel

Preface

The distribution of land plays a fundamental role in how cities and landscapes are shaped and used. Property titles in land are among the best legally protected things a person can own. However, land is also a scarce resource. This puts land in a fraught relationship between public and private interests and makes the careful management of the resource more difficult. It is the task of spatial planners to walk this tightrope. To do so, planners have a variety of instruments at their disposal – however, they sometimes have a lot of discretion to select the ones that fit the best and sometimes none at all.

> *It's not the one building the flat,*
> *not the one owning the house,*
> *but the one who owns the land,*
> *who decides the development of our cities.*
> (Opening of Bernoulli's book *Towns and the Land* (1946). Own translation)

Although Hans Bernoulli and other land reformers have suggested a radical change in land policy, the stance we take in this book is more pragmatic. We seek to explore three things to better understand how planners can strategically use instruments of land policy to deal with scarcity of land: (1) the basic mechanisms of how instruments impact scarcity, (2) the strategic use of the instruments, and (3) the differences in uses of the instruments in different countries.

Where does the curiosity of the editors and authors of this book come from? The simplest answer is that the International Academic Association on Planning, Law, and Property Rights (PLPR) inspired this book. The association was set up in 2007 as a platform to examine the difficult relationship between public and private interests in the use of land (www.plpr-association.org). It therefore bridges the disciplines of planning and law with a cross-national comparative perspective. From the beginning, passionate academic debates on instruments of land policy have been a key element to the annual conferences.

Numerous books on specific instruments, such as takings, compulsory acquisition, or land readjustment, provide input for such debates. But an international book that discusses and reveals the strategic way those instruments are used in land policy was lacking. We consider such a book important because all too often discussions on instruments of land policy focus on technical implementation details, neglecting the political and strategic dimensions.

Instruments of land policy do not function in a vacuum as they are embedded in specific societal, economic, and political contexts. These contexts often fed the lively debates at PLPR. Therefore, it was our aim to capture at least part of these debates in a structured format in this book. We chose to challenge authors to not only describe the basic mechanisms of the instruments, but also to discuss the strategic use of them for dealing with issues of scarcity. We would like to thank all the colleagues – many of whom became friends – who accepted the rules of this format and contributed as authors to this book. This book does not aim to be a comprehensive overview of all existing instruments of land policy, nor is it a systematic comparison between countries. We do intend, however, to initiate a debate on instruments that acknowledges the power discrepancies between planners, landowners, and the other major actors who shape spatial development.

Many esteemed personalities from the field provided us with inspiration and critical feedback and inspired us to soldier on with this project – in particular we would like to thank Barrie Needham and Peter Knoepfel for their timely and sound advice. To make this book possible we also relied on many invisible helpers to whom we would like to express our gratitude: Liz Stitt, our language editor, and the student assistants at Bern University (Moritz Iseli, Andrea Weber, and Sybille Vogel). We would also like to thank Martin H. Hartmann for the cover photo. Finally, we would like to thank our friends and family who had to put up with the unforeseen consequences of a project that became bigger and more time-consuming than we initially expected.

Jean-David Gerber, Thomas Hartmann,
Andreas Hengstermann
Utrecht and Bern, August 2017

Reference

Bernoulli, H. (1946) *Die Stadt und ihr Boden (Towns and the land)*, Verlag für Architektur, Erlenbach-Zürich.

Part I
Introduction

1 Land, scarcity, and property rights

Thomas Hartmann and Jean-David Gerber

Land policy and scarcity

Scarcity of land is the result of a political process. Only goods and services that are used up through consumption (subtractability) can become scarce (Ostrom et al. 1994).[1] Scarcity is usually thought to be found in situations where limited resources are confronted with demands (or needs) that outreach the available supply. But the story becomes a bit more complex if the rules and regulations that support the (unequal) appropriation and distribution of resource units are taken into account in the analysis, which a political approach to scarcity does.

Scarcity of land is not good or bad per se. This depends on the perspective and the policy goals one hopes to achieve. The reason why land dedicated to single-family homes becomes scarce is a matter of land use planning regulations (i.e. zoning for residential housing) and property rights. These institutions create exclusivity and lead to a situation where the supply does not meet the demand. Institutions governing land uses substantially contribute to the rivalrous character of the land. Because resource scarcity is mediated through institutions, it is always politically and socially constructed (Drahos 2004; Fuys and Dohrn 2010; Hess and Ostrom 2003).

Planning is about creating or alleviating scarcity of land according to politically defined spatial development objectives. By so doing, planners need to interact with, and sometimes confront, property-right holders. This is where power games come into play. Planning is about finding ways to deal with power grounded in strongly protected property rights. Otherwise, stalemate situations develop and land use plans remain paper plans.

This book explores the strategies used by planners to reinforce their position in front of other well-protected interests. In particular, this book aims to discover how planners can use different policy instruments, coming from either public or private law, to support the implementation of land use plans. The selection of policy instruments is often presented in a functionalist approach as if it depended merely on technical choices (Lascoumes and Le Galès 2005). However, instruments are not neutral; they correspond to specific interpretations of the role of the state and/or its private partners

(Salamon 2000). This makes land use instruments inherently normative and political. Today, local authorities appear to be caught between competing interests – private vs. public, efficiency vs. accountability, long term vs. short term, property rights vs. public policies, command-and-control vs. partnership, accumulation strategy vs. incentives to remain 'slim' – all of which have an impact on spatial development. In this context, public policy instruments have both a technical and a social dimension: they structure the social relationship between a public authority and the target groups according to the representations and meanings that they are carrying (Lascoumes and Le Galès 2005). As such, the selection of policy instruments generates political activity.

Land use plans are a source of legitimation for an intervention in the allocation and distribution of use rights to land. But this intervention faces many obstacles, creating situations of scarcity because plots of land are not available for the intended development goals. This book asks: how can public intervention strategically manage the scarcity of buildable land, either increasing or decreasing it, in order to promote, overall, a more sparing use of resources? This question follows three underlying objectives.

The first objective is to understand how different policy instruments can impact scarcity of land. The way different categories of instruments regulate use rights is conceptualized in the next chapter, which distinguishes four paths of intervention. We will see that public actors make use of a broad set of policy instruments to implement spatial planning objectives. Public policy instruments can either increase scarcity (mainly through different mechanisms restricting landowners' freedom to develop) or reduce it (e.g. by increasing allowed density or preventing land hoarding). These instruments provide governmental or municipal actors legitimate intervention ways to effectively influence the way land is allocated and distributed.

The second objective is to stress that policy instruments are political in nature: public intervention creates losers and winners. In other words, policy instruments lead to a (partial) redistribution of use rights to the land. This book does not aim to provide best-practice examples. Planners' activities are embedded in specific and complex institutional settings, which make it impossible to provide one-size-fits-all solutions to issues of scarcity, as each context is unique. Therefore the aim is to put forward a particular – strategic – way of thinking about policy instruments. Instruments can strategically be mobilized by planners and other actors involved in planning to reinforce their position in a given context in such a way that the implementation of politically defined development objectives becomes possible.

The third objective is to highlight the creativity that is needed to fight against scarcity. Policy instruments can be rediscovered after periods of oblivion, transposed from a rural to an urban setting, combined with other in a complex intervention strategy, and so forth. In this sense, this books aims to bring together examples from different national contexts in order to raise the awareness on how specific instruments are used by planners in other countries.

This volume will not question or address the spatial planning objectives followed in a specific municipality or country, and thus it will not address the question whether the goals are good or bad. Rather, we take the objectives of these public policies as given, since they are the result of a (parliamentary) socio-political compromise at a given time and scale. This book looks at the rationale of the different instruments of land policy and how they are used strategically in different contexts.

Changing notions of scarcity

In most national settings, land use planning instruments have been crafted in a context of land profusion and economic growth. During the past century, all Western countries have developed a system to shape their spatial development. Planning acts were passed, planners were trained through academic planning schools, and planning departments were established at all levels of government. Systems have been established to control urban growth and address related topics such as housing, transportation, environmental issues, and many more. The policy instruments that were invented and implemented proved to be quite effective when it came to shaping the expansion of urban areas at the edges of cities. Greenfield development is something that planners know how to deal with!

However, this context has changed. Today, actors in charge of planning must learn how to deal with scarcity. They are increasingly confronted with the challenge of brownfield development, redevelopment, mixed-use development, and urban land reconversion or densification. Many European cities have reached their maximum spatial expansion and are focusing on reshaping their urban core or industrial areas. Even where economic growth is still a given, the actors of land use planning struggle with this new focus on the redevelopment of pre-used plots. Besides managing technical challenges such as contamination, neighbour conflicts, noisiness, and so forth, understanding the structure of the underlying property rights is crucial for the success of planning projects. Planning frequently fails to cope with the complexity of property right arrangements, as its instruments are traditionally adjusted to deal with the simple property rights related to former agricultural land. One of the central challenges of the new scarcity situation is that land use planning now needs to address the complex property rights situations that characterize the already built environment. More than ever, effectively steering spatial development requires a keen understanding of the tight interactions between land use planning and property rights.

In a context where greenfield development always becomes more problematic because of the high resource consumption that is bound with it, building land becomes scarcer. This book claims that this scarcity is mostly constructed by the complex entanglement of property rights that characterize the already built environment. Controlling urban sprawl, promoting densification of already built areas, and encouraging brownfield redevelopment are undertakings that all need to address the complexity of property rights relations. For different reasons, planners have often ignored the reality of complex property right situations. A better understanding of the nexus between planning, property rights, and scarcity is of utmost importance for spatial development today and in the future.

This book

The challenges of land as a scarce resource differ in various national contexts, and strategies to deal with it vary accordingly. This book highlights how planning practices and scarcity interact with one another. Therefore, instead of systematically comparing a specific instrument (e.g. land readjustment or long-term building leases) in a number of different national settings, this book deliberately aims to present a broader range of instruments illustrating the nexus of scarcity, planning, and property rights. What is gained in scope would be lost in depth of analysis if the different national settings were not carefully chosen in accordance with each country's experience with a given instrument. In the selection of the cases presented in the next chapters, we looked for contrast in the use of instruments. Rather than selecting an 'average' case, we chose particularly eloquent situations to assure that the mechanisms at play would be more easily identifiable (Yin 2009).

Each chapter is discussed in a commentary written by an author of another national background, where the particular instrument is regarded from a different perspective. Different interpretations of the situations presented are also given by the fact that the contributions of this book were written by scholars from different disciplines (planners, lawyers, sociologists, political scientists, geographers, economists, etc.). The goal is to encourage the dialogue between national settings and between disciplines interested in planning. This enables a deeper understanding of the rationales of the different instruments and nurtures a broader academic and policy-relevant debate on the management of building land as a scarce resource – an issue that is of increasing importance worldwide.

Note

1 This purely economic perspective on scarcity can be challenged from various points: the Netherlands are a paramount example to illustrate that land can indeed be produced – whole cities exist on produced land. Also, the amount of land can be changed due to various environmental phenomena – sea level rise or volcanic activity. So land is not necessarily scarce per se.

References

Drahos, P. (2004) The regulation of public goods, *Journal of International Economic Law*, 7(2), 321–339.

Fuys, A. and Dohrn, S. (2010) Common property regimes: Taking a closer look at resource access, authorization, and legitimacy, in: German, L., Ramisch, J.J. and Verma, R. (eds) *Beyond the biophysical: Knowledge, culture, and politics in agriculture and natural resource management*, Springer, London, New York, 193–214.

Hess, C. and Ostrom, E. (2003) Ideas, artifacts, and facilities: Information as a common-pool resource, *Law and Contemporary Problems*, 66, 111–145.

Lascoumes, P. and Le Galès, P. (2005) *Gouverner par les instruments*, Presses de Sciences Po (P.F.N.S.P.), Paris.

Ostrom, E., Gardner, R. and Walker, J. (1994) *Rules, games, and common-pool resources*, University of Michigan Press, Ann Arbor, MI.

Salamon, L. M. (2000) The new governance and the tools of public action: An introduction, *Fordham Urban Law Journal*, 28(5), 1611–1673.

Yin, R.K. (2009) *Case study research: Design and methods*, 4th ed., Sage Publications, Los Angeles, CA.

2 Land policy

How to deal with scarcity of land

Jean-David Gerber, Andreas Hengstermann, and François-Xavier Viallon

Introduction: from land use planning to land policy

Land use planning is the 'process by which public agencies, mostly local governments, determine the intensity and geographical arrangements of various land uses in a community' (Fulton 1999: 7). In this book, land use planning is not framed by a scientific theory, a design activity, or a 'value-neutral' technique. It is understood as a *public policy*. As such, it aims to solve a public problem usually connected with inefficient use of public infrastructure or with the insufficient coordination of land uses that, for instance, leads to sprawl or induces nuisances. As a public policy, it draws its legitimacy from a legal basis (e.g. a constitutional article or the land use planning law), defines the public actors in charge of implementation (e.g. planning agency), and provides them with a budget, different competencies, or means of action. Through different *policy instruments*, a public policy aims 'at modifying the behavior of social groups presumed to be at the root of [. . .] the collective problem to be resolved (target groups) in the interest of the social groups who suffer the negative effects of the problem in question' (Knoepfel et al. 2007: 24). Land use planning has typically developed a series of hierarchical plans (policy instruments) to control the actions of those actors, namely the landowners, whose effective behavior has been identified as leading to uncoordinated growth. Therefore, landowners can be identified as the *target groups* of the land use planning policy (Knoepfel and Nahrath 2007). However, due to their strong position as titleholders, they are well equipped to resist. Here lies the conundrum of plan implementation: how can comparatively weak political-administrative actors impose land use restrictions (plans) on strongly protected target groups?

Historically this problem was de facto mitigated through a focus on areas with little conflict potential. At the margin of cities, new development could take place on greenfields where complexity was low and resistance weak. Similarly, large-scale redevelopments in American cities tended to take place in neighborhoods of lower socio-economic level with weak political connections (Bullard 1983; Wei and Knox 2015).

In a context of resource scarcity, this strategy that avoided directly facing the power of landowners or their representatives was reaching its limits.

But planners are typically insufficiently equipped to deal with power issues; they may sometimes feel helpless in front of the hidden power games at play in complex urban environments (Flyvbjerg 2006). However, the growing scarcity of land available for development in cities led to deep changes in the planning field. Land is more and more seen as a resource that needs to be properly managed, not only to comply with sustainability standards, but also to reduce the cost of an expensive way of life based on resource squandering.

In parallel to this changing reality of the planning field, theoretical concepts needed to evolve as well. In this chapter, we present four complementary 'shifts' or 'turns' that took place in the planning field – (1) the resourcial turn, (2) the institutional turn, (3) the actorial turn, and (4) the instrumental turn – and show how they have paved the way to the *land policy approach*. The main objective behind these theoretical considerations is to demonstrate that land policy is more than just an opening of land use planning towards other policy fields or property rights. While land use planning traditionally focused on the definition of development objectives, land policy focuses on their achievement. In this sense, while land use planning is about social or technical problem solving, land policy focuses on the actors and their interests in land. These actors actively devise strategies, e.g. select specific policy instruments, in order to bring their plan to life. In this book, we aim to show that land policy introduces a new paradigm putting strategic actors at the centre of the analysis. This analytical shift has great relevance not only for planning theorists, but also for practitioners.

This chapter is structured as follows: first, we define land policy (section 2). Land policy does not refer to a specific mode of regulation defined in the law. It refers to the strategic combination of instruments carefully thought through by public authorities in order to impose themselves in front of other private (or public) interests and reach public planning objectives. The next sections go back to the four shifts that led to the emergence of the land policy approach.

Second, we discuss the resourcial turn in planning. We show that sustainability objectives challenge planners (section 3). Land is more and more considered a resource that needs to be properly managed in order to meet quantitative and qualitative development objectives. This aids in generating new forms of scarcity: sustainability objectives constrain development because they reduce the set of available solutions due to stricter criteria. Scarcity is a source of conflicts among competing users.

Third, we present land use planning as a regulating intervention taking place within a tight web of existing rights and interests (section 4). To understand the full implication of land use planning and to measure its impact on sustainability, it is necessary to analyze institutions – the 'rules of the game' – and understand their repercussions. These rules are not only grounded in public law (public policies), but also in private law (property rights).[1] Property rights play a central role in explaining the outcomes of planning activities. Whenever possible, strategic actors try to rely on property rights because they are much more resistant to change than public policies (van der Molen 2015).

Fourth, we discuss the human factor, which explains the difference between formal rules and their implementation (section 5). Land use plans are never implemented one to one. Power issues explain the fundamental difference between plan making and plan implementation. Public and private actors strategically activate certain rules ('institutional shopping') to defend their specific interests and to protect their particular use of the land.

Finally, we explain why an instrumental perspective in planning makes it possible to evaluate the different 'tools' or instruments that actors can use to either reinforce plan implementation or to delay it (section 6). Approaching public policies through instruments has a main advantage (Hood 1983): it provides a framework for the analyst to grasp the diversity of modern governments' operations. In view of the overwhelming complexity of social control through governments, an analysis in terms of instruments gives structure to this complex reality and reduces it to a relatively small set of basic tools.

Land policy – a shift of paradigm

'Land policy' is not a new term, but its definition varies depending on the context and the specific authors. Generally, there is an agreement that 'the term "land policy" commonly covers land development issues that are broader than land use' (Alterman 1990: 16). The concept of land policy aims to move the implementation of spatial development objectives towards a broader perspective than just land use planning alone, taking into account, in particular, the property-right dimension. The following sections will show that the land policy approach results from a broader shift of analytical focus in spatial research. As we show that land policy is more than an extension of land use planning, we also contend that resources, actors, and institutions – including property rights – are determining factors in explaining the outcomes of land policy processes.

By land policy, we mean all the political-legal measures implemented by a municipality to deal with the issue of land scarcity – thus attempting to match the real supply with the potential supply of parcels (Hartmann and Spit 2015). An active land policy refers to *all public decisions and actions aiming to implement politically defined spatial development objectives through changes in the use, distribution and value of land* (Hengstermann and Gerber 2015). Planning is often directed at avoiding undesirable developments (e.g. excessive development of agricultural land, uncoordinated settlement expansion). Land policy focuses on the actual implementation of planning objectives (e.g. high quality inward settlement development, coordination between housing and infrastructure supply, provision of socially fair housing).

With this definition, we refer to initial debates on land policy that took place through the first half of the twentieth century (George 1879; Howard 1898; Bernoulli 1946) and then to the public policies studies as a subfield of planning research that have arisen since the 1970s (Epping 1977; Seele 1979; Lichfield and Darin-Drabkin 1980). At the same time, we connect to an international debate and go beyond national discussions, which all have their own specificities. For instance, in the Netherlands, land policy has a much narrower definition as a tool used by municipal authorities to simultaneously coordinate development and boost public revenues (Needham 1997; Buitelaar 2010). In contrast, in the U.S., 'land policy' is used in connection with land distribution issues (e.g. the Homestead Act 1862 and the Federal Land Policy and Management Act 1976) and urban economics (e.g. Lincoln Institute for Land Policy).

Our understanding of land policy might be closer to the definitions used by international organizations. According to the European Commission,

> land policies determine who has legal rights of access and/or ownership to certain resources and under what conditions, and therefore how these productive assets are distributed among diverse stakeholders. Land policies therefore express, implicitly or explicitly, the political choices made concerning the distribution of power between the state, its citizens, and local systems of authority.
>
> (2004: 1)

The European commission continues: 'Land policy aims to achieve certain objectives relating to the security and distribution of land rights, land use and land management, and access to land, including the forms of tenure under which it is held' (2004: 3).

Land policy is not a public policy, but a strategy. It puts actors at the centre and analyzes how some of them activate, combine, or avoid specific rules, i.e. mobilize a strategic set of policy instruments in order to implement politically defined spatial development objectives. Therefore, land policy rests on a careful appraisal of power relationship between actors. Planners are often not the most powerful players because they are not titleholders, but they can combine instruments, including private-law instruments, in order to support the implementation of planning objectives.

Land policy, both as a strategy and as an analytical concept, evolved out of the observation that planners are not well equipped to deal with the complex institutional situations resulting from resource scarcity, which in turn results from competition on uses and vested interests in land. The land policy approach aims to put asymmetric power distribution in the centre of the analysis and to give planners the analytical tools to deal with it. As such, we defend the idea that land policy evolved out a shift of paradigm in land use planning. In times of scarcity and corresponding latent conflict linked with complex webs of intermingled rights such as they exist in the urban environment, planning is about the institutional creativity of public and semi-public actors who are able to get their agenda through thanks to a detailed appraisal of power relations and a carefully considered strategy combining different policy instruments.

The resourcial turn in planning

In order to be sustainable, development should meet the needs of the present generation without compromising the ability of future generations to meet their own needs (Brundtland Report 1987: 51). The sustainability discourse has brought to a broader audience the message that resources can be depleted, that growth might have limits, and that our society has the responsibility to manage resources for the long run.

The resource-based approach promoted by the sustainability discourse is also justified by a pragmatic consideration of which lands are subject to different kinds of competing uses that lead to rivalries or conflicts. The main characteristic of the resource-based approach is that it places the human subject at the centre of the analysis (Zimmermann 1951). The resource-based approach relies on a constructivist perspective: a resource emerges from a relational process linking an 'object' – that can be material or non-material (water, soil, forest, landscape), constructed (housing, building land, infrastructure), or social and cultural (know-how, knowledge) – and an economic, cultural, or ecological 'production system' producing goods and services to satisfy human needs (Kébir and Crevoisier 2004; Kébir 2010). According to this constructivist and relational perspective, 'resources are not automatically viewed as factors with an inherent use-value and predetermined application. [. . .] The use-value of a resource depends upon the social context within which goals and capabilities are shaped' (Bathelt and Glückler 2005: 1547).

In a finite global ecosystem, resources are finite as well. Various forms of scarcity coexist. There are forms of absolute scarcity because of objective planetary boundaries: land is scarce because of its non-reproducibility. The total amount of land may not be extendable, but its quality is modifiable through human intervention. Even more central to our discussion, land of a given quality may be available, but access to it might not be possible. The constructivist definition of resource incites the analyst to adopt a constructivist approach to scarcity as well. One can thus distinguish socially or politically constructed forms of scarcity leading to relative forms of scarcity rather than absolute ones and contributing to time-limited, cyclical, or structural scarcities. Even in countries where land is not seen as a scarce resource, housing shortages or lack of green spaces exist in given locations. In any case, scarcity is closely related to the institutions regulating uses, but also to those leading to exclusive appropriation of resource units at the expense of redistribution (Sen 1981).

Faced with risks of scarcity, we can observe the establishment of more or less complex and constraining devices to regulate the rival uses of the resource. Land use planning's main objective is precisely to allocate use rights to spatial resources in order to minimize conflicts. The issue of the sustainability of a resource system is approached differently depending on whether resources are renewable or recyclable or not, whether units of the resource are substitutable or not, or whether users can be excluded or not. Use rights allocation is an easy process if resources are plentiful; it becomes much more conflicting if resources are scarce (Ostrom 1990). This is the new context that land use planning has to deal with when shifting the focus from greenfield development to the management of the built environment.

The institutional turn in planning

Questioning the sustainability of resource uses also implies that the institutions governing land uses be analyzed (North 1990; Gerber et al. 2009). Land use planning takes place within a tight web of existing rights and interests. A careful analysis of the architecture, operation, coherence, or regulation capacities of these devices needs to be carried out in order to understand the full implications of each planning intervention.

Land use planning as a public policy

Policy analysis consists in the 'study of the action of public authorities within society' (Mény and Thoenig 1989: 9). Appraising land use planning as a public policy means seeking to comprehend the complex functioning of the state 'in action', starting with the public and private actors involved in spatial planning, their resources, and the institutions that govern their actions. Political institutions, such as public policies, property rights, the division of competences among political levels, or procedural rules, are analyzed from the perspective of the constraints and opportunities they offer to the actors involved in planning.

Land use planning as a public policy can be defined as a series of intentionally coherent decisions or activities taken or carried out by planning administrations and authorities at different levels of government, whose resources and interests vary, with a view to resolving in a targeted manner the politically defined problem of uncoordinated land development. Hierarchically organized plans are the classical instruments of land use planning (Bühlmann et al. 2011; Bassett and McNamara 1940; Booth 1995). Among them, the zoning plan plays a central role because it is binding to landowners. Plans are the responses by public authorities to the problem of uncoordinated spatial development that might result from the involvement of unrestrained property titleholders (Adams et al. 2002; Jacobs and Paulsen 2009). Coordinating housing, industry and infrastructure development, securing density-related objectives, and fighting against uncoordinated spatial development that leads to urban sprawl, and so on, are the main objectives of land use plans.

The proposed definition of land use planning as a public policy leads to a type of analysis ultimately focusing on describing, understanding, and explaining the workings of the planning process as a part of the political administrative system and its interactions with private actors. Planners, who have long focused on the policy dimension of planning, have often underestimated the role played by property rights (Jacobs and Paulsen 2009; Hartmann and Needham 2012). While land use planning traditionally focuses on the definition of planning/development objectives, a broader institutional perspective in planning analyzes *all rules and regulations*, including those based on property rights that impact spatial development.

Planning at the interface between public policy and property rights

Because it takes place at the interface between two major sources of legal constraint – property rights and public policy – land use planning translates the logic of one intervention into the other, and vice versa, mainly through delivering individual building permits (Gerber et al. 2011). Property rights are necessary, because they define the precise plots where planning decisions become concrete. They play an important role in protecting the way planning decisions materialize, and make planning decisions robust (Davy 2012). Planning would lack legal durability if it took place in a context where property rights were not clearly defined: such constellations would hamper investments in, and betterment of, the land (Soto 2000).

Finding a socially and politically acceptable balance between the defence of private and public interests is a never-ending challenge (Booth 2002). Strong property rights encourage and protect long-term investments in property (Davy 2012: 1–2; Steiger 2006). However, contemporary planning theory often criticizes property rights as being too inflexible to effectively cope with uncertainties, deadlock situations that hamper changes (Hartmann and Needham 2012; Gerber et al. 2017), changes in economic conditions (e.g. brownfield redevelopment), and evolution of political objectives (e.g. discussions about densification). Of course, in the same way that the state can create, define and shape property rights, the state can also terminate them under specific circumstances (e.g. construction of roads, railways). However, because of the constitutional guarantee of private property, termination enables the dispossessed titleholder to file claim for just compensation (Cooter and Ulen 2004). As depicted by the concept of 'incrementalism' (Lindblom 1959), planners, as public decision-makers, often have limited room for manoeuvre at their disposal.

Four paths of interventions

Figure 2.1 shows how land uses can be impacted by public interventions. Depending on the type of law (public or private) and their effects on the

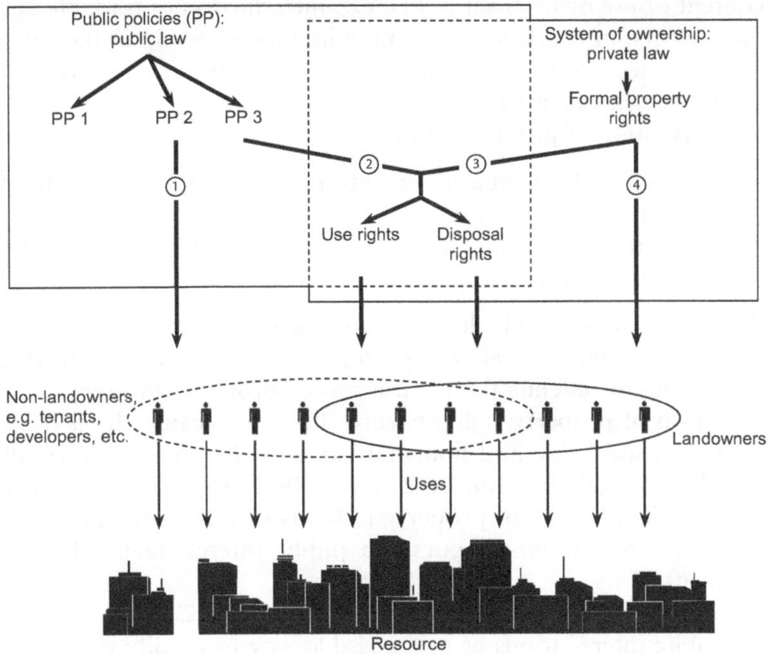

Figure 2.1 The behaviour of actors using the resource land can legally be constrained by (1) policies with no impact on the content of use or disposal rights (e.g. information, incentives), (2) policies with an impact on the scope and content of use or disposal rights (e.g. zoning), (3) re-definition of property rights with an impact on the scope and content of use or disposal rights (e.g. tradable development rights), and (4) redefinition of the structure of the distribution of property titles (e.g. expropriation)

property title, we identify four paths of intervention which influence the behaviour of landowners, developers, or investors towards land (Knoepfel et al. 2001; Doremus 2003; Gerber et al. 2009).

The state can influence the behaviour of landowners and other resource users through four paths:

1 Policies with no impact on the content of use or disposal rights, e.g. information campaigns, economic incentives (tax or subsidies).
2 Policies with an impact on the scope and content of use or disposal rights (e.g. zoning, land readjustment) leading to:

   - Regulation of use rights without infringing on formal ownership, e.g. limitations on the right to access the land, to emit pollutants, to build through different command-and-control instruments.
   - Regulation of disposal rights: prohibition of sale to certain purchasers (e.g. foreigners, non-farmers), etc.

3 Legal redefinition of property rights with an impact on the scope and content of use or disposal rights, e.g. introduction of tradable development rights, introduction of condominium ownership in the civil code, new right to expropriate 'rogue neighbors', or pre-emption rights (right of first refusal) granted to municipal authorities.
4 Redistribution of property titles:
   - Limited and punctual intervention, e.g. formal expropriation, targeted purchase of land.
   - Radical and profound intervention: privatization or nationalization (with or without compensation).

Policy interventions which have no impact on property rights (e.g. incentives) are comparatively easier to get through a parliament than initiatives aiming to redefine the institutions of property. In many countries, the definition of property rights hardly changes, because the delicate balance between use value and financial value of the land is the result of a subtle political-legal compromise (Harvey 2008). Direct redefinition of the structure of distribution of property rights is rare as well, except in large development projects which pursue a public interest (e.g. infrastructure development).

Figure 2.1 places land use plans (arrow 2 in Figure 2.1) in a broader context of public interventions as one possible way to modify the uses of the resource land. Planning competes with other interests that materialize in different public policies (agriculture, defence, transportation, etc.) and in the definition of the institution of property. An actor-centered analysis aims to link these different interests with the strategies of the actors defending them.

Actorial turn in planning

Actors and institutional rules

The neoinstitutionalist paradigm postulates that the actors and the institutions influence each other; the actors are influenced by the formal rules, while at the same time the rules evolve because of the actions and decisions of the actors. Neo-institutionalism has a different meaning in political science, economy, or sociology (Lowndes 1996; Koelble 1995). The prefix 'neo' distinguishes it from the classic institutionalism, which postulates that democratic rules determine collective decisions, and that actors limited by the institutional framework will act in compliance with the formal rules. In this context, the work of the policy analysts consists of describing, in a legalistic language, the functioning of institutions (Knoepfel et al. 2007: 102; Thelen 2003). But the question then arose as to what extent the institutions supervise, direct, or even determine the social or political decisions and actions of the individuals concerned.

Actors – more specifically, 'resource users' – have some leeway within a given set of institutions (Bourdieu 1986: 40). Actors use a given institutional context to develop strategies and use their power to shape decisions according to their interests; simultaneously the institutional framework also shapes their preferences, their perception, and their awareness of public problems. For instance, planners under pressure by new management standards focusing on cost effectiveness will not consider long-term public investments in the same way they would where the political majority targets sustainability objectives. Although actors are not entirely free, their behaviour is never completely determined by formal rules of law. A process of reformulation and adjustment of formal rules takes place at the time of their implementation. Actors never let go (Knoepfel et al. 2007: 41). Actors are never passive in relation to the rules: they adopt an active behaviour that gives them the potential to modify the content of the rule, both during adoption and implementation.

Three positions can be identified that explain the differences between rules and their implementation (Lascoumes and Le Galès 2007). First, actors may ignore the content and norms of policies and therefore not refer to them when attempting to solve conflicts or rivalries. This option should not be overlooked in the highly complex legal settings of advanced democracies. Second, actors may know the content of norms and policies but resist their application, with more or less success depending on their political strategies and power. Third, actors may divert the content of norms and policies according to their own objectives. They may resist the implementation of a rule by invoking another rule, by assuming that their behaviour will remain unpunished, or by choosing not to activate a rule (Schweizer 2015).

Actors have to comply with the new regulations, but they simultaneously enjoy a degree of autonomy allowing them to implement their own strategy. The degree of autonomy they have varies according to the degree of legal protection of their interests and the amount of power they have (e.g. in terms of information, organization, or personnel). Therefore, Figure 2.1 illustrates a bidirectional process. From a top-down perspective, formal institutions constrain the behaviour of resource users if they are defined as the target groups of a public policy. In contrast, from a bottom-up perspective, actors always attempt to resist when their interests are put at risk. Because this process is a game with several rounds, Figure 2.1 should also be understood dynamically. Implementation efforts always result in a compromise between political-administrative actors and target groups. Even if phases of greater stability can be observed, this compromise is constantly renegotiated as other legal or societal norms evolve and change.

In this regard, both formal and informal rules are important. Institutions encompass both formal rules, which have been explicitly and legally formalized, and implicit or informal rules, which correspond to commonly shared standards. Formal rules facilitate or limit the political participation of certain actors. By institutionalizing the relations of power between social groups, institutional rules contribute to the stability and foreseeability of the system. In times of rapid global change, the stability of formal rules can also become a problem if they lead to inefficiencies or incoherencies (Gerber et al. 2017).

Power asymmetries in planning

Planners have long known the importance of power in planning (Castells 1977; Harvey 1978; Fainstein and Fainstein 1979). However, planners have always been ambivalent about power (Friedmann 1998). The works of communicative theorists (Forester 1989; Healey 1997) stress the importance of power, but because of their focus on Habermasian communicative rationality, they tend to remain strongly procedural, calling for deliberative fora, without the substantive understanding of realpolitik (Flyvbjerg 1998). Flyvbjerg (2006) calls for a better acknowledgement in planning 'for the working of power and for the passionate engagement of stakeholders who care deeply about the issues at hand' (p. 363).

The land policy approach relies on a detailed understanding of existing norms and institutions and aims to understand how public and private actors develop concrete political-legal strategies for the implementation of societally defined spatial development objectives. Formal and informal institutions inform about the *institutional opportunity structure* within which actors develop their strategies (Vatn 2009).

While land use planning law is regularly amended, and while zoning is revised every 15 years or so, property rights are stable over decades or more. Both the legal definition of the institution of property and the (socially unequal) distribution of ownership titles are stable over time. Therefore, a power asymmetry exists between landowners and non-landowners. The interests of landowners are well protected in the long term by an institution that barely changes and guarantees full compensation in case of expropriation. This is the situation that planning administrations face every day.

This brings us back to the fundamental conundrum of plan implementation: how can comparatively weak political-administrative actors (the planners) impose politically and societally defined spatial development objectives on strongly protected target groups (the landowners)? The instrumental perspective in planning provides some answers.

Instrumental turn in planning

In order to solve a public problem, a public policy defines the collective problem requiring resolution and identifies the target group, whose behaviour is thought to be the cause of the problem (Knoepfel et al. 2007). Each public policy also establishes *how* the problem can be resolved. In other words, it defines the means of public intervention, or public policy instruments that will influence the activities of the target groups so that these will be compatible with the political aims (Knoepfel et al. 2007: 59). This section focuses on the policy instruments in the land use planning policy. We refer to the renewed interest in policy instruments of spatial development as the *instrumental turn in planning*.

Instrument typologies

Attempts to classify policy instruments pursue mainly two objectives (Hood 1983; Hood and Margetts 2007): first, making sense of the complexity of government intervention by looking at it through a set of generic predefined instrument types; second, picking the right tool for the job by comparing and assessing their selection and the effects they produce.

A common and frequently mentioned typology is E. Vedung's threefold classification of instruments *carrots, sticks, and sermons* (Vedung 1998). The idea is that three ways exist to exert power on subjects and make them comply: (1) the coercive power of the stick, characterized by (the threat of physical) sanctions, frustrations, and force, e.g. if developers do not comply with a building permit (threat to demolish); (2) the remunerative power of the carrot, which controls the material resources and their allocation, e.g. when the state grants tax cuts to new industries, or defines additional taxes on cars with high emission; and (3) the normative power of the sermon, which contains the allocation and manipulation of symbolic rewards, such as when eco-efficient initiatives are shown as examples by public authorities.

Refining this approach, Pierre Lascoumes and Patrick Le Galès (2007) distinguish among two broad types of state intervention: (1) historic classic routine intervention relying on a legal basis, including (i) legislative and regulatory 'command and control' instruments and (ii) fiscal and economic tools; (2) less authoritative conventional intervention such as (i) 'govern and contract' approaches including agreement and incentive-based instruments, (ii) communication and information-based instruments that rely on audience and opinions, including citizens' rights to access information, and (iii) de jure and de facto standards and best practices negotiated among private actors (among target groups, and with third parties).

These typologies classify instruments in a generic manner, but they do not explain the reasons of instrument selection, nor the effects instruments produce.

Ways to analyze policy instruments

Three research questions complement the issues left open by the generic tool classification approaches (Hood and Margetts 2007): Why do decision-makers chose certain instruments over others? What instruments are the most effective in solving a given problem? How does instrumental change explain broader change of perception of a given public problem? These three questions result in three complementary research streams. Each stream relies on a distinct conceptual framework that puts the variable 'instruments' at a different spot: the first stream conceives an instrument as a dependent variable, the second treats it as an independent variable, and the third stream defines an instrument as an intermediary variable.

The dependent-variable approach focuses on actors' perceptions of instruments in the political decision-making process (Linder and Peters 1989, 1990). According to Linder and Peters, four main attributes play into the trade-offs policymakers face when adopting a policy instrument: (1) the administrative and implementation costs linked with the instrument (resource intensiveness), (2) the degree of selectivity and flexibility when defining the instrument's target groups (targeting), (3) the market or state orientation of the instrument (degree of constraint), and (4) the instrument's visibility, as well as the adverse effects it may produce (political risk). Underlying and empirically tested hypotheses show that policymakers tend to adopt instruments (1) whose implementation can be delegated to an existing administration, (2) that would face minimal resistance from the target group, (3) that comply with the ideology of the political majority in power, and (4) that have already been experienced elsewhere (Varone 1998; Kuhlmann and Wollmann 2013).

The independent-variable approach focuses on the effects of policy instruments on the policy's target group. Policy instruments are conceived as a 'method through which collective action is structured to solve a public problem' (Salamon 2002: 19). This conception of instruments also includes broader political institutions, which *structure* interactions among individuals: one can mention the type of organization in charge of implementation (e.g. public, central, agency, independent regulator, private, local), procedural rules that shape the political process, and other general rules, such as the nature of the political regime in place (e.g. central, majoritarian) or societal conceptions of property, justice, and administration.

The intermediary-variable approach relies on a more holistic conception of instruments (Lascoumes and Le Galès 2007; Halpern et al. 2014). Instruments are conceived as technical and social devices that organize social interaction between public authorities and target groups based on the representations and meanings instruments carry in the eyes of the actors who decide upon their adoption and their implementation. Therefore, instruments are conceived as *markers of change*: they crystallize a political compromise on specific public problems in a certain moment in time, and produce effects of their own. Such a perspective allows for long-term analysis of the conception and (re-) orientation of public problems, of the evolution of public policies, and of the effects they produce.

The land policy analyst's perspective

In a land policy perspective, accounting simultaneously for both instruments stemming from public policies and instruments stemming from property rights is central. The exposed typologies and approaches each offer respond to different questions and help define a suitable approach to land policy analysis. This book focuses on instruments that (1) are already formally adopted by national governments, (2) contribute to the resolution of a public problem, *and* (3) are implemented in emblematic situations in a specific moment in time. Therefore, the perspective adopted defines policy instruments as an independent variable.

However, even once an instrument is adopted, uncertainties in the balance of power remain: instruments create inertia to outside pressure and induce conflicts of interests; they foster a particular representation of the issue at stake; they also induce a particular framing of the issue, and a specific explanatory model rationalizing the understanding of the issue (Lascoumes and Le Galès 2007: 10). The selection and use of policy instruments is often presented functionally, as though the choice only depends on mere technical questions (Lascoumes and Le Galès 2007). However, instruments are not axiologically neutral; they correspond to a particular understanding of the public problem, to a specific interpretation of the role of the state and/or its private partners, they denote a precise conception of intervention mechanisms, and they are value loaded (Salamon 2002; Landry and Varone 2005). Public policy instruments structure the social relationship between a public authority and the target groups according to the representations and meanings that they are carrying (Lascoumes and Le Galès 2007). As such, the selection of policy instruments generates political activity.

Accounting for power games around the instrument does not stop with the instrument's choice or adoption, but continues during the implementation stage. Even once an instrument is adopted, it might be mobilized (or not) by actors, depending on their strategies. One policy instrument might be preferred over another instrument, or the instrument might be circumvented, or diverted, from its original purpose, or passively implemented by actors (Schweizer 2015).

Instruments and instrument shopping

Questioning the contribution of policy instruments to solve a given public problem requires one to account simultaneously for organizational types, general rules, and procedures (Hood and Margetts 2007: 168–169). In this book, we rely on the framework depicted in Figure 2.1 which encompasses the entire legal framework – public policies and property rights – regulating the use of the land resource (Gerber et al. 2009). Instruments are appraised separately according to the four paths of intervention defined in Figure 2.1. Such an approach makes it possible to include private law instruments into the analysis of regulations and sets the focus on the actors' games surrounding instrument implementation. Instruments are defined as 'the detailed forms of intervention or measures planned to fulfil the objectives of a public policy'; they are 'means used to motivate those affected (particularly target groups) to comply with the policy provisions' (Knoepfel et al. 2007: 156–157).

In order to account for the strategic thinking of actors underlying each policy implementation process, we introduce the concept of *instrument shopping*. In reference to the concept of venue shopping, defined as 'the activities of advocacy groups and policymakers who seek out a decision setting where they can air their grievances with current policy and present alternative policy proposals' (Pralle 2003: 233), instrument shopping can be defined as the actors' choice of specific instruments over others, based on the objectives they want to achieve (Benda-Beckmann 1981). The term stresses the fact that (1) instruments have to be activated by actors, (2) actors select the instruments strategically according to their specific interests, and (3) the actors operate within a given framework that simultaneously limits the actors' understanding of the problem and the strategies available. In fact, strategic thinking of actors is limited by a lack of thorough information on all available instruments, by actors' preferences for certain types of outputs or styles of political intervention, and the ideological concerns conveyed to the constituency when using a specific instrument (Pralle 2003: 240–241).

In contrast to land use planning approaches, which traditionally focus on the definition of planning and development objectives, land policy analysis insists on the adoption and implementation of instruments in order to solve a public problem and to achieve the objectives. The distinct consideration of instruments, together with the concept of instrument shopping, allows an accounting of all policy instruments that both political-administrative actors and target groups use (or not) to achieve their objectives, and the strategies and power games underlying their implementation. The choice of embedding public policy analysis in a land use planning perspective is intended to fill the existing gap in the literature on land policy instruments implementation.

Note

1 Public policy relates to public law, which involves the state using its authoritative power, including regulatory statutes, penal law, and other laws of public order. It is distinguished from private law, which deals with the relationships between individuals (i.e. property law, the law of contracts, torts, and obligations). Public policies and property rights are the two main types of formal rules that actors can mobilize to defend their use interests in the land resource.

References

Adams, D., Disberry, A., Hutchison, N. and Munjoma, T. (2002) Vacant urban land: Exploring ownership strategies and actions, *The Town Planning Review*, 73(4), 395–416.

Alterman, R. (1990) *Private supply of public services: Evaluation of real state exactions, linkage, and alternative land policies*, New York University Press, London, New York.

Bassett, E.M. and McNamara, K. (1940) *Zoning: The laws, administration, and court decisions during the first twenty years*, Russell Sage Foundation, New York.

Bathelt, H. and Glückler, J. (2005) Resources in economic geography: From substantive concepts towards a relational perspective, *Environment and Planning A*, 37(9), 1545–1563.

Benda-Beckmann, K. von (1981) Forum shopping and shopping forums. *Journal of Legal Pluralism and Unofficial Law*, 13(19), 117–159.

Bernoulli, H. (1946) *Die Stadt und ihr Boden (Towns and the land)*, Birkhäuser Verlag, Basel, Berlin, Boston, MA.

Booth, P. (1995) Zoning or discretionary action: Certainty and responsiveness in implementing planning policy. *Journal of Planning Education and Research*, 14(2), 103–112.

Booth, P. (2002) From property rights to public control. *Town Planning Review*, 73(2), 153–170.

Bourdieu, P. (1986) Delegation und politischer Fetischismus, *Ästhetik und Kommunikation*, 16(61/62), 184–195.

Brundtland, G.H. (1987) Our common future – call for action, *Environmental Conservation*, 14(4), 291–294.

Bühlmann, L., Haag, H., Jud, B., Kissling, S. and Spori, N. (2011) *Einführung in die Raumplanung (Introduction to land use planning)*, VLP-ASPAN, Bern.

Buitelaar, E. (2010) Cracks in the myth: Challenges to land policy in the Netherlands, *Tijdschrift voor Economische en Sociale Geografie*, 101(3), 349–356.

Bullard, R.D. (1983) Solid waste sites and the Black Houston Community. *Sociological Inquiry*, 53(2–3), 273–288.

Castells, M. (1977) *The urban question*, MIT Press, Cambridge, MA.

Cooter, R. and Ulen, T. (2004) *Law and economics*, Addison-Wesley, Boston, MA.

Davy, B. (2012) *Land policy: Planning and the spatial consequences of property*, Ashgate, Farnham, Surrey.

Doremus, H. (2003) A policy portfolio approach to biodiversity protection on private lands, *Environmental Science and Policy*, 6, 217–232.

Epping, G. (1977) *Bodenmarkt und Bodenpolitik in der Bundesrepublik Deutschland*, 67, Duncker & Humblot, Berlin.

European Commission (2004) *EU guidelines to support land policy design and reform processes in developing countries*, COM(2004) 686 final, elaborated by: EU Task Force on Land Tenure led by Poul Nielson (DG DEVCO).

Fainstein, N.I. and Fainstein, S.S. (1979) New debates in urban planning, *International Journal of Urban and Regional Research*, 3(1–4), 381–403.

Flyvbjerg, B. (1998) Empowering civil society: Habermas, Foucault, and the question of conflict, in: Douglass, M. and Friedmann, J. (eds) *Cities for citizens: Planning and the rise of civil society in a global age*, John Wiley, New York, 185–211.

Flyvbjerg, B. (2006) Bringing power to planning research: One researcher's praxis story, *Journal of Planning Education and Research*, 21(4), 353–366.

Forester, J. (1989) *Planning in the face of power*, University of California Press, Berkeley, CA.

Friedmann, J. (1998) Planning theory revisited, *European Planning Studies*, 6(3), 245–253.

Fulton, W. (1999) *Guide to California planning*, Solano Press, Point Arena, CA.

George, H. (1879) *Progress and poverty: An enquiry into the cause of industrial depressions, and of increase of want with increase of wealth: The remedy*, K. Paul, Trench & Company.

Gerber, J.-D., Knoepfel, P., Nahrath, S. and Varone, F. (2009) Institutional resource regimes: Towards sustainability through the combination of property-rights theory and policy analysis, *Ecological Economics*, 68(3), 798–809.

Gerber, J.-D., Nahrath, S., Csikos, P. and Knoepfel, P. (2011) The role of Swiss civic corporations in land-use planning, *Environment & Planning A*, 43, 185–204.

Gerber, J.-D., Nahrath, S. and Hartmann, T. (2017) The strategic use of time-limited property rights in land-use planning: Evidence from Switzerland, *Environment and Planning A*, 49(7), 1684–1703.

Halpern, C., Lascoumes, P. and Le Galès, P. (2014) L'instrumentation et ses effets: Débats et mises en perspectives théoriques, in: Halpern, C., Lascoumes, P. and Le Galès, P. (eds) *L'instrumentation de l'action publique: Controverses, résistances, effets*, Presses de Sciences Po, Paris.

Hartmann, T. and Needham, B. (2012) *Planning by law and property rights reconsidered*, Ashgate, Farnham.

Hartmann, T. and Spit, T. (2015) Dilemmas of involvement in land management – Comparing an active (Dutch) and a passive (German) approach, *Land Use Policy*, 42, 729–737.

Harvey, D. (1978) On planning the ideology of planning, in: Burehell, R.W. and Sternlieb, G. (eds) *Planning theory in the 1980s*, Rutgers University Center for Urban Policy Research, New Brunswick, NJ, 213–234.

Harvey, D. (2008) The right to the city, *New Left Review*, 53, 23–40.

Healey, P. (1997) *Collaborative planning: Shaping places in fragmented societies*, Macmillan, London.

Hengstermann, A. and Gerber, J.-D. (2015) Aktive Bodenpolitik – Eine Auseinandersetzung vor dem Hintergrund der Revision des eidgenössischen Raumplanungsgesetzes (Active land policy – a discussion in the light of the revision of the Swiss Land Use Planning Law), *Flächenmanagement und Bodenordnung (FuB)*, 6, 241–250.

Hood, C. (1983) *The tools of government*, Macmillan Education, London.

Hood, C. and Margetts, H. (2007) *The tools of government in the digital age*, Palgrave Macmillan, London.

Howard, E. (1898) *Tomorrow, a peaceful path to social reform*, Swann Sonnenschein, Londres.

Jacobs, H.M. and Paulsen, K. (2009) Property rights: The neglected theme of 20th-century American planning, *Journal of the American Planning Association*, 75, 134–143.

Kébir, L. (2010) Pour une approche institutionnelle et territoriale des ressources, in: Maillefert, M., Petit, O. and Rousseau, S. (eds) *Ressources, patrimoine, territoires et développement durable*, Peter Lang, Bruxelles, 69–86.

Kébir, L. and Crevoisier, O. (2004) Dynamique des ressources et milieux innovateurs, in: Maillat, D., Camagni, R. and Mattéaccioli, A. (eds) *Ressources naturelles et culturelles, milieux et développement local*, EDES-GREMI, Neuchâtel, 261–290.

Knoepfel, P., Kissling-Näf, I. and Varone, F. (2001) *Institutionelle Ressourcen-Regime. Institutionelle Regime für natürliche Ressourcen: Boden, Wasser und Wald im Vergleich*, Helbing & Lichtenhahn, Basel, 11–48.

Knoepfel, P., Larrue, C., Varone, F. and Hill, M. (2007) *Public policy analysis*, The Policy Press, Bristol.

Knoepfel, P. and Nahrath, S. (2007) Environmental and spatial development policy, in: Klöti, U., Knoepfel, P. and Kriesi, H. (eds) *Handbook of Swiss politics*, NZZ Verlag, Zürich, 705–733.

Knoepfel, P., Nahrath, S., Savary, J., Varone, F. in collaboration with Dupuis, J. (2010) *Analyse des politiques suisses de l'environnement*, Rüegger Verlag, Zürich, Chur.

Koelble, T.A. (1995) The new institutionalism in political science and sociology, *Comparative Politics*, 27(2), 231–243.

Kuhlmann, S. and Wollmann, H. (2013) *Verwaltung und Verwaltungsreformen in Europa: Einführung in die vergleichende Verwaltungswissenschaft*, Springer, Wiesbaden.

Landry, R. and Varone, F. (2005) Choice of Policy Instruments: Confronting the Deductive and the Interactive Approaches, in: Eliadis F.P., Hill, M.M. and Howlett, M. (eds) *Designing Government. From Instruments to Governance*, McGill-Queen's University Press, Montréal.

Lascoumes, P. and Le Galès, P. (2007) Introduction: Understanding public policy through its instruments – from the nature of instruments to the sociology of public policy instrumentation, *Governance*, 20(1), 1–21.

Lichfield, N. and Darin-Drabkin, H. (1980) *Land policy in planning*, Allen, London.

Lindblom, C.E. (1959) The science of 'muddling through', *Public Administration Review*, 79–88.

Linder, S. and Peters, G. (1989) Instruments of government: Perceptions and contexts, *Journal of Public Policy*, 9(1), 35–58.

Linder, S. and Peters, G. (1990) *Policy theory and policy evaluation: Concepts, knowledge, causes, and norms*, Greenwood Press, New York.

Lowndes, V. (1996) Varieties of new institutionalism: A critical appraisal, in: *Public Administration*, 74, Blackwell Publishers Ltd., Cambridge, MA, 181–197.

Mény, Y. and Thoenig, J.C. (1989) *Politiques publiques*, Presses Universitaires de France, Paris.

Needham, B. (1997) Land policy in the Netherlands, *Tijdschrift voor economische en sociale geografie*, 88(3), 291–296.

North, D. (1990) *Institutions, institutional change and economic performance*, Cambridge University Press, Cambridge.

Ostrom, E. (1990) *Governing the commons: The evolution of institutions for collective action*, Cambridge University Press, Cambridge.

Pralle, S.B. (2003) Venue shopping, Political strategy, and policy change: The internationalization of Canadian forest advocacy, *Journal of Public Policy*, 23(3), 233–260.

Salamon, L. (2002) The new governance and the tools of public action: An introduction, in: Salamon, L. (ed.) *The tools of government: A guide to the new governance*, Oxford University Press, New York, 1–48.

Schweizer, R. (2015) Law Activation Strategies (LAS) in environmental policymaking: A social mechanism for re-politicization? *European Policy Analysis*, 1(2), 132–154.

Seele, W. (1979) Bodenpolitik für Stadt und Land, *Vermessungswesen und Raumordnung*, (8), 387–400.

Sen, A. (1981) *Poverty and famines: An essay on entitlement and deprivation*, Clarendon Press, Oxford.

Soto, H. (2000) *The mystery of capital: Why capitalism triumphs in the West and fails everywhere else*, Basic Books, New York.

Steiger, O. (2006) Property economics versus new institutional economics, *Journal of Economic Issues XL*, (1), 183–208.

Thelen, K. (2003) How institutions evolve: Insights from comparative historical analysis, in: Mahoney, J. and Rueschenmeyer, D. (eds) *Comparative historical analysis in the social sciences*, Cambridge University Press, New York, 208–240.

van der Molen, P. (2015) Property and Administration: Comparative observations on property rights and spatial planning with some cases from the Netherlands, *Administration & Society*, 47(2), 171–196.

Varone, F. (1998) *Le choix des instruments des politiques publiques*, Haupt, Bern.

Vatn, A. (2009) An institutional analysis of methods for environmental appraisal, *Ecological Economics*, 68(8), 2207–2215.

Vedung, E. (1998) Policy instruments: Typologies and theories, in: Bemelsman-Videc, M.-L., Rist, R. and Vedung, E. (eds) *Carrots, sticks and sermons: Policy instruments and their evaluation*, Transaction Publishers, New Brunswick, NJ, London, 21–58.

Wei, F. and Knox, P. L. (2015) Spatial transformation of metropolitan cities, *Environment and Planning A*, 47(1), 50–68.

Zimmermann, E. W. (1951) *World resources and industries*, Harper and Brothers, New York.

3 Instruments of land policy

Four types of intervention

Andreas Hengstermann and Thomas Hartmann

To explore how planners can strategically manage the scarcity of land in order to promote a more sparing use of resources, this book focuses on policy instruments. Each contribution from the different authors focuses on a specific instrument, which are classified according to the four paths of intervention identified in the previous chapter:

- Part II: Instruments that regulate land uses using public policy without impacting property rights
- Part III: Instruments using public policy that impact the scope and the content of use or disposal rights
- Part IV: Instruments that redefine property rights and that impact the scope and the content of use or disposal rights
- Part V: Instruments that redistribute property rights.

For each of the four types of intervention, there are three to four representative instruments presented. The aim of this volume is not to provide a comprehensive and exhaustive list of instruments. Rather it aims to capture how different types of instruments have been or could be used strategically in different contexts or countries.

For each instrument, a whole chapter describes the basic mechanisms through which scarcity is impacted using four criteria derived from policy analysis: effectiveness, efficiency, legitimacy, and practicability (Salamon 2002). To reflect on potential strategic uses of the instrument in other nations, the main chapter is complemented by contrasting and concise commentaries from two different countries. This approach intends to illustrate that, although the basic mechanisms are often similar, the use of the instrument varies depending on the national political-legal context or the planning problem at stake.

The following are the instruments and countries that were selected.

Instruments that regulate land uses using public policy without impacting property rights

(1) **Reference land values.** Information about actual values of specific parcels and general knowledge of the development on the land market are

important for a functioning market. This is what economists predict when referring to transaction costs. Some countries decide to collect and publish information on land market and actual transactions. This is done for various reasons. In 1960, Germany introduced a system of public reference land values to prevent speculation on the land market. *Winrich Voß* and *Jörn Bannert* illustrate empirically how it works in relation to land policy. Within Europe, Sweden is among the few countries with detailed and elaborated public information on land markets. *Thomas Kalbro* and *Leif Norell* note what happens when the land values are determined by the tax office and not published by the planners. Reference land values also exist in Taiwan. As *Tzuyuan Stessa Chao* reports, the assessment of the land remains the crucial challenge – from a technical point of view as well as from political perspective.

(2) **Added value capturing.** Changing zoning causes huge changes in the economic value of a parcel. Capturing this planning gain has been discussed by planners and politicians for decades. *François-Xavier Viallon* shows some Swiss examples on the instrument of added value capturing (in other contexts referred to as betterment tax). This instrument is topical, because in Switzerland it was established in the national law in 1979 but substantially reformed recently in 2014. Nevertheless, there is great interpretation leading to leeway for municipalities when practically applying the instrument to realize their strategies. The arguments for and against this instrument in the Netherlands are presented by *Erwin van der Krabben*. The debate illustrates that, in fact, land value taxation and value capturing are in some way similar, but the conflict lines about the instrument are different. In England, the instrument has an even longer tradition, as *Janet Askew* shows describing the changes and development of the instrument over time.

(3) **Land taxation.** Shaping taxes according to policy goals is a classical economic way of influencing behaviour of specific groups of people. *Fabian Thiel* and *Fabian Wenner* show how land taxation is used to achieve the realization of planning goals. In their case study of Estonia, they describe one of the very few examples in the world where a land value tax system has been established. The system was created in 1990s to reduce urban sprawl and uncontrolled land consumption. *Dirk Löhr* then highlights how taxes on landed property are currently discussed in Germany, where questions of effectiveness and justice dominate the debate. *Antonia Layard* contrasts land value tax with the variety of financial incentives that exist in England.

Instruments using public policy that impact the scope and the content of use or disposal rights

(4) **Negotiated land use plans.** Land use plans are the most standard instrument of land use planning. The plan defines zones and corresponding (potential) development rights. The Netherlands apply land use plans in a specific manner: *Joost Tennekes* reports how negotiated land use plans have worked

there for over the past two decades. For the Dutch context, this form of land use plans provides an efficient, effective, and accepted form of cost recovery for the municipalities. In Austria, similar discussions are ongoing. *Alois Humer* discusses how municipalities use more private law approaches in local planning decisions. In Canada, public interests are achieved by negotiating with land owners and investors. As *Marko Marskamp* of Canada presents in a case study, the interplay between a public law instrument (land use plans) and private law arrangements via negotiation even has its own name: Vancouverism.

(5) **Urban growth boundaries.** To address especially the arising problem of urban sprawl, an explicit determination limiting the expansion of cities can be used to complement the zoning plan. Portland is an outstanding example in the U.S. for having realized an urban growth boundary. *Edward J. Sullivan* explains how this exceptional instrument works on the municipal level. He reflects on juridical levers as well as challenges that occur when using the instrument to capture urban sprawl. In the contribution from the Netherlands, *Leonie Janssen-Jansen* and *Wendy Tan* describe how the Dutch deal with urban growth without an urban growth boundary. In Germany, a more formalized instrument exists. *Martin Wickel* explains how regional land use plans within the German system establish similar boundaries for municipal development, but work differently at the same time.

(6) **Land readjustment.** Land readjustment is a scheme that reshapes property structures that are inappropriate for the designated land use. This instrument has gained popularity in an increasing number of countries. Portugal adopted land readjustment as an instrument of land policy some years ago. *Beatriz Condessa, Ana Morais de Sá, Joana Almeida,* and *José Antunes Ferreira* report how the introduction of the instrument came with high expectations, hoping to have found a good response to the aftermath of the financial crisis in 2008 – and the huge challenges that are faced when the instrument is applied in real life. In contrast, in Germany the instrument has existed for over 100 years and is the standard instrument of planning presently. Against this background, *Theo Kötter* adds a number of key factors, such as the question of coercive participation. The Netherlands is currently experimenting with land readjustment in the urban realm. *Sanne Holtslag-Broekhof* gives an overview of this current debate. She explains whether land readjustment should be established and could form a risk-free alternative to the hitherto practiced active land policy.

(7) **Building obligation.** Whereas the preparation of a zoning plan is an active process, its implementation is – in most cases – passive. Building obligations set time limits to overcome this passivity and to guarantee its implementation by forcing landowners to comply with the land use plan. This instrument is currently tested in Switzerland in some cantons (regions). *Andreas Hengstermann* reports first practical experiences, including assumed effects. The instrument exists only in a few other countries, among them Germany, where it was introduced in 1971. *Michael Kolocek*

reflects on reasons why it has barely been used since then. *Harvey M. Jacobs* reflects an American perspective where such an instrument is unthinkable and would probably be a shock.

Instruments that redefine property rights and that impact the scope and the content of use or disposal rights

(8) **Pre-emption rights.** To achieve a desired land use, the state may directly intervene and become landowner. In France, the government can pre-empt land acquisitions for agricultural or housing policy purposes and even for building land reserves. *Romain Melot* presents a case study from the region of Paris, where housing scarcity occurs and public bodies prevent speculations on land prices with this instrument. In Switzerland, pre-emption rights are applicable to deal with scarcity of land. *Stéphane Nahrath* reports how in Geneva effects occur anticipatory, even without actually enforcing the instrument. Public bodies strategically use the instrument as a threat to prevent rising prices. The instrument has a totally different connotation in Serbia. *Sofija Nikolić* explains from the former socialist country that the reservations against the instrument are high, but nevertheless it still exists for specific issues of scarcity of land.

(9) **Tradable development rights (TDR).** The TDR instrument redefines property on land in a way that the development rights can be traded independently from the remaining rights. This solution aims at the problem-solving forces of the market and has been discussed in many countries. Nonetheless, only a few examples of TDR are actually implemented. The instruments stems from the U.S., so *Thomas Skuzinski* and *Evangeline Linkous* illustrate along four different cases how it works there. The examples show that the system is closely linked to the legal nature of development rights. Israel tried to follow the U.S. example. *Nir Mualam* uses the example of Tel Aviv, to show how development rights are distributed and traded as incentives and can also counter-finance the preservation of historic buildings. Canada adopted TDR as well. *Eran S. Kaplinsky* discusses several projects with different goals. His commentary shows a variety of models and crucial parameters.

(10) **Long-term land leases.** Another way of re-defining property rights is based on the separation of the rights in land and the rights in building on land. In France, the instrument of long-term land lease (sometimes referred to as heritable building rights or long-term ground leases) has a long tradition. *Sonia Guelton* and *Vincent Le Rouzic* present two specific cases where they describe how the disconnection of the financial value of land from the use value fosters affordable housing in Paris and homeownership in Lyon. The authors point out how control by the public sector is a key success factor. Relying on a Swiss example, *Jean-David Gerber* describes the ongoing debate on the introduction and extension of long-term land leases by

municipalities. In Australia, the interest in the instrument is continuously increasing, as *Rebecca Leshinsky* reports.

Instruments that redistribute property rights

(11) **Strategic land banking.** Public land banking is based on strategic purchases of land on the free market by a public authority to use the land for specific projects or to build up reserves. This is meant to foster a quick implementation of future planning projects. In the Netherlands, land banking is often used on the municipal level. As *Tejo Spit* describes, some provinces have additionally started to use this instrument for specific purposes. For Great Britain, *Deborah Peel* points out that even though the public sector is the largest land owner in the UK, there is a huge implementation gap. The key question for her is how to successfully incentivize the involved parties to build. Taking the American perspective, *Richard K. Norton* describes that public planning does not play as prominent a role in shaping land use patterns in the U.S. However, public land banking, in a very narrow sense, is sometimes used to fix a dysfunctional tax foreclosure process, not to coordinate and speed up private development projects that advance municipal planning as for example in the Netherlands. The application of land banking thus depends not on technical or legal issues, but crucially is influenced by cultural and political aspects in the respective country.

(12) **Expropriation.** This is one of the standard instruments of land policy. To mobilize parcels that are required to realize planned public projects, the instrument of expropriation exists in all states. However, the interpretation of when its application should be allowed is very different, as is the terminology. Expropriation means the transfer of property rights from the original parcel owner to the state. In Germany, the hurdles for expropriation are high because private property is well protected. *Juliane Albrecht* describes the legal challenges in setting up a just and effective procedure of expropriation. The instrument is mainly used for transport projects. *Barrie Needham* outlines a more pragmatic approach in the Netherlands, with a broader understanding of public purposes. Expropriation can be applied for housing or even shopping centres. In contrary, the understanding of public purposes justifying expropriation is much narrower in the U.S., as described by *Dan Tarlock*. Land can only be expropriated for infrastructure projects such as pipelines.

(13) **Nationalization of land.** In cases where private land patterns lead to overexploitation of the resource, a nationalization of land might be a solution. *Greg Lloyd* reports from Scotland that public interest in land can be secured through public landownership. *Jirina Jilkova* reminds us that although land nationalization might be a promising instrument for some situations, the historic experiences of the Czech Republic and other former Soviet countries, where collectivization was implemented on a large scale

and destroyed social structures, has had negative impacts on nonmarket services of land as a resource. A different situation can be found in Greece where, after the economic crisis, neoliberal policies increased political-economic uncertainties even more. The aftermath continues to be balanced by even further privatizations. *Konstantinos Lalenis* reflects on this trend and refers to the issue of nationalization of land. From a post-socialist perspective, nationalization of land appears far less tempting.

Not all of the discussed instruments exist in all countries, some are rather specific, such as urban growth boundaries (UGB) or building obligations. Others, such as negotiated forms of land use plans or expropriation, can be considered standard instruments of land policy, available in most countries. The scope for discretion for choosing a specific instrument differs according to national legislation. The contributions of this book reveal that, even if an instrument exists in similar forms in different countries, it is often used differently by planners. International comparison shows that many problems faced by planners in connection with land scarcity are similar, but the responses are often different. This is one of the reasons that make the comparison presented in this book topical.

Reference

Salamon, L.M. (2002) The new governance and the tools of public action, in: Salamon, L.M. and Elliott, O.V. (eds) *The tools of government: A guide to the new governance*, Oxford University Press, Oxford, New York, 1–47.

Part II

Regulating land uses without impacting property rights

4 Reference land values in Germany

Land policy by market transparency

Winrich Voß and Jörn Bannert

Introduction

In Germany the system of reference land values was established by law more than 50 years ago to support market transparency and to avoid speculations with land. The stakeholders of a well-functioning urban land market are in need of reliable information about the current price level of developed land. Reference land values are available for each neighbourhood (areas of comparable location quality) and are evaluated and published by official valuation boards periodically. This chapter examines the impact of this tool under the perspective of land policy. A case study near Hanover illustrates the results. Different and opposing impacts are extracted. In the balance, the usage of reference land values by market participants and the evaluation by the valuation boards will converge to market value.

Market transparency is one of the preconditions of a well-functioning real estate market. Market transparency is created by market information that is easily available to everyone; market information should include indicators on supply, demand, prices, and transactions. This information may be published by private stakeholders as well as by public institutions (Gudat and Voß 2012).

In Germany, market transparency is created by market information from the private segment, but especially by the work of special administrative units called Boards of Expert Valuers (*Gutachterausschüsse für Grundstückswerte*). One of their tasks is to derive and publish 'reference land values' according to different locations in each German municipality. Reference land values are important orientation guides for real estate market participants, such as municipalities, developers, investors, or private persons.

This contribution investigates the influence of reference land values on the land market, especially the relation to land prices, and examines the question: do reference land values affect land prices? The following research questions are at the centre of interest:

- How are reference land values established today?
- What is the part/function of reference land values in the market system today?

- How do reference land values influence the market? Do they have a land policy effect?

To examine possible land policy effects, the chapter analyzes the different methods of the evaluation on the one hand, and the way market participants usually make use of the reference land values on the other hand. This is based on the current legal base and practice in view of the historic intentions when introducing reference land values in Germany. To illustrate the market effects of reference land values, a case study of a residential area in a medium-size town near Hanover, Lower Saxony, is shown. For each year since 2005, the average price level based on purchase prices for building land will be compared with the fixed reference land values. It is differentiated between private landowners, municipalities, and professional players. The chapter derives some conclusions about the influence of reference land values on the local land market.

The system of reference land values in Germany

The first German Federal Building Code (*Bundesbaugesetz*) in 1960 introduced reference land values as an instrument to create market transparency. Reference land values are determined by the entrusted Boards of Expert Valuers (*Gutachterausschüsse für Grundstückswerte*). Reference land values refer to average prices for unbuilt, completely developed plots. They compare areas with a comparable standard of land use (reference land value zone, e.g. a residential neighbourhood) and are determined by a range of purchase prices from this area within the past year. The law publishes the results, and everyone is able to extract information for his/her purposes.

The Boards of Expert Valuers are established in different administrative sectors throughout the country. In Lower Saxony, they are organized at the cadastral offices as part of the federal state; in other federal states (*Länder*), they are established at the county level. The work of the Boards of Expert Valuers has to be independent from the policy of their respective administrative unit. All members of the boards are appointed – usually for a five-year period – and have to be experienced in land and property valuation. The boards consist of experts from different professions in an interdisciplinary mixture – surveyors, architects, civil engineers, bankers, real estate agents, developers, urban planners, agricultural and forestry experts, employees of tax authorities, building authorities, and planning authorities. Each Board of Expert Valuers is responsible for running their database – the Automated Transactions Register – publishing market reports, determining reference land values (at least every two years), deriving important data regularly necessary in property value determination, and further tasks (Kertscher et al. 2011).

Within the determination process, the Boards of Expert Valuers are also using information about urban land use planning (detailed land use plans).

Using this information, combined with purchase transactions in these areas, reference land value zones are created. Therefore, reference land value zones combine similar land values based on comparable type and degree of land use. A reference value for each zone is then calculated relating to a reference plot. In summary, each reference land value zone is represented by the mean value of current property transactions and a reference plot regarding the urban land use situation (Figure 4.1).

In Germany, the online platform *BORIS* was created by the Boards of Expert Valuers with the aim of presenting the fixed reference values and giving access to everyone (in some federal states, such as Lower Saxony, for a fee; Wanzke 2006). In Figure 4.1, the reference land value zones in the city centre of Hanover are shown with their specific value (euro per square meter). 'MK' core area (*Kerngebiet*) stands for the dominant type of land

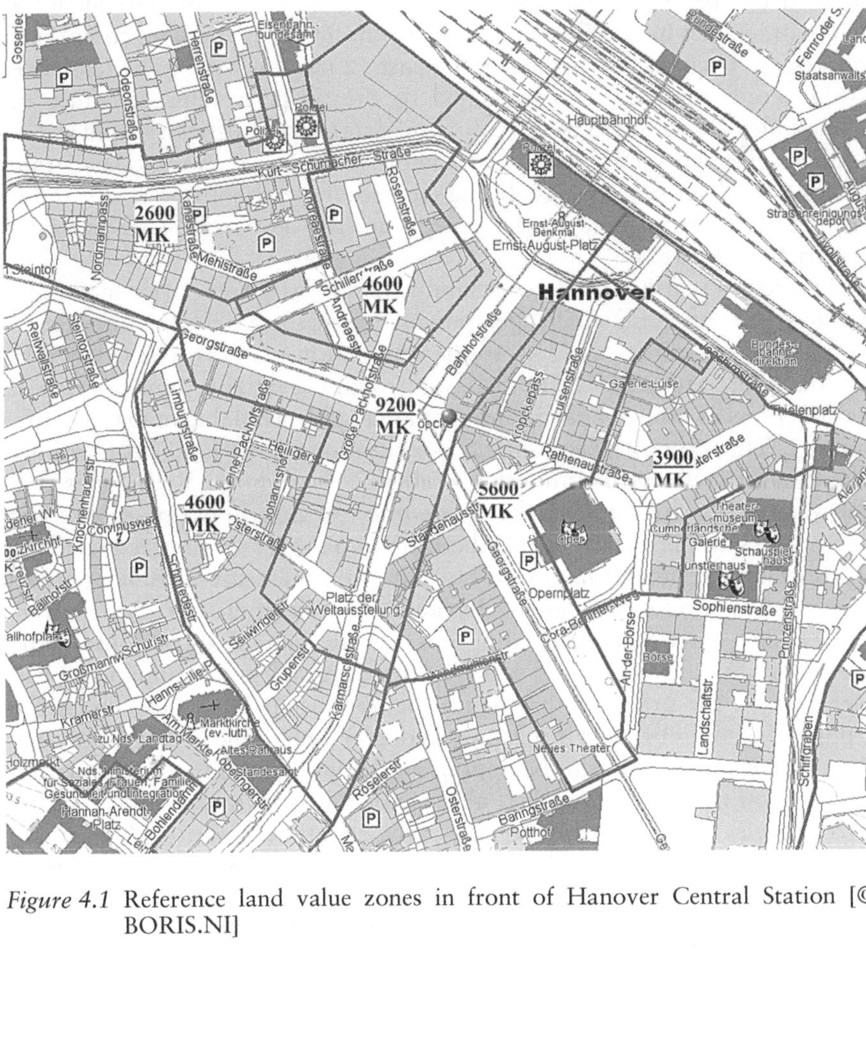

Figure 4.1 Reference land value zones in front of Hanover Central Station [© BORIS.NI]

use in each zone. Often typical characteristics of the plots are reported additionally, e.g. permitted floor space ratio or typical size of a plot.

In Germany, reference land values have to be determined at least every two years (§ 196 German Federal Building Code). In Lower Saxony, the Boards of Expert Valuers determine reference land values once a year. Reference land values have to be determined for building land and should be determined for agricultural land. The reference land values refer to 1 square meter of site area and include all development costs (fully developed plot) (§ 21 Niedersächsische Durchführungsverordnung des BauGB 2005).

The determination of reference land values is based on information from the Automated Transaction Register and other, for the valuation required data, like land price index series or conversion coefficients. All notaries are required by law to copy each property sale contract and send it to the local Board of Expert Valuers. The Boards of Expert Valuers register all property sale contracts in the Automated Transaction Register. But only purchase agreements are used. Unusual or personal factors are disregarded. Reference land values have to be determined primarily using the sales comparison approach. The purchase values of the past 12 months have to be referenced (using conversion coefficients suited to the property characteristics and using index series suited to the valuation date) and statistically analyzed for outliers. Reference land value zones with only a few or no purchase transactions are determined by analyzing changes in neighbouring zones and by using index series suited to the general market development (Bodenrichtwertrichtlinie 2011).

The determination of reference land values from current price material of the past year often is a challenge. In many towns the number of transactions of cases of unbuilt land is low, so the transaction prices from the last three to four years are used. Other methods are taking into account prices from transactions of built-up properties that are readily available in many market sectors. Thus, the market-compliant separation of the land proportion in the total property price is another challenge. In addition to the sales comparison approach (*Vergleichswertverfahren*) for determination of reference land values and property values, there are two more standardized valuation approaches for determination of built-up properties: the income approach (*Ertragswertverfahren*) and the replacement cost approach (*Sachwertverfahren*). All three standardized approaches are defined by statutory order (ImmoWertV). The choice of which of these approaches is going to be used depends on the property that has to be appraised. The sales comparison approach should be used if there are enough comparable transactions. If an investment property has to be appraised, the income approach is used. The application of each approach is also regulated by statutory order (*Sachwertrichtlinie, Ertragswertrichtlinie, Vergleichswertrichtlinie, Bodenrichtwertrichtlinie*). The Boards of Expert Valuers support the work of commercial valuers by publishing important benchmarks as all-risk-yields (income approach) or market adaptation factors (cost approach).

Importance and genesis of reference land values

Reference land values today are relevant in different fields, e.g. the determination of fair market values, the fiscal and property tax valuation, the assessment of locations for urban and regional development, and especially for enhancing the transparency of the real estate market (Kleiber 2016: 1132). They are well known and often used to orientate oneself in the price level of land.

Additionally, reference land values are important in the budget control of German municipalities and state bodies. They are obliged, by budgetary law, not to sell building land under the market value, represented by reference land values. Hereby, reference land values have a direct link to local land policy, but a municipality's range to dampen land prices is very limited. Reference land values easily allow for checking the range of selling prices.

The first demand for official market information originated from tax issues. The official collecting of transaction prices started in Germany with the Prussian tax reform in 1893 and its technical instruction concerning the initial estimation of property values. The introduction of reference land values in the reconstruction period after World War II arose in consequence of a former edict about price freezing. In 1936, price increases for developed land were officially forbidden; the 'Reichscommissioner for pricing' determined the prices and supervised the compliance. After 1952, the edict about price freezing was no longer used, and it was finally abolished in 1960 (Kertscher et al. 2011).

But while preparing the new Federal Building Code (*Bundesbaugesetz*) during the 1950s – a very interesting period of land policy discussions – the government became worried about uncontrolled increases of land prices in the new market economy. The building boom in the 1950s and the former price freezing for land caused a parallel market. So an official monitoring of the market activities – including price collection system, reference land values, and local valuation boards – was thought to improve market transparency with additional information about volume and price level of market activities. The intentions of the new Federal Building Code were 'the real estate observation, the creation of market transparency and the absorption of vibrations on the market' (BT-Drs 336 1958: 106). This was an initiative of the conservative parliamentary group (CDU/CSU). Therefore, it was necessary to get reliable information about the 'new real estate market' based on notarial purchase agreements and to publish the derived information in the form of the first market reports available for all participating players on the real estate market (GAG 2016). The intention was to strengthen market transparency by publication of reference land values based on a collection of transaction results; it was not intended to implement a tool to directly influence market aspects, e.g. to dampen land prices.

The impact of reference land values should be limited to the aspect that – after the long period of controlled market forces – they could counteract in case of unclear perceptions about value relations for the involved parties. If scarceness dominates market conditions, the seller often is in a stronger position; here an improved market transparency by offering reference land values could help keep a fair balance between seller and buyer (Kleiber 2016: section 196).

The regulations of the Federal Building Code concerning reference land values have proven their worth over more than 50 years. The main amendments of the Building Code in 1976 and 1986 added small modifications only. The 2009 amendment focused on the competencies concerning the determination and uniformity of reference land values at the national administrative level (Voß, EZBK 2016, section 192–199; Kleiber 2016: 1133f.).

In the past two decades, the technical 'state of the art' has grown rapidly – especially at 'the new media sector'. That's why the publishing platforms were extended and online platforms like *BORIS* were created in addition to the 'classic analog' products, e.g. maps (Figure 4.1) or market reports.

Another important result of the boards' activities relevant to market transparency is an index of property price development within the region. Currently there are many discussions about the strong land and property price increase in German towns.

Today experts from federal, state, and local authorities confirm that the 1960 aims of the foundation of the Boards of Expert Valuers in creating market transparency have been achieved. The products from the Boards of Expert Valuers have been established (Kleiber 2016; Voß 2011).

Case study: relation of reference land values and market price

Based on an empirical investigation, literature-based assessments, and the experience of the authors the question of the effects of reference land values on land policy will be discussed. An investigation area with available information in Langenhagen-Kaltenweide was chosen, where building land has been developed in several steps since 2005.

Different participating players act on the real estate market, and each participating player may use reference land values with different intentions. The participating players can be divided into three groups: profit-oriented participants, nonprofit-oriented participants, and natural persons. The group of profit-oriented participants includes e.g. investors, developers, banks, housing companies, and sometimes municipalities. The group of nonprofit-oriented participants includes e.g. municipalities or municipal housing companies. The group of natural persons includes private purchasers, private sellers, or private persons, who want to get information about the real estate market.

In the investigation area the following players are acting on the real estate market (offering fully developed building plots): housing companies ('KSG Hannover'), private landowners, and the municipality of Langenhagen itself. The following analysis differentiates according to these market players.

Presentation of the investigation area

With more than 53,000 residents, Langenhagen is one of the biggest municipalities in the Hanover region. The region of Hanover includes 21 municipalities and is the regional development authority of Lower Saxony's capital city area. Most of the residents in Langenhagen live in the centre. About 7,250 residents live in the district of Kaltenweide, which is the investigation area (Langenhagen 2016a).

To develop building land especially for families with children (the aim of the local land policy), Langenhagen decided to create plots in Kaltenweide in several steps, starting in 2005. Since the development area is located in the reference land value zone of Kaltenweide, the reference land values are available from the yearly review of the valuation board. In the next step, all plot purchases in that zone from 2005 until 2015 are selected from the Automated Transaction Register.

Transactions – selection criteria

For selecting suitable property transactions from the Automated Transaction Register the following selection criteria are used: within the reference land value zone of Kaltenweide, property purchase agreements between 1 January 2005 and 31 December 2015 are selected. Only property purchase agreements without unusual circumstances or value-affecting specialities in small housing estate areas or private home areas with upmarket standard are selected.

According to these selection criteria the Automated Transaction Register provides suitable transactions for building land. It is very important that value-affecting specialities are disregarded.

The database delivers 691 property purchase agreements in 11 years. For each year there are enough purchase agreements for a reliable statistical evaluation (on average about 60 transactions per year).

In the next step, possible outliers have to be eliminated from the annual samples. A property purchase agreement is defined as an outlier, if the individual value lies outside the calculated range according to the following formula:

$$\textit{Value Range} = \textit{Mean Value} \pm 2.5 \times \textit{standard Deviation } \sigma$$

For each year a value range is calculated. Each purchase data out of this range is eliminated and a new value range is calculated (iterative process). This methodology is also used by the Boards of Expert Valuers to detect outliers and is 'state of the art'.

Evaluation of property transactions in comparison with reference land value

Table 4.1 gives an overview of the average transaction prices. A difference is made whether the seller is a natural person, the municipality itself,

Table 4.1 Mean purchase prices and reference land values

Year	*Reference Land Value*[1] *(€/m²)*	*Mean Price Level (€/m²)*	*Seller Natural Persons*	*Seller Municipality*	*Seller Housing Companies*	*Seller Other Legal Persons*
2005	165	173	–	170	173	–
2006	165	175	–	–	175	175
2007	165	173	–	151	174	–
2008	165	172	–	–	172	–
2009	165	171	–	–	171	–
2010	165	170	–	–	170	–
2011	165	171	161	–	171	–
2012	165	170	–	172	170	–
2013	165	186	–	195	181	–
2014	170	191	–	190	192	–
2015	185	–	–	–	–	–

[1] Published by the Board of Expert Valuers Hameln-Hannover

Table 4.2 Number of property transactions per seller

Year	*Outliers*	*Natural Persons*	*Municipality*	*Housing Companies*	*Other Legal Persons*
2005	1	0	17	104	0
2006	8	0	0	64	1
2007	8	0	1	44	0
2008	7	0	0	64	0
2009	0	0	0	79	0
2010	1	0	0	103	0
2011	1	1	0	56	0
2012	2	0	4	75	0
2013	2	0	14	23	0
2014	0	0	7	4	0
2015	0	0	0	0	0

a housing company, or another legal person. For each group and year, the price level is calculated on the basis of the mean value of all purchase values (without outliers) and will be compared with the reference land value.

Before these results can be interpreted, it has to be examined as to how many property transactions are sold by which seller. Table 4.2 shows the number of property transactions (without outliers) for each year by seller.

The marked results are statistically insecure, because there is only one property purchase agreement in these years. So these three price levels have to be interpreted very carefully.

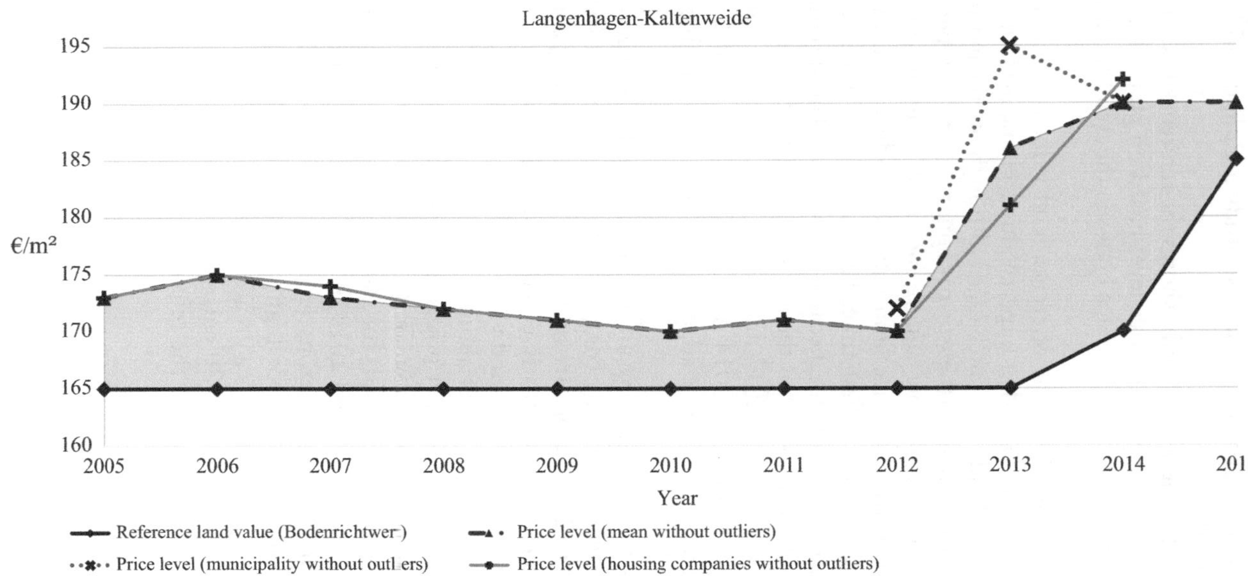

Figure 4.2 Reference land value and mean price level [own presentation]

Between 2005 and 2013, most of the plots were sold by housing companies. In 2005, 2012, and 2013, the municipality of Langenhagen has a significant share of the plot sales. Unfortunately, the group of private landowners (natural persons, one plot sale in 2011; other legal persons, one plot sale in 2006) is not relevant in the case study area and will be ignored for further investigations.

In figure 4.2 the line with rhombs shows the reference land values, the line with triangles shows the mean price level based on plot sales by all institutions. There is a systematic difference between the two lines marked in grey color.

Between 2005 and 2013 the reference land value is constant (165 euros per square meter). The Board of Expert Valuers Hameln-Hanover decided to keep the reference land value unchanged although the mean purchase prices were higher in these years (10 euros per square meter or 6 percent in 2006, but decreasing to 5 euros per square meter or 3 percent in 2010–2012). Starting in 2014, the reference land value was adjusted to the mean price level of plot sales for the first time, because the difference between price level and reference land value became significant. The difference between these lines are mostly equal but there is still a constant price level difference between 5 to 10 euros. In 2013 and 2014 the mean price level for all plot sales increases strongly. In 2014 and 2015, the Board of Expert Valuers raised the reference land value adapting the increase of the mean price level for plots.

The graphs for plot sales by all institutions and housing companies are mostly equal, because housing companies having the largest share of all plot sales. In 2008 to 2010, there are only plot sales by housing companies. The gradients of the lines are mostly equal until 2012 and show, a price level difference between reference land values and mean price level for all institutions or housing companies of about 5 to 10 euros.

Starting in 2012 the market prices strongly increased in Langenhagen, a trend which could be noticed in Germany's housing market at all.

The graph (mean price level) for plot sales by municipality can only be calculated between 2012 and 2014, because in these years there are more than three purchase transactions (compare Table 4.2). In this time the municipality sold the plots for higher prices than the housing company (compare Figure 4.2). There is a greater price level difference (20 euros difference for all plot sales and 30 euros difference for plot sales by municipality) in these years because the reference land values were adapted with delay.

Discussion

Although the case study is a single case with specific involvement of the municipality and a housing association (municipality is the dominating associate), the detected gap between sales prices and reference land values seems to be a typical situation according to the experience of the authors.

The following aspects need to be mentioned:

- The legal base of reference land values and of Boards of Expert Valuers does not strive for direct influence on real estate markets. They are obliged to picture market trends and activities in a neutral manner. The general autonomy of the boards and the interdisciplinary composition of their members is essential and has been a standard for over five decades.
- However, from the beginning, the understanding of reference land values seems to be predominantly that of a smoothing tool for volatile market trends. That is why reference land values often operate as 'vibration absorbers' with the aim to cover price fluctuations carefully and significantly (Dietrich and Voß EZBK 2016, secs. 192–199). This function impacts reference land values in both directions; it is not limited to dampening effects. In the first decade of the current century in more than a few regions property prices decreased in Germany; here it would be possible to show the absorber effect in case of decreasing market trends.
- The case study of Kaltenweide shows a lag of reference land value behind the average market value. The difference between the linear trends is small, but significant. The Boards of Expert Valuers are used to determine reference land values conservatively and in a manner that will not strengthen speculative trends in market development. Therefore, the Boards of Expert Valuers mostly prefer to determine reference land values a little bit under the estimated mean price level for building land.
- The lag in the case study area comes to an amount of about 5–10 euros per square meter or 3–6 percent of reference land value. This is not a representative result, but it is ranked to be a small range in view of typical accuracy levels of property valuations. In a long discussion related to the amendment of BauGB valuation regulations 2009, a range of 20–30 percent was discussed as the target heterogeneity of land values within one reference land value zone (Kleiber 2016: 1134).
- The results of the case study of Kaltenweide show a 'temporal shift' between the reference land value and the calculated mean price value for each year since 2005. The mean price level (linear trend) is a result of supply and demand for building land and is influenced by the economic climate on the real estate market. The temporal shift arises because the reference land values are determined every 12 or 24 months. During this time period, the economic climate on the real estate market continues to develop but the reference land value is frozen for 12 months (e.g. in Lower Saxony) or 24 months. The temporal shift expands if the Boards of Expert Valuers determine the reference land values at least every two years. A minimizing of the temporal shift is possible if reference land values are verified at least twice a year.
- The 'temporal shift' is relevant in periods of strong changing of prices as the increasing trend in German cities since 2010. The shift is caused by the estimation methodology of the reference land values due to the valuation date. For example, the price material of the year 2016 is analyzed and

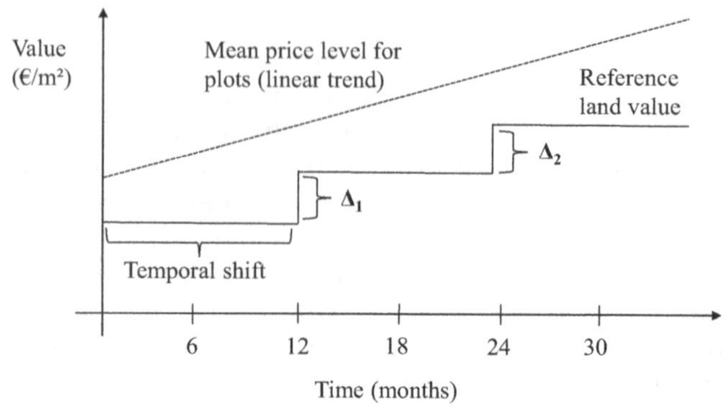

Figure 4.3 The temporal shift [own presentation]

updated to the valuation date (31 December 2016). This result is published in 2017 as the valid reference land value. A competent use of the data would require a time adaptation to each respective valuation date.
- The different participating groups make use of reference land values in different intentions.

The profit-oriented participants want to achieve high profits from their invested capital and usually negotiate higher selling prices for developed plots. Therefore, profit-oriented participants understand the reference land values as the lowest threshold for their calculations. Many participants add as a minimum the amount of their profit surcharge to the reference land value.

The nonprofit-oriented public participants (like municipalities or municipal organizations) are obliged by budgetary law to operate profitably. They regularly orientate selling prices for developed plots on reference land values as fair market values. Budgetary law does not allow selling prices less than the adapted reference land values. Housing companies, nonprofit-oriented participants, and even municipalities often negotiate higher selling prices when the market participants will accept a higher selling price in view of the current conditions on the real estate market.

The group of natural persons is often clueless about a fair market value. If they get the information about relevant reference land values – easily today by internet – and this level meets their beliefs, they interpret the reference land values as possible purchase prices at a minimum level. Sellers feel more satisfied if the contracted price is higher than the reference land value. On the other hand, buyers often agree to pay slightly more than the reference land value because of the opinion that reference land value level is seen as the minimum rate.

Conclusion – do reference land values affect the land market?

Taking into account the different aspects and arguments discussed above, in summary a systematic dampening effect of reference land values is not reasonable. The dictum of the valuation boards and the process of estimating reference land values lead to cautious estimations of reference land values on the one hand, often with a time delay to market development. On the other hand, the stakeholder groups – even nonprofit parties – understand reference land values as the lowest possible price, which they wish to exceed more or less. In the balance of these two contrary effects, the result of the different aspects of reference land values on the behaviour of the market participants will converge just near to market value. Nevertheless, the discussion additionally shows that some expert knowledge is necessary to use the information from reference land values in an appropriate way (e.g. time relevance and valuation date).

All in all, reference land values are an important and market-compliant instrument in Germany to support the real estate market information; they are able to support the legal request to create transparency on the real estate market. Due to the independent nature of the Boards of Expert Valuers, there is no general land policy influence by the determination of reference land values. In times of strong land and property price increase, reference land values are even more important for creating transparency on the real estate market. Although improvements are discussed, the reference land values are established and well proven in Germany; today they are of valuable use in the society and are not up for debate.

Acknowledgement

The authors would like to thank the Board of Expert Valuers Hameln-Hannover for selecting the purchase transactions with the selection criteria from the Automated Transactions Register and for providing the needed information for the empirical investigation.

References

Bodenrichtwertrichtlinie (2011) *Bodenrichtwertrichtlinie in der Fassung vom 11.01.2011* (online) available at: www.bundesanzeiger-verlag.de/fileadmin/BIV-Portal/Bildervorschlaege/PDF/Bodenrichtwert-richtlinie.pdf (accessed 21 October 2016).

BT-DRS 336 (1958) *Entwurf eines Bundesbaugesetzes* (online) available at: http://dipbt.bundestag.de/doc/btd/03/003/0300336.pdf (accessed 2 March 2017).

Dieterich, H., Voß, W., EZBK (2016) *Ernst/Zinkahn/Bielenberg/Krautzberger: BauGB Kommentar, Loseblattsammlung*, Verlag C. H. BECK, Munich.

GAG (2016) *50 Jahre Gutachterausschüsse für Grundstückswerte in Niedersachsen, Festschrift* (online) available at: www.gag.niedersachsen.de/ gutachterausschuesse/102587.html (accessed 14 October 2016).

Gudat, R. and Voß, W. (2012) *Endbericht zum Forschungsprojekt Weiterentwicklung der Markttransparenz am Grundstücks- und Immobilienmarkt* (online) available at: www.gih.uni-hannover.de/uploads/tx_tkpublikationen/ endbericht_markttransparenz_2012.pdf (accessed 15 February 2017).

Kertscher, D., Liebig, S. and Klein, T. (2011) 50 Jahre Gutachterausschüsse und Grundstücksmarkttransparenz – Rückblick und Bilanz am Beispiel des Landes Niedersachsen, *Zeitschrift für Geodäsie, Geoinformation und Landmanagement*, 2011(6), 344–351.

Kleiber, W. (2016) *Verkehrswertermittlung von Grundstücken: Kommentar und Handbuch zur Ermittlung von Marktwerten (Verkehrswerten) und Beleihungswerten sowie zur steuerlichen Bewertung unter Berücksichtigung der ImmoWertV*, Bundesanzeiger Verlag, Cologne.

Kleiber, W. and EZBK (2016) *Ernst/Zinkahn/Bielenberg/Krautzberger, BauGB Kommentar, Loseblattsammlung*, Verlag C. H. BECK, Munich.

Langenhagen (2016a) *Facts about the town* (online) available at: www.langenhagen.de/index.phtml?mNavID=1620.1&sNavID=1620.15&La=1 (accessed 25 October 2016).

Niedersächsische Durchführungsverordnung des BauGB (2005) *Niedersächsische Verordnung zur Durchführung des Baugesetzbuches in der Fassung vom 24.05.2005* (online) available at: www.nds-voris.de (accessed 21 October 2016).

Voß, W. (2011) *Transparency of property markets – the 1. national level market report*, paper FIG Working Week Marrakech, 18–22 May, Marrakech, Morocco, (online) available at: www.fig.net/resources/databases/srl/index.asp (accessed 19 February 2017).

Voß, W. and EZBK (2016) *Ernst/Zinkahn/Bielenberg/Krautzberger, BauGB Kommentar, Loseblattsammlung*, Verlag C. H. BECK, Munich.

Wanzke, H. (2006) *BORIS.NRW – the information system on standard land values in North-Rhine-Westphalia, Germany*, Paper XXIII FIG Congress, 8–13 October 2006, Munich, Germany (online) available at: www.fig.net/resources/databases/srl/index.asp (accessed 19 Feruary 2017).

A Swedish perspective on reference land values: transparency by tax policy

Thomas Kalbro and Leif Norell

Establishment of reference land values

In Germany, as described by → *Voß and Bannert*, reference land values are determined by the entrusted Boards of Expert Valuers, which are established in different administrative constellations throughout the country. For example, in Lower Saxony they are organized at the cadastral offices as part of the federal state. The determination of reference land values is based on information from the Automated Transaction Register and values are primarily determined by using the sales comparison approach.

In Sweden, reference values are basically related to the property taxation system, but are today used for a number of purposes. The assessed so-called tax value corresponds to 75 percent of the market value. The total tax value consists of two parts – a land value and a building value.

The tax assessment is drawn up and approved by the Swedish Tax Agency, with the assistance of the National Land Survey (*Lantmäteriet*). Single-family houses, terraced houses, and condominiums are assessed every three years, whereas properties for industry, agriculture, and forestry are assessed every six years.

In short, as a result of the property tax system, Sweden is divided into a number of 'value areas with reference values' (*värdeområden och riktvärdekartor*) with equal conditions related to the type of property, site area, water and sewage status, construction year, standard of buildings, and so forth. As we understand, this principal system is a very similar system to what Voß and Bannert describe.

The information with property tax values is publicly available through the Tax Agency.[1] Furthermore, sales taking place within the area are continuously reported, as can be exemplified by Figure 4.4. If we compare Figure 4.4 with Voß and Bannert's, it seems that the underlying ideas in Sweden and Germany are more or less identical.

With this basic information it is possible to analyze property values in different ways in a value area, a municipality, a region, or the whole country. This can be exemplified by Figure 4.5, which shows an index series of prices for single-family houses, second/holiday homes, and apartment

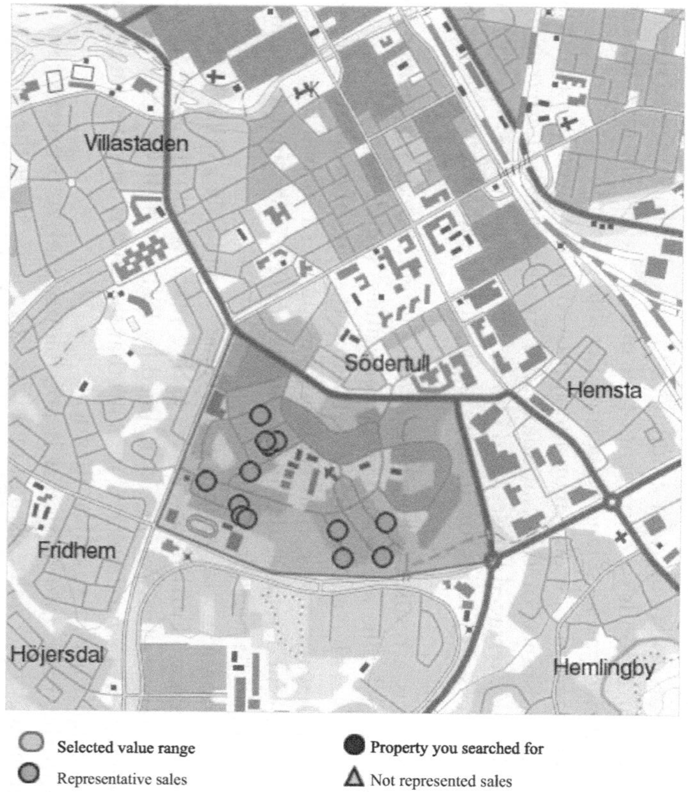

Value range number: 2180017

Date title deed	Purchase price	T/K-tal
2013-09-25	1 875	0,84
2013-07-01	1 725	0,78
2013-05-31	3 700	0,65
2012-01-16	3 400	0,72
2012-01-02	2 200	0,84
2011-12-01	3 500	0,61
2011-09-30	2 600	0,74
2011-09-30	2 400	0,70
2011-08-15	1 830	0,79
2011-08-15	1 675	0,75
2011-07-20	2 200	0,69
2011-06-01	1 550	0,75
2011-04-15	2 225	0,73

Figure 4.4 Publicly available property tax values (www.skatteverket.se)

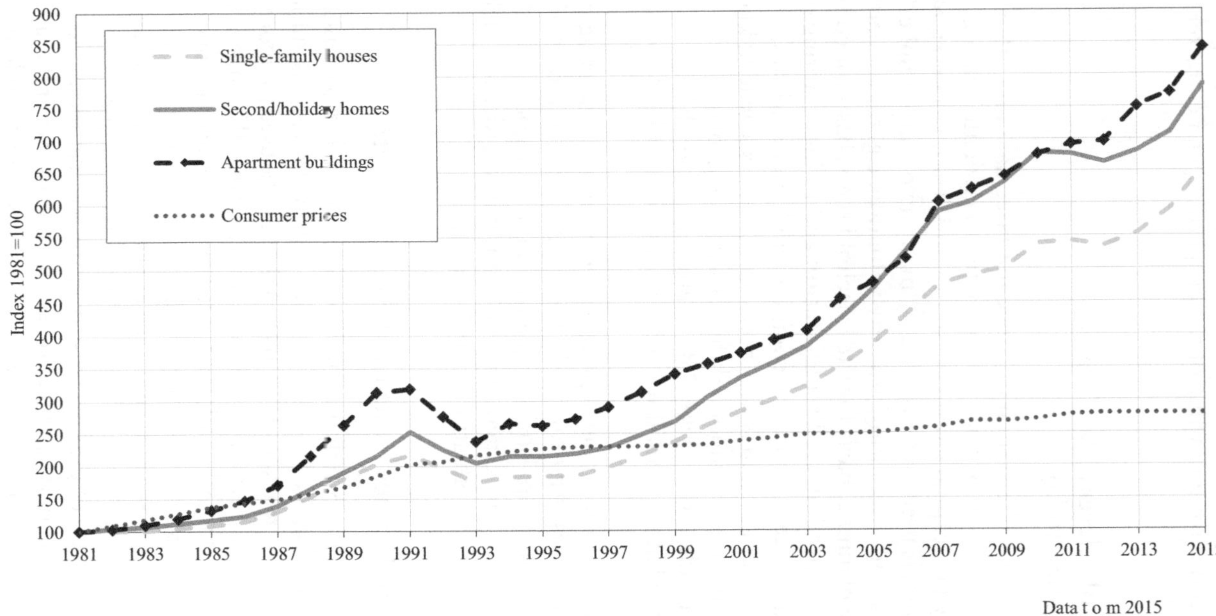

Figure 4.5 Price development in Sweden from 1981 to 2015

Source: Statistics Sweden (*Statistiska Centralbyrån*, www.scb.se)

buildings between 1981 and 2015. This price development is compared to the increase in consumer prices (Statistics Sweden 2017).

The index series above is based on the prices (K) for each property sold in relation to the respective tax value of the properties (T), i.e. the relationship between K/T.

The function of reference land values in the market system today

As mentioned earlier, the system of collecting price data and other features related to properties was originally constructed to facilitate taxation of properties (property tax, capital gains tax, stamp duty, etc.). However, today the data in the system is used and analyzed by many actors in a number of ways as a basis for measures requiring property valuation, e.g. for property acquisition, land use planning, basis for site leasehold rents, basis for compulsory acquisition compensation, credit information and rating, granting of credit/mortgaging, insurance purposes, accounting, and price statistics.

Since the price information is easy accessible, there is a general knowledge of the property price levels among different actors, e.g. planners or developers who are dependent on market information to make the right decisions. Shall we initiate planning? Shall we acquire this piece of land? Within what price range?

In many cases general property price information is the starting point for more detailed analyses. An example is when a property or a part of a property *can be* acquired compulsorily, e.g. a road. Initial negotiations about the price can be based on this general information, but in order to reach a final agreement more precise valuations may be required.

Do reference land values influence the land market?

Unlike in Germany, the Swedish system of reference value/tax value has no intention of influencing the land market. But it provides very useful information to the actors in the market – information that can be used for more detailed analyses in different respects. Nevertheless, we can draw the same conclusion as Voß and Bannert do: 'All in all, reference land values are an important and market-compliant instrument to support the real estate market information.' The transparency of the Swedish land market also reveals that land prices, generally speaking, are quite low compared to other Western European countries. Despite the background of price increase over the past decades, land is affordable for a large portion of the population in most areas, even if the situation in metropolitan areas, such as the Stockholm region, is more troublesome.

Note

1 Available at: www.skatteverket.se/privat/sjalvservice/allaetjanster/tjanster/vardeomradenochriktvardekartor (accessed 14 June 2017).

A Taiwan perspective on reference land values: the hare and the hedgehogs – chasing real price levels with public market information

Tzuyuan Stessa Chao

How to put a proper price on a plot of land is always one of the difficult tasks for many countries with limited land resources. It is generally considered as the core context of how a political regime manages and controls its property right system and land value. As in Germany, the system of establishing reference land values is for enhancing the transparency and fair transactions of the land market. Thus, in most Asian countries, i.e. Japan, South Korea, and Taiwan, governments have often intervened in land markets due to the rapidly increased development tension and scarce land resources.

Through regulatory systems and land policies, Taiwan has established a very comprehensive land value assessment system. In 1954, the Equalization of Land Rights Act (TELRA)[1] was enacted as the highest legal instruction for land policies in Taiwan. Considering the scarcity of land and following the landownership nationalization basic principle in the Constitution of Taiwan, TELRA set up two clear aims: (1) any land use shall maximize its possible profit and (2) the extra profit generated from land use shall feed back to the public. Four tools were established to ensure every land policy followed TELRA accordingly. They are land value assessment, taxation according to the land value declared by the owner, the government's purchase right of land at the declared land value, and the land value increment to the public. These four tools have been executed for more than 60 years as the land management system in Taiwan. Other related laws, including the Land Act (1930) and Land Tax Act (1977) have followed TELRA in a general sense. Accordingly, there are three types of land value provided by the government on every plot of land in each city or municipality of Taiwan: publicly announced land value, current assessed land value, and market transaction value. They are used for different purposes, such as annual taxation or transaction taxation. Publicly announced land value is the reference for the government to charge land tax annually from landowners. Current assessed land value is the taxing reference for land value increment tax, which only occurs when the land goes through transactions and, according to the Land Tax Act, all increment profits from a land transaction are taxed to fulfil the policy set by TELRA of extra profit generated from land being shared with the public. It is similar to the land transaction tax in many Western countries.

The above two land value types were designed to discourage land speculation by lowering the owning cost and increasing the transaction cost. For a long time, the current assessed land value was expected to be appraised as close to the market price as possible, but that idea failed due to the pressures from economic development. Thus, land speculation and serious property affordability issues are two concerning consequences. The central government did not request that every market transaction value be reported by the new owner of the land to establish market value transparency until 2012. Since 2016, such reported market value has been considered as one of the value references for land value increment tax. All three types of land value are announced and updated by the government officially and regularly. They are also available online for the general public to inquire about the value of their own properties and properties in the surrounding areas. According to TELRA, all land plots in the territory of Taiwan have to be assessed and have a 'publicly announced land value' first. Such land value shall be reassessed once every three years after its initial assessment or reassessment (art. 14). Cities and municipality governments are responsible for the land value assessment and follow a five-step procedure (art. 15). The land administration department in every city is in charge of land value assessment, and they collect the average transaction prices of different land use and income values of land occurring in the past 12 months by land value sections. Similar to the German system, Taiwan also has a 15-member independent Land Value Evaluation Committee composed of government officials, land value experts/appraisers, academic scholars, and local representatives to be the final decision-maker of the value to be announced. On the other hand, since the current assessed land value serves as a reference value for land increment tax, it has to be updated more frequently and reflect the actual market value to some standard. It is announced on an annual basis.

One of the long-lasting debates in Taiwan is that both publicly announced land value and current assessed land value have always been underestimated due to political reasons and the intense land development pressure for economic prosperity. Hence, unlike Voß and Bannert mentioned in the chapter that market values usually are very close to reference land values in Germany, in most cases, publicly announced land values in Taiwan only match 20 percent of the actual market transaction price, according to an official report by the Ministry of Interior in 2016. In Taiwan, the publicly announced land value assessment is local government's duty, as the land tax is the local tax. Given that the Land Tax Act has provided the basic land tax rate as 10 percent of publicly announced land value, most local governments have been hesitant to appraise land value close to the market price for various reasons. There are worries of political corruption and possible negative impacts on the property market. As a result, most landowners are sitting on a large amount of land by paying very little annual land tax. This actually violates the national policy of avoiding land monopoly. Clearly, the laws are consistent with land policy in Taiwan, but the enforcement at the local level is very poor. As a consequence, many cities and municipalities are in financially vicious circles since they can never receive sufficient land tax revenue for future urban construction expenses. The average revenue from land tax from all 22 municipalities in Taiwan accounts for approximately 20 percent of total annual government income in 2016. The reason for underestimated current assessed land value is almost always the same: poor enforcement. Although Taiwan has clear land policy goals at the national level to prohibit land speculations by charging higher land transaction tax to increase transaction cost, when it comes to local government's assessment results of current assessed land value, it is always underestimated. As a result, with low transaction costs, land speculations become unavoidable.

Another controversial debate regarding the land value is about the need for real estate market transparency. Until 2012, the actual market transaction prices were not available for the general public to query in Taiwan. It is actually a consequence of the aforementioned problem. Since the owning cost of the property is very low, properties are increasingly considered as good investment objects instead of places to live. In fact, in the past 20 years, the homeownership rate in Taiwan has never dropped to 80 percent or below, which is higher than most countries around the globe (The Executive Yuan, Taiwan 2014). As a result, issues of housing affordability have gained tremendous attention, and the property market is practically controlled by big developers and investors, especially in the capital cities such as Taipei. The urgent need for an open access platform where all market transaction prices are available within a certain periphery of a property in order to make the fair real estate market assessment has been urged by the real estate scholars and the general public. Therefore, the Ministry of Interior finally amended TELRA and established an open access platform for Actual Price Registration of Real Estate Transactions in 2012 (Ministry of Interior, Taiwan 2012). Since then, every property transaction price is required by law to be reported to the platform within 30 days from the transaction completion. However, such system is still criticized by experts for two major flaws. First, prices for the pre-sale housing units are not clearly regulated and do not have to report the price until two to three years from the time that the actual transaction happened. For those pre-sale housing transactions, the actual market price has a time-lag of at least two years, which causes confusion of immediate property market prices. Second, the rental market prices are also not required to be revealed in the platform. A lot of tenants, who are usually the middle or lower income groups, still face the disadvantages of negotiating rental prices due to the lack of actual rental market price information. After four years of operation, the official impact evaluation of the market price transparent policy on the real estate market is still being undertaken by the Ministry of Interior in Taiwan.

The perception of land value and ways to evaluate land value in Taiwan may not be significantly different from Germany mentioned in the chapter. The case study of Taiwan reflects both similarities and differences between

Taiwan and Germany in terms of land value assessment. There is no doubt that both countries are working towards a more transparent and healthy real estate market and are expecting to lower the possibility of land monopoly and market speculations that could interfere with property affordability and the right to live. However, the differences between the two countries can be observed from two major perspectives: land policy goals and land market speculations. The fundamental differences of political reality and development density between the two countries affect the relationship between land value assessed by the government and the actual transaction value in the real estate market in each country. Taiwan, as a small island famous for high population density and development pressure, faces greater challenges of land scarcity than Germany especially. Even with stronger government intervention through law and a land value assessment system, it is still very difficult to stop market speculation trend due to the high investment profit.

Note

1 The Equalization of Land Rights Act 2011, Ministry of the Interior, Taiwan, available at: http://law.moj.gov.tw/Eng/LawClass/LawAll.aspx?PCode=D0060009 (accessed 14 June 2017).

References

Executive Yuan, Taiwan (2014) *The survey of family income and expenditure*, Bureau of Accounting and Statistics.

Ministry of the Interior, Taiwan (2012) (online) available at: http://lvr.land.moi.gov.tw/homePage.action (accessed 14 June 2017).

Ministry of the Interior, Taiwan (2016) *The final report of land value assessment 2015* (online) available at: www.land.moi.gov.tw/pda/content.asp?cid=14&mcid=184 (accessed 14 June 2017).

5 Added value capturing in Switzerland

How much is enough?

François-Xavier Viallon

Institutional determinants of economic land value

In Western conceptions of land property, the concept of economic land value can be traced back to Roman times, when it was defined in the three components of property: in the *usus* and in the *fructus*, i.e. in the use(s) that one can make of its property and the subsequent value one can gain from these uses; and in the *abusus*, i.e. in the right to sell and destroy property, and in the added or reduced value that results from the exercise of this right.

In the modern conception of land property, economic land value is conditioned by two broad institutional factors. The first one is the property rights system. Through a set of instruments, such as acquisition, sale, and mortgage of land, property rights make the circulation of capital through land possible, and, in addition, grant a financial leverage to the property titleholder, which can be reinvested (Harvey 1982). The second institutional factor is public policy. Through zoning and land service, land use planning policy defines development rights to landowners, and ensures the accessibility and effective usability of the land. Other public policies also influence the economic value of land. Through the variation of tax rates, fiscal policy makes specific locations more or less attractive for inhabitants and companies. Further, the construction of transport infrastructure increases the value of nearby land (e.g. Cervero and Murakami 2009). The point is that value creation on land is widely conditioned by public planning and action, and tightly intertwined with the property rights system. Therefore, value capture does not only refer to the levy of the increment in land value caused by planning decisions, but questions more broadly the appropriation of land rent.

This contribution analyses two value capture instruments of Swiss land policy and their influence on land management. The argument is divided into three parts. The first part reviews existing value capture instruments in Swiss land policy on federal and cantonal level and presents recent legal changes. The second part presents two examples of value capture tools in practice, focusing on the strategies pursued by authorities, and the means they have in order to implement these tools. The third part discusses the potential of value capture instruments in order to achieve a more sustainable use of land, considering their practicability, efficacy, efficiency, and legitimacy. It turns out that resource use and value control are intertwined and should be coordinated over time in order to use land sparingly and satisfy societal needs.

Overview of value capture instruments in Switzerland

Referring to the criterion of time, one can classify value capture instruments into two categories. The first category encompasses *punctual* value capture instruments stemming from the federal spatial planning act and the cantonal planning and construction acts. These instruments are linked with a zone change or the attribution of additional development rights to a plot and the effective use of these rights by landowners and developers. The second category refers to *durative* value capture instruments. These capture on a recurrent basis (annually) part of the land rent, and thus constitute a land use steering tool that public actors can use for achieving land policy goals. These instruments are mostly defined in cantonal and communal fiscal legislation.

Punctual value capture instruments

A preliminary remark emphasising the intertwine of public policies and property rights eschewed previously is that value capture tools from land policy discussed thereafter are secured by a legal mortgage, that is to say, a property rights obligation in favor of the concerned authority securing the payment of the due value capture. In Swiss law, a legal mortgage is prioritised to all other mortgages and generally does not require to be entered into the land registry.

Tax on added land value created by zoning

The main value capture instrument of Swiss land policy is the tax on added land value created by zoning. The first spatial planning act proposal elaborated in 1974 introduced the instrument in order to separate planning from property issues (Nahrath 2005). The idea was to create a federal compensation mechanism that captured part of the value induced by the definition of new building zones in order to compensate their reduction elsewhere. The funds collected by the instrument were meant to grant authorities the means to distribute, remove, and relocate development rights without infringing the guarantee of ownership, which prescribes that, under specific conditions defined by case law, a full compensation is due to the landowner from whom authorities remove development rights. Without such compensation mechanism, authorities would have been limited in the fulfilment of land policy objectives – such as the dimensioning of building zones according to societal needs, and their rightful location, because they could not have undone past zoning choices.

However, the 1974 legal proposal was rejected after the referendum launched by federalist milieus and economic interests linked to real estate and construction. The spatial planning act adopted in 1979 left the implementation of the tax on added land value to the cantons, that is to say to the member states of the Swiss Confederation. Over the past 35 years, only 4 of 26 cantons implemented the instrument:

- The city canton Basel introduced a tax on added land value created by zoning in 1977 and uses it today. It applies a uniform 50 percent tax rate on the difference between old and new land market values, both to new building zones and to up-zoning changes. The amount of funds collected varies depending on the construction activity, as the tax is only due when landowners or developers effectively use the granted rights. The funds collected are intended for surrounding green spaces, and thus indirectly benefit both the investor and inhabitants (Poldervaart 2016).
- Canton Bern implemented in its cantonal law the tax on added land value in 1985. However, the canton delegated its implementation to the communes, also on a voluntary basis. The research results of the instrument's implementation in canton Bern are shown further later in this chapter.
- Introduced in 1986, the tax on added land value created by zoning in Neuchâtel taxes 20 percent of the added value created through the planning measure. The funds collected are used to compensate reduced values created through planning, help farmers to acquire land, or for land use planning measures decided by the canton or the communes. The time of taxation is decided by the cantonal administration, but occurs at the latest when the plot is sold.
- In Geneva, the tax was introduced in 2011 and fixed a tax rate of 15 percent that applies only to new building zones. The money collected is primarily dedicated to housing and compensation measures resulting from planning decisions. A lump sum discount rate of 30 francs per square meter is granted in the calculation of the added economic value created through zoning. Note that in specific zones, land price calculation does not refer to market value, as in specific zones, land prices and rents are capped by law.

Since the 2014 revision of the federal spatial planning act (SPA),[1] the tax on added land value created by zoning has become mandatory in all cantons. In case of non-implementation, no new zoning operations are allowed (art. 38a SPA). The minimal taxation rate has been set at 20 percent of the added land value (art. 5 SPA). The tax is due when the land is developed or sold. The tax produce is mainly destined to compensations due to planning measures that are equivalent to an expropriation, but also to the protection of fertile land, and to the better use of existing building zones including brownfields and low-density zones. A consultancy estimated that a 20 percent tax rate on new building zones will generate around 2 billion francs per year in Switzerland (BSS 2011).

Extended land service tax

In Switzerland, as opposed to the tax on added land value, land service taxes are conceived as *value recovery tools*. Federal spatial planning legislation sets the objective of making the landowners financially participate to land service from which they gain specific and particular advantages. Most cantonal laws have a set of instruments that allow communes to recover the investments made in land service such as roads, water and sewer connection, electricity, street lights, and so forth. Other public infrastructure that does not only service specific plots, such as schools, sports facilities, bus stops, and green spaces, are generally financed through the produce of regular taxation.

However, from the 1980s onward, certain communes in canton Vaud, when they granted new or additional development rights to a plot, started negotiating informally with developers for a lump sum agreement financing public infrastructure beyond land service, such as green spaces and parks, bus stops, and schools. In 2007, the developer of a wider project refused to pay the sum the commune claimed, arguing that there was no legal basis (Berta 2016). The tribunal proved him right, arguing that the contractual capture of added value required the commune to allocate the money to specific infrastructure, and not just put it aside for undefined purposes of public planning or the realisation of public infrastructure, as the commune partly did.

Consequently, the cantonal law was changed in 2011: it formalised communal practices through the introduction of a specific instrument in the cantonal law on communal taxes called *extended land service tax*. On average, urban communes that use the instrument tax around 30 francs for each additional square meter of gross floor area dedicated to activities and 140 francs per square meter for housing.[2] The tax difference between distinct uses is explained by the additional infrastructure housing requires (such as day care centers and schools). The target groups are all landowners, with the exception of authorities, churches, and private landowners pursuing an aim of public interest. The maximum sum to be taxed is capped at 50 percent of construction cost of public infrastructure linked to the zoning operation. These are, in decreasing order of costs: schools, kindergartens, bus stops and other transport related infrastructure, green spaces. The controversy that appeared while applying the tax to (semi-)public landowners is illustrated later in this section.

Since the 2014 federal revision of the spatial planning act and the obligation to implement the tax on added land value created by zoning, canton Vaud has two levies for taxing value increments due to zoning. Current cantonal legislative proposal has limited the combined taxation rate of both instruments to 50 percent of the added value created by the zoning operation.

Although not presented in detail here, other punctual fiscal tools taxing transactions exist: a real estate gains tax, which is digressive over time (from a 50 percent tax rate for less than two years possession in canton Geneva, to less than 5 percent for 20 years possession) and a property transfer tax (generally between 1 and 3 percent of the transaction price). Inheritance tax is almost nonexistent.

Permanent value capture instruments

A consultancy estimates that approximately 18 percent (14.5 billion francs) of all fiscal revenues in Switzerland (82 billion francs in 2006) are linked to land and real estate (Wüest und Partner 2006). Two main instruments (and a set of fiscal deductions not presented here) allow capture value:

- The land property tax (a wealth tax specific to land property),[3] which accounts for roughly 16 percent of land-linked revenues (2.3 billion francs);
- The land property income tax, which is mostly collected through the regular income tax or benefits tax, and accounts for 84 percent of land-linked revenues (12.2 billion francs).

Land property tax

The land property tax taxes annually the value of plots. It is defined by cantonal legislation – 6 of 26 cantons do not have such instrument at all (Waltert et al. 2010). The tax relies on the official land value, which in most cantons is underrated: these can refer to the acquisition price – notwithstanding the date of acquisition, or to an irregularly adjusted, and in most cases significantly underrated, but still updated land value (see for example Steuerverwaltung des Kantons Bern 2009). Taxation rate is usually defined in per mill of the land's value.

Land property income tax

Depending on cantonal and communal tax rates, but also between natural and legal persons, income taxation varies substantially from 13 percent to 36 percent of the yield (Wüest und Partner 2006). Certain moral persons with special statuses benefit from a negotiated tax. Further, a wide range of organisations are exempted from the land property income tax: authorities, churches, national pension funds, health care funds, and other organisms pursuing goals of public interest or nonprofit goals. When declaring the income earned through real estate, landowners and investors subtract maintenance cost and interest paid on mortgages from the declared revenue.

Main insights from permanent value capture instruments can be summarised as follows: communal, cantonal, and international tax competition induce an overall reduction of tax rates (Dafflon 2015). The latter is reinforced by the increased mobility of individuals across territories, that put forward the low costs of living in order to attract new inhabitants (Segessemann 2016). Therefore, the capture of landowners' windfall profits is competing with other factors, such as territorial attractiveness, and local policies, which can favor "housing as a mean of wealth creation and economic boosterism" (Segessemann and Crevoisier 2016: 1401).

Value capture in practice

Two emblematic implementation cases of punctual value capture instruments are presented: the voluntary tax on added land value in canton Bern, and the extended land service tax in canton Vaud. The goal of this section is to reveal actors' strategies in implementing these instruments in a federal state like Switzerland.

Voluntary tax on added land value created by zoning in canton Bern

Since 1985, cantonal Bernese spatial planning legislation granted to the communes the possibility to levy part of the added value created by planning measures through a *tax on added land value created by zoning*. As a reminder from the first section, the gains collected through this tax are primarily aimed to compensate landowners who suffered a loss of value from a building zone reduction, and thus enhance the capacity of authorities to implement land policy.

The present analysis deals with Oberaargau, a peri-urban region composed of 47 communes in canton Bern (Viallon 2016a). In a context of demographic and land price stagnation, institutional fragmentation, and strong communal autonomy in land use planning and fiscal matters, the implementation of non-mandatory value capture instruments failed in a wide number of cases. In fact, 20 years after canton Bern introduced the tax on added land value, only 18 communes in this region had implemented the tax in their building regulations.

The communes that introduced the tax are mainly those that have over-sized building zones. According to federal legislation, building zones are over-sized when they exceed communal needs for the next 15 years (art. 5 SPA). The outstanding fact is that these communes introduced the tax only *after* the definition of their building zone, from the 2000s onward. Consequently, the initial aim of the instrument – the collection of funds in order to financially compensate building zone reductions – could not be fulfilled, as subsequent zoning operations were very limited due to already over-sized building zones. This leads to an ironic situation, where the tax on added land value created by zoning was implemented in reaction to the problem it intended to solve in the first place.

In cases where the instrument was implemented, the funds collected through the instrument served other purposes than building zone reduction: part of the funds provided by the instrument were used as a substitute for the land service tax: the money collected paid land service – sometimes the one directly benefitting the landowner – or other communal infrastructure. Further, local authorities were free to fix the land values used as the tax base. This led in certain cases to an effective taxation of 21 percent of the added land value instead of the 30 percent contractually fixed (Viallon 2016a).

Overall, the implementation of value capturing instruments on the communal level faced high reluctance because it directly challenged local interests of both landowners and communal authorities: the former perceiving the capture of part of their gains as 'robber barony', the latter being put under pressure by fiscal competition and territorial attractiveness.

Extended land service tax in Vaud

The definition of the extended land service tax in canton Vaud's legislation occurred in 2011 (art. 4B LICom).[4] Since that year, the instrument's use has spread across a wide number of urban communes, in particular in the agglomeration of Lausanne. The case of the redevelopment of Malley, an industrial brownfield in the center of the agglomeration that has lost part of its former land uses, is of particular interest, because of the implementation of the tax on public and semi-public landowners: the ownership structure to be regulated by the future local development plan Malley-gare is composed of Lausanne, the urban center of the agglomeration (130,000 inhabitants), and of the Swiss Federal Railways. The land is located on the communal territories of Renens and Prilly, two smaller neighbor towns (20,000 and 10,000 inhabitants, respectively). Until today, legal uncertainty exists on the necessity for public landowners to pay the tax. The present case shows how the (semi-)public landowners used a set of policy resources in order to minimise the amount of value taxed (Viallon 2016b).

Malley's outstanding location in the center of the agglomeration, between the train lines and a subway line, and the reduced industrial activity present on site – the public gasworks closed in 1977, and the slaughterhouse closed in 2002 – led to the elaboration of several architectural competitions and master plans in order to redevelop the area. Most important, the canton obtained federal funding for the construction of a regional train stop adjacent to the area, thus pushing towards land redevelopment.

Turning to the implementation of the extended land service tax, cantonal law states that authorities and their subordinated entities, as well as private entities working in the public interest (such as pension funds, churches, social security funds, health care funds, nonprofit moral persons working in culture) are exempted from the tax (art. 90 LI).[5] Therefore, Lausanne and the SBB would be considered exempted from the tax. However, uncertainty prevailed on the objectives pursued by the two landowners: are these in the public interest or not? Both Lausanne and the SBB intended to lease their land to private developers through a building right, and neither the provision of surfaces for activities nor for housing are legally recognised of public interest.

Nevertheless, the question was not settled, and both the communes and the landowners mandated a legal expertise in order to clarify the matter. As one could have expected, both parties received contradictory legal advice leading to a stalemate. Instead of publicly exposing their divergences and losing time in front of a court, the actors agreed to negotiate the amount that would be paid.

The criteria to be used for fixing the amount of tax to be paid depended on the future uses of the buildings (housing being more expensive than activities due to the schools that are linked to it), but also on other factors, such as soil pollution: these costs had a significant impact on the project development, as landowners have the legal obligation to remediate the heavily polluted soils. In order to reduce remediation costs, authorities and landowners mandated several soil expertises determine the location and depth of pollution, and thus provide a wide amount of information allowing first to estimate excavation and remediation costs, and second to adapt the location of constructions within the development plan as well as their type (e.g. limitation of underground constructions). But the calculation of remediation costs, and of those linked to the development, required an organisational capacity that the territorial communes did not have, or at least did not allocate to the project. Consequently, an information asymmetry between authorities and landowners appeared, and the latter used it during negotiations in order to inflate costs linked with remediation and development and thus keep the taxed amount at the lowest level possible.

Another result of negotiation, which is possible by law, is the five-year delay granted to landowners for the payment of the extended land service tax, once the first building permit is delivered.

The negotiations' financial result, in particular the amount of value captured, depends on how the added value and the costs are calculated (Table 5.1). If one considers solely the extended land service tax, the instrument captured 2.9 percent of the added land value induced by the local development plan Malley-gare (Table 5.2). If one considers the extended land service tax jointly with the railway underpass, which is not part of regular land service according to federal legislation (and as a consequence financed through the added value captured), then the amount of added value taxed corresponds to 17.6 percent of the overall added land value created by zoning.

If one considers that the extended land service tax solely applies to the part of the local development plan that belongs to the semi-public landowner SBB (in the hypothesis that Lausanne, as public landowner, is exempted from the tax), then the amount of added land value taxed is around 8 percent. If the costs of the railway crossing are included in the calculations, then the percentage of value capture increases up to 22 percent.

Table 5.1 Surfaces and gross floor areas of the local development plan Malley-gare (Viallon 2016b)

Surfaces and densities	*Total*	*CFF*	*Lausanne*
Constructible ground surface of the local development plan	10,600 m²	7,551 m²	8,665 m²
Old gross floor area	15,200 m²	7,100 m²	8,100 m²
New gross floor area	52,500 m²	20,500 m²	32,000 m²

Table 5.2 Land values, costs and taxes in the local development plan Malley-gare in the landowners' perspective (Viallon 2016b)

Values and costs	*Total*
Old land value	10.0 M CHF
New land value	34.4 M CHF
Added land value	24.4 M CHF
Planning costs	0.3 M CHF
Remediation costs	2.4 M CHF
Connection tax	0.7 M CHF
Land service tax	2.1 M CHF
Railway underpass	3.6 M CHF
Extended land service tax	0.7 M CHF
Estimated annual rent on building right	4.5% × 34.4 M = 1.55 M CHF

If the extended land service tax had been fully applied (30 francs per square meter for activities, and 140 francs per square meter for housing), 3 million francs would have been collected, and a taxation percentage of 12 percent (respectively 27 percent if one includes the railway underpass) could have been achieved.

Notwithstanding the percentage of taxation considered, this case has showed that a wide part of the added valued created by authorities remains in the hands of the landowners. In fact, using a capitalisation rate of 4.5 percent – a common rate for publicly attributed building rights (Cour des comptes du canton de Vaud 2011) – value captured by authorities is recovered through the land rent within three years.

Effectiveness, practicability, and legitimacy of punctual value capture tools

The two value capture instruments presented above provide a set of insights to be discussed and compared based on the criteria of practicability, effectiveness, efficiency, and legitimacy.

The empirical analysis of the tax on added land value and of the extended land service tax has shown a set of elements. In terms of practicability, we learned that the legal definition and choice of implementation of land policy instruments at local level reduces their chances to be used by authorities, and facilitates the circumvention of the instruments' initial purposes by landowners. Circumvention strategies are evident in the case authorities do not have a clear and explicit legal basis, but also occur when the instruments' modalities are unclear: for example, the tax base, as well as the percentage or monetary value of the tax, should be explicitly defined in regulation in order to reduce loopholes. As we have seen in the Bernese case, the tax on added land value requires precise information on land values before and after the zoning operation, which are not systematically available in Switzerland, and whose collection involves administrative costs. The Vaud case showed that the extended land service tax requires information on the production costs of communal infrastructure, but also on the production costs of the landowner/developer. Information asymmetry in favor of the landowner or developer tends to reduce the instruments' potential effects. And the provision of such information requires shared information between actors, but also personnel.

But exhaustive and stringent regulations, available information, and personnel are not enough to guarantee the instruments' effectiveness. Both instruments capture part of the land rent and redistribute it to other (land) policy objectives. Therefore, their effects on land depend on how the funds they collect are used. The Bernese tax on added land value created by zoning has shown that the implementation of compensation instruments at local scale face high controversy, both due to landowners and authorities. This issue was however solved with the 2014 revision of the federal spatial planning act, which has now defined the instrument as mandatory. Nevertheless, the collection of the tax on the cantonal level is incongruent with the scale of the problem it intends to solve, namely the reduction of over-sized building zones, which is a typically Swiss land policy issue. These over-sized building zones are mainly present in peri-urban cantons, and no inter-cantonal redistribution of the funds collected is planned (for example, between urban and peri-urban or mountainous cantons). As a whole, the tax on added land value created by zoning and the funds captured enhances authorities' margin of maneuver when adapting land policy, and in particular zoning plans, to socio-economic changes. Thus, it allows to reduce the gap between zoning and effective land use and fosters a more economic use of land. The extended land service tax provides a mean for funding public infrastructure that benefits the neighbourhood and the wider urban agglomeration. It passes part of the costs of urbanisation initially carried by local authorities on to the landowners. The instrument's effects on land depend on local political objectives (urban growth, reuse of brownfields, etc.), but are not tackled directly by the instrument.

In terms of efficiency, the tax on added land value created by zoning has moderate administrative costs (due to value assessment) and potentially a high punctual financial return, depending on the percentage of windfall profits taxed. A similar reasoning can be applied to the extended land service tax, although the tax as defined by canton Vaud limits the effective amount to be captured to 50 percent of the costs of infrastructure whose construction is due to the increase of development rights. The method used in order to calculate the amount due for each type of infrastructure (schools, kindergartens, green spaces, bus stops) refers to an average price paid per person by the commune over a 15-year period for making the different services available.

One could argue that it could be easier to capture the added value through durative value capture instruments, such as the land tax or the income tax. In the absence of detailed analysis on the instruments' perceptions hold by policy makers, we can hypothesize that whereas a tax increase would produce highly visible changes in the communal budget and require an additional fiscal effort from all communal contributors, the tax on added land value and the extended land service tax are applied in a far less visible manner on very specific landowners who are granted substantial development advantages. The very limited implementation of the tax on added land value in Oberaargau's communes shows the lack of acceptance the instrument faces. The 40-year gap between the instrument's initial proposal in federal legislation (1974), and its mandatory definition (2014) further reveals how vested landowners and financial interests are to land property income.

In regard to the taxes' legitimacy, the lack of clear attribution of the funds reduces the acceptance of value capture tools, whereas the specific allocation of funds (for example, in a perimeter where it benefits the landowners) eases their acceptance. This issue becomes salient when considering that in canton Vaud, the extended land service tax was initially used without any legal basis because it leads to the emergence of joint interests between developers (to additional rights) and authorities (to more captured value).

Prioritising land uses with a high added economic value also leads to the eviction of uses with lower added economic value. Therefore, value capture should be not an objective per se. It is the question of the objectives of value redistribution, and of *value control*, that are central to land policy. The examples from canton Vaud show that value capture instruments whose funds are allocated to a specific and spatially defined (preferably local) purpose – and produce low redistributive effects – are more legitimate than those meant to achieve general objectives in nonspecified spatial perimeters that produce high redistributive effects. Hereby, they confirm the key role of redistribution inherent to all political processes (Schneider and Ingram 1990).

In Switzerland, the legal amount of rent that a property titleholder is entitled to is not settled legally. In a 1979 decision on the constitutionality of levying land value increments due to zoning (BGE 105 Ia 134), the Federal Tribunal solely stated that the legal guarantee of ownership obligates the legislator to protect the substance of property and the possibility to increase wealth. This leaves a wide margin of maneuverability to future political choices, and to the appropriation or control of rent by the actor(s) and for the purpose(s) considered the most legitimate. As prospective thought for future (re-)development projects, the implementation of the tax on added land value that, in Switzerland, will now apply to all new building zones defined in the future, and that will capture 20 percent of value increment, does not appear as problematic, in particular if compared to the percentage of value capture that prevails in other countries (Altermann 2012).

Notes

1 Federal Spatial Planning Act (SPA) (*Raumplanungsgesetz, RPG*) of 22 June 1979, SR 700.
2 For reference, a square meter of gross floor area in an urban center around Lake Geneva, as in the case of Malley, is around 3,100 francs per square meter for activities and 2,500 francs for housing.
3 An additional wealth tax considering the entirety of wealth and not only land property exists in certain cantons and is to be added to the land property tax. In 2006, the fiscal revenues it generated were around 2 billion francs.
4 Loi vaudoise du 5 décembre 1956 sur les impôts communaux (LICom), SR-VD 650.11.
5 Loi vaudoise du 4 juillet 2000 sur les impôts cantonaux (LI), SR-VD 642.11.

References

Altermann, R. (2012) Land use regulations and property values: The 'Windfalls Capture' idea revisited, in: Brooks, N., Donaghy, K. and Knaap, G.-J. (eds) *The Oxford handbook of urban economics and planning*, Oxford University Press, Oxford.

Berta, E. (2016) Nyon ou la recherche de l'équilibre par les conventions, *Collage*, 2016(3), 16–20.

BSS (2011) *Konzepte zur Bauzonenverkleinerung. Abklärung der monetären Folgen und der Wirksamkeit von vier verschiedenen Konzepten*, Schlussbericht zuhanden des Bundesamtes für Raumentwicklung (ARE), Basel.

Cervero, R. and Murakami, J. (2009) Rail and property development in Hong Kong: Experiences and extensions, *Urban Studies*, 46(10), 2019–2043.

Cour des comptes du Canton de Vaud (2011) *Droits de superficie octroyés par les collectivités publiques vaudoises*, rapport numéro 19 du 13 décembre 2011, Lausanne.

Dafflon, B. (2015) *Panorama Des Impôts Suisses. Du Local Au Fédéral, Entre Équité et Concurrence: Quels Enjeux?*, Domaine public, Lausanne.

Harvey, D. (1982) *The limits to capital*, Basil Blackwell, Oxford.

Nahrath, S. (2005) Le rôle de la propriété foncière dans la génèse et la mise en oeuvre de la politique d'améagement du territoire: quels enseignements pour la durabilité des aménagements urbains? in: Da Cunha, A., Knoepfel, P., Leresche, J.-P. and Nahrath, S. (eds) *Enjeux du développement urbain durable. Transformations urbaines, gestion des ressources et gouvernance*, Presses polytechniques universitaires romandes, Lausanne, 299–328.

Poldervaart, P. (2016) Abgabe schafft grünen Mehrwert für alle, *Collage*, 2016(3), 13–15.

Schneider, A. and Ingram, H. (1990) Behavioral assumptions of policy tools, *The Journal of Politics*, 52(2), 510–259.
Segessemann, A. (2016) De La Production à La Consommation: Le Rôle de l'économie Résidentielle Dans Le Développement Régional, Université de Neuchâtel.
Segessemann, A. and Crevoisier, O. (2016) Beyond Economic Base Theory: The Role of the Residential Economy in Attracting Income to Swiss Regions, *Regional Studies*, 2016, 1–16.
Steuerverwaltung des Kantons Bern (2009) *Erläuterungen zum steuerlichen Bewertungssystem von Grundstücken und Liegenschaften im Kanton Bern*, March, Bern.
Viallon, F.-X. (2016a) *Implementation of redistributive land policy instruments in urban spaces: The case of Oberaargau (1990–2014)*, Working paper de l'IDHEAP, 2016(6), Lausanne.
Viallon, F.-X. (2016b) *Implementation of redistributive land policy instruments in urban spaces: The case of Malley*, Working paper de l'IDHEAP, 2016(7), Lausanne.
VLP-ASPAN (2015) *Prélèvement de la plus-value dans les différents cantons*, état au 03 décembre 2015, Bern.
Waltert, F., Pütz, M., Böni, R. and Seidl, I. (2010) *Fiskalische Instrumente und Flächeninanspruchnahme, Eidgenössische Forschungsanstalt für Wald, Schnee und Landschaft WSL*, Bundesamt für Umwelt BAFU, Bern.
Wüest und Partner (2006) *Immo-Monitoring*, 2006(3), Zürich.

A Dutch perspective on added value capture: how far can you go?

Erwin van der Krabben

In 1879 Henry George advocated, in his famous work *Progress and Property* (George 1879), the introduction of a land value tax – also referred to as a 'single tax' on land. Before him, Adam Smith had already called it 'the perfect tax' (Smith 1776; Webb 2013) because of its economic effects. George argued that because the supply of land is fixed and its location value is created by communities and public works, the economic rent of land is the most logical source of public revenue. While most taxes distort economic decisions and suppress beneficial economic activity, land value tax is payable regardless of how well or poorly land is actually used. Noble Prize winner William Vickrey believed that

> removing almost all business taxes, including property taxes on improvements, excepting only taxes reflecting the marginal social cost of public services rendered to specific activities and replacing them with taxes on site values, would substantially improve the economic efficiency of the jurisdiction.
>
> (Vickrey 1996: 603)

Despite the strong economic arguments in favor of land value tax as the main – or single – revenue source for public finance, and despite (ongoing) debates in many countries around the world to introduce land value tax, only few countries actually implemented land value tax (but never as a single tax), including some states in Australia, Hong Kong, Taiwan, Colombia, Denmark, and Mexico (Andelson 1971).

The introduction of a land value tax in Switzerland can be related to these theoretical discussions. The Swiss case is interesting from at least two different perspectives. First, the introduction of – or better, attempts to introduce – a land value tax has led to political controversy in other countries as well. To place the Swiss case in an international context, I will briefly refer to the (political) objections that arose after related proposals to 'cream off' the planning gain, which arises when permission to develop land is granted, in the UK and the Netherlands. Second, the Swiss case of introducing a land value tax system provides an interesting insight into the practical aspects of implementing such tax.

Before introducing the UK and Dutch political debates with regard to taxing development gain, it is useful to distinguish this tax on development gain (or land value tax) from (1) developer contributions (or obligations) to plan-related infrastructure costs (from which the developer will benefit directly) and (2) property tax. Most countries use some kind of system to make developers contribute to the infrastructure costs related to a plan. They are often discussed in a technical sense, but the political dispute about them is usually limited. Property tax is a general tax based on property value and is not meant to cream off development gain (although they do to a certain extent, if there is a property value increase because of a development).[1] Perhaps the most documented dispute over taxing development gains took place in the 1940s in the UK after publication of the Uthwatt Report in 1942. The Uthwatt Committee discussed among other things the introduction of a betterment levy to capture the planning gain – quite similar to the Swiss land value tax. A betterment levy was introduced in the 1947 Town and Country Planning Act. However, the political controversy about the new regulation became clear soon after, when the subsequent Conservative government immediately decided to abolish it by passing the 1954 Planning Act. Internationally less known is the political crisis that developed in the Netherlands in 1977, after incompatible views had arisen with respect to land policy between the Labour Party and the Christian Democrats that formed a coalition at that time. The debate was not about introducing a land value tax, but about a related theme: the compensation to be paid in case of expropriation. While the Labour Party wanted a compensation based on the value of the land in its original use (the planning gain as the result of the government decision to change the use of the land would go to the state), the Christian Democrats did not want to change the existing regulation that prescribes compensation based on the market value of the land (the planning gain would remain with the owner that would be expropriated). The coalition partners couldn't agree on the method to define compensation (which added up to some other disagreements within the coalition) and decided to step down. Compensation for expropriation would continue to include planning gain. Since then the issue has hardly been touched upon in Dutch politics. In 2008 a new land law was introduced, but this land law was meant to offer a legal basis for charging developer obligations and did not touch upon the issue of taxing development gains.[2] Political debate regarding the present revision of the expropriation law – as part of the law on land and property ownership (*Aanvullingswet Grond en Eigendom*), which will replace both the 2008 land law and the current expropriation law, which will be, in turn, part of the new Law on the Environment (*Omgevingswet*), expected to be implemented in 2019, also ignores this topic. My impression is that in the Netherlands – though the country is sometimes considered a *planning paradise*, with strong planning legislation – a similar proposal to introduce a land value tax, as in Switzerland, is unthinkable, because of the legal view that all value increase, including planning gain, rightfully belongs to the property owner.

The implementation of a land value tax – as probably any other tax – also raises questions with respect to the practicability, effectiveness, efficiency, and legitimacy of such a tax. The Swiss case illustrates quite convincingly that these aspects may cause problems. For instance, it seems to me that the practice in some places to informally negotiate a lump sum contribution to finance infrastructure beyond land servicing costs makes the value capture system quite inscrutable. Moreover, an efficient and fair land value tax system requires precise information on land values before and after a change in the zoning plan. According to Viallon, such information is not systematically available in Switzerland, and high administrative costs will be involved when a more standardized system would be introduced. And finally, it is claimed that legitimacy issues may appear. The use of land value tax may bring local authorities to prioritize land uses with a high added economic value, because it will give them higher revenue compared to uses with lower added value.

The 'solution' sought in the Netherlands with respect to practicability issues regarding charging development contributions (which is different from a land value tax) has been to make it as transparent as possible. All types of costs that can be charged to private developers have been described. Before plan approval can take place, all plan-related costs must be covered. The extent to which private developers must contribute to these costs depends on three criteria: profitability, proportionality, and accountability. In addition, a maximum has been set to the size of the contribution: it can never exceed a level that would lead to a financial loss for the private developer. In such a situation, the municipality must find other ways to cover these extra costs (or decide not to approve the plan). Developer contributions to plan-related infrastructure can be forced, according to the law, but only when a voluntary agreement cannot be reached. This provides possibilities for negotiations between the municipality and private developers (which are not very transparent), which may include adjustments to the real estate program (density, housing mix, etc.) and/or adjustments to the infrastructure. After the introduction of this legislation in 2008, both municipalities and private developers seemed to be more or less happy with the system. It wasn't until a few years later that the first problems arose. While the traditional comprehensive development plans usually made it possible to calculate all infrastructure costs in advance, the 'organic', bottom-up developments that have become more dominant now in urban transformation projects often do not allow calculating these costs in advance because it is frequently unknown at the start of the plan what will be developed. Another problem is that, even if the municipality would be able to define all necessary infrastructure works, it would be obliged to guarantee covering the costs itself because it is unknown who will develop. The aforementioned 'land and property ownership law' offers some solutions to this. However, as the minister responsible for spatial planning has stated herself in the explanatory memorandum for the draft version of the law, another problem remains to be solved. Where Dutch cities in the past usually were able to raise sufficient revenue for covering infrastructure costs by relying on the combination of income from land sales, contributions by private developers and national government subsidies, this has become quite uncertain for the future (with possibly large variation among cities regarding the size of the problem). Income from land sales is substantially lower than it used to be, national subsidies for urban renewal are no longer available, and with (less profitable) urban transformation projects now becoming more dominant, contributions by private developers may decrease as well. The minister acknowledges the problem, but has not yet suggested any solutions to it.

Notes

1 There is also much international debate about property tax, particularly in developing countries, mainly in relation to public finance and municipal fiscal health, but I leave that aside.

2 Dutch municipalities, however, made use of another strategy to capture planning gain. By the commonly used public land development model they were able, as landowners, to keep most of the planning gain. Since 2008 (the global economic and real estate crisis), municipalities have become much more reluctant to use this development model because of the financial risks involved.

References

Andelson, R.V. (1971) *Land-value taxation around the world*, Wiley Blackwell, Hoboken, NJ.

George, H. (1879) *Progress and poverty*, The Country Live Press, New York.

Smith, A. (1776) *The wealth of nations*, Wordsworth Editions Ltd.

Vickrey, W. (1996) The corporate income tax in the U.S. Tax System, *Tax Notes*, (73), 597–603.

Webb, M. (2013) How a levy based on location values could be the perfect tax, *Financial Times* (accessed 23 March 2017).

A British perspective on added value capture: ups and downs during its history

Janet Askew

In the UK, there is a long history of using planning instruments to tax betterment and capture value that comes about as a result of changing the use of land (via planning policy or planning permission). Alterman (2012) refers to Britain as the 'world's former laboratory of betterment-capture instruments'. Indeed, the power to use such instruments was first introduced in 1932, since which time it has been evolving. This is particularly pertinent to the Swiss case of value capture, which was first mooted in 1974, but has not yet been implemented across the whole country (*see* → *Viallon*). It is not an easy instrument to devise. Methods and regulations to capture value continue to be debated in many countries, with much experimentation with new approaches (Hobma et al. 2014). This is true of the UK, and current regulations employ a mixture of negotiation and a financial levy.

The question is, how much does the land value capture instrument contribute to land scarcity? It is important to comprehend some fundamental differences between the English planning system and those of other countries to fully understand how the instruments work. This is relevant to the debate on land value capture instruments. The instruments are created by central government and apply to the whole country. How are they regulated? What is the process by which they are applied? The Town and Country Planning Act of 1947, which is the basis upon which planning law is based, nationalized development rights (Booth 2003), meaning that individual property rights do not assume such great importance in relation to town planning as elsewhere in the world. Two other features distinguish the British planning system. The first is the centralisation of planning regulations that have to be adhered to by planning authorities; local regulations cannot be made. In this, England differs considerably from the Swiss system, where local regulations and local taxes can be imposed. Second is the requirement for a development plan to be produced and, after a lengthy process of consultation, adopted as a statutory document. This is the primary material consideration for decision-making. There is no legally binding plan. The main difference between the English system and others is the point at which the decision to build is taken. The decision is discretionary; the absence of an up-to-date land use plan does not eliminate the ability to develop, rather it means that other material considerations are taken into account before permission to develop is granted, resulting in considerable negotiation during the process. The development plan often includes value capture policies that enhance the ability of the local authority to seek developer contributions, and negotiation is often protracted.

The history of land value capture in England has meant that there have been many attempts over the past 80 years to introduce methods of taxing betterment, with successive governments repealing old laws and introducing new ones. The property boom of the early 1970s saw an increase in the use of planning gain and the idea of capturing value was encapsulated in Section 52 of the Town and Country Planning Act 1971. Debate and controversy have continued ever since, with numerous changes to the instruments, and successive governments have tried to find a way to regulate for a fair system to overcome perceptions that there was widespread extortion in planning gain (Cullingworth and Nadin 2006). During the ensuing years, there was increasing use of planning gain agreements, with considerable objection by developers and communities to their implementation. In particular, the agreements were inconsistent, not transparent, and not measured. In order to regularise them, the Town and Country Planning Act 1990 included a new Section 106 that related to planning gain agreements, accompanied by various statutory orders that laid down tests to ensure fairness, necessity, and proportionality of the gains sought.

Despite this, debate and objections continued and, in particular, there was concern that the Section 106 agreements were overly complex, resulting in lengthy and costly negotiations (DCLG 2008). Such criticisms raised questions concerning their effectiveness, integrity, and sustainability. The legitimacy of the negotiated outcome based upon both the appropriateness of the proposed agreement was queried, as well as the ability to directly link the settlement with the proposed development (Moore and Purdue 2012). Challenges to the courts to interpret and mediate unreasonable demands were increasing, and the process was becoming expensive (Askew and Sheppard 2014).

More specifically, two aspects to planning agreements began to crystallise. The first is linked to the idea that the uplift in land value should be taxed. This relates to early ideas about betterment due to changing designations of the use of land, and is called 'punctual' value capture by Viallon. In England, successive governments have mostly avoided direct land taxes, leaving any uplift in value to be achieved by negotiation.

The second aspect might be termed 'cost recovery', which became more prevalent with the cutbacks in public sector funding, resulting in local authorities needing to secure finance for associated infrastructure, sometimes directly associated with a new development, sometimes not. During the 1990s and early 2000s, demands for cost recovery grew, including the ability for local authorities to collect cash directly. Further evidence that the system was not working very well was confirmed when local authorities were found to be underspending and sitting on the surplus, despite serious shortages of funds for public services.

To overcome these issues, in particular to standardise demands for social housing and infrastructure, and to clarify the use of planning gain, a law in the Planning Act 2008 introduced one new instrument – the Community Infrastructure Levy (CIL). It amended the use of the Section 106 agreement with regard to its use for affordable and social housing provision.

The Community Infrastructure Levy is more akin to a development tax and requires the local authority to prepare a mandatory charging schedule, accompanied by a 'Regulation 123 List' of developments for which the levy will be used. While the list states what the Community Infrastructure Levy is collected for, it does not necessarily apply to infrastructure directly associated with the development upon which the tax is levied. There are some limited powers to allow for different tax percentages to be set locally, so that poorer areas wanting to encourage investment can set their Community Infrastructure Levy at zero. The fact that the money is not used directly for the benefit of the actual development, but as a contribution towards new infrastructure across the council area has already attracted criticism from developers. This was an issue in the Swiss canton Vaud. To date, there has been a lack of ambition on the part of local authorities in England, and the lists produced contain a preponderance of road schemes and traffic improvements, although they are able to include new schools, parks, flood defences, or social care facilities (Askew and Sheppard 2014). As an incentivisation measure, a portion of these funds is allowed to be given to smaller communities who are preparing a neighbourhood plan.

Section 106 agreements remain flexible, are not mandatory, are open to negotiation, and are only for related off-site works and affordable housing. Long-standing objections of uncertainty have not been overcome. As a result, there continues to be debate and concern over the use of value capture and cost recovery instruments, with developers objecting to the imposition of two separate 'taxes'. Of great relevance to this is the fact that for the first time, the viability of a development has become a material consideration in decision-making. The National Planning Policy Framework (DCLG 2012) has a policy that allows developers to argue that a development would be rendered unviable if Section 106 agreements are deemed to be unreasonable, particularly in the area of affordable housing. Viability for developers is a crucial part of the government's housing strategy (Housing White Paper, DCLG 2017) and this affects the local authority's ability to achieve affordable housing in a development. Many developers simply argue that they cannot afford the social element.

Unlike in Switzerland, developers and planning authorities in England are accustomed to the use of different instruments for the capture of value. While there is considerable debate about how best to do this, it is accepted by all stakeholders that these instruments will be applied. As a result, there is no avoidance of them and although arguments persist in negotiations, their desired achievements are compromised by viability issues.

There is little evidence to suggest that value capture instruments in England are the cause of land shortages, nor that they in any way exacerbate scarcity of land. England has a long history of cost recovery and betterment taxes and, for over 80 years, it has been devising and amending ways of recovering the uplift in value of land. Developers assert that there is a scarcity of land in England, but they do not blame instruments of value capture. Rather, they blame the bureaucracy of planning for delays in achieving permission to develop, protracted negotiation being one of their main complaints. But their ire is mainly directed at models that constrain city growth, most particularly countryside and green belt designations.

Land value capture is not a static instrument in England. The latest instruments are being scrutinised for their effectiveness, and reviews and policy statements are common. What is certain is that planning gain instruments are not currently demonstrating success in helping to resolve the housing crisis.

References

Alterman, R. (2012) Land use regulations and property values: The 'Windfalls Capture' idea revisited, in: Brooks, N., Donaghy, K. and Knaap, G.J. (eds) *The Oxford handbook of urban economics and planning*, Oxford University Press, Oxford, 755–786.

Askew, J. and Sheppard, A. (2014) England, in: Hobma, F. (ed.) *Internationale vergelijking financiering en kostenverhaal bij organische gebiedsontwikkeling*, Report for the Ministry of Infrastructure and Environment of the Netherlands, TU Delft, The Netherlands, 63–106.

Booth, P. (2003) *Planning by consent – the origins and nature of British development control*, Routledge, Oxford.

Cullingworth, B. and Nadin, V. (2006) *Town and country planning in the UK*, Routledge, Oxon.

DCLG (2008) *The community infrastructure levy*, HMSO, London.

DCLG (2012) *The national planning policy framework*, HMSO, London.

DCLG (2017) *Fixing our broken housing market*, White Paper, HMSO, London.

Hobma, F., Askew, J., Mitschang, S., Santing, J., Schwarz, T., Sheppard, A. and Verbist, S. (2014) *Internationale vergelijking financiering en kostenverhaal bij organische gebiedsontwikkeling* (International comparison of funding and cost recovery in organic area development). Technical Report. TU Delft.

Moore, M. and Purdue, M. (2012) *A practical approach to planning law*, Oxford University Press, Oxford.

6 Land taxation in Estonia

An efficient instrument of land policy for land scarcity, equity, and ecology

Fabian Thiel and Fabian Wenner

Introduction

Object-based taxes such as taxes on real estate (i.e. buildings, land, or both) belong to the most traditional and established forms of taxation in many legislations (Norregaard 2013: 7). Several forms of real estate taxation can be differentiated, especially nonrecurring and recurring taxes. The most significant nonrecurring taxes are levied when ownership of real estate is transferred, e.g. in the case of the 'Grunderwerbsteuer' (property transfer tax) in Germany or the 'stamp duty' in the UK, or when significant changes in development potential or admissibility occur, as in the case of development levies in the UK. They are usually one-off fees conditional and proportional to a property rights change. As transaction costs, they might form a hindrance to otherwise viable development schemes. More important for public revenues are recurring real estate taxes, which are typically levied annually and unconditionally.

Both usually amount to a legally determined share of the value of the taxed asset. Hence it is of paramount importance how this value is determined, especially for landowners. Often authorities use mass appraisal procedures (UBC 2003; Löhr 2010) for the assessment, but methods and tax bases differ widely across countries – some only take into account the buildings on a plot of land, some only the land component disregarding buildings, and some use a combination of the two, or they rely on other criteria as proxies (Table 6.1). While some methods are designed to take into account the particularities of each single case, most use crude approximations like the size of a building, or the number or floor space of rooms to determine the tax base, i.e. the value of the taxed object, to facilitate administrative procedures. Hence, mass valuation always faces a trade-off between efficiency and justice (Oates and Schwab 2009; Löhr 2010).

Many tax systems also set varying rates for different land use classes, e.g. agricultural or urban land plots (Netzer 2003). All these set screws influence land policy and urban development though the setting of (dis)incentives for property owners and buyers, often unintended. However, there is a growing awareness in both developing and developed countries for the need of an

Table 6.1 Examples of different forms of real estate taxation

Type	*Real Estate Tax Base*			
	Property (Land and Buildings)	*Only Buildings*	*Only Land*	*Other*
Recurring	• Property Tax • (Income Tax)	• 'Mansion Tax' • Municipal Service Fees	• Land Value Tax • Unused Land Tax	• Site Tax • Simplified Property Tax • Municipal Service Fees
Nonrecurring	• Property Transfer Tax • Development Fee • Wealth Tax • Inheritance Tax	• Value Added Tax	• Betterment Tax	

active use of these set screws as a tool for land use and settlement policy, in addition to the generation of revenues.

Compared to other recurring and nonrecurring taxes, all real estate taxes share certain particularities that are often used to legitimise them: they are object based, buoyant, local, and progressive. Object-based taxes are impersonal: the payable amount does not depend on individual solvency, leading to relatively predictable revenues, also since the taxed object cannot be 'hidden'. Buoyancy means that real estate prices generally increase relative to general economic growth, which leads to synchronously increasing tax revenues. Real estate taxes are organized as local taxes in many countries, often as the only or most important independent source of local revenue (Maurer and Paugam 2000: 1–2). Since the value of real estate generally reflects the local endowment with infrastructure and public services and the demand for housing, taxes on it can be seen as proportionate service contributions to municipalities as the providers of most public services. Progressive taxes rise with wealth, and real estate owners usually have above-average financial resources.

In addition, the better the municipal and rural services – financed by taxation – the higher might be the property value and thus the property tax rendering for the state revenues, and vice versa. Hence, public administration should have a vested interest in a fair, regular, efficient, functioning real estate taxation system that produces stable revenues.

However, scrutiny is needed whether a certain tax-base choice is lifting or depressing prices and rents, and if the effect is similar or differs depending on the type of land. The consequences of a change of land tax can cause societal conflicts if the tax base generates systematic advantages or disadvantages, e.g. regarding landowners and renters, landowners and the public administration, or winners and losers within the group of landowners. Such shifts of tax burdens can be intended or unintended. Any form of real estate tax is also always an attenuation of property rights. Hence, it needs a sound justification and fair and transparent implementation.

To sum up, nonrecurring real estate taxes might prevent market adjustments but are of minor fiscal importance for communities, while recurring ones are part of the framework that determines the viability of developments for landowners. Real estate taxes are predictable, local, and progressive.

Focus: land as a tax base

In the following chapters we want to focus on recurring real estate taxes that use land as a tax base, since such systems show particular inherent benefits for a successful land use policy, as we will demonstrate. It responds to issues of land scarcity, equity, and ecology, and supports urban planning and land policy (Netzer 2003; Thiel 2008). For example, it is thought to increase building density and mobilize brownfields in developed countries, to curb land speculation and ownership concentration that causes price hikes, and reduce urban sprawl and greenfield development. In the following, we will describe two sub-types of land-based taxes in more detail.

Unused land tax

Some jurisdictions have introduced a special recurring tax that is only levied on land that is determined by public authorities as 'not used'. Scholars, for example in Germany, have proposed such a tax as a 'second best' option to spur brownfield reuse and the closure of building gaps in cities (Dieterich and Josten 1998). The tax on unused land, however, is disputed, since a clear definition of 'unused' is often difficult. Instead, the tax authorities especially in developing countries could consider different strategies dealing with the phenomenon of land speculation, for example by selling or leasing state land to private investors (in particular for foreign direct investment, or FDI) under the condition that the desired development of the land has to be granted by the landowner/investor within a certain period. If the landowner/investor fails to fulfil this condition with the consequence that the land remains 'unused', this plot may fall back to the government. The investor would receive the investment back that he paid for the land, but without compensation for the unearned 'windfall profit'. In order to avoid such discussions, the 'naked' land should be taxed without regarding the actual use – it should be a land value tax (LVT).

The tax on 'naked' land: land value tax (LVT)

For the land value tax (LVT), taking only site (land) values without buildings or other improvements is characteristic. The LVT was highly influenced by Henry George (1879) and his 'single tax' approach as a de facto value capture instrument, meaning a recurrent tax by which annual 'windfall profits' on landownership from community growth or public investment are consequently taxed away. Windfalls are caused by increased land values and demand for land by private and institutional investors, for example insurance companies or real estate investment banks. Today, basic information on land and property sale prices records and on land valuation systems and techniques for real property taxation are given in Germany, but there are measurement problems and city- and country-specific peculiarities as well as political obstacles against land value taxation.

Accessibility gains through public infrastructure projects lead to higher local demand and higher asking prices for land (Coleman and Grimes 2010), which is not captured by building-based taxes. The opposite is true for public measurements that lead to value losses, in which case the tax burden decreases. A municipality will thus be incentivized to avoid value-reducing plans. LVT was highly influenced by the book *Progress and Poverty* from Henry George (1879). George developed a 'single tax' approach as a value capture instrument based on the land value only, without improvements or salaries, meaning a recurrent tax by which annual 'windfall for wipe-out' profits on landownership from community growth or public investment are consequently taxed away (Andelson 2000). George considered the land and its commodities (oil, gas, minerals, etc.) as a gift of nature and as such owned by the whole community (Blackledge 2009: 12). Hence, the value of a site is calculated out of the net present value of the extra surplus – a surplus that normally can be achieved through public land use planning without any investment by the landowner.

The rate for the LVT is generally fixed, without being changed according to the actual use of the site. A fixed tax rate always results in the same tax burden for the owner. The owner of the land cannot avoid the tax if it has the character of a fixed cost (Coase 1960; Mill 1848/1987). The only way to lower the effective burden of the tax is to use the site efficiently. While a tax on buildings only in theory leads landowners to mandate less and smaller new buildings to avoid taxes, taxes on land do not distort the market equilibrium, considering that land supply is fixed and perfectly inelastic. Potential rent-seeking processes cause windfalls by increased land values and demand for land for construction or agriculture investments.

Regarding land speculation, it can be argued that 'land hoarding' of undeveloped urban land for later use or sale becomes more expensive due to higher costs, requiring landowners to use their land more profitably and efficiently (Cocconcelli and Medda 2013: 393, 398). Land speculators can shift to other asset classes if land value increases are consequently taxed away through regular reassessments of land values. The result is a reduction of demand and prices as well as attenuated price cycles on the land markets. Finally, the use of public revenues generated through the tax also has a profound influence on its social merits.

The burden of a land tax falls entirely on landowners; a land tax is neutral. According to John Stuart Mill, the property tax supports utilitarian justice. It helps to maximize the 'greatest happiness of the greatest number', since the utilitarian moral means the use of the individual utility plus the social utility. Additionally, Mill supported the idea of the taxation for windfall profits and increased values of real estates through a house-tax: 'A house tax is a nearer approach to a fair income tax than a direct assessment on income can easily be' (Mill 1848/1987: 843). It does not distort economic decisions and thus does not generate an excess burden.

A number of arguments have been brought forward against the LVT. Most important, from a social justice viewpoint it could be argued that LVT encourages – or at least, does not halt – 'gentrification' since individual landowners and renters often cannot prevent land values in an area from rising even if they wanted to. This especially affects asset-rich and income-poor households, who might be forced to move. Supporters of LVT argue that this is merely a conflict of two perspectives on social justice: adequate contribution based on fair present value versus the right to a familiar neighbourhood and established social bonds (Maurer and Paugam 2000: 9). Another important objection is that LVT can distort urban development when modelled with multiple time-steps. Mills (1981) and Lim (1992) argue that, when uncontrolled, landowners are encouraged to develop their land prematurely to realize the 'best use' early on, which might not be the best use in a later time step, when it becomes too expensive to change. Finally, Song and Zenou (2006) find that apartment size decreases with high building-based taxes, which might offset the building density effect of a land value tax. Banzhaf and Lavery (2010: 175) also identify an inverse dwelling-size effect for LVT, that is offset by the densifying effect in a study of Pennsylvanian municipalities.

Today, basic information on land and property sales, on land valuation systems and techniques for property tax and land value tax, are limited in most developing countries. In the future, much more detail is needed to justify the sustainability of a future simple revenue generation system, for example through computer-assisted mass appraisal options (CAMA) that are based on the IAS-defined market value. The assessment of the tax base could be carried out by committees according to the blueprint of the German land assessment boards (*Gutachterausschüsse*; see § 192 Federal Building Code (*BauGB*)), which are public land assessment service agencies. These boards of surveyors collect data of all land transactions and set out annual guiding values of unimproved land (*Bodenrichtwerte*) for zones of plots with similar characteristics. Surely, the theory and practice of land taxation, combined with the Ricardian rent in particular of unimproved land, is highly controversial. Much more detail is needed to justify the sustainability of a future simple revenue generation system (Löhr 2010; Thiel 2011).

Land valuation: the basis for land taxation

Land taxation needs a sound valuation system. A just valuation needs to be accurate, but efficiency requires simplifying methods. It has to be carefully taken into account how much simplification is just and reasonable without a violation of the essential principle of equality in taxation, and if there are any distortions of the market to be considered (e.g. a tax wedge). Mass valuation always faces a trade-off between efficiency, predictability, and justice. Additionally, valuation and taxation follow different purposes. We need to be careful about the dangers that arise when the two are mixed up.

However, the estimation of land values is particularly complicated, since there is no unambiguous, single 'land value' for a plot. Instead, land values comprise ecological, economic, and social meanings that mirror the complexities and varieties of land policy (Bromley 2008; Thiel 2008; Dye and England 2009; Oates and Schwab 2009). For taxation purposes, the economic value is of special importance. Controversies about the economic land value or about the exchange value between Adam Smith, David Ricardo, John Stuart Mill, John Locke, or Karl Marx – the classical or neoclassical economists and political philosophers – mirror the difficulties in explaining the creation of the land value or the ground rent (Davy 2012; Thiel 2011). The land valuation system in Germany, for example, implemented the fair market value according to the International Accounting and Valuation Standard or the valuation standards of the Royal Institution of Chartered Surveyors (RICS; Blackledge 2009: 124–132; UBC 2003). Moreover, different developing countries have different stages of institutional development and governance; there is hardly any 'one size fits all' approach for property taxation, and different cultures have to be taken into account (Netzer 1998; Andelson 2000; Netzer 2003; Bird and Slack 2004; Cornia and Riddell 2008; Löhr 2010). Before implementing land taxation, some basic questions have to be answered, depending on the local circumstances: Which tax is easy to administer and to assess? Which tax base is justifiable? Which brings sustainable and high fiscal revenues? Will the tax be accepted and be easily understood by the taxpayers and the taxation departments? Also, the impacts on distribution and social consequences have to be assessed before taxation. These and other aspects need systematic analysis and examination.

Land valuation applications consist of two general families of worldwide surveyors' activities: appraisal and assessment. Both techniques are based on the same foundations and are thus subject to the same methods of valuation. Appraisal uses detailed expertise, while assessment uses a mass application through coded structures. Mass appraising aims at private expertise, while an assessment is ordered from a governmental authority in view of territorial inventory and ad valorem taxation on immovable properties. Assessment is covered by law (land valuation ordinance) and submitted to a specific national policy; such a policy is limited to assessment practices

(Appraisal Institute of Canada and Appraisal Institute 2005; Blackledge 2009). Taxation and valuation are based on a sophisticated assessment and appraisal for the rate-setting process.

Appraisal is a formal opinion of value prepared as a result of a retainer, intended for reliance by identified parties, and for which the appraiser assumes responsibility. Appraisal involves selective research into appropriate market areas, the use of appropriate analytical techniques, and the application of knowledge, experience, and professional judgement to develop an appropriate solution to a specific appraisal problem (UBC 2003). The appraiser provides the client – private and public – with an opinion (in fact, an estimation; hence, the thumb is the most important part of the appraiser's body) of the value on an immovable property that reflects market evidence. For example, an appraisal for tax purposes would require an opinion of investment value or some other properly defined value of an identified interest in real estate at a specific date for specific objectives (for insurance and relocation purposes, or property tax appeals).

Assessment is the act of valuating the totality of the properties within a global territory by using mass appraising applications and processes. Assessment is mainly done as a base for ad valorem property taxation. It should be regularly actualized (UBC 2003; Thiel 2008; Blackledge 2009). Data actualization is permanently done; value actualization is done on a fixed cyclical base, varying from yearly to once every three or five years. The quality of the results is inferior to the appraisal data, but the assessment has the advantage of producing permanent inventories and statistical data covering the entire country. Furthermore, assessment produces a neutral base for annual property taxation. Assessment is mainly done to finance municipalities, to support the cadastral actualization or specific types of infrastructure. The better the municipal services are, the higher might be the property value and thus the tax rendering.

As an interim conclusion, instruments of appraisal and assessment require market monitoring and data storage in a timely and updated manner of the purchase prices, rent prices, and statistics regarding construction materials. The land information system (LIS), consisting of cadastral maps and land registry, serves both as data storage and land valuation mapping to combine property and site-related data (e.g. size, location, condition). Actualization of data will secure the updating of data bases and ensure the integrity of the tax base on immovable properties to distinguish between data assessed values. It is, in any case, essential to actualize the existing databases (DB) in order to gain updated land values.

Case study: Estonia

Estonia is currently the only country in the European Union applying a land value tax without any other form of additional real estate taxation. After the post-socialist revolution of 1991, the country quickly reoriented itself as a 'Nordic country' and embarked on liberal and streamlined pro-investment policies, often with the support of Western advisors, despite harsh economic conditions. This desire for a streamlined 'no red tape' approach, rather than land policy or urban planning goals, was also the reason for Estonia to introduce LVT in 1993. It applies only with few exemptions for land used for roads, churches, cemeteries, embassies, and nature reserves, though recent changes allow waivers for owner-occupied homes and pensioners. Municipalities are free to set a tax rate between 0.1 percent and 2.5 percent of the assessed land value per annum (Tiits 2006; Estonian Tax and Customs Board 2013).

Responsible for the valuation of land is the National Land Board. Valuations are based on transaction databases; municipal governments have to approve the valuation presented to them by the board. Stamp duties and similar transaction fees for land are very low to ensure the use of correct purchasing prices in contracts. The law does not prescribe a regular valuation interval. Instead, assessments have been performed sporadically in 1993, 1996, and 2001. Because land values have risen considerably since 2001, economists and researchers have called for a revaluation, but this is politically less viable the larger the gap between current market value and assessed value gets (Tiits 2006). The omitted revaluations may even have contributed to the speculative bubble in and after 2007 (Cocconcelli and Medda 2013: 393).

LVT revenues were localized in 1995 because the municipalities still lacked a distinct and adequate source of income, and real estate taxes are appropriate local taxes. However, the share of LVT on local government revenues today is only between 5 percent (large towns) and 30 percent (rural areas), and even with the tax today it is estimated that only 10–20 percent of all municipalities are financially sustainable (Tiits 2006: 14). This underfunding of municipalities (Jaakson 1996a: 341; Ott 1999: 45) leads to calls for an increase to the municipal tax base through a reintroduction of a property value tax (Trasberg 2004). At the same time, Estonia is one of the countries with the lowest share of real estate taxation revenues in total tax revenues (OECD 2014).

Planning initially had a weak role after 1990 due to its association with socialism, and planning decisions were handled laxly and in favour of private landowners in the years after independence. Unclear landownership and lengthy restitution processes further complicated the situation (Jaakson 1996b: 3–4). As a result, urban sprawl characterized the first phase after Estonian independence. On the other hand, a simultaneous trend became apparent in the 2000s: multi-family houses and even Soviet-style high-rise blocks started to dominate housing construction again (Tammaru et al. 2009: 423). Inner-city densification and the replacement of old wooden buildings by higher, more robust structures denoted urban development in Tallinn (Ruoppila 2006: 208–211).

Compared with other cities in the Baltics, Tallinn today shows a denser development and a higher share of multi-family homes (Wenner 2016).

However, while fully unused brownfields are rare in Tallinn, some are only used as fee-based parking sites, pointing to the fact that buildings are not necessarily the most profitable use for land. One possible explanation is that LVT in Estonia is not high enough to exert enough pressure on landowners for more land use intensification in central locations. At 1 percent of the market value in many localities, with prices assessed the last time in 2001, and since 2012 with tax exemptions for owner-occupiers, its steering power is too weak to compete with the desire for the single-family home.

Conclusion

Our review allows a number of conclusions; some policy priorities and consequences follow. We have shown that certain real estate tax configurations, especially land-based taxes and their varieties, have beneficial influences on urban development both in theory and, albeit only with slight evidence, in the practical case of Estonia. However, particular attention has to be paid to the underlying valuation and control regime and the tax base, since every tax can be distorted if the valuation is carried out irregularly or infrequently.

How can better governance be achieved in view of land scarcity on the one hand, uncontrolled land consumption and urban sprawl on the other, and a socially still unbalanced distribution of property rights for land? Private landowners mostly hope to increase and collect the ground rent ('rent seeking'). Land policy must ensure that (part of) these profits, sometimes triggered by public investments, are regained for the public to generate revenues for local governments through appropriate taxation, and to use the set screws presented in this chapter to simultaneously encourage sustainable urban development. Land value taxation is an efficient instrument to do so, since it requires little administrative effort (at least in developed countries) and generates few distortions in the market while being able to raise substantial revenues.

References

Andelson, R.V. (2000) *Land-value taxation around the world*, 3rd ed., Wiley, Malden, MA.

Appraisal Institute of Canada and Appraisal Institute (2005) *The appraisal of real estate*, 2nd Canadian ed., Real Property Ownership and Interests, University of British Columbia, Vancouver.

Banzhaf, H.S. and Lavery, N. (2010) Can the land tax help curb urban sprawl? Evidence from growth patterns in Pennsylvania, *Journal of Urban Economics*, 67, 169–179.

Bird, R. and Slack, E. (eds) (2004) *International handbook of land and property taxation*, Edward Elgar, Cheltenham.

Blackledge, M. (2009) *Introducing property valuation*, Routledge, New York.

Bromley, D.W. (2008) Land and economic development: New institutional arrangements, in: Cornia, G.C. and Riddell, J. (eds) *Toward a vision of land in 2015, international perspectives*, Lincoln Institute of Land Policy, Cambridge, MA, 217–236.

Coase, R. (1960) The problem of social cost, *Journal of Law and Economics*, 3, 1–44.

Cocconcelli, L. and Medda, F.R. (2013) Boom and bust in the Estonian real estate market and the role of land tax as a buffer, *Land Use Policy*, 30(1), 392–400.

Coleman, A. and Grimes, A. (2010) Betterment taxes, capital gains and benefit cost ratios, *Economic Letters*, 109(1), 54–56.

Cornia, G.C. and Riddell, J. (eds) (2008) *Toward a vision of land in 2015, international perspectives*, Lincoln Institute of Land Policy, Cambridge, MA.

Davy, B. (2012) *Land policy: Planning and the spatial consequences of property*, Ashgate, Farnham.

Dieterich, H. and Josten, R. (1998) *Gutachten zur Einführung einer Bodenwertsteuer – Daten zur Auswirkung einer aufkommensneutralen Bodenwertsteuer in ausgewählten Städten*, Bonn.

Dye, R.F. and England, R.W. (eds) (2009) *Land value taxation, theory, evidence and practice*, Lincoln Institute of Land Policy, Cambridge, MA.

Estonian Tax and Customs Board (2013) *Home owner's land tax exemption in Tallinn* (online) available at: www.emta.ee/?id=25511 (accessed 18 August 2014).

George, H. (1879, reprinted 1997) *Progress and poverty*, Robert Schalkenbach Foundation, New York.

Jaakson, R. (1996a) From Marx to market: Deciding the urban form of post-Soviet Tallinn, *Estonia, Journal of Urban Design*, 1(3), 329–354.

Jaakson, R. (1996b) Planning the future and the future of planning in the Baltics, *Journal of Baltic Studies*, 27(1), 3–20.

Lim, D.H. (1992) The nonneutrality of land value tax – impacts on urban structure, *Journal of Urban Economics*, 32(2), 186–194.

Löhr, D. (2010) *Land conversion out of control – how to achieve better governance*, Paper presented at the FIG conference, Sydney, 2010 (online) available at: www.fig.net/pub/fig2010/papers/ts03e%5Cts03e_loehr_4666.pdf (accessed 1 July 2016).

Maurer, R. and Paugam, A. (2000) *Reform toward ad Valorem property tax in transition economies: Fiscal and land use benefits*, The World Bank – Land and Real Estate Initiative, 13 (online) available at: http://www wds.worldbank.org/external/default/WDSContentServer/WDSP/IB/2003/07/23/000112742_20030723105938/Rendered/PDF/253930Urbanbackground13.pdf (accessed 21 August 2014).

Mill, J.S. (1848) *Principles of political economy and chapters on socialism*, Reissued ed. 2008, Oxford University Press, Oxford.

Mills, D.E. (1981) The non-neutrality of land value taxation, *National Tax Journal*, 34(1), 125–129.

Netzer, D. (eds) (1998) *Land value taxation: Can it and will it work today?* Lincoln Institute of Land Policy, Cambridge, MA.

Netzer, D. (eds) (2003) *The property tax, land use and land use regulation*, Studies in fiscal federalism and state-local finance in association with the Lincoln Institute of Land Policy, Edward Elgar, Cheltenham.

Norregaard, J. (2013) *Taxing immovable property: Revenue potential and implementation challenges*, IMF working paper (online) available at: www.imf.org/external/pubs/ft/wp/2013/wp13129.pdf (accessed 19 February 2016).

Oates, W. E. and Schwab, R. M. (2009) The simple analytics of land value taxation, in: Dye, R. F. and England, R. W. (eds) *Land value taxation, theory, evidence and practice*, Lincoln Institute of Land Policy, Cambridge, MA, 51–71.
OECD (2014) *Taxes on property as a percentage of GDP* (online) available at: www.oecd-ilibrary.org/taxation/taxes-on-property_20758510-table7 (accessed 1 July 2016).
Ott, A. F. (1999) Land taxation and tax reform in the Republic of Estonia, *Assessment Journal*, January/February, 40–49.
Ruoppila, S. (2006) The increase of urban inequalities in Tallinn – Does EU accession change anything? in: Altrock, U., Güntner, S., Huning, S. and Peters, D. (eds) *Spatial planning and urban development in the new EU member states: From adjustment to reinvention*, Ashgate, Farnham, 201–254.
Song, Y. and Zenou, Y. (2006) Property tax and urban sprawl – theory and implications for US cities, *Journal of Urban Economics*, 60(3), 519–534.
Tammaru, T., Leetmaa, K., Silm, S. and Ahas, R. (2009) Temporal and spatial dynamics of the new residential areas around Tallinn, *European Planning Studies*, 17(3), 423–439.
Thiel, F. (2008) *Strategisches Landmanagement, Baulandentwicklung durch Recht, Ökonomie, Gemeinschaft und Information*, 2nd ed., Books on Demand, Norderstedt.
Thiel, F. (2011) Property entails obligations: Land and property law in Germany, *European-Asian Journal of Law and Governance*, 1, 78–94.
Tiits, T. (2006) *Land taxation reform in Estonia*, paper presented at the conference 'Making the Property Tax Work in Developing and Transitional Countries', 15–17 October 2006, Stone Mountain, Georgia (online) available at: www.andywightman.com/docs/Estonia_landtax.pdf (accessed 1 July 2016).
Trasberg, V. (2004) Property and land taxation in the Baltic States, *Journal of Property Tax Assessment and Administration*, 1(2), 31–43.
University of British Columbia (UBC) (ed.) (2003) *Real property assessment*, Real Estate Division, University of British Columbia, Vancouver.
Wenner, F. (2016) Sustainable urban development and land value taxation: The case of Estonia, *Land Use Policy*, online first, doi: 10.1016/j.landusepol.2016.08.031.

A German perspective on land taxation: political inertia and debates on social and distributional aspects

Dirk Löhr

Discussion in Germany

In June 2016, the finance ministers of the German states agreed upon a reform of the property tax base. This was the provisional end of a debate lasting 20 years. However, the final decision of the German parliament (*Bundestag*) is still pending. The reform was necessary since the old tax base is widely considered unconstitutional. It is based on values from 1964 for West Germany and from 1935 for East Germany. Just like the existing tax base, the new tax base will also include the value of the land (using guiding land values, or *Bodenrichtwerte*) and the improvements ('compound tax base' or 'property tax' in → *Thiel and Wenner*, Table 6.1). However, within the new tax base the valuation of the improvements is done in a crude way using a rough cost approach. The new property tax will be revenue neutral, which means that the overall property tax burden will not increase.

Opposition to the legislative proposal comes from two states (Hamburg and Bavaria) with high land values and also from lobby groups, particularly in the housing sector. It appears that Hamburg and Bavaria are afraid of a worse position in the federal financial equalization scheme; generally a higher property tax burden should be avoided due to the updated land values. Bavaria, for instance, proposes a property tax based on the physical size of the building and the plot without considering the value of real estate (see → *Thiel and Wenner*, Table 6.1, 'Simplified Property Tax', rightmost column, 'Other'). This means, for example, that a house owner in the center of Munich has to pay the same as somebody in the spatial periphery with a fraction of the market value of his real estate if the size is the same. It is hard to imagine that such a tax would be constitutional.

Another opposition group is trying to achieve a taxation of land without including the building values. The tax base can either be the pure land value (see → *Thiel and Wenner*, Table 6.1, column 'Only Land') or a combination of land value and plot size. The promoters of this proposal are organized in a campaign called '*Grundsteuer: Zeitgemäß!*',[1] representing, among others, mayors, environmental protection organizations (*NABU*, *BUND*), the tenants' organization (*Deutscher Mieterbund*) and a renowned economic research institute (*Institut der Deutschen Wirtschaft*, Cologne). Compound tax bases in general and the legislative proposal of the German finance ministers in particular are criticized for various reasons: The more valuable an improvement, the more tax has to be paid. An efficient use of a site, such as filling a gap between buildings or extending a building, would cause higher taxation. Furthermore, there is almost no pressure to bring underused or unused real estate into use. In contrast, the tax is lowest if a site is kept idle. Thus the land market remains immobile. Compliance with the land use plans is 'punished' with higher taxes. At the very least, the finance ministers have accepted the criticisms in that they are willing to consider combining their proposal with a tax on unused land for certain zones (see → *Thiel and Wenner*, Table 6.1). Moreover, within a compound tax base of the legislative proposal, the highest share of a compound tax base falls on buildings. Since the supply of buildings is elastic to a certain degree, a 'compound' property tax on buildings can be shifted to the tenants. In contrast, if the land use planning is strict, the supply of land is inelastic. That's why a pure land value tax (LVT) can hardly be shifted to the tenants. Moreover, the difficulties of a mass appraisal are not so much caused by land as by the building. The legislative proposal is based on the gross floor area. However, one and the same gross floor area might go hand in hand with completely different residential quality. Staggered stories, 'captive rooms', and other special features of a building cannot be considered within a mass appraisal. The legislative proposal provides standard values for the construction costs, which are classified into three different categories according to the year of construction. However, this classification is so crude that new buildings are systematically overvalued. On the other hand, no market adjustment is done. As a consequence, the tax values of buildings in the periphery also appear to be systematically too high. For these and other reasons, the valuation of the buildings is systematically biased.

Reflection

Comparing a 'tax on naked land' with a compound property tax (→ *Thiel and Wenner*, Table 6.1), the result is as follows:

> Regarding effectiveness, property taxes, as well as other taxes, might either be used to feed the public budget or to generate incentive effects. Both the LVT and a compound property tax have to be considered primarily as a fiscal instrument. However, both may influence the real estate market. Most of the differences in real estate values between regions as well as over time are caused by differences in land values. Since an LVT aims to divert land rents into the public purse, it may dampen price hikes and speculative activities if the rates are high enough. Moreover, unlike a compound property tax, an LVT supports compliance with the land use plans: those who use the sites with lower intensity than

determined in the plan have to pay the same as with an efficient use – in contrast to a compound tax base.

Looking at efficiency, an LVT is a neutral tax if it is combined with strict land use planning. In this regard it is also different from a compound tax base because it doesn't cause any excess burden (→ *Thiel and Wenner*). Sometimes it is even called 'super-neutral' (Dwyer 2014: 764), since it actively promotes efficiency, for example with the use of the land scarcity factor, and may remove existing distortions. Moreover, the Henry George theorem suggests that as a result of a shift to LVT, the size of settlements gets closer to optimality. Thiel and Wenner refer to the opinion that LVT may distort intertemporal decision-making. On closer scrutiny, Tideman already showed in 1995 that possible distortions are not caused by the LVT itself but by market imperfections. Concerning a compound tax base, most economists agree that a compound tax base causes distortions, referring to the matters discussed. For instance, it basically hampers investments in buildings. However, some supporters of a compound tax base stress that the building component may serve as a proxy for the congestion costs of settlements and reflect the actual use of infrastructure. However, the land value also reflects the congestion effects. In this regard, it is superior to building values (e.g. in the case of vacant houses). Considering the actual use of infrastructure, usage-based fees are preferable anyway.

Regarding legitimacy, the valorization of land in favor of the private owner is predominantly caused by public services, besides other factors such as agglomeration of qualified workforce or efforts of neighbors (e.g. well-tended gardens). This means the value of land is the result of (positive) external effects. This is why an LVT might be interpreted as a means to internalize at least a share of these external effects to the causer, which is the public. Those who get higher benefits from the public pay more (principle of equivalence). In contrast, a compound tax base based primarily on the value of the building implies that the privately created value of the building is socialized and most of the publicly created land value is privatized. Of course, transition rules are also necessary for an LVT. For decades, politics promoted the guideline of a detached single-family house with a large garden. For income-poor and asset-rich people (→ *Thiel and Wenner*, ch. 2.2.), like an elderly widow, the change of paradigm may cause hardship if a new paradigm of dense settlement is incentivized by LVT.

In terms of practicability, an LVT would be based on guiding land values for sites (see → *Thiel and Wenner*, ch. 2.2.). These values are already comprehensively available in Germany due to the public property assessment boards (*Gutachterausschüsse*). However, the quality of values is not always satisfying, since the functioning, the financial and personal endowment, and the organization of the assessment boards differ from state to state. However, given the necessary political will, these shortcomings could be removed easily. Despite these imperfections, the standard land values are supposed to comply with the legal requirements for standardization regarding mass appraisals. Using the guiding land values, municipalities simply would have to choose a tax rate and put it on this tax base. In contrast, the aforementioned legislative proposal will take some ten years in order to complete the valuation. This delay is mainly caused by the difficulties of appraising the buildings. It remains to be seen whether the result of the appraisal is in line with the requirements of the constitution.

Conclusion

Closer consideration reveals many advantages of an LVT compared to a compound property tax. It is superior in terms of effectiveness, efficiency, legitimacy, and practicability. However, an LVT is not a silver bullet. According to the Tinbergen rule, independent policy goals should be pursued with different, independent instruments. Taxes may have two potentially conflicting tasks: feeding the public budget and incentivizing the desired behavior of the stakeholders. Both a compound property tax as well as an LVT should be primarily considered as a fiscal tool and not as a steering tool. Although an LVT supports land use planning, contributes to higher efficiency of the land markets and may remove some of the distributional bias (see below), it cannot replace complementary instruments. Also the success of an LVT depends on sound use of complementary instruments, in particular strict land use planning.

In contrast to the discussion in Estonia, where a 'red tape approach' should be avoided (→ *Thiel and Wenner*), the German discussion on property tax reform focuses on social and distributional aspects. Indeed, an LVT may help to rebalance the distributional bias to a certain degree. In Germany, as in many other countries, the winner in the struggle for income and wealth distribution during recent years has not been labor and capital but land. This perception was the rationale of the critics of Stiglitz (2015) and others on Piketty (2014). An LVT could help to redistribute income and value from land, since it redirects a share of the ground rents from private purses into the public budget. However, it doesn't lower the ground rents. This is why an LVT is not the right tool to control gentrification processes, as → *Thiel and Wenner* state. On the other hand, LVT stimulates the supply of housing and doesn't restrict it, unlike a compound tax base – with corresponding effects on the rents. Nonetheless, particularly the left-wing parties and groups in Germany prefer a compound property tax, since it is regarded as a first step into a more comprehensive wealth tax. Ironically, in Germany, an LVT seems to have more supporters in the conservative and liberal political spectrum, mainly due to its efficiency and simplicity.

The German discussion has been influenced a lot by extraneous considerations such as the position of the various states within the federal financial equalization scheme. Although a property tax is supposed to be a means of choice within competitive federalism, most of the finance ministers insisted on the dogma of the legislative responsibility of the federal government. As a result, a political consensus between the states was celebrated as a success, as an end in itself, without regarding the material result.

Note

1 See www.grundsteuerreform.net.

References

Dwyer, T. (2014) Taxation: The lost history, *The American Journal of Economics and Sociology*, 73, 664–988.

Piketty, T. (2014) *Capital in the twenty-first century*, Belknap Press, Cambridge, MA.

Stiglitz, J. E. (2015) Thomas Piketty gets income inequality wrong, *Salon.com*, 3 January, San Francisco, CA: Salon Media Group Inc. (online) available at: www.salon.com/2015/01/02/joseph_stiglitz_thomas_piketty_gets_income_inequality_wrong_partner/ (accessed 11 November 2016).

Tideman, N. (1995) *Taxing land is better than neutral: Land taxes, land speculation and the timing of development*, Lincoln Institute of Land Policy (online) available at: http://schalkenbach.org/rsf-2/wp-content/uploads/2014/07/Tideman-1995-Taxing-land-better-than-neutral.pdf (accessed 11 November 2016).

A British perspective on land taxation: politically unpopular

Antonia Layard

In England, land is required for new housing projects. However, while the grant of planning permission remains a function of the state (generally the local authority), it is private developers who currently build around 84 percent of all new housing in England (DCLG 2016). So, as in the case of Estonia in the contribution by *Wenner and Thiel*, it is essential to mobilize private developers to make efficient use of land. There are widespread suggestions that there are sufficient planning permissions in existence (the Local Government Association estimates 465,000 permissions are currently unused; LGA 2016) and that there are market explanations for limited supply. However, increasing households and the market dynamics in a primarily speculative housing market in England lead to prices that continue to rise both for home ownership (by 8.3 percent from September 2015–16) and for rental (by 14.1 percent from 2011–2016, or 9.9 percent excluding London; ONS 2016), as well as for agricultural land (Savills 2016). Given rising prices and a lack of clarity over market dynamics, could a change in taxation bring more land to market (and so reduce prices)? One change might be to alter taxes on exchange value (nonrecurring taxes) to provide nudges to bring more land to market. A second type of land tax change is to alter taxes on use value (or recurring taxes). In England these include council tax or business rates for property, with failed proposals for a so-called mansion tax, land-banking, and research on land value taxes. There are also underused provisions that enable local authorities to bring empty dwellings back into active use and occasional proposals to tax land banking. This commentary discusses how these different forms of taxation – as introduced by → *Thiel and Wenner* – could relieve the scarcity of building land in England.

Nonrecurring taxes

Starting with English exchange taxes capital gains taxes are charged on a wide range of assets (including share income, savings and profits from asset sales), although there is an exemption for individual private homes (§ 222 Taxation of Chargeable Gains Act 1992). For older homeowners contemplating 'downsizing', there are no financial disincentives as a consequence of capital gains tax. For landowners, however, notably farmers selling farmland for housing, there will be a liability to capital gains tax (currently up to 28 percent after allowances). There are of course exemptions, including entrepreneur and rollover reliefs, which may reduce this dramatically. While reducing capital gains tax might incentivize sale, enabling owners to keep a larger proportion of their gain, there is significant anecdotal evidence (Hetherington 2015) that farmers and landowners are not retaining their land as result of the consequences of taxation but, instead, in hope of higher profits still to come. Reducing capital gains taxes would by no means incentivize landowners to sell.

Similarly, inheritance tax, which is collected on the death of a landowner, might be altered to incentivize owners to sell before death, bringing land for housing onto the market. With an elderly electorate, this could be politically controversial, and in recent years individual inheritance tax liabilities have been reduced, introducing larger nil-rate bands as well as allowing transfers between spouses (the objective is to achieve £1 million tax-free by 2020–21). For farmers, there are further exemptions still, since inheritance tax is not payable if agricultural uses are continued on the land within two years of the owner's death. However, inheritance tax receipts were around £4.9 billion in 2016–17, an increase of over 26 percent compared to 2014–15, the consequence both of higher asset values as well as an increase in the number of deaths producing receipts (HMRC 2016). While there are then political advantages in reducing inheritance taxes at a time of rising house prices, from a policy perspective this has not been tied into incentivizing house sales and downsizing to any significant degree. As such, changes would lower tax revenue significantly while being unlikely to bring new land sales, given sellers' expectations at times of ever-rising property prices.

The third form of exchange tax on land in England is stamp duty land tax. This is levied on sales of new properties or sites. It is a staggered system, with a nil-rate band up to £125,000, and a top band of 13 percent over £1.5 million (in 2016–17). The tax has been seen as a disincentive to sale. The influential Mirrlees review, for example, could find 'little to say in its defence' and recommended that it be abolished (preferring a housing services tax [for domestic property] and a land value tax [for business property] instead; Mirrlees and Adam 2010). Stamp duty land value tax could, perhaps, be tweaked in order to incentivize sales, thereby bringing larger houses onto the market for families. For example, since April 2016, buy-to-let landlords and second homeowners have been subject to an additional 3 percent stamp duty when buying properties.

However, once again, however economically flawed, it is unlikely that the stamp duty land tax would be abolished at time of trade deficit, austerity, and financial uncertainty. In 2015–16, £7,310 million of stamp duty land tax was paid on 1.18 million residential transactions, with £3,370 million on 114,000 non-residential transactions (HMRC 2016b). Rates of stamp duty land tax might be reduced for those wishing to buy a smaller property, incentivizing downsizing. So far, however, while advocates have called for such a change, no such suggestion has been made by government (the 2017 Housing White Paper 'Fixing Our Broken Housing Market' makes no such suggestion, for example). Reducing stamp duty might incentivize sales by increasing the profits companies or individuals would make if they sell, but if vendors believe that there are more profits to be made by hanging on (and with ever-increasing prices this is likely), it remains economically rational not to sell, even if exchange value taxes are reduced.

These three exchange taxes then – capital gains tax, inheritance tax, and stamp duty land tax – while all politically contentious, bring in significant revenue and are all politically sensitive. Since taxation is only a proportion of the profit sellers receive on sale, any nudge effects of altering taxation rates will only be effective if they are sufficiently persuasive to counter the attractions of hedging against inflation at a time of steadily rising land and housing prices. Reducing exchange taxes to encourage greater land supply is not currently on the political radar.

Recurring taxes

Turning then to taxes on use value (or recurring taxes), the most notable intervention here is council tax, which in 1993 replaced Margaret Thatcher's widely loathed 'poll taxes' after widespread political discontent and riots. Council tax is imposed in eight bands (A–G) that have not been adjusted for inflation since their initial introduction in the Local Government Finance Act 1992. Re-banding is contentious, as owners who have improved their property, and so might go up a band as a result of their properties greater attractiveness, would be taxed for their investment. With huge cuts imposed on local authority revenues, as well as increasing local costs, notably at the moment for care for the elderly, there are consistent suggestions for ways to increase council tax and thereby increase taxation of use value. These proposals are, however, spectacularly politically unpopular.

The commercial equivalent use tax is business rates, payable to local authorities at fixed rates based on a rateable value (as assessed in 2008 and not updated since then). This is multiplied by centrally set figures (which are not particularly transparent). Again there are exemptions for small or rural businesses, if the land is owned by a charity, in Enterprise Zones, where new business is spatially encouraged, or where it is empty for three months. The greatest exemption, however, is for agricultural land, which is not subject to business rates. While this may be beneficial for asset-rich, cash-poor farmers, with agricultural land increasingly bought as a wealth shelter (and then worked by tenant farmers), there are increasing concerns about the lack of use taxes on agricultural land (Hetherington 2015).

Other initiatives to tax use have also been unsuccessful. The so-called mansion tax, an annual levy on properties worth over £2 million, was first proposed in 2009 by the then opposition Liberal Democrats and taken up as a central pillar of Labour's election campaign in 2015. It was wildly unpopular, criticized as damaging England – and particularly London's – attraction to international entrepreneurs and investors as well as being a tax on success, potentially bringing in only £1.2 billion. Similarly, proposed taxes or management orders for 'land banks', owned but not developed by construction companies, retailers, or land traders, have also been unable to find the requisite political support. While Labour politicians have suggested imposing fines or compulsorily purchasing unused sites in land banks, commercial arguments have held sway with the current government. Lastly, a parliamentary bill to undertake research on land value tax met with criticism and a lack of political success. Such use value taxes are perceived to be attacks on ambition and success and portrayed accordingly, particularly in some parts of the press (Land Value Tax Bill [HL] 2014–15).

There has also been a lack of political will to use policy tools for repurposing underused land. One policy intervention, for example, is the Empty Dwelling Management Orders, introduced in the Housing Act of 2004. Their objective was to start a dialogue between homeowners who were leaving properties empty, living elsewhere, and were to be used very much as a last resort. The orders were an attempt to balance property rights with sustainable land use (and so are considered to be human rights compliant). Initially, properties only had to be empty for six months before an order could be contemplated; however, following negative media coverage and a change in government, in 2012 this was changed to properties empty for two years and only if the buildings were magnets for vandalism, squatters, or other forms of anti-social behaviour (House of Commons Library 2016). While these orders are potent devices at a time of severe housing shortages, they are rarely used.

Conclusion

To conclude, then, reforms in taxation are both politically contentious, with significant lobbying by key industries, notably commercial housebuilders and farmers. Infrastructure projects are more likely to be able to use processes of compulsory purchase, which while being locally politically contentious have national governmental support. The provision of new housing, however, which is so desperately needed, is primarily reliant on private land trades and construction. With land prices so high – and rising – the nudge effects that might be gained by lowering exchange value taxes are offset by owners' expectations of higher asset value growth and hedging against inflation.

There are certainly greater possibilities in using use value measures, whether introducing either a land value tax or imposing business rates onto some agricultural land, in incentivizing land sales, bringing more land to market. Such changes could affect asset-rich, cash-poor elderly occupiers and farmers and would, once again, be politically contentious. However, such innovations could provide significant incentives for sale, bringing more land to market, if the political will could be found. This could considerably reduce the price of land and so bring down housing costs, which are currently limiting choice and quality of life for so many.

References

DCLG (2016) *2014-based Household Projections: England*, 2014–2039.

Hetherington, P. (2015) *Whose land is our land?* Policy Press, Bristol.

HMRC (2017) *Inheritance Tax Statistics* 2014–15.

HMRC (2016) *Annual Stamp Tax Statistics* 2015–2016.

HMRC (2017) *Capital Gains Tax rates and annual tax-free allowances.*

House of Commons Library (2016) Briefing Paper, No 04129, 24 June 2016, Empty Dwelling Management Orders (EDMOs).

LGA (2016) *Responses to the housing and planning bill*, House of Lords, Report Stage.

Mirrlees, J. A. and Adam, S. (2010) *Dimensions of tax design: The Mirrlees review*, Oxford University Press, Oxford.

National Statistics (2015) *2012-based Household Projections: England*, 2012–2037, 27 February.

Office of National Statistics (ONS) (2016) *2016 House price index*, September.

Savills (2016) *Market survey UK agricultural land.*

Part III

Steering land uses through regulation impacting property rights

7 Negotiated land use plans in the Netherlands

A central instrument in Dutch 'active' and 'passive' land policy

Joost Tennekes

Introduction

Since the beginning of the 1990s, land use plans that are negotiated between a municipality and private sector companies, agreed upon in a contract under private law (hereinafter 'negotiated land use plans'), play a central role in Dutch municipal land policy. The legislator's preference for this instrument has been foundational for Dutch cost recovery law and its reforms in 2008 and 2016.

In this chapter, the preference of Dutch government, both state and municipality, for this particular instrument will be explained within the institutional framework on land policy and cost recovery. As will be shown, the lack of good alternative instruments for cost recovery, and the possibilities for capturing the value increase of the land, both play a key role. But the tension that results from the fact that municipalities use both private law *and* public law instruments has been criticized by planning professionals, administrative courts, and parliamentarians. Is the public interest of good spatial planning compromised by municipalities acting under private law?

A representative database of negotiated agreements is not available for quantitative or qualitative research. Therefore, empirical research on these negotiations is difficult, although some studies have tried to detect their importance indirectly (Woestenburg and Van der Krabben 2013; Buitelaar and Witte 2011). The method used in this chapter is to analyze what constitutes the incentive structure for actors involved in the process, in particular the municipality, and to illustrate it through discussions in parliament, court decisions, and a case study.

The instrument of the negotiated land use plan is described in the context of *two* Dutch practices. The first is that of 'active' land policy, the most common way of urban development in the Netherlands (section 3). The second practice is 'facilitating' land policy (section 4), which has slowly become more important since the 2000s. In *both* practices, negotiations with private sector developers over the land use plan and developers' obligations is a crucial step, which will be illustrated by the case of the 'Overstad' development project in the city of Alkmaar in section 5. After going into more detail on the issue of legitimacy of the instrument in section 6, an assessment of the use of negotiated land use plans in the Dutch context will be given in the concluding section. But first, the role of the land use plan in Dutch development-led planning will be introduced.

The role of the land use plan in Dutch development-led planning

Planning in the Netherlands can be characterized as 'development-led' and not 'plan-led' (Buitelaar et al. 2011). In most cases, land use plans are made only upon a concrete building initiative for development. Municipalities do *not* adopt a land use plan and then wait for developers to come. Until the 1990s, the building initiative came from the municipality itself. Since then, it has been mostly initiatives by the private sector in close cooperation with the municipality.

The dominant image of the municipality's role in urban development in the Netherlands is that it should not only manage autonomous growth but should have an active role. It should stimulate and direct urban development, in order to (1) reach housing production objectives and safeguard the public interests of concentrated development and the prevention of sprawl; (2) see to a proper layout and design of the area, integrating infrastructure and public services within the greater spatial context; (3) guarantee the provision of social housing; and (4) last but not least, organize the production of all these together. Within this frame, the municipal task does *not* end by guaranteeing the right amount of building land to become available for potential developers. The municipality's efforts should aim at guaranteeing that houses are *actually* built, within an environment that meets numerous *policy objectives* (integration, high quality public space, and social equality), and *on time*.

In the decades after World War II, development-led planning expressed itself in what in the Dutch context is called 'active land policy'. The municipality acquires all the land necessary, changes the land use plan, develops the land and sells it to developers, be it private companies or housing corporations, and so forth. Since the 1990s, the role of the municipality has changed, because it did not own all the land, or even any land at all. The function of the land use plan then changes into guiding the behavior of *the owners*, who, according to Dutch law, cannot be obliged to build. In that case, the adoption of a land use plan then often is preceded by other agreements under private law that deal with the aforementioned public interests. The public competency of changing the land use plan becomes the key trump card of the municipality in its private-law negotiations with developers.

Table 7.1 shows four practices of urban development situations, departing from the assumption of (a) two kinds of municipal land policy (active and passive) and (b) two kinds of land use plan (those that have been adopted without prior negotiations with potential developers, and negotiated land use plans). Quadrants 1, 3, and 4 all describe situations that conform to

Table 7.1 Four practices of urban development in the Netherlands. The grey quadrants correspond to different forms of 'development-led' planning, the white to 'plan-led' planning.

	Active land policy: municipality (co-)owns the pooled land at some point in the development process	*Passive land policy: municipality does not (co-) own all land at any point in the development process*
Changing land use plan (public law) without negotiation over contracts with developers (private law)	1. Traditional situation of full active land policy	2. 'Facilitating' land policy – public law cost recovery
Contracts (private law) signed between municipality and developers before changing land use plan (public law)	3. PPP (building claim model, joint venture model)	4. 'Facilitating' land policy – private law cost recovery

the tradition of development-led planning either because (a) the municipality itself takes the initiative (quadrant 1) or (b) the municipality ensures, before the land use plan is being changed, that private sector activity will take place (quadrants 3 and 4). Only quadrant 2 describes a situation in which the realization of the plan is still open. This situation is very rare in the Netherlands.

Negotiated land use plans in the context of 'active' municipal land policy

During the 1990s, market actors started to speculatively buy land on a much larger scale than before. With development companies owning land on strategic positions at many locations, it had become impossible for the municipality to acquire the necessary land without entering into negotiations about the land use plans in relation to future building possibilities. Therefore, during the '90s, new forms of active land policy developed, that were based on cooperation between municipality and private sector companies (Public Private Partnerships; quadrant 3).

In the *building claim model*, private landowners negotiate with the municipality, sell their land to the municipality, which develops the land and sells serviced, zoned building land back to its contract partners at an agreed price (or according to an agreed price mechanism) that is high enough to recover costs for public services and public housing. In the *joint venture model*, the municipality and private landowners together establish a private law developing company, pooling the land and developing it. This entity may then sell the land to others or develop the real estate itself.

One of the factors that might have supported the municipal preference for active land policy (although in a new form) was the increasing financial potential of urban development. As house prices started to rise dramatically in the period 1995–2008, land value was pushed up. The Public Private Partnerships enabled the municipality to not only recover the costs for public services and social housing, but also to get a share of the (planning) gain. During this period, income from land development played an important role in the general municipal budget (Korthals Altes 2008), paying for other municipal services (BHV 2013; Muñoz Gielen and Van der Krabben 2015). Although it constituted only a small percentage in the total of municipal revenues, it was important 'extra' money in surplus of the 'normal' central government grants and municipal taxes (Tennekes et al. 2015).

Negotiated land use plans in the context of passive ('facilitating') land policy

The Public Private Partnerships of the 1990s and 2000s may have been successful in terms of housing production and municipal revenues, but they still had some important flaws. One of them was that 'free riding' still occurred: private developers that did not contribute enough for public services from which they benefitted. This prompted the legislator to reform the law in order to make the municipality less dependent on the success of negotiations with developers. Attempts to attain this by enhancing municipal pre-emption rights were not effective enough (Groetelaers 2004), and the only existing instrument for compulsory contribution by developers, the betterment tax (*baatbelasting*) was practically useless for the purpose (Schep 2012). Therefore a new instrument for cost recovery had to be created for passive, or 'facilitating', land policy.

There were also doubts about the legitimacy of negotiated land use plans. The municipal competency to prescribe the use of land is a privilege it has as a public body. Yet, it uses this competency as a trump card in its negotiations with developers with the purpose to sign a private law contract. In the white paper on improving cost recovery law (VROM 2001), the government itself mentions the problem that has come to be known as the 'double hat' problem: the municipality wears a public hat and a private hat at the same time, regulating land use as a government body and earning money as a landowner, respectively (Van Rij and Korthals Altes 2010). Government is both regulator *of* the game and player *in* the game. The white paper states as follows: 'There is the danger that the municipality operates too much out of motivation of profit, and too little on grounds of the policy goals' (Ministry of Housing 2001: 10).

After many years – in which the alternative of a purely public system was also discussed (Koeman et al. 2008) – parliament decided in 2005 in favor of a 'mixed system' in the land development law, coming into force in 2008.

In this system, the municipality is obliged to recover the public costs from developers. It is, however, free to organize cost recovery by *private law*, with all the advantages of freedom of contract. When no agreement can be reached with all developers in the area, the municipality has to set up a contribution scheme under public law for the whole area, which stipulates the obligatory contribution for all developers, but it is only collected from developers with whom no agreement is made.

Although the municipality is free to choose the way of public cost recovery from the beginning, refraining from negotiations with landowners, the minister explicitly states that contracts under private law are the preferred option, and that he expects that in the overriding majority of cases cost recovery will take place through contracts.

In the public-law variant, there is a balancing of all costs and revenues of the whole area, so that owners of a high potential, low cost plot contribute relatively more, thus discouraging the 'cherry-picking' of plots by developing companies. Moreover, the amount of the contribution is proportionally related to the extent that the developer profits from the public services. As the contribution scheme is set up for an entire area, this prevents costs being passed on to developers with whom a municipality does not reach agreement. A public scheme does not mean that former agreements under private law lose their validity. Nor does it mean that an additional contribution can be asked from contract partners, in case the privately agreed obligations are lower than the contribution according to the public scheme. Vice versa, developers cannot claim lower contributions when the public scheme demands lower contributions than they agreed to give under private law. The explanatory memorandum explicitly states that these differences have to be considered as normal 'market risks' for the contract partners, i.e. municipality and developer (Brand et al. 2006).

In the major reform of 2016, in which planning law is integrated in a general 'living environment law', the basics of this system of cost recovery have been maintained, although some amendments are made that make cost recovery under public law easier (Sorel et al. 2014).

Although after the law reforms of 2008 (and 2016) cost recovery under public law has become a more viable option than before, in the great majority of urban development projects private contracts are used. Between 2008 and 2011, in 97 percent of the projects cost recovery was arranged via private contracts (negotiated land use plans in active *and* passive land policy, cf. quadrants 3 and 4 in Table 7.1, or land sales under full active land policy, quadrant 1), and only 3 percent through public law (Buitelaar et al. 2012a).

This preference of municipality for private agreements is quite understandable, as public cost recovery has a couple of restrictions. And although these constraints may 'cast their shadow' over private law negotiations (Buitelaar et al. 2012a), influencing the content of the private contracts, still the private agreements may offer less constraints. The most important constraints imposed by public cost recovery are as follows:

- The contribution that a municipality may demand is strictly limited to recovery of the costs actually made. Capturing the value increase of the land is forbidden.

- The scope of cost recovery is limited by a governmental list of kinds of costs, and a prescribed way of calculating costs. Costs for sewerage, for example, can be included, but costs for many other public services, for example school buildings, cannot.
- Cost recovery for public investments that are made at some distance from the development, or made at a later moment but still benefit from it, is difficult. Many municipalities (38 percent in 2013) (BHV 2013) found it difficult to make a juridical sound claim for a contribution, linking the costs sufficiently to the land use plan (Muñoz Gielen 2013).[1]

In short, cost recovery under public law should be interpreted as a 'minimum variant' in comparison to the possibilities under private law. In jurisprudence, the administrative courts guard well the boundaries of this 'minimum'. This increases the judical risk for the municipality: flaws in the contribution scheme could easily lead to annulment of the whole scheme and the land use plan (Buitelaar et al. 2012a; Netjes 2013).

This preference for private law instruments also has to do with the required *flexibility* of the land use plan. The public contribution scheme has to be drawn up together with the land use plan, and because of the aforementioned balancing of costs and revenues for the whole area, this requires a highly detailed plan. However, during the past ten years or so, municipalities started to acknowledge the advantages of less detailed and more flexible plans. In this way, they could better accommodate changes during the development period.[2]

Negotiated land use plans after the economic crisis: the case of Overstad in Alkmaar

The financial crisis of 2008 and its consequences undermined the dominant practice of negotiated land use plans and Public Private Partnerships. Development companies reacted to lower consumer demand and the increasing difficulties to finance their projects, and drew out of many cooperation projects. Thus municipalities – still striving for urban residential development – lost their preferential partners, i.e. professional development companies. Lacking the funds to return to full active land policy, some invited new, often more small scale and non-professional developing actors, for example individual households (Buitelaar et al. 2012b; Sorel et al. 2014). As these generally are less able to act as partner in negotiations over the land use plans, public cost recovery via a contribution scheme (cf. quadrant 2) would seem the best adaptation to the new situation.

Empirical research is not abundant on whether this adaptation took place, and it shows a mixed picture. A master thesis research in The Hague (Grommen 2015) indeed suggests that there is a trend away from (large) projects, involving negotiation under private law. But in many other cases (Buitelaar et al. 2012b; Sorel et al. 2014), municipalities prefer to sell the land they have in property, also to non-professional developers, (quadrant 1), or wait for professional partners to negotiate the land use plan with (quadrant 3 or 4).

The example of the Overstad project illustrates that, in most cases, municipalities' answer to the crisis did not include a shift towards public cost recovery. Overstad is an old industrial area of approximately 30 hectares in the city of Alkmaar (100,000 inhabitants). In 2006 the municipality had a master plan made – not a formal land use plan, only a vision document – for a complete restructuring of the derelict industrial area into a lively quarter with primarily apartment buildings, and a large component of retail and cultural sites, including a cinema and a concert hall. The municipality had only acquired some plots. As it proved impossible to unite all the 42 landowners in order to pool the land and redevelop it, the municipality set up a joint venture with a consortium of development companies (Sturm-Reijnders 2010). The joint venture company was expected to succeed where the municipality had failed (maybe because some of these developers may have had separate agreements with the landowners). They were to buy the remaining land in the area, whereupon the municipality would change the land use plan and development would start.

As a consequence of the economic crisis, however, the joint venture company had to be dissolved. How to proceed? The municipality still wanted to develop the area, but now it had to be done in a more piecemeal way.

The decision the municipality took is illustrative for the dominant role of negotiated land use plans in the Netherlands. The municipality decided to adopt a land use plan that conserved present land use.[3] The land use plan was changed only for the land in municipal possession and for those plots for which already agreements had been made with the owners. At the same time, a new vision document was adopted, in order to 'invite' initiative for redevelopment. Contrary to the old master plan, in this document the present road structure and parcellation largely stayed intact. In this way, a redevelopment did not necessitate a pooling of land, nor large investments in the public infrastructure (Sorel et al. 2014). It could be done piecemeal, plot by plot. The municipality now could approach every landowner that wanted to develop individually, and negotiate under private law over developer obligations.

The municipality *did not* opt for public cost recovery through a contribution scheme, in combination with a new land use plan that upgraded the designated land use for all owners (and still retained the existing parcellation). Theoretically, that would have fitted perfectly with the goal of the municipality to redevelop the area in a piecemeal manner. But it preferred cost recovery under private law. As described earlier, this gave much more freedom in the negotiations with landowners. And it added to the flexibility: for a contribution scheme to be valid, it should be accompanied by very detailed land use plans, whereas in the present (non-binding) master plan, the land use could remain more open (Personal communication 2013).

Strategic choices between private or public cost recovery

The introduction in 2008 of a public law instrument for cost recovery has changed the nature of the legitimacy problem of the 'double hat'. Before 2008, the fact that municipality wore two hats at the same time involved two dangers. First, there was the danger that a municipality might be motivated too much by the financial aspects of planning, which would compromise the public interest of good planning; for example, by planning the most lucrative land uses on a particular plot (Van Rij and Korthals Altes 2010). Note that corruption, which means that public officials enrich themselves for personal or party gain, is only one form of this danger. Also when financial contributions of private developers are used only for democratically approved public goals, the interest of good spatial planning could still be compromised.

Second, there is the danger that the municipality will not act to the advantage, but to the *dis*advantage of a particular developer, forcing conditions on him/her that cannot be linked to the necessity of good spatial planning. Also in this way, the municipality misuses its competencies for another goal than for which it was given (*detournement de pouvoir*).

In both ways, this kind of planning is called 'planning in exchange for money' (*betaalplanologie*), which is forbidden in law and jurisprudence (Netjes 2013). And it applies not only to the situation where the municipality has financial *gain* through the transaction, but also when *only the costs* for public infrastructure are recovered.

But the very fact that, after 2008, the municipality has a *choice* between a private and a public way of cost recovery, changes its negotiation possibilities considerably. The 'double hat' problem changes from the municipality wearing two hats at the same time, to putting on the 'public hat' and its 'private hat' at its own will. In part, this is exactly what the legislator intended: the possibility of taking recourse to the contribution scheme was meant to function as a 'backup' to prevent free riding. But the facultative use of public competencies can also be misused. Two examples illustrate this new aspect of the problem of the misuse of public competencies.

Schobben (2016) comments on a decision of the court of administrative appeal in a case of a municipality that threatened to exempt the piece of land of a developer from the land use plan because no agreement over a contribution could be reached. The court reasoned as follows. Before 2008, the municipality could have successfully argued that it was lawful to exempt this particular piece of land, because otherwise the development project as a whole would be frustrated. This line of reasoning no longer holds. The mere fact that the municipality since 2008 has the option for a public way of cost recovery means that the municipality no longer can argue that the refusal of one private developer could delay the whole urban development. The municipality could have taken recourse to public cost recovery, *obliging* the landowner to a fair contribution according to the contribution scheme. Therefore, exempting the land from the land use plan was unlawful.

Whereas in the last case the public cost recovery as a second option weakens the bargaining position of the municipality, in other cases it reinforces it. A second example illustrates how the municipality's choice for public over private cost recovery can be motivated by its land positions. Consultant firm Deloitte (2011) shows a fictive case in which the land in possession of the municipality involves little development costs and high potential revenues, whereas the neighboring land in possession of a private company needs high investments and promises low revenues. When the municipality decides to make *two* land use plans instead of *one* (one for the plot owned by the municipality, the other for the privately owned plot), the municipality would get a higher contribution from the private owner in total (Table 7.2). In such a situation, municipalities could avoid negotiations and opt for public cost recovery, only in order to make use of the advantage of splitting up the land use plan. Although the delineation of the land use plan can be an object of review by the court and held against principles of the rule of law and good spatial planning, municipalities still have a lot of freedom in delineation.

Table 7.2 Fictive case of developer contributions in case of one or two land use plans

	Costs	*Revenues*	*Contribution Situation 1*	*Contribution Situation 2*
Plot A (municipality as land owner)	€2 M	€6 M	€4.8 M	€2 M
Plot B (private owner)	€6 M	€4 M	€3.2 M	€4 M
Total	€8 M	€10 M	€8 M	€6 M
Municipality (as public body) pays			€0	€2 M
Municipality pays in total			€4.8 M	€4 M

In plot A, 25% of the total costs are made, and 60% of total revenues. In plot B, 75% of the costs are made, and only 40% of total revenues.

In situation 1, there is only one land use plan and the owner . . . etc. the owner of piece A (municipality) contributes 60% of the costs, and the owner of piece of land B contributes 40%.

In situation 2, however, there are two land use plans and two contribution schemes. In area A, the total costs are recovered from the (the municipality itself). In area B, the private landowner contributes the maximum possible (that is, maximized to his revenues). Although the contributions are not sufficient to recover all the costs, in total the municipality pays now €2 M for area A (as land owner) and €2 M for the deficit in area B (as a public body), in total €4 M. This is less than the €4.8 M that it had to pay in situation 1.

Conclusion

Negotiated land use plans have been central in Dutch urban development from the 1990s onward. Although during this period economic circumstances and the juridical framework changed considerably, negotiation over the land use plan has remained a key instrument. The main explanation is that cost recovery via negotiations under private law has many advantages for the municipality, compared to public cost recovery, which was only introduced in 2008 and was constructed by the legislator as a 'minimum variant'. The freedom of contract under private law does offer the municipality more possibilities[4] but also more risk. Equal treatment of all developing parties in terms of financial contribution is not guaranteed, but the alternative public cost recovery instrument systematics of fair contributions sets some standards for private law agreements. The fact that private sector developers in almost all cases go along with private law agreements indicates not only their preference for influence and bargaining over preset rules, but points also to the successful practice of cooperation with the municipality that evolved over the past decades.

The popularity of private law negotiations is understandable due to its effectiveness, efficiency and practicality. Nevertheless, there has been discussion on some legitimacy issues over the last 20 years.

The *effectiveness* of the instrument of negotiated land use plan should be assessed against the policy objectives of timely production of houses in areas that are characterized by spatial integration, high quality public space, and social equality. Although it is not clear whether this can be attributed to this particular instrument, housing production in the period 1990–2008 has been high, although not as high as expected (Jókövi et al. 2006; Rigo 2007). Likewise, the policy's performance on objectives of integration, public space, and social equality goes beyond the scope of this chapter, but evaluations are rather positive (Rigo 2007). Although the large urban development projects have been heavily criticized by professionals of the discipline of urbanism, residents of these areas have on average been happy with their neighborhoods (Rigo 2007). Even after the crisis of 2008, as many municipalities encountered financial difficulties as a consequence of development risks they took, it was much more individual municipalities that were blamed for their decisions, not the system.

High *efficiency* has been an important reason for using negotiated land use plans. Dutch municipalities have a historical preference (De Klerk 2008) for cooperation with relatively large, professional development companies. These companies can realize economies of scale at the large urban development sites that are typical of the Netherlands (Tennekes et al. 2015), and they reduce (financial) risk. Full active land policy gave the opportunity for selection of these partners, but since this is often no longer possible, negotiated land use plans still give more control than taking a purely public role.

In terms of *practicality*, many organizational structures and routines have been developed over the past decades. In the bigger cities, special municipal land development companies work together with private sector companies, often in project organizations that are specially created for this purpose and paid out of the revenues of the development. In this way, expertise about contracting was built up and collective standards developed.

The most problematic is the assessment of negotiated land use plans on the criterion of legitimacy. It is important here to make the distinction between 'output legitimacy' and 'input legitimacy' (Scharpf 1999). The output legitimacy of the instrument has been very high, as it has effectively delivered housing projects. However, the practice of negotiating land use plans can be criticized in terms of input legitimacy, as the incentive to capture as much as possible of the value increase may collide with the interest of 'good spatial planning'. Although it is the city council that ultimately controls municipal decisions, negotiations themselves can be successfully screened off from the press and citizens, for example, because they could 'harm the interests of bargaining parties'.

All in all, the success of negotiated land use plans in delivering may have been the reason why criticisms of the 'double hat' of the municipality has not have much impact on the last planning law reforms.

Notes

1 Under public law, it is not possible to demand a preset contribution per square meter development, like the infrastructure levy in England or the *tax d'aménagement* in France (Hobma 2014). Only for really small projects is such a general 'forfait' per square meter possible.

2 Therefore, in the new law of 2016, the requirement of a simultaneous adoption of the land use plan and the contribution scheme has been eased, as it is now possible to postpone the adoption of the contribution scheme until further working out the land use plan.

3 As a consequence of law reform of 2008, all municipalities had to adopt an up-to-date land use plan for their whole territory. Otherwise, the city of Alkmaar could just have prolonged the old land use plan.

4 This freedom is not absolute: the municipality is bound to principles of good governance, and the contract has to be related to spatial measures (Netjes 2013).

References

BHV ruimte (2013) *Onderzoek forfaitaire bijdrage bovenplanse kosten en bijdrage ruimtelijke ontwikkelingen*, BHV Ruimte bv, Den Bosch.

Brand, J.A.M., van den Bregman, A. G. and de Groot, J. F. (2006) *De grondexploitatiewet: enkele verkenningen*, Instituut voor Bouwrecht, The Hague.

Buitelaar, E., Bregman, A., van den Broek, L., Evers, D., Galle, M., Meijer, T. and Sorel, N. (2012a) *Ex-durante evaluatie Wet ruimtelijke ordening: tweede rapportage*, PBL, The Hague.

Buitelaar, E., Feenstra, S., Galle, M., Lekkerkerker, J., Sorel, N. and Tennekes, J. (2012b) *Vormgeven aan de spontane stad, belemmeringen en kansen voor organische stedelijke herontwikkeling*, PBL/Urhahn urban design, Den Haag/Amsterdam.

Buitelaar, E., Galle, M. and Sorel, N. (2011) Plan-led planning systems in development-led Practices: An empirical analysis into the (lack of) Institutionalization of Planning Law, *Environment and Planning A*, 43, 928–41.

Buitelaar, E. and Witte, P. (2011) *Financiering van gebiedsontwikkeling. Een empirische analyse van grondexploitaties*, PBL, The Hague.

De Klerk, L. (2008) *De modernisering van de stad, de opkomst van de planmatige stadsontwikkeling in Nederland 1850–1914*, NAi Uitgevers, Rotterdam.

Deloitte (2011) Binnenplanse verevening op basis van de Grondexploitatiewet, *Grexpert Magazine*, 24, 1–2 (online) available at: www2.deloitte.com/content/dam/Deloitte/nl/Documents/real estate/deloitte-nl-grexpert-nummer-24–2011.pdf (accessed 21 August 2016).

Groetelaers, D. A. (2004) *Instrumentarium locatieontwikkeling. Sturingsmogelijkheden voor gemeenten in een veranderende marktsituatie*, DUP Science, Delft.

Grommen, E. (2015) *From integral to organic development? A study of area development approaches in The Hague*, Master thesis, Universite du Luxembourg.

Hobma, F.A.M. (2014) *Internationale vergelijking financiering en kostenverhaal bij organische gebiedsontwikkeling*, Department of Real Estate and Housing, Delft Faculteit Bouwkunde.

Jókövi, M., Boon, C. and Filius, F. (2006) *Woningbouwproductie ten tijde van Vinex*, Ruimtelijk Planbureau, Den Haag.

Koeman, N.S.J., Ten Veen, A., Van Angeren, J. R., Kortmann, C.N.J., Fransen, D.S.P. and Kaajan, M. M. (2008) *Parlementaire geschiedenis Wet ruimtelijke ordening*, Alphen a/d Rijn, Kluwer.

Korthals Altes, W. (2008) Actief grondbeleid betaalt zich terug, *Property Research Quartely*, 7(1), 22–27.

Ministry of Housing, Planning and Environment (VROM) (2001) *Op grond van nieuw beleid, Nota Grondbeleid*, White paper, The Hague.

Muñoz Gielen, D. (2013) Vergelijking nota's bovenwijkse voorzieningen, *Grondzaken in de praktijk*, August, 22–24.

Muñoz Gielen, D. and van der Krabben, E. (2015) *Finance of large public infrastructure after the economic crisis and the role of developer obligations in the Netherlands*, paper presented at the PLPR conference, 25–27 February, Volos, Greece.

Netjes, C. (2013) De dunne scheidslijn tussen kostenverhaal en betaalplanologie, *Grondzaken in de praktijk*, October, 12–13.

Rigo (2007) *Evaluatie verstedelijking Vinex 1995 tot 2005*, Eindrapport, Ministery VROM, The Hague.

Scharpf, F. (1999) *Governing in Europe: Effective and democratic?* Oxford University Press, Oxford.

Schep, A. W. (2012) *Naar evenwichtig bijzonder kostenverhaal door gemeenten: Bekostiging van voorzieningen met baatbelasting, grondexploitatiebijdrage, ondernemersfondsen en BIZ-bijdrage*, Eburon, Delft.

Schobben, R. (2016) *Gemeentelijke betaalplanologie aan banden* (online) available at: www.thuispartners.nl/nl-nl/1/203/gemeentelijke-betaalplanologie-aan-banden.aspx (accessed 31 August 2016).

Sorel, N., Tennekes, J. and Galle, M. (2014) *De bekostiging van publieke voorzieningen bij organische gebiedsontwikkeling*, PBL, Den Haag.

Sturm-Reijnders, M. (2010) *Gebiedsontwikkeling 2.0. Uitgangspunten voor een succesvolle samenwerking bij gebiedsontwikkelingen als gevolg vanthekredietcrisis*, Master thesis, Amsterdam School of Real Estate (online) available at: http://files.vastgoedbibliotheek.nl/Server/getfile.aspx?file=docs/MRE/10/Sturm-Reijnders.pdf (accessed 15 August 2016).

Tennekes, J., Harbers, A. and Buitelaar, E. (2015) Institutions and urban development: Understanding urban morphological differences between the Netherlands,

Flanders and North Rhine-Westphalia, *European Planning Studies*, 23(11), 2165–2183.

Van Rij, R. and Korthals Altes, W. (2010) Looking for the optimal relationship between spatial planning and land development, *The Town Planning review*, 81(3), 283–306.

Woestenburg, A. and van der Krabben, E. (2013) Een institutionele analyse van agrarische grondprijzen, *Real estate Research Quarterly*, Juni, 16–29.

An Austrian perspective on negotiated land use plans: a means for municipalities to mobilise building land

Alois Humer

The legislator is a municipality's best friend

From an Austrian perspective, there are several noteworthy aspects to the practice of negotiating land use changes in the Netherlands that make up the bigger picture: the legislator and control bodies in the Netherlands seemingly equip and empower the municipalities better to follow their mission of active urban development than their Austrian counterparts do. While the practice of 'active' land use policy is also common in Austria from the municipal side, the instruments in the Netherlands go much further, especially because the legislator provides the municipalities with both the option of public- and private-law-based land use contracts with developers/owners. This is the most distinctive difference and can be considered as a representative example of a more supportive jurisdiction for municipalities undertaking land use planning in the Netherlands, compared to a more hesitant interpretation of cases in Austria, especially by the Austrian Constitutional Court. In contrast to the more pragmatic approach taken in the Netherlands, concerns about legitimacy outweigh any other concerns of effectiveness, efficiency, or practicality in the Austrian situation. Within private law-based land use management, the Dutch municipalities not only enter into contracts with developers or owners – as Austrian municipalities also do – but often co-own the land and establish PPP, such as developing companies and so can co-profit from land value increase. Such a pro-active role is rarely taken by Austrian municipalities, who at times can rely on financial bridging support from their federal state governments in order to act as a landowner but who are far from the empowered Dutch situation whereby municipalities can generate considerable portions of their local budget from land use changes. Again, the legislator and above all the Constitutional Court do not enable the Austrian municipalities to profit from land use changes.

Why is the Austrian legal situation more rigid?

The motivation to set up private law–based land use contracts differs in the two countries. In the Netherlands, much more emphasis is placed on the financial aspects – infrastructure cost recovery, profiting from land value increase, and so forth – while in Austria, land use contracts are predominantly used to mobilise building land and interfere with an individual's decision about their land property, i.e. to set legal incentives to gently force private landowners to – possibly against their original will – construct buildings or sell instead of just hoarding the land. Therefore it is a fairly higher order problem of individual rights, which are safeguarded by the Austrian Constitutional Court, compared to possible financial detriments for landowners.

The legal, historical, and contemporary context of Austrian land use planning is essential for a general understanding of the current circumstances. First, land use planning is a federal matter. According to the constitution, there is no legal mandate at the national level; instead, all nine federal states of the republic formulate their own spatial planning laws and all the roughly 2,100 municipalities – around 80 percent of them counting fewer than 3,000 inhabitants – have self-governmental rights when it comes to local land use planning. Legislation is therefore heterogeneous, and implementation is in the hands of local authorities of sometimes very limited financial and professional capacity. Second, the historic burden of excessive zoning of building land that arose in the early phase of Austrian planning law and practice – between the 1950s and 1970s – is yet to be resolved. Today's 'building land paradox' is that while on the one hand there are countless unused plots of building land across the country, on the other hand there is a need for rezoning new building land in the land use plans. This is due to the high volume of land that has already been designated but is not available on the market, driving (speculation on) land value. The market for building land is therefore very passive. Consequently and third, in many cities and regions, affordable housing is growing scarce. There is, however, some indication that political will in the federal states and municipalities is increasing to actively address what has become a pressing social problem and mobilise building land, especially in the larger cities and densely populated Alpine valleys. Nevertheless, it remains difficult for local planning authorities to compel private landowners to develop their land.

In a legal understanding, Austrian land use planning is a 'negative planning' matter; the categories in the land use plan either propose or prohibit certain uses of land for the future, but the landowner is not obliged to implement it in the case of a change to a new land use category. This legal situation creates a very passive setting for the municipality whose aim it should be to realise the development of the territory according to underlying land use plans and other planning instruments. The Federal State of Salzburg was the first to attempt a legal solution, introducing land use plan contracts based on private law in the 1990s. The Austrian Constitutional Court repealed the law, as contracts were foreseen as being 'obligatory' for each and every land use change to building land. Learning from that, however, softer, 'facultative' versions are now in place in all nine state versions of planning law, allowing for a heterogeneous mix of various contract contents – depending on the state – for example, time-based mobilisation of building land, the selling of land to third parties who are willing to build up the land, co-financing of infrastructure and/or planning procedural costs, and so forth. Still influenced by the unexpected and discouraging verdict against the Salzburg planning law, one major uncertainty in Austrian planning laws centres on the legitimacy of such active land policy, especially as the Constitutional Court interprets planning laws so strictly to secure individual rights. The municipality's supreme public-private double position – as likewise discussed in the Dutch case – is of particular concern. The municipality is a state authority when changing land use plans and a private actor when entering into private law contracts with landowners that are based on designating certain building land. Private law contracts on mobilising building land must therefore withstand content-related checks of good spatial planning, or – legally speaking – fulfil the principles of legality and equality. For the problem at hand, this means isolating and prioritising the content-related planning decision of whether a plot is suitable to become building land from the contents of the private contract. The zoning of building land must be the sole precondition for the contract coming into force and nothing more. A rezoning of suitable building land into green land simply because the owner has failed to – example given – meet the contracted 5–10 year period in which to begin construction is an invalid reason. Instead, other potentially negative consequences for the private party should be imposed when the contract conditions are not met. Austrian planning legislators are currently considering enhanced tools for financial regulation, such as extra infrastructural fees for the time while building land remains undeveloped.

What are lessons from and for Austria and in general?

In light of comparably more pragmatic – due to the more finance-based and less private property-focused approach – Dutch active land use policy, further potential for Austrian land use practice might lie in private law contracts that include negative financial repercussions for the contracting parties. The current discussion in Austria of switching from private law–based land use contracts to a public law–based system of active land use policy will not change the situation significantly. Interestingly, however, Dutch planning law offers municipalities both options – a combined approach that has not yet been considered in Austria – in practice Dutch municipalities strongly prefer the private law land use contract system. Instead of changing the legal approach in Austria, it might be more advisable to orientate the conditions and objectives of the land use contracts towards more financial consequences and less interference into individual property rights of a landowner. The Constitutional Court would then presumably be able to interpret cases less rigidly. Additionally, successful practices in the nine different federal state planning laws should be mainstreamed across Austria, in favour of an easier, more consistent decision base for the Constitutional Court.

From a municipality-centred point of view, more financial resources – if not their own, then state or federal funds – could help to actively influence land use development significantly. In any case, active land use policy is more promising when done by local authorities of a certain financial and professional capacity. Therefore, enhanced inter-municipal or supra-local planning instruments and cooperation might strengthen the local authorities' position when it comes to negotiated land use planning.

A Canadian perspective on negotiated land use plans: discretionary zoning in Vancouver

Marko Marskamp

Introduction

The Dutch instrument of negotiated land use plans seems to respond well to a new, volatile land market characterized by diverse actors owning and developing land. The instrument's success, as *Tennekes* points out, is its ability to stimulate housing development without relying on institutional actors and comprehensive plans. Illustrating this is the redevelopment of a derelict industrial area where a city welcomed plot-by-plot rezonings and opted for cost recoveries under private law.

But how does the instrument of negotiated land use plans fare in situations of scarcity? What if this instrument is used to rezone plots not for large urban development projects but within existing neighbourhoods? Is this a useful tool to take up the challenge of infill and densification? The following explores the instrumentality of negotiated land use plans in dealing with scarcity by contrasting the Dutch experience with discretionary zoning in Vancouver, British Columbia (BC). This comparison is productive since Vancouver's city planning combines elements of an administrative and discretionary planning system.

Under the Vancouver Charter, the city of Vancouver enjoys discretionary planning powers not available to other municipalities in British Columbia. Of particular interest here are the city's two different cost recovery instruments: the Development Cost Levy (DCL) and the Community Amenity Contribution (CAC). The DCL is calculated in a formal way, for a limited range of costs, and can only be allocated to defined purposes – this is the standard across British Columbia. With the CAC however, the city of Vancouver can levy a negotiable tax on planning and development. It is this tool of discretionary zoning that will be discussed further to reflect on negotiated land use plans in the Netherlands.

Developer-led land use planning in Vancouver, BC

In both the past and the present, discretionary zoning is an important land use planning tool in Vancouver's city planning. It could be said that it has earned the city its signature planning style, also known as 'Vancouverism'. This model of urban planning and development is considered to originate in the transformation of the downtown area's brownfields and industrial waterfronts into compact clusters of residential and office towers with quality urban design at street level. Here, the city's preference for negotiating land uses and cost recoveries played an important role in directing the architectural form and urban design that are now all part of the city's iconic skyline. This type of urbanism continues to be associated with dense, sustainable, and attractive neighbourhoods, and is regularly celebrated with regards to Vancouver's ranking as a liveable city.

Today, discretionary zoning and CACs remain central to the planning and liveability of the city. With no citywide plan, the land use plan is one of the most important planning instruments. In terms of Tennekes's typology, Vancouver's city planning can be described as passive and development-led. Rather than pre-zoning certain districts, the city evaluates rezoning applications and negotiates developer contributions on a case-by-case, plot-by-plot basis – a practice locally known as 'spot-zoning'. With developer contributions adding up to almost 8 percent of the municipal budget, CACs are an important source of income for the city. For the present Council, they are used as a financial mechanism to improve housing affordability in the absence of senior government support for public housing.

However, now that the downtown area is widely considered 'built up', the practice of discretionary zoning in other areas predominantly zoned for single-family housing is increasingly debated. As the development pressure spreads across Vancouver, some claim that discretionary zoning undermines not only the identity of the neighbourhood but also the independence of the city from the development community and the equity of community deliberation in the face of large contributions. In other words, discretionary zoning might jeopardize the public interest of good spatial planning. To explore how this issue plays out in Vancouver's city planning is the topic of the remaining discussion.

Discretionary zoning: the case of a Downtown South rezoning

A good illustration of the Vancouver version of the 'double hat' problem is a complex rezoning in the Downtown South area in 2013. The site requested for rezoning is at the edge of a neighbourhood park and across the street from the developer's offices. At the time, a low-rise social housing complex stood on the site and the developer proposed to rebuild social housing on its own plot in exchange for a residential tower at the edge of the park. This project thus required a land exchange, requested increased density, and promised affordability; a mix that challenged the city's urban planning and business competences.

Following the first approval of the rezoning for the proposed tower, a group of local residents contested the Council's decision in the British Columbia Supreme Court. Within the planning administration, the project was split up in a rezoning application for the tower, a development application for the replacement of social housing and a land exchange contract between the city and the developer. The three different procedures have different degrees of openness: the rezoning application is subject to a public hearing and a decision of Council, the development application can be decided upon by the planning department autonomously, and the land exchange contract is settled by Council behind closed doors. The residents argued that the different procedures compromised public participation on the planning of the neighbourhood. The judge generally agreed and quashed the new zoning bylaw, stating 'Residents of the City have a right to voice in integrated projects of this kind, and a right to a fair opportunity to express themselves relative to the overall advantages and disadvantages of the proposal' (BC Supreme Court 2015: par. 118).

The city appealed, arguing that certain planning decisions cannot be delegated to the public and need to remain at the discretion of an elected Council and an expert planning staff. In their evaluation of the appeal, the judges largely followed up on this perspective, asking 'When, if ever, does a duty of procedural fairness arise from the exercise of business powers?' (BC Court of Appeal 2015: par. 1). They acknowledged that tension exists between the land use planning and business dealings of the city, noting 'Good business may not serve the same interests as good land use planning and development control' (ibid.: par. 61). Consequently, they argued for a careful separation between the legislative power and the business power according to the requirements and regulations set out in the Vancouver Charter. Attempting to resolve the 'double hat' problem, the judges thus maintained, 'What is required of a municipality in such situations is to ensure that it manages the conflict, that it not let its business interests overwhelm its duty to make good law' (ibid.).

When in 2012 the city was looking for a new director of planning, it advertised the profile of an experienced city planner but with 'strong business acumen and change management capabilities to deliver on a mandate of transformation of the processes and technologies supporting the City's primary revenue generating business' (City of Vancouver 2012; cited by Spaxman 2014). The above presented rezoning controversy, however, has, in part, triggered the retirement of the then hired general manager of planning and development. Since 2016 the planning department has been split up in the department of planning, urban design, and sustainability, and the department of development services, buildings, and licensing. This newly created administrative division aims to improve the city's legitimacy in balancing the public good understood in terms of both the fit and finance of planning proposals.

Conclusion

Over the past few decades, the city of Vancouver has gained an international reputation for compact, attractive, and sustainable urban planning. Discretionary zoning is an important instrument in this achievement. It has been effective in maintaining a standard of urban design while producing a high quantity of housing in a short amount of time. Moreover, backed by a strong planning vision, discretionary zoning has been efficient in redeveloping together with a few big developers large parts of the city's downtown. Only recently is the experience with this instrument in the outer neighbourhoods zoned for single-family housing regarded as problematic. While discretionary zoning allows for the consideration of redevelopment on a plot-by-plot basis, the speculation on increased density inflates land values overall. As such, it counters its other mechanism of improving housing affordability through developer contributions.

As in the Dutch case, it is eventually the legitimacy of this instrument that is most complicated. The recent organizational separation between planning and development can be seen as an attempt to adapt the instrument to a new context. In the absence of a citywide plan but in the presence of well-developed rezoning procedures with specialized planners and advisory bodies, discretionary zoning remains practical for planning (future) land uses. Yet, the case illustrated that the blurring of good spatial planning and business acumen affects the public confidence in the institutional planning expert. Observing planning proposals turning into legal issues, discretionary zoning might thus better deal with scarcity when both the examined land uses variances and the calculated developer contributions are politically as well as legally defensible.

References

British Columbia Court of Appeal (2015) *Community Association of New Yaletown v. Vancouver (City) 2015 BCCA 227*. CA42560, Vancouver, BC.

British Columbia Supreme Court (2015) *Community Association of New Yaletown v. Vancouver (City) 2015 BCSC 117. S143452*, Vancouver, BC.

Spaxman, R. (2014) *It is no longer the olden days* (online) available at: https://pricetags.wordpress.com/2014/09/25/ray-spaxman-it-is-no-longer-the-olden-days/ (accessed 22 May 2017).

8 Urban growth boundary in the U.S.

Managing land scarcity in the Portland region

Edward J. Sullivan

Oregon's urban growth management experience sets it apart from other land use planning and regulatory programs in the U.S. The Oregon land use program has endured for more than 40 years, suffering the vicissitudes of multiple constitutional attacks and legislative adjustments. Oregon's policy protects most rural lands suitable for resource use (Sullivan and Eber 2009: 2; Sullivan and Somolou 2011: 181). It also seeks to be efficient in spending limited public funds to expand public facilities and services when lands are urbanized (Sullivan and Clark 2013: 413). This chapter examines one aspect of that statutory regime in one area of the state – growth management in the Portland Metropolitan Area, the state's most populous region. Under that regime, each city must have an urban growth boundary (UGB) separating urban from rural lands. This separation has profound implications for landowners, as a rural designation would not allow most commercial or industrial uses or dense housing. In lieu of establishing a UGB for each city, Oregon statutory law delegates to an elected regional body, Metro, the power to set a regional UGB for the 23 cities and the urban portions of three counties within that region. The process has been in place for nearly 40 years and is accepted by public and private interests, as it allows for cities to plan for and provide public services and facilities and for landowners and developers to have a modicum of investment certainty. Because of the impacts on these public and private interests (especially land values), UGB changes are carefully watched and sometimes hotly contested. Because urban growth boundaries provide for a transparent planning and public infrastructure process, it is superior to other instruments for growth management in the U.S. that are less certain, such as adequate public facilities regulations, concurrency requirements, or urban service boundaries, all of which depend on the ability of the applicant to assure infrastructure, or population caps or growth management caps, which are artificial and arbitrary growth limits on development. Moreover, as demonstrated by its long-time acceptance and effectiveness, the system works. In fact, in the past 40 years, the 'population of the Portland metro area has grown 60 percent, while the UGB has expanded just 14 percent' (Green 2015).

We begin with a brief description of the Oregon planning system and the unique planning regime for the Portland metropolitan region as it has evolved over the years, the current regional and state agency development and review of growth management policy for the region, and an evaluation of that policy as it relates to land scarcity. While land is relatively abundant in Oregon, especially given the state's relatively low population density, the problem of land scarcity relates more to population trends, which bring new residents in disproportionately large numbers to the already relatively densely populated area between Portland and Eugene, which measures about 200 by 100 miles (322 by 161 kilometers) in length and width. The rapid population expansion in that area results in competition between the existing natural resource base in that area (supporting agriculture and forestry), which is a significant part of the state's economy, and the efficient and economic provision of public facilities and services to a compact urban area.

As detailed in this chapter, the Oregon planning program has devised several strategies dealing with land scarcity over the past four decades. Taken together, these strategies provide a unique constellation of growth management tools to create the grounds for an economically efficient and socially just public policy for land use. Many of these tools may be taken for granted in other places. Not so for the U.S., where land policy is the province of the various states, as the federal government has made only limited forays into land use (e.g. telecommunications and housing discrimination). While the federal government does have extensive powers to regulate commerce and to assure the civil rights of individuals (including rights to property), tradition places the resolution of most land use controversies with state governments. In turn, most states have delegated powers over land use to local governments, although state legislatures remain free to reallocate those powers to state and regional agencies.

Background: the Oregon land use system and the Portland region

The Oregon planning system

This section provides a brief description of the Oregon land use system. Under the Oregon Constitution (1859 as amended), a bicameral legislature enacts laws and the governor is generally responsible for assuring their execution. A Supreme Court, along with lower courts, adjudicates disputes over the constitutionality, validity, and interpretation of legislation. While the governor is responsible for the execution of laws, those laws will frequently delegate powers and responsibilities to state agencies to deal with day-to-day issues. These agencies frequently have the power to enact administrative rules, which have the force and effect of law, to interpret and implement statutory law, and to adjudicate disputes within the scope of their powers, all subject to judicial review. This structure is fairly common among American states. Similarly, unless a federal statute or constitutional provision is involved – an infrequent occurrence – most disputes are grounded in state law.

Under legislation enacted in 1973 and amended thereafter, a state agency, the Land Conservation and Development Commission (LCDC) served by staff in the Department of Land Conservation and Development (DLCD), has the responsibility to adopt and enforce binding land use policies (hereinafter 'Goals') and subordinate administrative rules, and to adjudicate certain planning disputes (*Oregon Revised Statute* 197.040). Because it was the product of state legislation, LCDC, albeit controversial, had political legitimacy and may be checked by the other branches of government – the governor appoints and can remove members of the commission, the legislature may change laws and affect policy by controlling expenditures and approving (or not) appointments to the governing body. The courts review, with an appropriate level of deference, the decisions of the commission. By using a state agency to set land use policy, rather than completely delegating that power to local governments, Oregon follows a less traveled path among the states as one laboratory for democracy.

LCDC Goals setting state land use policy fall into five categories: the planning process (Goals 1 and 2), resource lands protection (Goals 3–5), human interaction with the environment (Goals 6–8 and 13), urbanization (Goals 9–12 and 14), and Goals relating to special areas (Goals 15–19). For purposes of this chapter, the most noteworthy planning tool of the Oregon program is the urban growth boundary (UGB), a legally binding, legislatively created line adopted under Goal 14 ('Urbanization') that separates 'rural land' from 'urban land' (Dep't of Land Conservation and Dev., *Oregon's Statewide Planning Goals and Guidelines*, 2010).

The distinction is profound: land outside the UGB cannot be developed for urban uses, absent a goal exception, a very difficult process (*Oregon Revised Statute* 197.732; *Oregon Administrative Rule* 2014 s.660–014–0040). Conversely, there must be sufficient urban lands to accommodate long-term urban needs and populations, but those lands must be used efficiently.

To assure compliance with the Goals, the state has established processes that require local governments to adopt binding comprehensive plans and to implement those plans with land use regulations that are consistent with the local governments' plans (*Oregon Revised Statute* 197.175(1)–(2). State agencies are generally required to make their programs and actions consistent to those local plans that have been 'acknowledged' or certified by LCDC as complying with the Goals (*Oregon Revised Statute* 197.180). All of Oregon's 242 cities and 36 counties have had their plans and regulations 'acknowledged' by LCDC (Dep't of Land Conservation & Dev., Acknowledgement Scoreboard). Once these local plans have been 'acknowledged,' the statewide planning goals drop out as independent criteria for local regulations and actions because they are incorporated in the binding comprehensive plans. The state system, however, is subject to additional rules to meet the special needs of its largest population center. It is to this particular planning regime that we now turn to explore how land scarcity, in the Oregon sense described above, drives one experiment in a regional planning process.

The Portland metropolitan region

Understanding the evolution of the Metropolitan Service District (Metro) as a policymaking entity is important in order to understand growth management in the Portland metropolitan area. Metro stands alone among planning regimes in Oregon and the nation. With its population, economic domination, and the sheer size of its landmass, Metro is unique in Oregon. It is currently the only democratically elected regional government in the U.S., and it has the power to influence or decide significant land use and transportation planning issues (Abbott and Abbott 1991). Today, Metro encompasses 24 cities and the urban portions of three counties on the Oregon side of the Columbia River. The City of Vancouver and Clark County, Washington, lie across that river and are also part of the larger metropolitan area but are outside the jurisdiction of both Metro and the State of Oregon. The task of determining the extent that urban growth should be permitted in the Oregon portion of the Portland region is made particularly difficult by the fact that the same land in the region is usable for both agriculture and urban development.

Legislation for metropolitan growth management – delegations and expectations

A new metropolitan planning paradigm

In May 1978, the voters of the Portland urban region approved the foundation of the current version of 'Metro' (the former Metropolitan Service District) with an elected governing body and regional planning powers (Abbott and Abbott 1991: 11–12). In 1979, the Oregon legislature gave Metro the specific power and task to establish and amend as necessary a regional UGB (*Oregon Revised Statute* 268.390(3)).[1]

Metro thus derives its land use planning power from statutes, the Oregon Constitution, and a charter approved by regional voters in 1992. The charter considerably enhanced the ambit of Metro's power by exercising its home rule self-governance powers under the Oregon Constitution and defining Metro's mission as 'planning and policy making to preserve and enhance the quality of life and the environment' (*Metro Charter* 2003). Furthermore, the Metro charter placed the burden on Metro to develop and adopt ordinances that require coordination of local comprehensive plans that must 'substantially comply' with a Regional Framework Plan (RFP) applicable to the entire region (*Oregon Revised Statute* 268.380 and .390(4)), necessitating that every local plan and land use regulation also comply with the RFP within two years[2] (*Metro Charter* 2003 s.5(2)(e)). State law also gave Metro the authority to review city and county plans and land use regulations to ensure their compliance with the Regional Framework Plan, as well as the ability to remedy any inconsistencies between local plans and the Regional Framework Plan (*Oregon Revised Statute* 268.390).

Metro's regional framework plan and decisions on local comprehensive plans also must go through a similar process of acknowledgment or review. The plan, implementing ordinances, and land use decisions must be consistent with statewide planning goals, as are any decisions by Metro on city or county plans, regulations, and actions; each process is subject to review. The original Regional Framework Plan is described by law (*Oregon Revised Statute* 197.015(16)) and was acknowledged by LCDC in 2000 (*Oregon Revised Statute* 197.274). However, the Regional Framework Plan is not the kind of comprehensive planning function undertaken by local governments. Rather, it deals with regional issues, including the regional UGB.

The Regional Framework Plan sets forth the responsibilities of Metro and those cities and counties within its jurisdictional boundaries. It includes various functional plans that deal with diverse matters such as transportation and air and water quality. The text of the functional plans determines how it binds local comprehensive plans and implements regulations. Much like the Regional Framework Plan itself, these functional plans are also subject to both acknowledgement and periodic review. One of those functional plans, the Urban Growth Functional Plan, requires Metro to adopt a UGB in compliance with the statewide planning goals. As noted earlier, while Metro itself does not have a 'comprehensive plan' as other local governments such as cities and counties do, the UGB for the area must be incorporated into the comprehensive plans of the cities and counties of the region. The cities and counties in the region are responsible for adopting and enforcing plans and land use regulations that meet the statewide planning goals. Metro has the authority to coordinate those plans and to deal with specific regional planning issues. Similarly, notwithstanding Metro's regular periodic review obligations, it must also re-submit to the periodic review process before LCDC any time it seeks to add more than 100 acres to its UGB or establish an urban reserve.

Growth management and urban growth boundary changes

Growth management growing pains

By statute, Metro must review its UGB every five years to ensure it has 20 years of available buildable residential lands (*Oregon Revised Statute*

197.299(1), (2), 5(a)). If there is a deficit in the available buildable land from the land needed for the 20-year period, Metro must take steps to meet that deficit within two years following its analysis, including implementing performance measures to increase land use efficiency within the UGB, which generally leads to requiring increased density. These performance measures must be identified and reported to LCDC every two years. The net effect of these measures often would require local governments in the region to increase the residential densities under their plans and land use regulations.

In recent years, Metro has complained that this five-year review is a heavy burden and untenable because of the relatively short time for completion and the significant cost of the analysis. Metro has insisted that as it completes one such analysis, it must immediately begin another. In response to these complaints, in 2007, Metro received an additional two-year extension on its original two-year analysis requirement in order to work on its urban and rural reserves. A six-year analysis requirement is now provided. As described below, the Oregon Legislature has imposed multiple reviews on Metro to assure there is an adequate supply of residential, commercial, industrial, and employment land available for the region.

Required reviews of the Metro urban growth boundary

Beginning in 1995, the Oregon Legislature has enacted mechanisms to assure that certain UGB, including Metro's are more rigorously reviewed than others and that Metro in particular has sufficient buildable land to meet regional residential needs. In this context, 'sufficient' means enough lands to satisfy owner and renter land needs over the 20-year planning period (Goal 14, *Oregon Administrative Rule* s.660–015–0000(14)). One of these efforts, applicable only to Metro and other cities with a UGB containing a population of 25,000 or more, requires Metro, or a covered city at any periodic or other 'legislative' review of its plan involving its UGB and the state's housing goal, to demonstrate that its plan 'provides sufficient buildable lands within the UGB to accommodate estimated housing needs for 20 years (*Oregon Revised Statute* 197.296(2)). The analysis of the sufficiency of the existing UGB and sufficiency of buildable lands is fairly detailed with respect to the methodology used and required data. If the analysis shows the housing need is greater than the housing capacity, Metro, or the local government, must undertake remedial actions to amend its UGB, attempt to use land within its existing UGB more efficiently, or both. Similarly, after using the analysis, Metro or the covered city must determine the overall average density and mix of housing types for residential development of needed housing types to occur to meet housing needs over the next 20 years. If that density is greater than the actual density of development, or if that mix is different from the actual mix of housing types under the analysis, the local government, as part of its periodic review, must adopt measures that 'demonstrably increase the likelihood that residential development will occur at the housing types and density and at the mix of housing types required to meet housing needs over the next 20 years' (*Oregon Revised Statute* 197.296(7)).

While the foregoing apply to Metro and larger cities outside the Portland region, beginning in 1997 the Oregon Legislature has enhanced its expectations of Metro by requiring that the regional government undertake other specific tasks, including analyzing its UGB and buildable lands analysis every six years, stipulating that, if the housing capacity of the regional UGB is less than the need shown in the analysis, Metro must take certain actions (such as requiring local governments to increase density in their plans and regulations and leaving it to the market to provide development opportunities) to remedy one-half of this deficiency within one year of completing the analysis, providing that every two years Metro compiles and reports to DLCD regarding certain 'performance measures' (*Oregon Revised Statute* 197.299(1)–(2)(a), 197.301(2)). These measures are, on their face, 'informational,' but are presumably used to evaluate how well Metro will respond to any of its self-reported deficiencies in housing needs for the 20-year period going forward.

Metro has unique responsibilities to remedy, as opposed to report, insufficient buildable land capacity. Before Metro undertakes its reporting on performance measures, it must determine whether any necessary remedial actions to amend its UGB, attempt to use land within its existing UGB more efficiently, or both, are sufficient to meet that deficiency – if not, Metro must undertake 'corrective action,' including a corrective plan and schedule for action to be submitted with its performance measures report (*Oregon Revised Statute* 197.302(1)). Following submission of the plan and schedule, Metro has two years to meet the identified housing needs under penalty of LCDC issuance of an enforcement order to require such an outcome.

Metro's analysis, reporting, and remedial requirements make it important that it use the best data, analyze that data well, and assure that its UGB contains sufficient buildable land for a rolling 20-year period. Although the tasks are arduous (Sullivan 2015: 473), the potential penalties for failure, both political and economic, have served to keep Metro responsive in administering its urban growth policies. As demonstrated below, now that the initial UGB has been acknowledged, these policies are most vulnerable in dealing with amendments to that boundary and in designating urban and rural reserve lands.

Urban and rural reserves

In 1993, the Oregon Legislature overhauled legislation dealing with the requirements and methods of providing urban services by special districts and local governments (Act of Sept. 10, 1993). As further revised in 1997, this legislation authorized cities in all parts of the state, in conjunction with the relevant county, to establish 'urban reserve' areas outside existing UGB, and it also allowed LCDC to require the designation of urban reserves in certain cases. Urban reserves were designed to be areas into which a UGB would expand, if a need existed, beyond the 20-year UGB period. The urban reserve designation process allowed for nominating lands to be added to the UGB beyond those already designated for inclusion in existing UGB for a 20-year period, a victory for developers, who would otherwise generally be required under the 'land priorities statute', discussed below, to avoid good resource lands for future UGB additions. The concept was to provide certainty to both urban service providers and to the agricultural industry by setting out where urbanization would and would not extend.

This legislation followed LCDC's 1992 adoption of rules for designating urban reserves. Because investors speculate on which lands will be included in the urban reserve or UGB and, because land value is a function of scarcity and the real estate market and because that market is profoundly affected by the nature of uses permitted (urban vs. rural), there is a strong incentive to follow the actions of Metro and local governments in dealing with the UGB and urban reserves that warranted legislative intervention. In 1995, the Oregon Legislature provided that urban reserves were the presumptive candidate lands for inclusion if and when the Metro UGB was expanded, thus reducing the speculation every two to five years over which particular areas might be added to the UGB (*Oregon Revised Statute* 197.298). Otherwise, a 'land priorities statute', which made parcelization and soil types the principal factors for UGB expansion, had became the dominant factors in the location of UGB. However, the legislature concluded that urbanization should not be governed exclusively or even predominately by these factors.

Following Metro's remand in its first (unsuccessful) effort to designate urban reserves in *D.S. Parklane, Inc. v. Metro*, 994 P.2d 1205 (Or. Ct. App. 2000), the Oregon Legislature enacted S.B. 1011 in 2007 to provide additional authority and flexibility to the urban reserve process; the authority and flexibility was particularly for the benefit of Metro and to allow designation of urban reserves for a 20- to 30-year period (i.e. lands for an additional period beyond the 20-year period used to assure sufficient lands within a UGB (*Oregon Revised Statute* 195.145(4)). S.B. 1011 also provided for 'rural reserves,' or lands that would not be included within the UGB for the same period for which urban reserves were designated. Metro was the driving force behind the adoption of this legislation.

At Metro's behest, S.B. 1011 authorized LCDC to adopt a special set of rules (not exclusively based on soil types or parcelization) for Metro to follow in carrying out this legislation. Metro had claimed that both the UGB's initial allocation and subsequent amendment processes were exceedingly complicated, time-consuming, and did not meet regional residential land needs, noting that the regional agency was mandated to review its UGB every five years (*Oregon Revised Statute* 197.299). Although this five-year review requirement is focused only on residential review, Metro took it upon itself to conduct a comprehensive review of all urban land needs (*Oregon Revised Statute* 195.141(1)). During the process, S.B. 1011 allowed the three counties in the Metro region to enter into an intergovernmental agreement to designate both urban and rural reserves in order to pre-emptively select lands where future urbanization was very likely to occur (urban reserves) and where urbanization would be held back for up to 40 to 50 years (rural reserves). Proponents claimed that designation of these lands would allow local governments an added flexibility in planning for future growth, while at the same time giving the agricultural industry and natural resource areas an additional protection beyond the existing legislation that provided an alternative method to designate urban reserves found in existing rules.

Administrative rules filled in the gaps of the legislation. LCDC granted Metro the regulatory authority to designate both urban and rural reserves in a new and alternative process that would apply only to Metro, an authority reflected in the rules (*Oregon Administrative Rule* s.660–027–005–.080). In the alternative process, urban reserves may be selected only by Metro through inter-governmental agreements with the affected counties. In contrast, the counties, through intergovernmental agreements with Metro, may select rural reserves (*Oregon Administrative Rule* s.660–027–020(1), (2)–.0030). Moreover, both Metro and the counties involved must undertake citizen involvement and coordinate with affected cities in the area, as well as school districts and other state agencies.

S.B. 1011, and the administrative rules subsequently adopted by LCDC to implement it, provided a significantly different process to designate urban reserves in the Portland region from other areas of the state. Whereas under the 1993 legislation, an urban reserve designation is based on the 1995 statutory priorities for adding land to a UGB, the rules specifically applicable to the Metro region appear to allow for a more subjective process. Metro must base its urban reserve decisions on 'consideration' of eight 'factors.' Metro has a similarly detailed system for designation of rural reserves (*Oregon Administrative Rule* s.660–027–0050 and 0060).

The reason for the differences in the two reserve regimes was a perceived need to give Metro additional flexibility in its designations, as the region had to deal with 25 cities (now 24) and three counties, all of which had different objectives and needs. Metro must enter into agreements with each of the three counties in the region to establish a simultaneous, concurrent, and coordinated urban and rural reserves process (*Oregon Revised Statute* 195.143, 195.145(1)(b)).

In June 2010, Metro, in conjunction with the three counties within the Portland region, concluded a lengthy process for adding urban and rural reserves for the area and sought LCDC review and approval of that work, which occurred in August 2012. A number of disappointed interests (landowners not included in urban reserves, conservation and agricultural interests contending the urban reserve areas were not sufficiently justified, and some cities who did not want to be saddled with provision of urban services to areas included in urban reserves) appealed LCDC's order to the Oregon Court of Appeals, which handed down its decision in *Barkers Five, LLC v. Land Conservation & Dev. Comm'n*, 323 P.3d 368 (Or. Ct. App. 2014) on 16 January 2014, reversing and remanding the order on several grounds.

The court upheld LCDC's interpretation of the relevant statutes, as well as their administrative rules implementing those statutes. While none of the rural reserves was remanded, the court found that a portion of the Washington County urban reserves, and smaller portions of those for Multnomah and Clackamas Counties, was insufficiently based.

Washington County, on the western edge of the Metro UGB, had the greatest difficulty before the court. This county has highly suitable classes of agricultural soils in the Willamette valley, but also had seen the fastest growth in jobs and population. Washington County sought to add significant amounts of urban reserve lands to be converted into urban lands as soon as less than a 20-year supply remained and the county was anxious to add to its tax base by including lands that could be used for its growing high-tech industries (Sullivan 2012). The deficiency in the county's methodology, which Metro and LCDC had accepted, was its *addition* of factors not contained in the urban reserve statutes or rules, which the court called 'pseudo factors,' to evaluate candidate lands for urban reserves, perhaps to manipulate the outcome. In any event, according to the court, this methodological flaw required remand. In contrast, the issues relating to Multnomah and Clackamas counties related to findings applying the reserves factors to specific areas, rather than to any methodological flaw.

It just so happened that the Oregon Legislature was in session when the Oregon Court of Appeals rendered the *Barkers Five* decision. Responding to concerns that the remand would be lengthy, contentious, and expensive (Gaston 2014), the Oregon Legislature chose to step into the role of arbitrator. The result was a quickly enacted 'grand bargain' that placed a significant amount of the contested land proposed by Washington County for urban reserves into a rural reserve, adjusted other land allocations and the UGB in that county, and effectively nullified some of the more contentious issues that would have been difficult to deal with on remand (Act of April 1, 2014, ch. 92, 2014 Or. Laws 252–56 (2014)). While the 'quick fix' provided by the legislature dealt with most of the immediate problems, the question of practical precedent for resolution of future land use disputes by the legislature is troubling, as it may presage a land use regime not based on thoughtful planning as has been the case to date, but on the political urges of the moment.[3]

Conclusion: metropolitan growth management – planning for change

The Portland metropolitan area regional planning process has been sanctioned by state law for more than 40 years and has transitioned from an informal voluntary process to one overseen by an elected regional body – planning and administering regional land use, transportation, and air and water quality plans (*Metro Charter* 2003). That process also provided for the establishment and change of a regional UGB. Several observations may be gleaned from the experience of regional planning in the Portland metropolitan area:

1 *Overall, the regional system works.* Having an elected body to deal with the regional aspects of planning, the provision of public services and facilities, and the establishment and change of a UGB gives legitimacy to that body's actions. Additionally, the election of the councilors by district, excluding the regionally elected presiding officer, gives the council a perspective from all parts of the region, as well as greater political legitimacy. No other region in the country has a comparable (or better) process for urbanization. However, it is true that the Portland metropolitan area has soils suitable for farm and forest use at the periphery of its UGB, but those will inevitably be lost to urbanization once need is shown. The locational factors in the boundary amendment process and the urban reserve factors mitigate both the amount of resource lands lost, as well as diverting boundary changes to lesser quality soils where possible.

2 *Regional planning is political.* Planning cannot be divorced from the aspirations, proclivities, and prejudices of elected officials and the people they represent. Multnomah County is dominated by urban development, especially in Portland. Washington County to the west is the major growth engine of the region, adding jobs and population, and aggressively asserting its economic and political clout. Clackamas County has also added population and jobs and is in competition with Washington County for growth. Some cities in the region prefer to grow, while others prefer to be left alone. Some rural property owners want to redesignate their lands to facilitate urban uses; others prefer to farm or to enjoy rural peace. Homebuilders, developers, and landowners desire certainty. These attitudes reveal themselves in the oft-contested efforts to add to urban reserves or the UGB. Planning law does not erase these attitudes, but subordinates them to a common set of criteria or factors by which decisions can be made and evaluated in similar terms. For the system to work, the decisions must be articulated in those same terms.

  Similarly, the attention of the legislature is better suited towards the structure and policy of the urbanization process in the Portland Metro Area, as opposed to the details over the inclusion or exclusion of particular lands as in the recent 'grand bargain' affair. While the process is indeed political, these decisions are best made under criteria that go beyond raw political power.

3 *Rules are better than ad hocery*. Planning law is a branch of administrative law. Courts defer to planning agencies formulating policy or undertaking rulemaking, while the application of policy, in a contested case or otherwise, is more closely scrutinized to assure that policy is met in the context of the individual decision. Like many states, Oregon has an Administrative Procedures Act applicable to state agencies (*Oregon Revised Statute* 183.310–502). In the land use field, Oregon also has detailed requirements for local government land use decision-making. However, in an effort to make it easier for Metro or other local governments to make land use decisions more immune from judicial review, the Oregon Legislature has been known to fiddle with review bodies and standards, with no appreciable change of results.[4] That fiddling more recently included the use of 'factors' for UGB changes, instead of criteria. However, *Barkers Five* indicates the appellate court will not lessen its scrutiny for that reason.

4 *The process for changing UGB must be rationalized*. Amending the regional UGB has many moving parts, with 25 cities and three counties, in addition to Metro, being involved. Goal 14 requires consideration of both the need for additional land, as well as where that additional land may be added. In addition to any other regional or local considerations, the Oregon Legislature has provided priorities for lands to be added to the UGB over and above the Goal 14 requirements. Conflicts between a former version of Goal 14 and the statutory priorities have led to a need for mind-numbing detailed findings. There may be help on the horizon with the passage of legislation allowing LCDC to adopt administrative rules to provide more confidence that additions to UGB will be upheld in exchange for cities following a more formulaic methodology based on data that takes much of the political pressures out of UGB decisions (Act of July 1, 2013, ch. 575, 2013 Or. Laws 1–12 (2013)). Time will tell whether the UGB change process has become even more complicated by this legislation.

5 *How often must metro review and act on boundary changes?* Metro is obliged to review and respond to its housing capacity, needs analyses, and analysis of residential buildable land supply at least every six years (*Oregon Revised Statute* 197.299(2)(b)). Metro must also report to LCDC every two years regarding a number of legislatively designated 'performance measures' (*Oregon Revised Statute* 197.301–.302). If Metro determines a deficiency in residential land supply, it must submit a report outlining corrective action, and it must also make an additional report on those actions within two years. These actions are neither easy nor cheap. If contested, the end of one such review may coincide with the beginning of the next, which is wasteful and difficult for all participants.

Moreover, it may be questionable from a planning standpoint whether two years or six years is a viable metric for items that deal with many moving parts and vague parameters.

6 *Conversion of urbanizable to urban land must be factored.* The Oregon system has never dealt adequately with the conversion of land from urbanizable to urban. Goal 14 defines 'urbanizable land' as:

> Urban land that, due to the present unavailability of urban facilities and services, or for other reasons, either:
>
> (a) Retains the zone designations assigned prior to inclusion in the boundary, or
> (b) Is subject to interim zone designations intended to maintain the land's potential for planned urban development until appropriate public facilities and services are available or planned.
>
> (Dep't of Land Conservation & Dev., *Oregon's Statewide Planning Goals & Guidelines, Definitions, 2010*: 8)

Over the past 20 years, these lands are best described as those added to a UGB and do not yet have adequate public facilities and services. The problem is developing a strategy for the urbanization of these lands, particularly as to their allocation of uses and provision of public services and facilities. Goal 14 states blandly:

> Land within urban growth boundaries shall be considered available for urban development consistent with plans for the provision of urban facilities and services. Comprehensive plans and implementing measures shall manage the use and division of urbanizable land to maintain its potential for planned urban development until appropriate public facilities and services are available or planned.
>
> (Goal 14)

Metro has made provisions for planning for these new areas (*Metro Code* 2014 s.3.07.1105–1140). The code requires a 'concept plan' in advance of annexation of an area to the UGB, which requires coordination with affected local governments and a strategy for bringing urban facilities and services to the area. But the relationship of providing public facilities and services to lands already within the UGB and more speculative planning for providing for those facilities and services to urban reserves and in annexing those lands to the UGB has not been adequately explored. This appears to be the new frontier of growth management law in the Portland metro area.

Much has been done over the past 40 years in growth management in Oregon generally, and the Portland Metro area in particular. Nevertheless, change and the types of growth facing the region will require even bolder steps to meet the demands of the future.

Notes

1 This allows Metro to expand its own boundaries by Council action, so that when urban land is added to the regional UGB, Metro's boundaries expand as well (codified as amended at Or. Rev. Stat. §§ 268.347, .354, and .390 (2013)).

2 This allows Metro to require city and county plans to conform to its 'functional plans', one of which is the Urban Growth Functional Plan (UGFP)); id. § 268.390(7)(a) (giving Metro the ability to require individual land use decisions to conform to the UGFP).

3 It is not as if the notion of legislative intervention into local land use matters is entirely unprecedented. Oregon has an often-overlooked history of preempting planning by ad hoc siting decisions of particular uses. See generally Cogan Owens Cogan, Final Report, Energy Facilities Siting Task Force: Report on Land Use Issues 17–19 (20 June 1996), available at www.oregon.gov/energy/Siting/docs/TFR/TFR_T.pdf.

4 In 2007, the Oregon Legislature used a series of 'factors' to be applied to urban and rural reserve cases and directed appeals in those cases to the Court of Appeals perhaps to give those decisions a more deferential review and avoid the use of a system in which failure to meet any one criterion would be the basis of remand. See Act of June 28, 2007, ch. 723, §§ 3, 6, and 9, 2007 Or. Laws 1885–89 (2007) (codified as amended and revised at Or. Rev. Stat. §§ 195.141, .145 and 197.626). The Oregon Legislature made further revisions to this last statute in 2011, so that Metro's urban growth boundary decision was subject to Land Conservation and Development Commission review and then judicial review. See Act of June 23, 2011, ch. 469, 2011 Oregon Laws 1384–88 (2011). The *Barkers Five* decision appears, if anything, to make decision-making more complex.

References

Abbott, C. and Abbott, M.P. (1991) *A history of metro* (hereinafter Metro History) (online) available at: http://library.oregonmetro.gov/files//abbott-a_history_of_metro_may_1991.pdf.

Gaston, C. (2014) Oregon house passes land use 'Grand Bargain' in unanimous vote, *OregonLive*, 28 February, 5:43 PM, available at: www.oregonlive.com/politics/index.ssf/2014/02/oregon_house_passes_land_use _g.html.

Green, J. (2015) *Do urban growth boundaries work?* American Society of Landscape Architects: The Dirt (online) available at: https://dirt.asla.org/2015/05/04/do-urban-growth-boundaries-work/ (accessed 25 August 2016).

Sullivan, E.J. (2012) The quiet revolution goes west: The Oregon planning program 1961–2011, *Marshall Law Review*, 45(357), 372–374.

Sullivan, E.J. (2015) Urban growth management in Portland, Oregon, *Oregon Law Review*, 93(455), 473.

Sullivan, E.J. and Clark, B.H. (2013) A timely, orderly, and efficient arrangement of public Facilities and services: The Oregon approach, *Willamette Law Review*, 49(411), 411–475.

Sullivan, E.J. and Eber, R. (2009) The long and winding road: Farmland protection in Oregon 1961–2009, *San Joaquin Agricultural Law Review*, 18(1), 1–69.

Sullivan, E.J. and Somolou, A. (2011) Preserving forest lands for forest uses – land use policies for Oregon forest lands, *Journal of Environemntal Law & Litigation*, 26(179), 181–258.

Law

Act of April 1, 2014, ch. 92, 2014 Or. Laws 252–256 (2014).

Act of July 1, 2013, ch. 575, 2013 Or. Laws 1–12 (2013) (amending sections 197.015 and 197.298 of the Oregon Revised Statutes).

Act of July 13, 1995, ch. 547, § 5, 1995 Or. Laws 1399 (1995) (codified at Or. Rev. Stat. § 197.298).

Act of July 15, 1979, ch. 402, § 1, 1979 Or. Laws 491 (1979) (codified as amended at Or. Rev. Stat. § 268.390(3)); Act of June 2, 2009, ch. 216, § 3, 2009 Or. Laws 725 (2009).

Act of June 28, 2007, ch. 723, § 1, 2007 Or. Laws 1885 (2007) (codified as amended and revised at Or. Rev. Stat. § 195.145(4)).

Act of Sept. 10, 1993, ch. 804, 1993 Or. Laws 2530–37 (1993) (generally codified as amended and revised at Or Rev. Stat. §§ 195.020-.085, .145, and .210-.235).

Code of the Metropolitan Service District (Metro Code), Metro Council (online) available at: www.oregonmetro.gov/metro-code (accessed 25 August 2016).

Dep't of Land Conservation & Dev., Acknowledgement Scoreboard *D.S. Parklane, Inc. v. Metro*, 994 P. 2d 1205 (2000)

Dep't of Land Conservation & Dev., *Oregon's Statewide Planning Goals & Guidelines*, Definitions, p. 7 (2010).

Metro Charter (2003) 6 January (online) available at: www.oregonmetro.gov/metro-charter (accessed 25 August 2016).

Oregon Administrative Rules, Oregon Secretary of State (online) available at: http://sos.oregon.gov/archives/Pages/oregon_administrative_rules.aspx (accessed 25 August 2016).

Oregon Revised Statute, Oregon Secretary of State (online) available at: www.oregonlegislature.gov/bills_laws/Pages/ORS.aspx (accessed 25 August 2016).

A Dutch perspective on urban growth boundaries: from containing to stimulating growth

Leonie Janssen-Jansen and Wendy Tan

Within international planning educational circles, the Netherlands has long been held up as an exemplar of effective national and regional land use planning practices. Well-known examples are the water management policies (van der Cammen and de Klerk 2012). The clearly defined administrative hierarchies, the policy consistency, and the management of the land resource with governmental controls in planning have been praised in planning literature. The Dutch planning system is seen as a great example for other countries, just as Sullivan's Portland example (Bontje 2003; Fainstein 2005). The urban growth boundary (UGB) of the Regional Framework Plan of Portland is likewise one of the most outstanding elements of the land use planning system in State of Oregon. This is an example of an instrument accompanied by many other complementary ordinances, regulations, and rules that together result in a desired planning outcome. The UGB is therefore often compared to national planning instruments in the Netherlands intent on enforcing a strict boundary between the urban and the rural. In the Netherlands, this divide has always been a keystone concept of the land use planning system, which is to keep as much open space 'open' as possible, while concurrently address the need for expansion and growth by ensuring enough land for residential development in a context of land scarcity in the upcoming decades. This is a similar situation to Portland where the growth necessary for the next 20 years needs to be balanced by the geographical constraints of the nature and agricultural areas. Although the regional UGB enjoys statutory status in Portland, regional coordination is considered an informal norm within the Netherlands. For example, certain provinces keep to an 80–20 rule, whereby the majority of new developments should take place within existing urban contours. The regional focus of Portland's planning system is relevant for international planners as most land use issues tend to cross administrative borders in nature and involve more than a single government level. On the surface, the Dutch planning system might not have much to offer as compared to Portland as the legal force is maintained mostly at the local level in the form of municipal land use plans (Needham 2016). Although the 2008 revision of the planning law (WRO 2008) does enable regional and inter-municipal zoning plans that can be brought forward by multiple municipalities or proposed by the Dutch regional government – the province – this instrument has been hardly implemented. From the provincial perspective, 'overthrowing' municipalities is politically not popular; municipalities – and their governors – focus on the land in their municipality as they are accountable for planning within the municipality, not outside.

There is however a 'hidden' story here. Dutch planning has been increasingly based on neoliberal idea waves (Janssen-Jansen 2016), with the right-wing national government abandoning national planning in 2010 while handing over the complete control of spatial planning to the provincial authorities. Surprisingly, there hardly have been any protests against this neoliberal overturn of planning that designates a larger role to private actors in planning, concurrently with a withdrawing government.

Managing growth in the Netherlands

As one of the world's most densely populated countries, averaging 504 inhabitants per square kilometer (Statistics Netherlands 2017), land for development is scarce in the Netherlands. With a decentralized parliamentary democracy functioning with three tiers of government, the national government (*Rijk*), the intermediate level governments (*Provincies*), and the local governments (the municipalities – *Gemeenten*) are all active in Dutch planning processes. The 12 Dutch provinces should not be seen as city-regional governments such as Metro – the Metropolitan Planning Organization for the greater Portland region – as the Netherlands lacks a city-regional administrative system or the legal force to enact planning policies at that level. The regional tier functions rather with collaboration and consultation then through enforcement. The three distinct government tiers – national, provincial, and local – all have their singular responsibilities within a multi-levelled co-governance system, with their individual competencies and authority stipulated in the Dutch Constitution, and further elaborated in the Province Act (*Provinciewet*) and the Municipality Act (*Gemeentewet*). Between 1965 and 2008, development growth was controlled through regulations and policies at those distinct levels based on the Spatial Planning Act of 1965 (WRO). Although the Dutch planning system then and now still has a clear policy hierarchy where each planning level is monitored for consistency with goals set at a higher level, only the local land use plan made by municipalities is legally binding. This legal detail is often overlooked when assessing Dutch planning. The lack of a regional entity such as the unique Metro, the lack of enforcement at regional level with only legally binding instruments at local level, fuels intermunicipal competition for development and regional real estate markets.

From containing to stimulating growth

The famous reputation of Dutch planning was built upon the technocratic plans and ideas from the 1960s and 1970s – the period famed for 'bundled deconcentration' (*gebundelde deconcentratie*) where in suburbanization outside towns and cities is concentrated. This policy, presented in the Second National Policy Document on Spatial Planning (Ministry of Housing and Spatial Planning 1966), shows similarity with the UGB as used in Portland. The idea was to avoid excessively high densities in the main cities due to population growth, which was then forecasted as 20 million inhabitants in the year 2000, while concurrently avoiding sprawl by separating the urban from rural/non-urban land and introducing new towns.[1] This is similar to postwar Portland, where the protection of land for food production was a major incentive to manage and control growth by incentivizing growth only in certain allocated growth poles. Unsurprisingly, soon after the implementation of the 'bundled deconcentration' policies, the planners' assumption of jobs accompanying population growth turned out to be unfounded and that the population forecast that was a point of departure turned out to be enormously exaggerated. The current Dutch population stands at 17,108,799[2] (Statistics Netherlands 2017), falling short of the predicted 20 million inhabitants. In addition, the jobs were not located where population growth was, contributing to additional commuting traffic and resulting in congestion problems. This resulted in the concept being unrealistic and ineffective before it was fully implemented. In comparison, Metro did better on this account with a strong infrastructure emphasis in their growth management plans (Tan et al. 2013).

In the 1970s – when regional planning started in Portland – the famous Dutch blueprint planning approach began to change towards adaptive and process-based planning. In the 1980s following a neoliberal political turn including a reorganization of the welfare state, 'bundled deconcentration' was seen as bringing up lots of social costs. The concept was not entirely successful in containing urban sprawl and protecting green belts and resulted in financial problems for almost all growth poles. The relatively autonomous position of the Dutch municipalities in land use planning – with instruments as active land policy and the resulting growth orientation of them – has been attributed as the reason for the failure to contain urban sprawl despite the slower than expected growth. Despite their international reputation, the Dutch national and provincial authorities are weak while the municipalities have the real power in land use planning. Dutch spatial planning laws will be revised in 2019, when all laws relevant to land use and environment will merge into the Environment and Planning Act to expedite the planning process by reducing the number of procedures to expedite sustainable development with attention to environmental quality and societal needs with an integral approach (Ministry of Infrastructure and Environment 2017). This new approach, born from neoliberal politics with their demand for a larger role for the market and less regulation, is a major change in Dutch planning. The consequences for planning of its implementation have been under-researched until now, as the focus still remains on the legal aspects. The upcoming law requires municipalities to produce a local environmental plan to regulate which land is designated for a particular activity and how the land can be used for this. Every development application will need to be considered and assessed on the basis of the provisions contained within this land use plan. If a proposed development is allowed within the terms and provisions of the plan, the building permit needs to be granted; and if not, it will be denied. An appeal mechanism and an exemption procedure have been built into the current planning system, in which any proposed development not meeting the terms of the local environmental plan could still be approved by the council who could amend the legally enforceable plan for areas of any size if the development was viewed favourably. Under the new Act, local authorities will have even more discretionary power in land development decisions. As argued in the commentary by → *Holtslag-Broekhof*, urban development is very attractive for municipalities not only because of the intended growth, but also due to the active land policy of the municipalities where there is often a 'develop-as-much-as-you-want' perspective at the local level instrumental to the financial health of a municipality. This perspective stimulates the increasing development-led practice in which political decisions often favour market developments overruling the spatial plans and policies that might consider societal factors, resulting in expansions of Dutch 'growth boundaries' at the local level.

From the 1990s onward, Dutch politics (and subsequently the planners) have developed land use planning policies that no longer focus on containing growth but rather try to refocus growth towards the cities instead. Just like in Portland with its 'build Portland up, instead of out' motto, compact city policies re-emerged as market developers took on a greater role in development.

In Portland, where the expansion of the growth boundary – 35 times more since the 1970s – is a regional decision allowing for a balance of interests such as environmental protection or availability of low-income households despite strong development pressures. Smaller pieces of rural land are often transformed into urban land despite the abundance of land in the greater Portland region in comparison to cities in the Netherlands. The boundary is thus not as strict as it is often perceived or communicated. This is part of the system as the land included within the UGB is subjected to a 20-year development reserve. Clear and hard boundaries might be necessary in some places to avoid environmental damages, but the need to accommodate development norms and guidelines about how and where to allow new developments is just as important.

One might argue that the focus on increasing urban density – partly to render transit-oriented development profitable – occurs at a cost to housing affordability and the pushback on low income housing as rents are raised. This is however an incomplete equation if one does not take into account transport, health, and energy costs or the quality of the environment. It is important to comprehensively and regionally assess the spatial impact of growth. Land use planning in the Netherlands is statutory as in Portland, and just as contested as the average government action. Compared to Germany, this contestation is much more pronounced in the Netherlands where the continuance of planning is debated. The national overview is already diminished due to neoliberal attitudes in spatial planning policy, taking a big departure in the Dutch paternalistic blueprint planning approach from the 1950s and 1960s. Current planning might be building upon this strong planning history, but has evolved into a more modest government action with strong local programmatic autonomy. The relatively strict boundaries at the state-regional-local level in Portland with legal enforcement such as in Oregon therefore offers an interesting experience for the Netherlands instead of the other way around.

Notes

1 In the late 1950s and early 1960s, Dutch political choices for a spatially equitable distribution of sources of national wealth and a balanced national urbanization pattern resulted in an explicit deconcentration policy.
2 Accurate as of 15 May 2017.

References

Bontje, M. (2003) A 'planner's paradise' lost? Past, present and future of Dutch national urbanization policy, *European Urban and Regional Studies*, 10(2), 135–151.

Fainstein, S. (2005) Cities and diversity, should we want it? Can we plan for it? *Urban Affairs Review*, 41(1), 3–19.

Janssen-Jansen, L. B. (2016) Taking national planning seriously: A challenged planning agenda in the Netherlands, *Public Administration*, 64/3–4, 23–43.

Ministry of Housing and Spatial Planning (1966) *Tweede Nota over ruimtelijke ordening in Nederland*, Ministry of VROM, The Hague.

Ministry of Infrastructure and Environment (2017) *Revision of environment and planning laws: Spatial planning and infrastructure* (online) available at: www.government.nl/topics/spatial-planning-and-infrastructure/contents/revision-of-environment-planning-laws (accessed 15 May 2017).

Needham, B. (2016) How the Dutch want their land to be used: The content of Dutch spatial policy planning, in: *Dutch land use planning: The principles and the practice*, Chapter 2, Routledge, Oxon, New York, 46–91.

Statistics Netherlands (2017) *Population and population dynamics; month, quarter and year* (online) available at: http://statline.cbs.nl/StatWeb/publication/?VW=T&DM=SLEN&PA=37943eng&LA=EN (accessed 15 May 2017).

Tan, W.G.Z., Janssen-Jansen, L.B. and Bertolini, L. (2013) The role of incentives in implementing successful transit-oriented development strategies, *Urban Policy and Research*, 32(1), 33–51.

van der Cammen, H. and de Klerk, L. (2012) *The selfmade land: Culture and evolution of urban and regional planning in the Netherlands*, 1st ed., Spectrum, Houten.

A German perspective on urban growth boundaries: the answer of comprehensive regional planning

Martin Wickel

The German government has set a land thrift goal of reducing the conversion of land to land for building and infrastructure to 30 hectares per day nationwide by 2020. To reach this goal, many measures on various administrative levels must be taken. As an example, in the past ten years, the approach of focusing development within existing urban areas has been given great emphasis. The statute regulating local land use planning, the Federal Building Code (*Baugesetzbuch, BauGB*), has been amended several times to advance this goal. But local planning alone cannot be relied on to solve the problem; a supralocal approach is also required. Regional planning allows for the (effective) management of growth and, very often, shrinkage.

The Portland Region system has been tailored to provide an effective instrument to manage urban growth on a regional level and is considered to be successful in this respect. In the following section, some aspects of the Oregon system, its strengths and weaknesses as described by *Sullivan*, will be compared with the German system of regional planning. This comparison will allow some conclusions about the merits of the German system.

In Germany, regional planning is a well-established instrument. Regional plans are part of the system of spatial planning. The Spatial Planning Act (*Raumordnungsgesetz, ROG*), a federal statute, provides for a two-level planning system. This system, which is applied in 12 of the German states (*Bundesländer*), consists of statewide spatial plans as the first level and regional plans as the second level (§ 8 I ROG). The Spatial Planning Act creates a legal obligation to prepare regional plans. Exemptions from this system are not the expression of a fundamental breach of this system. Rather, the size or the structure of some states (the so-called town states – Berlin, Hamburg, Bremen – and the Saarland) do not sanction a two-level planning system. More than a hundred regional plans have been issued in Germany. The widespread acceptance of this system is not self-evident. The states would have the legislative power to divert from this scheme. None, however, has chosen to do so.

This nationwide legislative basis makes regional planning a common part of the administration of land use policies rather than making it an exceptional construction. It is not challenged politically or constitutionally. In this respect, it seems to be in a better position than the Portland system. Regional planning in Germany is insulated against the direct interference of the political legislator. That does not mean that the political process has no influence on regional planning. But this influence is channelled through criteria and objectives set by statutes or superior plans. It does not take the shape of direct interference as experienced in the Portland region.

Regional planning is a mandatory task for all 16 German states (*Bundesländer*) due to the federal Spatial Planning Act. The organization and the procedures, however, are subject to legislation on state level. Therefore, a broad variety of organizational models can be found. In most cases the states delegate the preparation of regional plans to planning associations, public entities that are founded for that purpose. In many cases municipalities and counties are members. An example for this can be found in Art. 8 Bavarian Spatial Planning Act (*Bayerisches Landesplanungsgesetz*). This applies, for example, to the Regionaler Planungsverband München, a planning association comprising the City of Munich and the surrounding counties, covering an area of roughly 5,500 square kilometers and with a population of around 2.5 million inhabitants. To entrust planning associations with the task of regional planning seems to be a parallel between the German system and Metro. Other examples can be found, however, in which the state administration itself prepares the regional plans (Schleswig-Holstein) or in which this task is delegated to the counties completely (Lower Saxony).

The planning associations normally have a so-called planning conference in which the counties and municipalities are represented. This is one interesting difference from Metro as a directly elected regional government. In Germany the planning conferences normally consist of representatives of the counties and municipalities. The Regionaler Planungsverband München, for example, has a conference with 194 members representing 186 municipalities and eight counties. The number of voting rights of one member depends on the number of inhabitants he or she represents. Although the members are not directly elected, this does not necessarily result in a lack of democratic legitimation. The representatives chosen by the members draw their democratic legitimation from the elections of office-holders on the local level who in turn appoint the representatives. The ways of choosing the members of the governing body, however, make a difference. As a representative of a municipality (or a county), the member of the regional planning conference is likely to represent the interests of the respective municipality. If directly elected, it seems more likely that the members of the planning conference emphasize the regional perspective since they draw their legitimation from an election that is more likely to have a regional focus. When members have a regional rather than a local perspective, the decision of the planning conference is more likely to be the best solution from the viewpoint of the region. The variety of different models in Germany, however, is broad. Planning associations with directly elected planning conferences can be found as well, prominent examples being the Region Hannover and the Verband Region Stuttgart.

Regardless the organization to the planning association, the municipal interests have a strong position in preparing regional plans. The ability to decide about local land use is a core element of the constitutionally protected right of self-governance of the municipalities (Art. 28 II Grundgesetz). Regional plans that interfere with local planning intentions and limit the leeway of local decision-making must be justified by overriding interests. The Spatial Planning Act emphasizes that when regional plans are being prepared, the requirements of local land use planning must be accommodated. The legislator provides for a system of countervailing influence (§ 1 III ROG). Besides this, regional plans, like all other land use plans, are subject to the principle of balancing (§ 7 II ROG). This requires that, throughout the planning process, all relevant interests be identified, weighed, and brought into a just and proportionate balance, and that this balance be reflected in the plan itself. In the sense of *Sullivan's* second conclusion, this is a way to rationalize the process of political decision-making with respect to land use interests.

The scope of regional planning in Germany goes beyond defining UGB. It encompasses settlement structures, open space structures, and space designated for infrastructures (§ 8 V ROG). Therefore, regional planning in Germany can be best compared to the Portland Regional Framework Plan. It is part of a planning hierarchy. Regional plans in Germany must comply with requirements set by national and state law as well as state wide spatial plans (§ 8 II ROG). At the same time, they set goals themselves, most important for local land use plans of municipals but for sectoral plans of other state entities as well.

UGB can be most closely compared to designations for the development of settlements (§ 8 V Nr. 1 lit. d ROG). These allow municipalities that may develop new areas to be distinguished from others that are restricted. The areas that are used for development can be restricted in regional plans as well. In this respect, regional plans include designations that serve a similar purpose as UGB.

UGB in the Portland region are binding, drawing a line between land that can be developed for urban uses and land that is reserved for other uses. The binding effect of designations in regional plans may vary. According to the Spatial Planning Act, regional plans can set objectives and principles of spatial development. Objectives of spatial development are strictly binding (§ 4 I ROG). Therefore, municipalities may not divert from boundaries that are drawn by objectives. In addition, a municipality must adapt its land use plans if an objective of spatial development requires it to do so (§ 1 IV BauGB). The legal requirements for setting an objective of spatial development, however, are demanding. Since no leeway is left for the following stages of planning, all aspects that are relevant must be weighed in the process of balancing. Principles of spatial development, on the other hand, must be considered in the planning processes that follow, however, it is possible for principles of spatial development to be outweighed by other aspects. Therefore, urban growth can be limited by regional planning. To which extent regional plans are binding can be decided by the planning entity.

There are, however, inherent limitations. One is the scale level of regional plans. Spatial planning, because it is supralocal planning, is barred from regulating small spatial details. For that reason, small settlement structures are sometimes not relevant for the regional planning level. The scale level makes it difficult to draw exact lines that distinguish land for urban or other uses.

This may be overcome if regional planning merges with the highest level of local planning. The Spatial Planning Act allows for this option (§ 8 IV ROG). Such plans serve as regional plans as well as joint local land use plans for several municipalities. Here, designations of the kind normally found in regional plans can be combined with more specific designations of local plans. Therefore, the boundaries of settlement areas may be prescribed in detail together with more specific designations about the permitted use (e.g. residential, mixed use, commercial/industrial). Although this kind of plan was established under the Spatial Planning Act in 1998, only two of these plans have been adopted so far (Regionaler Flächennutzungsplan Ballungsraum Frankfurt/Rhein-Main; Regionaler Flächennutzungsplan Städteregion Ruhr).

It can be noted that the organization of Metro seems to be better suited to cope with regional planning issues than most planning regions in Germany. In particular, the direct election of the governing body seems to be an advantage if the goal is to achieve the best result from the regional perspective, overriding conflicting local interests. Furthermore, regional planning in Germany, being comprehensive in nature, normally does not concentrate on one task the way that Metro seems to concentrate on UGB. The specific advantage of regional planning in Germany might be that it is not contested as an instrument. The Spatial Planning Act provides a national legislative basis, which has a levelling effect on the states. Regional planning in Germany is part of an administrative tradition in the field of spatial and land use planning that insulates it against interference by the legislature, at least to some extent. After all, the differences between the systems should not be overrated. In both cases, urban development is restricted by regional planning approaches, the most important aspect being that competition between municipalities and local interests is prevented from leading to unsustainable land use.

9 Land readjustment in Portugal

Theoretically attractive but eternally postponed in practice

Beatriz Condessa, Ana Morais de Sá, Joana Almeida, and José Antunes Ferreira

Introduction

In most developed and developing economies, public control over land use planning and urban development aims to strike a delicate balance between public and private rights over land. The tension between the public right to manage a resource as scarce and socially valuable as urban land and the protection of private property rights is framed in different legal, political, institutional, economic, and cultural environments that have evolved over time.

Land readjustment is an old technique for managing urban land, and it has received increasing attention over the past few years. It can be simply described as an urban development method that implies the property structure transformation and an equitable distribution of the development benefits and costs to all participants according to their initial contributions. However, the advantages of land readjustment go beyond the scope of land assembly. In fact, land readjustment can be an effective and equitable technique for capturing value increase in urban land and for promoting more self-financed urban development and public goods provision (Larsson 1997; Sorensen 2000; Hong and Needham 2007; Alterman 2007; Davy 2007; Turk 2008). Furthermore, by improving the rationality between land use planning, property rights, and value capture, land readjustment can be a strategic approach for local governments in promoting integrated planning policies for a more sustainable urban development, rather than simply being a technical tool. However, while in theory land readjustment provides an attractive land management and urban development tool, in practice, its effective application is rare among advanced economies (Alterman 2012).

In Portugal, land readjustment came into force in 1999. Before that, from the public interest's perspective, public administration was ill-equipped to control private sector-led urban development (Carter and Nunes da Silva 2001). In fact, municipalities planned urban development on mainly private land without effective tools to encourage private landowners' engagement with the plan or to force development and finance it. Consequently, urban land often remained idle due to speculative market behaviour, inappropriate property patterns, or the landowners' inability to reach consensus, leading to scarcity of urban parcels. Within this framework, urban areas were generally oversized in municipal master plans, allegedly to increase supply in the market and thus control speculative behaviours.

Urban land currently represents approximately 7 percent of the Portuguese territory and provides an accommodation capacity for almost 30 million inhabitants (DGT 2009),[1] whereas the Portuguese population is only about 10 million. In addition to the current declining demographic trends, the financial and economic crises also show that the context of *growth-dependent planning* (Rydin 2013) is no longer sustainable.

Broadly speaking, urban land scarcity is, therefore, not a *quantity* issue. Instead, it takes different forms and they all undermine land use planning and urban development: *location, timing*, and *quality*. Significant changes in land use policies and public planning strategies are required to tackle this problem. A shift from a *laissez-faire* to a public-led approach of urban management is fundamental and, in this sense, land readjustment can play a key role in mitigating urban land scarcity.

However, from the public interest's perspective, the results of land readjustment application are far from desirable (Condessa et al. 2015). With this background, the Portuguese land readjustment application in detailed plans will be discussed and it will be demonstrated how, even within an adverse environment for efficient and equitable land readjustment implementation, mainly due to some cultural, legal, and economic aspects, it is still possible to adjust this tool and overcome some key constraints by fine-tuning the current land readjustment legal system and practice.

Urban development in Portugal and land readjustment

In order to clearly understand the context in which land readjustment came into force in Portugal, this section summarizes the land use planning legal framework and the prevailing practice of urban development over the past five decades.

Although the equity principle first emerged in the Portuguese law in the late 1990s, some land readjustment experiences had already taken place before. The first one, pioneer even in international terms, was related to the plan for the rebuilding of Lisbon following the devastating earthquake of 1755. Indeed, this plan included a remarkable and a very avant la lettre system of compensations between the former property owners and the public administration (Ribeiro dos Santos and Sagarra i Trias 2011).

Despite having been a successful experience, since that time the usage of land assembly procedures occurred only in rural contexts. It was only in the second half of the twentieth century that some more informal land readjustment experiences took place in the reconversion and legalization of certain illegal settlements, supported by *bottom-up* initiatives that occurred without any legal framework, but that inspired the law that later came into force.

After the democratic revolution in 1974, a new legal framework for land policies came into force, with urban land scarcity being the main item on the agenda (Decree-Law No. 794/76). However, this law didn't provided for real effective land use tools to allow public-led initiatives. Thus, in the following decades, private developers controlled urban development through ad hoc land subdivision schemes, most not framed by any land use plans or assembling mechanisms.

Under these circumstances, local governments' ability to effectively manage land use and to regulate the real estate market was very limited. This caused large diseconomies of agglomeration (e.g. traffic congestion, pollution, and other negative externalities triggered by concentration dynamics), increased regional disparities, and channelled productive private investment and household consumption to land hoarding, particularly in the surroundings of the two main urban areas (Lisbon and Oporto). As landowners could retain their urban parcels off the market without any penalties imposed by public administration, hoarding behaviours prevailed and market prices increased.

It became clear then that when urban development is mainly controlled by the private sector, public-led initiatives to tackle urban land scarcity require effective land use tools, such as dispute resolution mechanisms (e.g. expropriation or compulsory sales) and value capture instruments (e.g. land and property taxation or other non-financial compensation mechanisms as land readjustment). That was not the Portuguese case.

In the late 1990s, a new legal framework for land use and spatial planning came into force. The previous three-tier planning system was strengthened to define the municipal land use patterns and establish the main framework for local government development control (Law No. 48/98 and Decree Law No. 380/99). According to this law, the municipal master plan (MMP), drawn by the municipality and applied to the whole municipal territory, was meant to be a *structural plan*, and as such, it should establish the strategic municipal planning policies (but not precise land allocations) and form the basis for more detailed spatial policies. According to that, municipal master plans were usually represented on a 1:25,000 scale or, less frequently, on a 1:10,000 scale. In accordance with the strategic options of the municipal master plan, the urban zoning plan (UZP) should be more accurate regarding land use zoning and should be represented on a 1:5,000 scale. At the bottom of the three-tier planning system, the detailed plan (DP) was designed as a development plan, and as such, it defines the urban design at the more detailed level and is represented on 1:2,000 or 1:1,000 scales. These three types of municipal plans are binding for both public administration and private property owners, but only the municipal master plan is mandatory for local governments.

However, municipal spatial planning has rarely gone beyond the municipal master plan. Two main reasons explain this. First, while urban zoning plan and detailed plan are optional by law, municipalities without a municipal master plan in force do not access European funds. Second, from the local government's perspective, the whole plan-making process is rather bureaucratic and consumes more than its fair share of financial and human resources. In this framework, it was sometimes unclear for the municipality how spatial planning options established by urban zoning plan and detailed plan could provide flexibility to cope with changing circumstances and new opportunities.

Given the scarcity of urban zoning plan and mostly of detailed plan, municipal master plan became the main instrument of municipal land use control (in most municipalities, the only one) thereby losing its strategic nature and taking a significant normative role. Its scope, though, is inadequate to address all the issues raised by urban development control, which mainly relate to the layout and densities of future developments.

Despite these limitations, public activity has focused on development control based on municipal master plans, while urban development has been mainly implemented through building and land subdivision permits issued by local governments to private developers neither framed by urban zoning plan nor by detailed plan. This type of practice has been legally framed by the so-called first generation of municipal master plan that defined oversized urban areas (with no demonstration of an effective demand on the market, or of their economic and financial viability), allegedly to avoid monopoly and speculative behaviours by the landowners, yet failing to accomplish it.

The implications of this practice are significant, namely on the effectiveness of dispute resolution mechanisms, such as expropriation (typically used in Portugal as the last resort when voluntary negotiations between local governments and private landowners fail). Contrasting with other European countries, according to Portuguese Expropriations Law, the *fair compensation* value regarding potential urban areas planned on municipal master plan corresponds to the full potential market value (including both the value defined according to the current use and the incremented value generated by the potential urban use proposed by land use municipal plans). As most urban areas planned on municipal master plan are neither framed by detailed plan, nor by urban zoning plan, land value estimations are usually based on the maximum gross floor area ratio (FAR) defined on municipal master plan for extensive urban areas that largely exceed the effective market needs.

Consequently, from the local government's perspective, expropriation is perceived as an expensive solution and often uncertain and risky. According to the law, the *fair compensation value* must be defined in line with the highest market values estimated from a comparable set of real property transactions. Due to the speculative market trends that prevailed approximately until 2009 (when the financial and economic crises hit the country) prices could vary significantly and were difficult to predict when parties went to court (Condessa et al. 2015). Additionally, real estate market inefficiencies were further amplified, as value capture tools were also ineffective.

The problem of urban land scarcity in Portugal is, therefore, not a *quantity* issue. Indeed, most of the areas classified as urban on the *first generation* of municipal master plan remain rural areas (either because there is no effective demand for promoting such urban development or because land hoarding behaviours are economically and financially more advantageous for landowners than development). This surplus of urban land became even more significant with the economic and financial crises.

However, paradoxically, affordable access to urban land, namely by local governments (e.g. to promote social housing or urban regeneration, or to provide for public infrastructures and facilities), still faces significant constraints that adversely affect the quality of life of all citizens. In this sense, the low level of housing affordability, for example, or the lack of aesthetic and functional quality of so many urban settlements, are forms of scarcity caused, among other factors, by inefficient public policies on land.

Within this context, land readjustment can play a key role, as a potentially efficient instrument to implement new urban developments provided that it is based on a solid coordination between land policies, land use planning, and the real estate market.

In fact, one of the public actors' main concerns of the late 1990s legal framework was to promote a shift from a 'non-systematic' urban development practice founded on ad hoc land subdivision projects, to what is considered as 'systematic urban development execution', which corresponds to the development of integrated urban operations, with mandatory assembly mechanisms, within spatial units specifically delimited for that purpose in detailed plan. The law introduced land readjustment, termed as *Perequação* (from the Latin expression *per aequere*)[2] to guarantee an equitable distribution of the benefits and costs from these joint operations. In fact, *Perequação* can be considered a broader concept than (*stricto sensu*) land readjustment, implying not only the property structure transformation in order to create suitable building plots (replotting) but also the redistribution of benefits (plots, development rights) and costs (infrastructure costs and development exactions).

Land readjustment legal framework

According to the 1999 Law, the main land readjustment objectives are (1) to redistribute the gains assigned by the plan to landowners; (2) to provide for municipal land or buildings for public infrastructures and facilities; (3) to avoid speculative behaviours like land hoarding; and (4) to increase municipal financial resources.

Land readjustment is ideally implemented in detailed plan due to its specific nature, contents, and scale, but it can also occur within spatial units only framed by municipal master plans or urban zoning plans. In every case, land readjustment always starts with an early identification of all property owners and of the spatial boundaries within which development will be implemented. The definition of these 'Execution Units' can be led either by the municipality or by private landowners. The law also adds that the Execution Units must cover more and less profitable uses, to ensure a harmonious urban development and a fair distribution of benefits and costs among landowners.

In each unit, the degree of involvement of both public and private agents must be stated. Three approaches are mentioned in the law as *Execution Systems – Imposition, Cooperation*, and *Private Initiative* – allowing for varying degrees of public and private intervention.

Under the *Imposition System*, the municipality takes the responsibility for promoting urban development, acting directly or through an urban development concession granted by local governments to a private developer, for which a public tender procedure is required. A third party, such as a professional developer – similar to the Spanish *Agente urbanizador* – might be involved. Landowners should sign an agreement proposed by the municipality within a set deadline and are expropriated if they do not do so. Under the *Cooperation System*, local government in cooperation with private landowners or investors carries out the land readjustment programming, whereby the rights and requirements are defined in an urban development contract between both sides. Finally, under the *Private Initiative System*, a voluntary landowners association elaborates and implements the project and meets all costs. The role of local government is thus reduced to the land readjustment administrative control.

The law also defines compensation mechanisms but they are neither mandatory nor quantified. The proposed mechanisms include the *average floor area ratio*, for the distribution of benefits, and both the *average land transfer for infrastructures and public facilities* and the *local infrastructures costs allocation*, as development exactions. Other compensation rules can be established, provided that the equity principle is respected.

In accordance with international practice (Alterman 2007; Davy 2007; Turk 2008), the law also suggests that two different criteria can be used in the compensation tools: the *relative size* or the *relative value* of the former land parcels. However, a clear framework for the economic valuation of the original landholdings or the final plots is not specified.

In the end, the serviced plots are allocated to the original landowners or private investors according to the previously defined compensation rules. When some landowners fail to collaborate, municipalities must apply expropriation, followed by public infrastructure provision. This alternative implies a strong political and financial commitment and the capability to bear all the risks (namely, not recovering the public investment), given the high costs often implicated in the expropriation processes.

One last remark must be made. Although the late 1990s legal framework aimed to provide renewed impetus to urban planning and challenge the prevailing ad hoc private-led urban development practice, land subdivision without assembly mechanisms remains framed by the law (Decree-Law

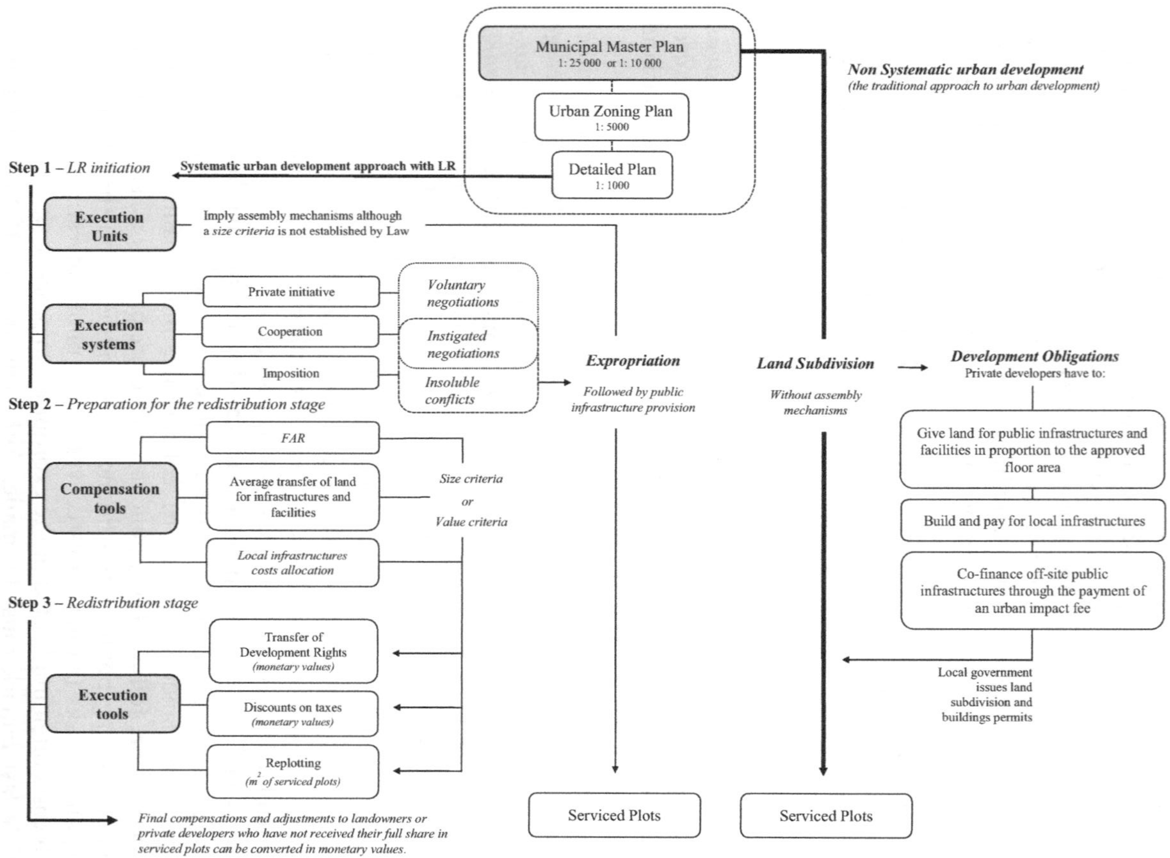

Figure 9.1 Legal framework of land readjustment and urban development in Portugal

No. 555/99), and it is usually more attractive to the private sector than land readjustment. In this case, private developers meet some development obligations, namely, providing land to the municipality for main public infrastructures and facilities in proportion to the approved floor area and guarantying the construction of local infrastructures at their expenses (e.g. local roads, sewage, water supply, or electricity). Additionally, they have to co-finance major off-site public infrastructures and facilities through the payment of an urban impact fee, which is levied in proportion to the authorized floor area.

Figure 9.1 systematizes the land readjustment legal framework and how 'systematic' and 'non-systematic' urban development can still coexist in Portugal.

Generally, it can be stated that the major contents of the land readjustment law seem to be in line with most of the legal requirements, considered fundamental by different authors, for a land readjustment efficient and effective application (Alterman 2007; Home 2007; Hong 2007; Needham 2007; Sorensen 2007; Louw 2008; Turk 2008; Souza 2011; Turk and Turk 2011). Nevertheless, in some instances, the unclear and insufficient degree of detail of the law, on the one hand, and the lack of coordination with other fundamental legal matters, on the other, has compromised land readjustment good practices. Moreover, because land readjustment practice is scarce, no case law has been developed yet.

Characterization of the Portuguese land readjustment practice

General overview of the land readjustment application

The methods used in the characterization of the Portuguese practice of land readjustment on detailed plan consisted of (1) a content analysis of the 371 detailed plan formulated and approved by the 1999 law (October 1999 December 2012) in mainland Portugal; (2) a survey (including both closed- and open-ended questions) conducted with municipal urban planning technicians on the adoption of land readjustment models, their potential and obstacles to their application (106 responses out of a total of 278 municipalities were received, corresponding to a 38 percent response rate); (3) interviews with 16 selected municipalities; and (4) two workshops with expert panels.

The 371 detailed plans refers to 152 of 278 municipalities (Figure 9.2a). Concerning detailed plan type of contents, it can be pinpointed that (1) urban expansion for residential or mixed use was the overriding type, showing that in the past decade, these plans remained more focused on urban land supply rather than in effective demand, which was very low; (2) 80 percent of the detailed plan was made up mainly on private land; (3) the detailed plan average size is 73.6 hectares (smaller areas are roughly the

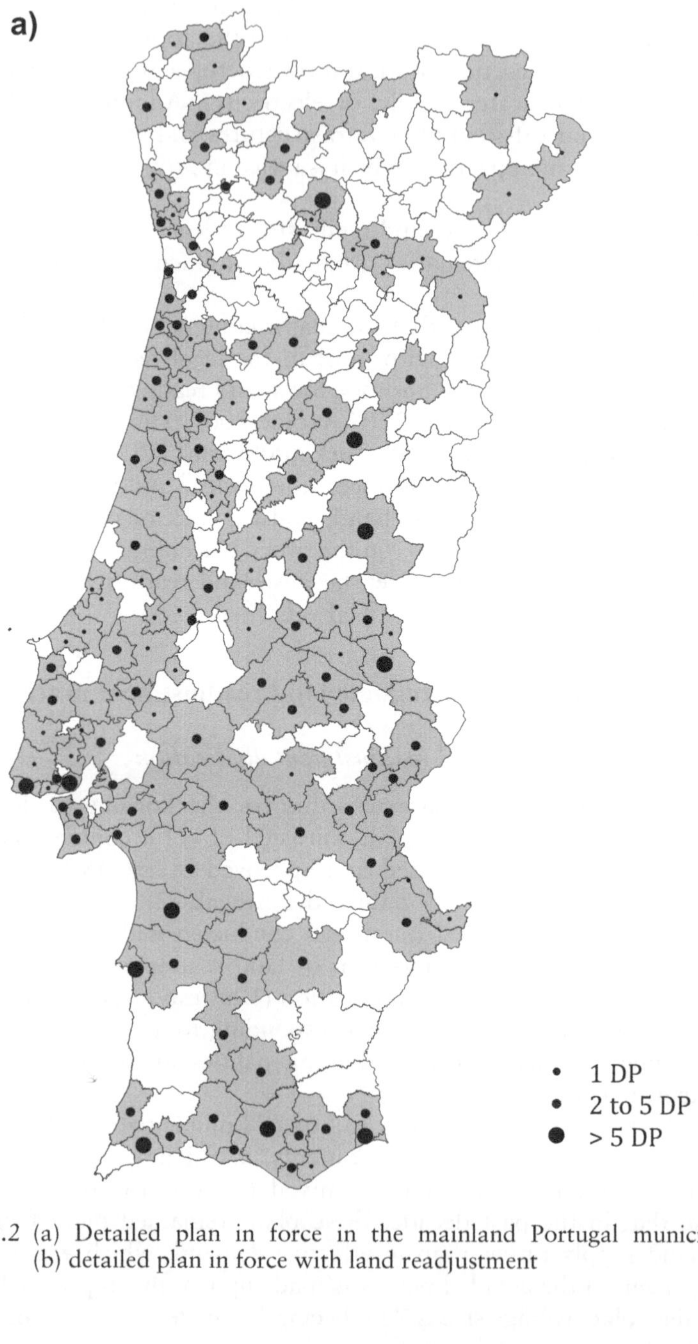

Figure 9.2 (a) Detailed plan in force in the mainland Portugal municipalities; (b) detailed plan in force with land readjustment

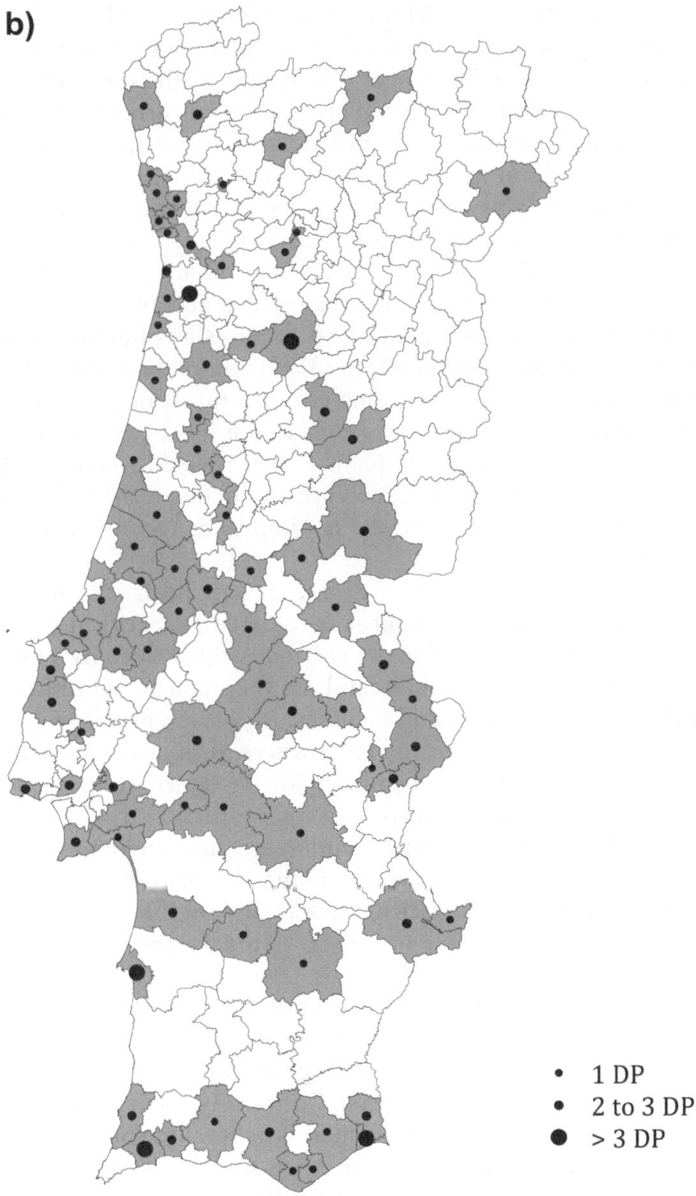

Figure 9.2 Continued

size of a city block, less than 1 hectare, while other areas can be larger than the urban area of a small municipality, with more than 1,000 hectares); and finally (4) the plan-making process was bureaucratic and lengthy, with an average period of 54 months. This analysis explains, to a large degree, why only few municipalities have more than five detailed plans and why 126 municipalities in mainland Portugal (45 percent of the total) did not enact any detailed plans during the period analysed. Concurrently, as mentioned earlier, land subdivision projects of private initiative frequently occurred on an ad hoc basis, without assembly mechanisms, because in most cases they refer to single parcels only framed by the municipal master plan.

From the perspective of both local governments and private developers, private land subdivision projects are commonly perceived as a more interesting urban development tool than a detailed plan: (1) it is not as time-consuming as a detailed plan; (2) it requires less human, economical, and financial resources; and therefore (3) it is more development oriented, allowing for more flexibility regarding effective investment opportunities.

Although land readjustment on detailed plan has been mandatory since 1999, only 36 percent of detailed plans (134) applied it (Figure 9.2b). This small percentage is partially explained because many of those detailed plans referred to only one landowner or did not imply changes in the former ownership structure.

Regarding land readjustment, a degree of consensus was noted on the survey analysis. Land readjustment is considered as a critical tool for promoting urban design quality, for the enhancement of the city's biophysical balance, and for providing public land for the implementation or renovation of public infrastructures and facilities. Moreover, as land readjustment ensures an equitable treatment of landowners, it is generally perceived as a critical tool to enforce the detailed plan implementation even when it implies a highly fragmented structure of the property.

Concerning land readjustment execution systems applied to each execution unit (private initiative, cooperation, and imposition; cf. section 3), the results show that this choice depends essentially on the municipality financial availability, on the number of owners and developers involved, and on the cadastral structure of the site area.

According to the interviews, an execution unit is typically implemented by private initiative when there is a strong private interest resulting in the agreement among owners and the plan proposal is of their own initiative (e.g. a detailed plan for touristic areas). Conversely, the imposition system is chosen when there is a strong public interest in development, when the owners fail to reach an understanding, or when the plan execution is unfeasible. Significant difficulties in implementing this system were mentioned: the adverse environment for urban development in the recent years (given the economic and financial crises) and the lack of financial capability of most municipalities that often hinders expropriation processes needed to solve dispute and conflict situations. As for the cooperation system, there were occasions when the municipality acted as a mediator over the disagreement among owners.

According to the survey (and later reinforced in the interviews), given the alternatives presented in a closed question, the main barriers to land readjustment implementation are as follows (see Figure 9.3): (1) the lack of a civic spatial planning culture and the discord among private interests and between private and public interests – often due to the gap between the plan provisions and the landowners' motivations/expectations; (2) the limited know-how in specific knowledge areas fundamental to land readjustment (land and property valuation and negotiation and conflict management) – in the interviews municipal technicians also identified as critical the lack of systematised land readjustment best practices that could support effective land readjustment implementation; (3) the insufficiency of endogenous municipality resources (financial, technical, or human); (4) the entrenched climate of mistrust between private agents and the central and local government – mainly caused by some unawareness relative to land readjustment; and (5) the difficulties in implementing expropriation (cf. section 2).

Other important interview results can be highlighted: difficulties in establishing a leadership role, other than the municipality's; the lack of private developers that take on the management role; and the difficulty in making these processes self-financeable and therefore feasible without a significant public investment component. The fact that the urban development compensations are usually paid to the municipality later than the incurrence of the most significant development costs and that there is a general lack of

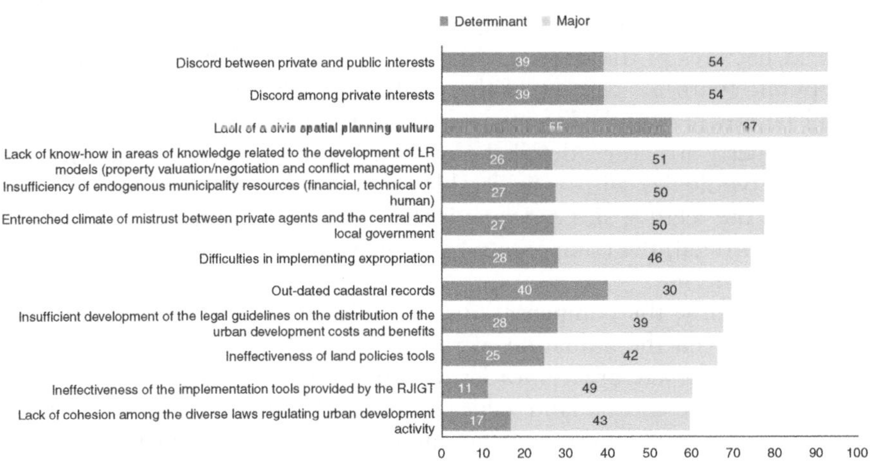

Figure 9.3 Municipal technicians' perceptions of the major and determinant land readjustment obstacles

commitment in ensuring the programmed execution make land readjustment risky for the municipality.

Finally, these obstacles to land readjustment are systematized in different categories according to their nature: Cultural; Economical; Legal; and Technical (Figure 9.4).

The interviews also point out some success factors: (1) the transparency and clarity of the rules throughout the entire land readjustment process; (2) the land readjustment model's simplicity (in particular with regard to the compensation mechanisms); and (3) the participation throughout the process and the sharing of interests, dialogue, and initiative.

The key changes needed to improve land readjustment effectiveness were also identified: (1) the redefinition of the expropriations law; (2) the definition of land readjustment compensation mechanisms based on the estimated economic value of both the former properties and the final serviced plots; (3) the banks' contribution in ensuring the financial risk in the plan's implementation; (4) the establishment of a platform for sharing examples of good practices regarding land readjustment; and (5) the existence of an interlocutor who takes on leadership of the process and establishes a relationship between the various stakeholders.

In line with some of the key factors aforementioned, two successful examples of land readjustment application will be summarized in the following section.

Some successful examples of land readjustment application

The land readjustment model for the expansion plan on the north of *Sines* (hereinafter detailed plan North) was founded on the cooperation system (for more details of the land readjustment model, see Condessa et al. 2015). The 35 hectares of the site area stretch over 34 landowners, two of whom are public (with 52 percent of the total area). The existence of large and small landowners with different expectations should be noted. As for the final property structure, detailed plan North encompasses several uses and building typologies with considerable market prices discrepancies. Hence, although the relative *size criterion* is the compensation method most often used in Portugal, the compensations in detailed plan North were based on the *value criterion*.

Consequently, the compensations to landowners correspond to the difference between the valuation attributed to each parcel and the average valuation of the site area. In order to enforce mutual trust between all the participants, the chosen land valuation method combines a set of objective criteria, based on the universal and online available tax land valuation tool.

This approach helped to increase transparency, reduce discretion, and to regulate the real estate market, reinforcing the environment of reliability throughout the whole urban development process.

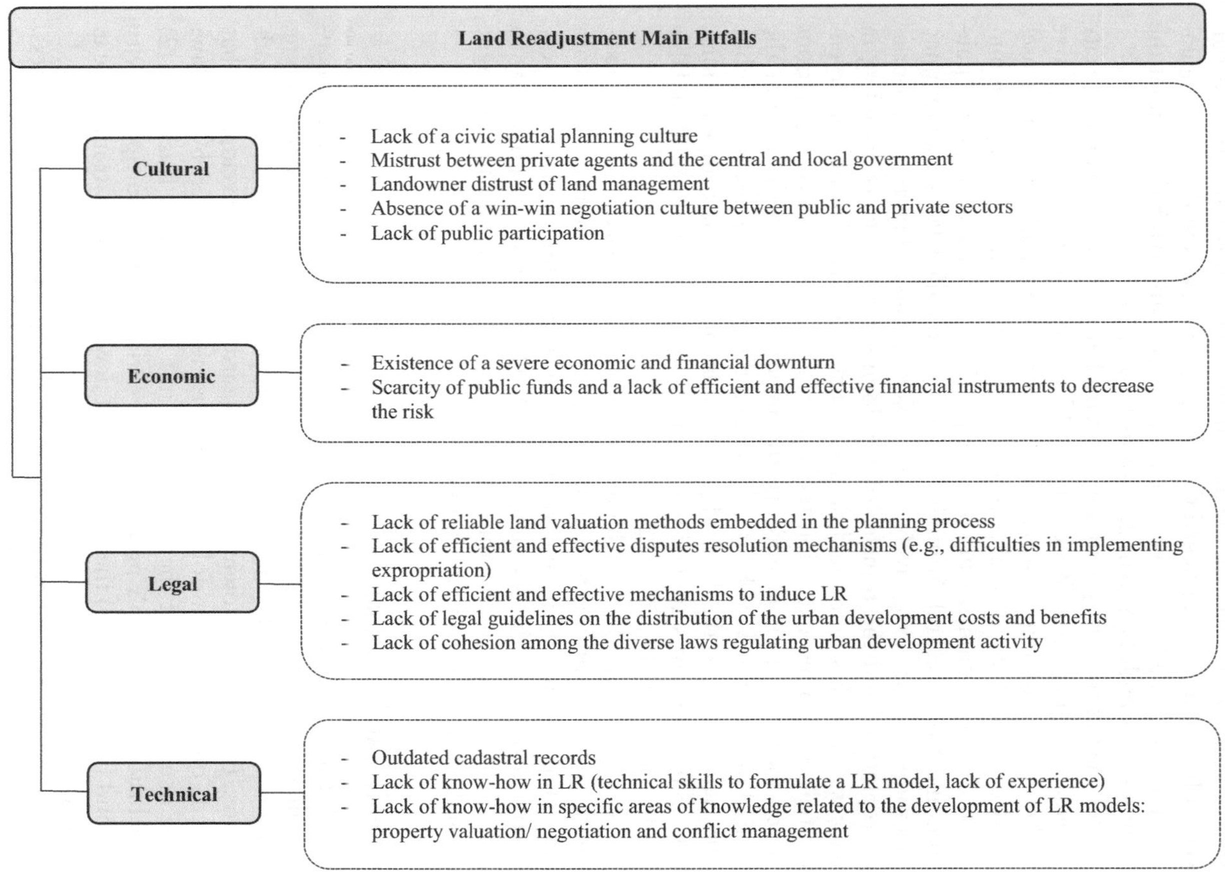

Figure 9.4 Major obstacles to land readjustment in Portugal

In short, the North of *Sines* detailed plan success factors are outlined as follows: (1) the uptake of an objective valuation model that calculated property and land values before and after the plan implementation; (2) early negotiations between all the participants that contributed to the urban design solution and strengthened the commitment levels in the implementation stage; and (3) a local government's proactive approach throughout the planning stages and the urban development process.

Under the imposition system, the *Aguieira* Park's detailed plan in the city of *Viseu* covers an area of 30 hectares and 26 landowners. Its main objective was the creation of a green urban area (a recreational park), but other uses were also allowed (residential and public facilities). With a strong commitment of the *Viseu* municipality and the possibility to access a specific public funding from Central Administration (the so-called Polis Programme), expropriation was extensively used. Nevertheless, besides expropriation, replotting and the transfer of development rights (corresponding in some cases to rights that could be used outside the detailed plan intervention area) were other execution tools chosen. Many previous negotiations between local government and private owners were held throughout the plan-making process, which later facilitated the transfer of areas for public facilities according to the detailed plan final layout. For the compensations, the floor area ratio was applied with correction factors on the nonbuildable agricultural and ecological reserve areas.

Some success factors can be highlighted in this case. *Viseu* is a municipality with strong tradition in planning (it is one of the municipalities with more detailed plans with land readjustment application and with a very proactive attitude in the planning process). There is also the possibility to access the Polis programme, implying heavy public funding and more agile plan-making and expropriation processes.

Discussion and conclusions

The publication of the new Basic Law on Land, Spatial Planning and Urbanism Policy in 2014, and the new Legal Framework of Spatial Planning Instruments in 2015, did not introduce significant changes in land readjustment. However, a growing concern regarding urban development has emerged, questioning the following requirements established by the law: (1) the demonstration of the plan's economic and financial feasibility; (2) the inclusion of the plan's program of execution in the municipal activity plans and budget; and (3) the regulation of new execution instruments (e.g. compulsory sale).

There is a clear paradigm shift regarding the urban development process, currently focusing on urban rehabilitation and regeneration. Urban sprawl is limited to exceptional cases: its economic and financial viability must be ascertained as well as the supply and demand levels and an execution time frame and a redistribution of benefits and costs must be established.

To a considerable degree, rising land values and a high demand for new urban parcels are the fuel that makes land readjustment an attractive proposition for landowners and real estate private investors. In Portugal, however, the existence of economic and financial crises that have negatively affected the real estate sector (including in the cities of *Lisbon* and *Oporto*) and thus the tax municipal revenues, on one hand, and the declining demographic growth trends, on the other, create an environment not conducive to land readjustment implementation.

In fact, in the past decade, due to the serious impacts of the financial and economic crisis, the demand on the real estate market decreased substantially. Banks are currently owners of a significant number of buildings and dwellings, which came into their possession because of repayment defaults.

Within this context, banks had no option but to put these properties on the market, causing a slump in the real estate market value not concurrent with an increase in demand.

Consequently, the real estate market plummeted. As the survey results show, land readjustment was scarcely used in Portugal in the past decade and one of the main reasons for that was the absence of demand for new urban development operations.

In any case, and despite the lack of a robust real estate market, some success factors can be identified that boost the land readjustment attractiveness to landowners, private developers, and local governments and help to create a 'win-win' culture between all the actors in the urban development process:

1 In most cases, landowners are not investors; therefore their goal is not to maximize the market value of land, but rather to optimize the usage value for themselves. It is paramount to increase the trust level between the other actors involved in the process, namely local governments and private developers, to make them receptive to the land readjustment, and for that the transparency and objectivity of the land valuation must be assured.
2 As urban development is mostly dominated by the private sector, the implementation of land readjustment is highly dependent on the extent to which local governments can successfully encourage landowners, developers, and investors to commit to the plan. Within this context, the expropriation legal framework must be reviewed in order to decrease the risk level to local governments when assessing the expropriation value before the decision of its implementation.
3 Not only more effective dispute resolution mechanisms are needed, but also strong incentives to urban development with land readjustment have to be created (e.g. urban, financial, or fiscal incentives), so that the net gains can be more appealing than the ones from land subdivision projects without assembly mechanisms.
4 Land readjustment usually involves private developers (investors) whose role is the management and financial support of the operation.

However, to increase the financial capacity of these developers, it is imperative to enhance the trust level of the financial entities (banks) in the management model implemented and in the management skills of these actors. Within this context, new management models must be developed and implemented and a public accreditation procedure for managers' entities is suggested.

5 The paradigm of the urban developing process has changed. Indeed, urban operations that turn rural land into urban land are no longer the core of urban land development, giving way to urban renewal or requalification projects. In this new paradigm, land readjustment effectiveness is even more challenging.

In other words, the so-called sleeping beauty of the urban development tools (Alterman 2012: 765) is theoretically attractive but eternally postponed in practice. When adjusted to build consensus and cooperation it can be improved, even in generally hostile environments, such as the Portuguese one. In this sense, despite some amendments needed to the existing legislation, the main focus should be on the modification of the established practices in municipal planning and management according to the success factors identified.

Notes

1 DGT (2009). Carta do Regime de Uso do Solo (*Charter of Land Use Regimen*) Directorate General for Spatial Policy.

2 This means to make an equal distribution between different parts or to deal fairly and equally with all concerned.

References

Alterman, R. (2007) More than land assembly: Land readjustment for the supply of urban public services, in: Hong, Y.-H. and Needham, B. (eds) *Analyzing land readjustment – Economics, law, and collective Action*, 1st ed., Lincoln Institute of Land Policy, Cambridge, MA, 57–85.

Alterman, R. (2012) Land use regulations and property values: The 'Windfalls Capture' idea revisited, in: Brooks, N., Donangy, K. and Knapp, G.J. (eds) *The Oxford handbook on urban economics and planning*, Oxford University Press, Oxford, 755–778.

Carter, N. and Nunes da Silva, F. (2001) Recent changes in territorial planning and the system for controlling urban development in Portugal, *Town Planning Review*, 72, 341–370.

Condessa, B., Morais de Sá, A., Cambra, P. and Antunes Ferreira, J. (2015) Land readjustment in Portugal: The case of Sines, *Town Planning Review*, 86, 381–410.

Davy, B. (2007) Mandatory happiness? Land readjustment and property in Germany, in: Hong, Y.-H. and Needham, B. (eds) *Analyzing land readjustment – Economics, law, and collective action*, 1st ed., Lincoln Institute of Land Policy, Cambridge, MA, 37–55.

DGT (2009) *Carta do Regime de Uso do Solo (Charter of land use regimen)*, Directorate General for Spatial Policy.

Home, R. (2007) Land readjustment as a method of development land assembly: A comparative overview, *Town Planning Review*, 78, 459–83.

Hong, Y.-H. (2007) Assembling land for urban development: Issues and opportunities, in: Hong, Y.-H. and Needham, B. (eds) *Analyzing land readjustment – Economics, law, and collective action*, 1st ed., Lincoln Institute of Land Policy, Cambridge, MA, 3–34.

Hong, Y.-H. and Needham, B. (2007) *International experiences in land readjustment*, Lincoln Institute of Land Policy, Cambridge, MA.

Larsson, G. (1997) Land readjustment: A tool for urban development, *Habitat International*, 21(2), 141–152.

Louw, E. (2008) Land assembly for urban transformation – the case of 's-Hertogenbosch in the Netherlands, *Land Use Policy*, 25, 69–80.

Needham, B. (2007) The search for greater efficiency: Land readjustment in the Netherlands, in: Hong, Y.-H. and Needham, B. (eds) *Analyzing land readjustment – Economics, law, and collective action*, 1st ed., Lincoln Institute of Land Policy, Cambridge, MA, 115–132.

Ribeiro dos Santos, M.H. and Sagarra i Trias, F. (2011) Trading properties after the earthquake: The rebuilding of eighteenth-century Lisbon, *Planning Perspectives*, 26(2), 301–311.

Rydin, Y. (2013) *The future of planning: Beyond growth dependence*, Policy Press, Bristol.

Sorensen, A. (2000) Land readjustment and metropolitan growth: An examination of land development and urban sprawl in the Tokyo metropolitan area, *Progress in Planning*, 53(4), 1–113.

Sorensen, A. (2007) Consensus, persuasion, and opposition: organizing land readjustment in Japan, in: Hong, Y.-H. and Needham, B. (eds) *Analyzing land readjustment – Economics, law, and collective action*, 1st ed., Lincoln Institute of Land Policy, Cambridge, MA, 89–114.

Souza, F. (2011) *Methods of urban planning: Land readjustment and urban redevelopment projects*, Paulo's Press, São Paulo, Brazil.

Turk, S.S. (2008) An examination for efficient applicability of the land readjustment method at the international context, *Journal of Planning Literature*, 22, 229–42.

Turk, S.S. and Turk, C. (2011) The annulment of land readjustment projects: An analysis for Turkey, *Town Planning Review*, 82, 687–707.

A German perspective on land readjustment: a proper instrument of modern urban governance for efficient land use

Theo Kötter

Meaning, principles, and procedure of land readjustment in Germany in the context of current urban development

Land readjustment has been applied in Germany for more than 115 years with great success in tackling the challenges of urban growth and urban renewal. The instrument developed from a prototype to an inalienable component of the urban land policy and urban development culture. Today it is regulated nationally by the Federal Building Code (*BauGB*).

The central reason for the development of land readjustment as a new instrument of land policy in Germany was the rapid growth of the cities and the great housing deficits in the nineteenth century. In view of the huge challenges of managing systematic and proper city extensions, despite the very small shareholdings, it became clear that there was a need for a new land policy tool with full acceptance of the landowners. To this end, the instrument of land consolidation, which was introduced for land management for agricultural purposes, was first set up. The successful application then led to the development of land readjustment for specific urban development purposes, which has been systematically developed to this day.

As in Portugal, the scarcity of suitable building land is still the driving force behind land readjustment. But there is no blueprint for its structure, procedure, and handling. This must be shaped by taking into consideration the regional cultural background and legal framework, political demands, and economical requirements of each country and its society. Therefore in this chapter only the principles and experiences of the German model of land readjustment will be depicted in order to give some suggestions and hints to be considered in the case of Portugal.

In Germany, mandatory land readjustment has proven itself as an officially conducted exchange of plots for the development of towns and villages. Its legal order consists of providing suitable properties in location, shape, and size for building or other purposes according to the binding land use plan. The current meaning of land readjustment becomes clear first in the context of the topical challenges of urban development, e.g. shortage of affordable housing, financing urban public infrastructure facilities, infill development, efficient use of the restricted resource land, and socially fair land use.

Land readjustment shows a high acceptance from landowners according to the following characteristics and principles:

- Property preservation principle: The property in the substance is basically not diminished and is preserved for the respective landowner.
- Solidarity principle: The areas for internal roads, green spaces, and other public infrastructure facilities, which predominantly benefit the residents of the land readjustment area, are provided in equal shares by all landowners.
- Private benefit principle: Land readjustment serves first private interests of the property owners and balances between them.
- Planning conformity principle: The legal relationships of the land, in particular the land borders, will be redesigned according to the regulation of the binding land use plan or the specific structure of the already built-up area.

One essential purpose of land readjustment is to provide areas for public infrastructure facilities according to the binding land use plan. This serves to balance the interests of the landowners as well, because the site development is an indispensable condition for the constructability of their property. However land readjustment cannot be conducted with the sole purpose to claim land for roads and green areas.

The great acceptance of the mandatory procedure of land readjustment mainly is the result of the so-called legal redistribution scales according to the regulations of the Federal Building Code. So after the fair deduction of land for the necessary public urban facilities, according to the binding land use plan, the remaining area is redistributed fairly to the owners taking into consideration that each owner has a claim to building land with at least the same value as his former property. The redistribution takes place either in the ratio of the values (value scale) or in the ratio of the areas (area scale) in which the land of the landowners stand before land readjustment. These redistribution scales are legally standardized by the Federal Building Code; however, a different scale can be stipulated with the landowners. In either case, the increase of value generated by the land readjustment, the so-called land readjustment advantage, must be compensated by a contribution by the owners in money or in land. The fair and, in general, accepted land redistribution is based on the clearly regulated valuation of the developing land before and the building land after land readjustment.

Another equally important success factor of land readjustment in Germany is the independent land readjustment committee, which is solely responsible for all decisions and results of land readjustment. In order to prevent conflicts of interest and to achieve the full trust of the landowners, this temporary body is staffed with experts and politicians and is not bound to the municipality landowner.

Topical discussion of land readjustment

The topical discussion to the land readjustment in Germany concentrates upon the following statements:

- 'The acceptance of land readjustment requires a strictly limited deduction of land for public facilities which serve common purposes of the owners' (section 55 II BauGB).

The maximum deduction should consider, on the one hand, the fundamental private benefit principle of land readjustment, so that the new plot must have at least the same value like the old property. On the other hand, the proprietary guarantee according to article 14 of the constitution as well as the property preservation principle of the land readjustment has to be taken into account. Therefore, deduction of land for infrastructure facilities must stand in an adequate relation to the advantages of the land readjustment. Hence, land deductions of more than 50 percent might be problematic.

- 'The land contribution taken from the landowners to compensate the land readjustment advantage must serve public interests.'

First of all, it must be stated that the choice of redistribution scale has to be justified by legal arguments and cannot by determined only by economic reasons. Objective decision criteria are expediency and legality. The area scale is legitimated, for example, if there is a considerable demand for land for social housing or for social infrastructure. The decision must be motivated by such public reasons and interests and cannot be justified by financial interests of the municipality.

- 'Under the umbrella of a mandatory land readjustment, arrangements and urban contracts with the landowners are also possible.'

The land readjustment law in Germany is flexible enough to allow arrangements with the owners under the umbrella of a mandatory land readjustment. Such urban contracts require the willingness of all partners to cooperate and accept the arrangement because of the win-win situation for all actors. The following arrangements have proved their worth: divergent redistribution scale, 100 percent bearing of the cost for planning, public infrastructure facilities, and necessary public amenities. An additional deduction of land for affordable housing can also play a central role, as well as types of renewal energy and construction obligations. In the end, with the so-called conjoint mandatory land readjustment, the arrangements are integrated into the land readjustment plan, so that no land transfer taxes and other public fees occur. Furthermore, there is an advantage in time and steadiness compared with a voluntary land readjustment, because the new legal property situation takes place immediately after the legal validity of the land readjustment plan.

- 'From the view of the landowners the mandatory land readjustment in some cases has objective advantages compared with a voluntary land readjustment.'

In particular, the mandatory land readjustment results in a significant reduction in the development time of land against a voluntary land readjustment if the number of owners is high and the interests are very inhomogeneous. Furthermore, it reduces the risk of a blockade by noncooperative owners. Finally it is also a fact, that it is quicker for the transfer of ownership to take place by means of the land readjustment plan, rather than by registering the new owner in the land register,

A mandatory land readjustment provides not only the necessary areas for public infrastructure facilities, but also condenses the municipal task of the development into a development duty, so that the roads and other public facilities are built shortly after the close of the land readjustment.

Costs also play a central role within the comparison. Compared with a voluntary land readjustment, there is no cost saving in a mandatory land readjustment if the property valuation is done in a proper way. The amount of the land readjustment advantage, which is taken by the municipality, is not less than the sum of charges in a voluntary land readjustment for measurement fees, notary public fees, consultant cost, land register fees, land transfer taxes, and management costs.

- 'There is no fundamental priority of voluntary land readjustment over a mandatory land readjustment.'

A land readjustment can be completely operated on the basis of an urban contract according to § 11 BauGB, which must be officially notarized. Usual arrangements comprise the agreement of all landowners and the municipality with the allocation of the new plots, the land values, the provision of land for public infrastructure facilities, with the 100 percent private cost bearing, and so forth. Such a voluntary land readjustment replaces mandatory procedure with all its regulations.

Voluntary land adjustment does have priority over mandatory land readjustment if there is already total cooperation between all landowners, land-rights-owners, and the municipality. The municipality cannot reject a voluntary land readjustment when a reasonable offer of the owners is given even if it could tax away the land readjustment advantage in money and/or in area in a mandatory procedure. Furthermore, the equal treatment of all owners must be guaranteed and the legally binding land use plan should be given for reasons of the legal security and realized in a proper way. Hence, in practice the voluntary land readjustment is limited to simple cases with homogeneous interests and few landowners.

In this context, it should be pointed out that the latest land readjustment in 2001 has expressly not qualified as expropriation by the Federal Constitutional Court. The land readjustment is legally classified as an instrument that primary serves to preserve private property and balance private interests.

Future relevance of land readjustment as an instrument efficient land use

The future relevance of land readjustment in Germany should be discussed with a view to a worsening target conflict. On the one hand, a sustainable spatial development might be forced to limit the further consumption of the resource land, and on the other hand, there is obviously an increasing demand of land for settlement and traffic purposes in growing metropolitan regions. This topic should be discussed relevant to the following theses.

- Thesis 1: The land readjustment in combination with the planning authority of the towns and municipalities will be necessary in the future to reach a social-appropriate land use and a fair balancing of interests.

Due to the necessities of each town, urban planning leads to accidental advantages and disadvantages for individual landowners. Land readjustment balances private interests, and it is therefore a permanent task to increase the acceptance of planning by the owners. For a demand-oriented supply with affordable housing, for the appropriate allocation of development costs as well as other demands on the use of land, the land readjustment makes an essential contribution that can be improved by cooperative arrangements. The municipality can gain cooperation and conclude contracts of the landowners through the targeted application of its planning authority.

- Thesis 2: Sustainable urban development needs the land policy instrument land readjustment.

The efficient use of land is seen as the epitome of sustainable spatial development. A land readjustment procedure allows a sparing and careful use of the limited resource land from an ecological point of view, and at the same time it ensures economically bearing and socially appropriate land use.

Land readjustment can contribute to these goals in urban infill development as well as in greenfield development.

- Thesis 3: For municipalities, an effective land policy instrument of enforcement will be indispensable in the future.

With the mandatory land readjustment according to Federal Building Code, the municipality has a land policy instrument, which allows it to strictly plan and to realize the objectives of urban development. The procedure can also be applied in other cases, for example, if not all owners are willing to cooperate. Additionally, numerous instruments exist for safeguarding the land readjustment that allow provisions for resolving individual blockades in order to satisfy the interests of the overwhelming number of landowners.

In the land readjustment plan, further stipulations can be included for the timely realization of the binding land use plan, especially building commitments, as long as the prerequisites are met. Meanwhile, a comprehensive and well-established jurisprudence is available on all disputes concerning the implementation, so that the procedures can be carried out in a legally secure manner.

- Thesis 4: The land readjustment corresponds with modern governance.

The land readjustment is executed by a specific land readjustment committee that does not belong to municipal administration, is not obliged by instructions from the municipality, and is filled with experts from the various relevant areas and representatives of politics. It can, therefore, act and decide on the interests of the landowners. This institutional and professional sovereignty leads to a high acceptance of the land readjustment committee.

The mandatory land readjustment is a constitutional procedure that ensures the rights of the parties on a large scale. On the one hand, there is intensive participation of the owners in the sense of information, consultation, and cooperation in all decision-making procedures. On the other hand, the owners have legal protection, and all administrative acts are open to the courts. A crucial point is that all forms of cooperation have priority over mandatory acts or can be combined. This flexibility makes land readjustment an appropriate instrument of modern urban governance.

The excellent analysis of the urban land market in Portugal done by Condessa et al. clearly shows the need for an effective and efficient instrument of land management to improve the procedure of urban land development. In order to achieve a successful urban development and at the same time to preserve public interests and to balance private interests, it seems to be useful to close the gap after the urban planning procedure by using an instrument such as land readjustment that has just been introduced.

A Dutch perspective on land readjustment: low practicability without mandatory legislation

Sanne Holtslag-Broekhof

Urban land readjustment in the Netherlands

In the Netherlands, land readjustment is perceived as the urban counterpart of land consolidation. While land consolidation has been used since 1916 to improve the agrarian parcel structure, and to realise spatial planning tasks in the rural areas, land readjustment has only been used scarcely. Just like land consolidation, land readjustment can help to realise spatial plans by exchanging ownership rights on land and buildings.

Traditionally, Dutch urban planning developments were primarily greenfield developments. These developments were often initiated by public institutions that acquired all property, serviced the land, developed it into buildable plots, and sold the buildable plots to developers. This approach enables the smooth readjustment of the parcels and is known as 'active land policy' (Needham 1997; Buitelaar 2008). Active land policy was used by Dutch public institutions to maintain control on spatial developments and to ensure the quality of the environment. Moreover, active land policy was attractive for its financial profits (Buitelaar 2008). To acquire land, public institutions have the ability to use voluntary purchase transactions, expropriation, or pre-emption rights, and to share the costs of land development (*kostenverhaal*).

Despite the diversity of land policy instruments to acquire land, a debate on the effectiveness of land readjustment and the necessity to introduce a land readjustment act has been going on. Since the economic crisis in 2008, decreasing financial means for urban renewal, a political desire to take a more facilitative role in urban developments, and the increasing number of planning tasks in urban areas all added to the current demand for new legislation on land readjustment. In 2015, the Dutch minister declared a plan to implement a new act for land readjustment in 2018. The design of the act was published for public consultation during the summer of 2016.

Land readjustment can enable area development by bringing owners who are willing to develop into position for development. The original landowners form the basis of the renewal process. An important principle of land readjustment is that none of the involved owners loses due to the readjustment process. In Portugal, the development benefits and costs are shared over all participants according to their initial contributions. In the Netherlands, there is no legislation that prescribes the share of the costs and benefits of land readjustment. The benefits and costs should therefore be divided according to the participants' own principles, as long as they all agree to these principles. Mostly, the costs and financial risks are for those who gain from the development. The land consolidation act determines that the costs of the consolidation are shared among the participants according to the usage they will have from the new parcel structure (*nut*). Land readjustment processes are generally based on public renewal tasks (i.e. the regeneration of a city centre, the renewal of a business district, or the modernisation of an urban district). Just as in Portugal, the readjustment process can be initiated and led by either the municipality or by private landowners. Because the land readjustment needs to be implemented on a voluntary basis, the readjustment usually consists of several cycles in which all owners share their personal wishes regarding their property. A readjustment plan – including the new parcel structure and the new landowners – is drawn up based on these wishes and the general renewal plans for the area. After the readjustment plan is made, the participants have the opportunity to respond and the plan may then need to be adapted based on their responses. This continues until all participants agree upon the readjustment plan. To prevent debate on the readjustment plan, prior to this cyclic process, principles for the plan may be established by all participants together.

Urban land readjustment as instrument for dealing with scarcity of land?

Today's Dutch land readjustment projects are located in different planning contexts, including business areas, housing, centre areas, recreation parks, and business districts. Most of the planning tasks are related to either restructuring or depopulation problems. Especially during these tasks, the use of existing land policy instruments can be risky and expensive. Restructuring tasks have always been complex and financially unattractive, but were in the past often financed by public subsidies or from the financial profits in greenfield developments. In the current circumstances, where these profits and subsidies do not exist, restructuring has become an increasingly complex task for municipalities. Depopulation tasks have been absent in Dutch planning due to yearlong population growth. This has resulted in planning tasks that mainly included urban growth, rather than renewal and regeneration tasks.

Hence, in the Netherlands, land readjustment is perceived as an instrument that may be useful in situations of vacancy, where the opposite of land scarcity is at stake.

In a small country with 17 million inhabitants, land scarcity is eminent to Dutch planners. Land scarcity is related to situations in which growth is desired, but the land available for this growth is scarce. In this context, developments are financially profitable, which makes the Dutch approach of active land policy again suitable. A Dutch approach that has been used frequently in situations of growth and fragmented landownership is public-private partnership. Within this approach, the formation of a development company can be argued to be a type of land readjustment. The development company is established to enable a smooth development and to share the risks, costs, and profits among two or more (public and private) parties. The parties may choose to bring their property into the development company and receive in return a share of stock in the company. This solves the problem of fragmented ownership and enables the share of financial risks. In the basis, the approach is very similar to the principles of land readjustment. However, there is one important difference: small private owners are never part of a development company and will always be acquired by one of the professional development companies or the government. This makes the process more practicable, but less democratic. Moreover, the process still starts with a traditional active land policy in which a few parties acquire land in an area. The financial risk is spread among this small group of developers (and often the municipality) but can still be considerable. Land readjustment could be an interesting alternative in which the financial risk and the financial profits would be shared among all initial landowners. However, it is questionable whether this approach will be used voluntarily by private development companies, as it would not only imply a division of the risk, but also a division of the profits.

Urban land readjustment: high legitimacy, low practicability

The current perception of the necessity for land readjustment mainly results from the current economic and political situation that does not allow public institutions to use active land policy. Municipalities are often not able to make the financial investment for land acquisition. Moreover, they are politically unwilling to take an active and risk-bearing role in the development. This implies that the main demand for a land readjustment act lays in its ability to share financial costs, gains, and risks, to effectively relocate owners and reshape parcels, and to decrease the development costs that occur during active land acquisition. The rationale for land readjustment is thus largely related to finances and to property relocation.

Because land readjustment is only starting to get explored, there are only a few complete examples of land readjustment. The following discussion on the effectiveness, efficiency, practicability, and legitimacy of land readjustment is based on the experiences in two finished land readjustment projects and the theoretical expectations on the instrument based on various experiences in pilot projects and simulation games.

The effectiveness of land readjustment is related to the realisation of the planning task. The content of the planning task obviously differs from case to case. Affecting the behaviour of the owners is a central element of the land readjustment instrument. As all interests are taken into account in the plan development during a land readjustment process, the attitude of the owners is in generally positive. The outcome of the readjustment process is more difficult to judge without real-life success stories. The question that is at stake here is whether the new property situation enables the realisation of the new plan. Currently it is difficult to determine whether the instrument will be more effective than other land policy instruments in urban renewal tasks. Overall the judgement on the effectiveness of land readjustment depends on its legal status. In order to be effective, all owners need to come to a voluntary agreement, which is often challenging. In rural areas this problem has been solved by legislation that enables compulsory consolidation if the majority of the owners agree with the plan and the plan serves the public gain. Currently, in urban areas, the only way to deal with landowners who are unwilling to cooperate in a land readjustment process is either to exclude them from the plan or to expropriate them. The exclusion of unwilling landowners may lead to a low effectivity, while an expropriation may lead to a low efficiency due to high costs.

The desire to develop with lower costs is an important argument in many projects to use land readjustment. This can be linked to the efficiency of land readjustment. According to the theory, land readjustment is more efficient than active land acquisition, as the costs of land acquisition can be saved and the effect would be equal. However, there is debate over the time frame of land readjustment and the costs the readjustment process incurs. If these costs are higher than the costs for land acquisition, land readjustment may be less efficient than its traditional counterpart.

The difficulties in land readjustment processes, past and present, may have to do with the practicability of land readjustment. The success of land readjustment depends on a good process, and this process increasingly lacks public actors. As there is no regulation on land readjustment, participants are left with many issues that need to be debated during the process, including the following: How do we organise ourselves? How do we ensure a democratic process? How do we divide the costs and profits? How much money do we have to invest? How do we ensure that all other owners keep their promises? Although there are answers to all of these questions in theory, there are no general rules that enforce the owners to work according to a certain approach. Therefore, all of these questions have to be dealt with in each project anew. This makes land readjustment a challenging process and not very easy to implement in practice. However, there may also be difficult factors inherent to all urban renewal tasks, such as fragmented landownership, numerous small land parcels, landowners' diverse interests, a high building density, polluted land, and mixed land uses.

The expected added value of land readjustment is mainly related to the distributional justice and democratic legitimacy of the method. Openness and transparency on both the finances and the division of interests, costs, and gains of the plans are expected to enable the democratic legitimacy, while a structural, proportional, and objective division of costs and gains should ensure the distributional justice of the method. Land readjustment is valued by its ability to enable bottom-up development that are initiated by the owners and facilitated by public parties. In contrast to the planning procedure during land acquisition and expropriation, landowners have a say on the development plan and can insert their own interest in the planning process. Moreover, land readjustment enables not only the equal division of cost and gains, but also the division of financial risks of urban developments, which is often seen as an important advantage compared to land acquisition.

References

Botman, J. J. (1984) *Stedelijke Herverkaveling Folkingestraat*, Bouwcentrum, Bureau voor onderzoek en beleidsadvisering, Literatuuroverzicht, Raad van Advies voor de Ruimtelijke Ordening, Centraal punt inspraak, 10(4), 35–38.

Bregman, A. and De Wolff, H. (2011) *Herverkaveling op ontwikkelingslocaties*, Onderzoeksinstituut OTB, Technical University Delft, Instituut voor Bouwrecht, Delft, 104.

Buitelaar, E., Segeren, A. and Kronberger, P. (2008) *Stedelijke Transformatie en Grondeigendom*, NAI Uitgevers and PBL, The Hague.

Needham, B. (1997) Land policy in the Netherlands, *Tijdscrift voor Economische en Sociale Geografie*, 88(3), 291–296.

10 Building obligations in Switzerland

Overcoming the passivity of plan implementation

Andreas Hengstermann

The building land paradox

Two points of view that, at first, seem paradoxical can be identified in discussions about spatial development in Switzerland. Some demand a reduction of the building zone, claiming that too much land is zoned. Others, however, demand an extension of the building zone, claiming that there is a lack of building land. In this case, there is more to those conflicting statements than mere different political viewpoints or an uneven distribution. They derive from a fundamental dilemma of spatial development that, as a public policy, defines the framework of expedient and lawful structural development, but whose implementation depends on the landowners.

At first it seems as if only a small part of the land is actually structurally developed. The land use statistics designate only 7.5 percent of the entire national territory of 41,284 square kilometers as settlement area (BfS 2013: 6, 7). However, the topographic conditions of Switzerland have not yet been taken into consideration here. Altogether, 10,458 square kilometers are considered not amenable for settlement (BfS 2013: 21). Of the land and forest areas, 4,385 square kilometers are protected as agricultural land, and 12,930 square kilometers are protected as forest (BfS 2013: 14, 17). Based on these numbers, the current settlements take up approximately one-third of the area amenable for settlement already.

At present, the actual building zone covers approximately 2,200 square kilometers, 27 percent of which is structurally undeveloped (ARE 2005: 33).[1] Thus by means of new construction in the existing building zone alone, housing for 2.5 million people can be created (ARE 2005: 37) – not taking into consideration the additional settlement densification of areas that do not exhaust the respective permitted utilisation. Therefore, the anticipated demand for building land is quantitatively secured until 2045, even in the event of the highest expected population growth scenario (ARE 2005: 33–37, combined with BfS 2015). These findings must be put into perspective if the distribution of building land reserves is taken into consideration – but it does not have to be reversed. Even in those regions where the demand for building land is high, building land reserves totalling from 12 percent (canton of Schwyz) to 18 percent (Agglomeration Fribourg) can be observed (Projekt RaumPLUS, published in Nebel 2014). So while the building zone is very large and often not structurally developed, there is a shortage of available building land. This excess demand leads to a steady increase in land prices.

For spatial development, these numbers pose a legitimacy problem. Since 1969, the Federal Constitution (BV) has been naming the economic use of land and its properly ordered settlement as its two primary goals (art. 75 BV), thereby establishing the legitimacy of extensive planning interference with the landowners' principal freedom to build. The main means of reaching both aims thereby is the principle of separability that, for each square meter, reviews if the land may be built on – or not.

From an institutional perspective, the cause of this paradoxical situation lies in the one-dimensional structure of the planning system. The classical planning instruments (most notably the land use plans) are not effective since they only regulate the rights of use of land property. They make offers to owners who are willing to invest but they do not actively control structural development (Dieterich 1983: 43). The level of property title remains untouched.[2] This means that spatial planning provides a framework for the landowner including provisions concerning the exercise of the freedom to build, but there is no building obligation. Planning, however, has to assume that the land is used entirely and consequently has to, for instance, measure dimension for the infrastructural development accordingly. While the landowners are faced with hardly any expenses for land property and can even directly capitalise the added value resulting from planning (for instance by means of mortgage), a chain of negative external effects is created. The municipalities are pressured into extending the building zone at the cost of agricultural land and into developing further land at a high cost to meet the building needs and to stifle the price development in the land and housing market. Under these circumstances, an extension of the building zone is not in the interest of the planning aims and has been prohibited since the partial revision of the Spatial Planning Act (SPA) in 2012. The affected municipalities therefore find themselves in a paradoxical situation in which, in theory, there is too much building land that may not be extended, while, in fact, there is too little building land that is effectively available. Therefore, it is possible to talk about the building land paradox (Davy 2000), a situation in which oversupply and undersupply coexist at the same time. The partial revision of 2012 tackles this problem by taking into consideration and promoting the availability of building land. One of the instruments designated for doing so is the building obligation.

Building obligation as an instrument of active land policy

All government decisions and measures that influence the use and distribution of land are considered part of the land policy. This very passive and extensive definition can be narrowed down. Active land policy only encompasses such government decisions and measures that actually intend to change use and distribution of land in order to implement the respective spatial development goals (Hengstermann and Gerber 2015). If spatial planning is understood as the public policies aimed at influencing type and degree of building and land use, only the land use rights, not the underlying property title, are influenced and taken into consideration. Besides, spatial planning, in the context of negative planning, is directed at avoiding undesirable developments (i.e. excessive development of agricultural land, unorderly settlement of the land), while land policy, in the context of active, positive planning, is directed towards the actual implementation of spatial development goals (i.e. high-quality inward settlement development, provision of socially fair housing).

Hence, the building obligation is an instrument that can be applied in the field of land policy. It is generally understood as a state intervention that creates either the sovereign or contractual obligation for landowners to use the land as building land within a certain period of time (Antoniazza 2008: 21–25) (also with different other and further subordinate definitions). Because of its effect mechanism, it can be used by planning authorities to liberate the realisation of the democratically determined spatial development goals (i.e. a compact settlement development) from the dependence on an individual landowner's decision.

Instrument sui generis between freedom to build and realisation of planning aims

The building obligation per se extensively interferes with the property guarantee. Even more so, the building obligation constitutes an unusual change to the property regime (Müller 1989: 173) that is particularly outstanding because Swiss law, besides the usual type of right of use, hardly knows any obligations to use. The building obligation is therefore a tool *sui generis* between the freedom to build and public planning aims. What is open to question is whether the fundamental right of freedom to build also unrestrictedly covers the freedom of nonutilisation or whether a restriction of property title can be applied, meaning that the right of nonutilisation ends if there are considerable consequences for the general public (unnecessary loss of agricultural land, unused connection to infrastructure and utilities) or private third parties (artificial lack of building land, high housing costs). Assessing this poses the biggest legal challenge of the instrument of building obligation. So far, this question has remained unanswered by the law and has not been reviewed by the Supreme Court. The Federal Supreme Court has so far merely emphasised that obligations to perform are classed among the title restrictions and that the building obligation can be applied for the sake of mobilisation of building land (Antoniazza 2008: 26, with reference to BGE 97 I 792, 795 and BGE 103 Ib 318, 326). The Federal Supreme Court has not yet assessed the proportionality in any concrete case.

Köhler believes that a building obligation has an expropriatory meaning but, contrary to expropriation, does not aim at revoking property but rather at making the owner use the owned land. Regarding the respective plot of land, it is not an interference similar to expropriation, but rather an administrative concretisation of the social obligation of property (1985: 17). Furthermore, he states that instruments like the building obligation come into consideration as suitable instruments for the municipalities to implement aims of planning and are essentially enforceable (1985: 110). Dieterich also brings forward the argument that a building obligation lies within the social responsibility of property, particularly in view of the fact that neither assets nor land are withdrawn but rather there is an increase in monetary value (1983: 45–46), evoking thoughts about the 'mandatory happiness' tool of land readjustment (Davy 2007). Therefore, a general disproportionality cannot be claimed (Müller 1989: 180) but rather depends on the specific situation (also for many other legal statements) (Antoniazza 2008: 26, 27). In areas characterised by a high demand, the instrument seems to be a suitable additional measure to realise high-density buildings at favourable locations. A further application of the building obligation, in areas not characterised by a high demand, would send wrong signals and would pose a breach of property guarantee (Antoniazza 2008: 227). The Federal Council agrees with this opinion and, besides proportionality and the predominant public interest, stresses that the building obligation has been created as a supporting instrument and that a comprehensive application is not planned. Under these circumstances, such an obligation serves the public interest of using the land efficiently and restricting land hoarding, and the Federal Council believes that the constitutional requirements for the interference with property guarantee are thereby met. The weighing of public interest in structural development and the constitutionally protected property guarantee can also be performed more precisely by means of a graduated formulation of legal consequences. In the event of a 'normal' lack of building land, fiscal measures should suffice. However, if there is an extraordinary interest in structurally developing certain building land reserves, cantonal law also has to include legal consequences that are suitable for enforcing structural development in the event that the land remains unused after a certain period of time (Federal Council Dispatch 2010: 1077).

Definition of legal consequences as a precondition of applicability

The setting of a certain period of time within which the land has to be structurally developed can be connected to different legal consequences in the case of noncompliance. Fiscal measures (directly by means of fines, indirectly by means of temporally graded betterment compensation), planning measures (de-zoning, non-zoning), and finally property measures (purchase right, expropriation) can be imposed. The construction and the principal applicability of this legal consequence are of utmost importance, as a comparison to the German planning and building law (section 176 BauGB) clearly shows. The provisions of this law concerning the building order and expropriation are not a graded, but rather a parallel procedure with distinct requirements and legal consequences (Stüer 1988: 37; Rothe 1986: 125 and also Federal Administrative Court judgement of 15.2.1990–4 C 41/87 published in NVwZ 1990: 658). Therefore, no possible sanctions beyond the general and applicable expropriation law arise from the German building order (Lücke 1980: 37, similarly Rothe 1986: 125–126). That is one of the reasons the German building order has hardly been practically applied in planning since its introduction in 1971 (Schäfer 1983: 22–27, 55; Lücke 1980: 2; Lobeck et al. 2006: 14) and frequently is referred to sceptically as a blunt sword (Stüer 1988: 337) or *lex imperfecta* (Lücke 1980: 37). Because of the close connection to the expropriation instrument, the instrument discussed in Switzerland more closely resembles the Vienna Building Code (§ 43 par. 5 BO) rather than the German building order.

Therefore, an applicable legal consequence must be integrated into the construction of the building obligation in Swiss Planning Law, even if it is the aim to reach the goals without its actual application (Schlichter 1993: 353, or as a concrete example, Menghini 2012: 10). The principal effect of the building obligation does not depend on the *actual application* but merely on the *applicability*, which, however, also includes an effective legal consequence (Dieterich 1983: 45, 49; Rothe 1986: 124–127; Schlichter 1993: 365–370 and many others). It can be applied by authorities as an indirect instrument to show the landowners that land is not a normal asset and that spatial development cannot entirely depend on the landowners' will (Müller 1989: 180–181). In the hands of a decisive municipality, the building obligation can become a practicable and usefully applicable instrument to achieve visible successes within a short period of time (Schlichter 1993: 375). However, concrete examples from communal practice are rare.

Legal development of the building obligation

When the revised Spatial Planning Act came into force, the building obligation received nationwide attention – and is thereby wrongly considered a new instrument. This mechanism was already included in the first draft of the Swiss Spatial Planning Act in 1974. The expropriation article (art. 35 SPA-1974) mentions an appropriate, officially ordered period of time as one requirement (par. 2). In addition to the rights, this also expressed the obligations of the landowners and was aimed at making sure that individual owners could not make the realisation of land use plans impossible. A referendum started by the *Ligue vaudoise* and the *Centre patronal vaudois*, supported by the Swiss Trade Association, was held against the law (and against this extensive expropriation article in particular) and the law was rejected by the people of Switzerland in June 1976 (48.9 percent voted yes).

Consequently, the Federal Council revised and edited the law and in particular the expropriation article massively. The officially ordered period of time was entirely removed (art. 5 par. 2 SPA-1979). The new, less tight version of the law was then passed by the Federal Assembly and came into force after the referendum obligation in January 1980. This means that the building obligation has not been integrated into the effective planning law at the federal level.

As a framework law, however, the Spatial Planning Act allows the cantons to pass further regulations in their own legislation. At least eight cantons have made use of this possibility and have passed provisions that include a building obligation or similar mechanisms. These provisions differ in significant respects, especially regarding the possible application scenarios and the legal consequence. Certain regulations only affect new zoning (Solothurn, Uri, Aargau, Fribourg) while others also apply within the existing building zone (Obwald, Neuchâtel, Appenzell Ausserrhoden, Grisons). The legal consequence is either de-zoning without compensation (Solothurn, Uri, Aargau), the reversal of zoning (non-zoning; Aargau, Fribourg) or the right to expropriate (Neuchâtel, Obwald, indirectly also Grisons). In the first two cases, an incentive to structurally develop the land is created by the threat of individual damage. However, in the case of noncompliance with the building obligation and the execution of this legal consequence, the public interest has not been reached. In fact, the opposite is the case: the desired compact settlement structure would not be reached in the new zone structure. Therefore, such a legal consequence does not work in accordance with the realisation of aims, which is why the proportionality and consequently the legitimacy have to be severely doubted. As a result, the Neuchâtel, the Obwald, and (indirectly) also the Grisons act differently. There, the regulations do not focus on penalisation but on the realisation of aims. For this purpose, authorities are granted the right to take, and this expropriation of property is to be compensated at full market value.

With reference to the cantonal experiences, among others, the instrument of building obligation was also rediscovered on the federal level. In 2008, the Federal Council presented a draft of a Federal Act on Spatial Development (SDA). The law was supposed to act as a total revision of the previous Spatial Planning Act and to also convey that with a new title. One explicit aim of this revision was to address the issue of land hoarding. A whole chapter, which also included the instrument of building obligation, was dedicated to the availability of building land. However, the Spatial Development Act draft proved not to be fully developed and was therefore rejected and dismissed by all political camps.

Instead, a draft for a partial revision of the Spatial Planning Act was presented in 2010 and passed by the Federal Assembly in 2012. The Swiss Trade Association called for a referendum against the new law and once again, the people of Switzerland had to vote on the Spatial Planning Act.

In March 2013, the law was passed with 62.9 percent at the ballot and came into force on 1 May 2014. The entire article concerning the building obligation is no longer included in this partial revision. Nonetheless, this mechanism has been integrated into the new, now applicable law in two different places and can be referred to as *actual* (art. 15) and *explicit building obligation* (art. 15a).

The conditions for the extension of the building zone include a small, but relevant change. In the old regulation, building zones encompassed those parts of land that will 'probably be needed and developed within 15 years' (art. 15 lit. b SPA-1979; own translation). According to the new regulation, land that 'will probably be needed, developed and *structurally developed* within 15 years' can be assigned to the building zone (art. 15 par. 4 lit. c SPA-2012; own translation; emphasis added). The addition of actual structural development makes an important difference. In the future, municipal planning authorities will have to legally secure actual structural development within 15 years already at possible assignment to the building zone. This makes the regulation similar to a deadline for structural development that is directly applicable and results in a withdrawal of zoning without compensation as a direct legal consequence in the event of noncompliance. With this little addition, the revised Spatial Planning Act has introduced an *actual building obligation* for the extension of the building zone.

In addition, the building obligation is also explicitly mentioned in the new article for the promotion of availability of building land (art. 15a SPA) in the revised Spatial Planning Act. The construction as a distinct article leads to the applicability of the regulations also on existing building zones. However, in comparison to the Spatial Development Act draft, the volume of regulations is a lot more limited and refers to the cantonal level in important aspects (Federal Council Dispatch 2010: 1076), which also leads to a relocation of political struggles.

Cantonal law allows for the responsible authority to set a deadline for structural development of a plot of land if this is justifiable based on public interest and, if this deadline passes and no structural development has taken place, the responsible authority undertakes certain measures (art. 15a par. 2 SPA-2012). The regulation includes two levels with different addressees. On the first level, the cantons are obligated to introduce a deadline instrument for structural development. On the second level, the municipal authorities are enabled to apply this instrument. The exact procedural steps and particularly the legal consequence in the event of nonperformance have to be determined first on a cantonal level before there is applicability.

Nonetheless, the instrument is introduced on the federal level by means of the partial revision – for new zoning as well as within the existing building zone. Onsite experiences will reveal the effects of this instrument in planning practice.

Experiences from the case example *Rothenbrunnen*

Embedding a building obligation into planning law does not necessarily mean a change in planning practice, which the German building order (which was introduced in 1971 and has hardly ever been applied), proves. It seems worthwhile to study a case example, and the one chosen for the purpose of this chapter is an example from Grisons. There, the law allows regulations that are subject to public law and do not require the owners' consent, which can also apply within the existing building zone and whose legal consequence is not restricted to automatic de-zoning (which is not desirable planning-wise). The municipality Rothenbrunnen has the most experience with the instrument in the canton of Grisons and was therefore chosen as an informative case example (see more detailed Hengstermann and Gerber 2017).

Municipal planning revision of 2010 as context

Rothenbrunnen is a small municipality with about 310 inhabitants in the Domleschg subdistrict in the canton of Grisons. In 2006, the total revision of municipal planning dating back to 1991 was initiated according to regular schedule. The defined aim of this revision was to achieve a steady population growth to reach 400 inhabitants, with a preference for families (Rothenbrunnen 2009: 7, 18; Menghini 2012: 8, 9). The rationale was to prevent the closure of rural infrastructure and local trade and to thereby keep the village alive. The municipality's official stated that if the envisioned development could not be realised, the municipality was at risk of collapse because school, kindergarten, the village restaurant, post office, and so forth might have to be closed down, which would hugely reduce the attractiveness of the municipality (Rothenbrunnen 2009: 9, 10).

By means of a simple trend calculation based on the aforementioned growth goal, the municipality deducted a building land demand of 1.4 to 1.5 hectares. The initial plan to generate this building land by means of an extension of the building zone was rejected by the canton in the course of the preliminary examination. The canton remarked that the envisaged growth was unrealistic and that the region would find itself confronted with a period of negative growth (Rothenbrunnen 2009: 9, 10). In addition, the canton remarked that sufficient space was available in the existing building zone and that that space needed to be mobilised first of all (ibid.). The municipality, however, decided to further pursue its aim, thinking that the aforementioned negative population forecast was not a determining factor for the municipality but rather a motivation to counteract the negative trend (Rothenbrunnen 2009: 9). But the growth had to happen within the existing building zone. The analysis of the building zones by an external planning office confirmed the canton's assessment that no extension of the building zone would be necessary (Menghini 2012: 8, 9). A total of 1.38 hectares of the residential zone that covers 6.4 hectares (about 22 percent of the area) is structurally undeveloped.

The predicted demand for building land (1.4 to 1.5 hectares) and the existing building land reserve (1.38 hectares) are nearly congruent in Rothenbrunnen. However, that reserve is hardly available (Rothenbrunnen 2009: 7), which leads to a building zone paradox. The lack of effectively available building land reserve makes the envisaged growth and the desired allocation to young families aimed at securing the rural infrastructure impossible. The general spatial development of the municipality and the realisation of planning aims therefore depend on the intentions of the individual landowners and are consequently, to a certain extent, 'heteronomous' (Rothenbrunnen 2009: 18).

To resolve this difficult situation, the municipal council openly threatened to de-zone the respective areas, explaining that 'existing building land reserves should principally only remain in the building zone if they are attractive and available' (Rothenbrunnen 2009: 8). A possible compensation was to be financed by means of betterment compensation of the areas zoned instead. The affected landowners opposed, whereby besides the fundamental argument ('My land must not be de-zoned') the abutters' individual interests (obstruction of view, expected increase in traffic) played a major role as well (Rothenbrunnen 2009: 11). At the municipal assembly, which was attended by two-thirds of the inhabitants, a broad coalition prevented a change to the building zone and, instead, the municipal council was assigned the task of implementing innovative and effective instruments to secure the areas in the existing building zone (Rothenbrunnen 2009: 14–16). The municipal council consequently decided to establish an active land policy and to adjust the building law accordingly. The instrument of building obligation was introduced as a central element. This was explicitly welcomed and not questioned at the municipal assembly (Rothenbrunnen 2009: 13) and the canton also regarded this tool as suitable, necessary, and proportional (ARE GR 2010: 4–14; Menghini 2012: 9).

Legal implementation of the building obligation in municipal building law

Since the revision of 2005, the planning law of Grisons has been prompting all municipalities to pursue active land and building land policies that are adjusted to the local conditions to promote the realisation of municipal planning aims (art. 19 KRG GR). This also encompasses the availability of building land. The cantonal law states that 'the municipalities take the necessary measures to ensure the availability of land for the designated zone purpose, in particular when it comes to zoning and re-zoning' (art. 19 par. 2 KRG GR; own translation). It seems that the instrument of building obligation is not included in this regulation and additionally, it only refers to the extension of the building zone. The wording *in particular*, however, also makes other approaches and applications possible. In reference to this open wording, the municipality Rothenbrunnen has developed a concrete form of the building obligation and has incorporated it into municipal building law as art. 22.

The content of the regulation provides for a multilevel procedure with various weighings of interest. First of all, it states that the building obligation does not automatically apply to the entire municipal area. Instead, the areas within the building zone that have to be secured as available building land will be marked in the zoning plan (par. 1). The municipality is granted the right to purchase these areas should the owners not sell or structurally develop them (par. 2). Legally, this right to purchase corresponds to an expropriation, but the municipal council has chosen a euphemism for political reasons.

The procedure in Rothenbrunnen provides for a two-level weighing of interests. First, it has to generally be weighed in which area the provision of the building obligation can be applied. This weighing is legitimised democratically at the ballot. Based on that, the municipality can order a deadline for structural development within two years, if the respective area has been part of the building zone for at least eight years and ready for structural development for five years and the demand for building land has to be confirmed. Additionally, another weighing of interests has to take place here, particularly focussing on the actual interests of the actual landowners. In case the conditions are met, the municipality can announce the takeover (par. 3). The area that has been taken over can then be taken over by the municipality at market value (par. 4) and can immediately be structurally developed (par. 5). A resale (with contractual building obligation with the new owner) is preferred, but not mandatory. This multilevel procedure aims at guaranteeing legitimacy and compliance, thereby politically enabling the applicability.

Actual experiences with the implementation

With the establishment of the building obligation in building law, 11 plots of land that fall within the regulation to secure the availability of building land according to art. 22 of the Building Law were recorded in the new zoning plan. All parcels of land had been connected to infrastructure and utilities: seven of them were immediately ready for structural development. For the other four, there existed a necessity for further planning (special land use plan obligation). Six years after the revision of the zoning plan, two of the seven parcels of land ready for structural development have still not been built on, four have been structurally developed, and one is currently being structurally developed – whereby a direct causal link between the structural development and selling activity and the building obligation cannot be proven without doubt. It is nonetheless noticeable that these activities temporarily followed the media reports on the building obligation. A formal deadline for structural development has not yet been ordered. The introduction of the instrument has raised the community's awareness of the social consequences of individual decisions, which created a pressure for justification (Menghini 2012: 11). In this respect it can be assumed that the awareness of the existence of the instrument alone had a psychological effect. The political opponents of this instrument (in particular the local liberal party and the Homeowner Association) only realised its scope after the appeal period and opposed it. However, there were no objections in cooperation with the concerned landowners.

Despite the introduction of this land policy measure, the superordinate aims of the municipal planning revision could not be reached. The additional structural development has not led to a growth in population because of demographic changes. Accordingly, the closure of the village shop, the post office, and the restaurant could not be avoided. Additionally, the loss of an important source of finance (the interest out of a local mineral water source) had a considerable impact on the municipal budget and has led to the decision to close the school as well. Finally, the political autonomy of the municipality is insecure, even though the threat of merger has so far been stopped at the ballot. After the introduction of the building obligation in Rothenbrunnen, further municipalities in the canton of Grisons (i.e. Flerden, Sils i.D., and Conters i.P.) have implemented this instrument in the municipal building law (Menghini 2012: 11).

Assessment of the building obligation as a land policy instrument

On a small scale, the example of Rothenbrunnen demonstrates a problem that undermines the legitimacy of spatial planning in all of Switzerland. What exists is a paradoxical situation in which the building zone is supersized while at the same time the demand for building land is not met. That means that both constitutional goals of spatial planning are not fulfilled. This paradox cannot merely be explained by means of a bad distribution of building land but is, on a small scale (like in the case example Rothenbrunnen), the result of a lack of effective availability of the building land. Spatial planning has not yet been able to solve this dilemma because its classical instruments primarily influence the land use rights without formulating the obligation to use the land and without taking into consideration the underlying property structures. Consequently, the realisation of the planning aims and public interests depends on the landowners' actions.

To resolve this dilemma, the revised Spatial Planning Act introduced the building obligation. Alongside future extension of the building zone, it has been mandated that land actually be structurally developed within 15 years, establishing a mandatory and directly applicable criterion that corresponds to a factual building obligation. In case of nonperformance, this precondition for the extension of the building zone shall be void and revoked ex post facto, whereby there is no entitlement to compensation. In addition, the building obligation has explicitly been introduced for the existing building zone, whereby this regulation at first requires a cantonal implementing law. The integral conflicts (in particular the question of legal consequence in case of nonperformance) have been re-located. According to Swiss law, the cantons are obligated to establish this instrument and the municipalities are authorised to apply it in a given case. The actual effectiveness of the tool can only be reviewed based on practical experiences in spatial planning.

The case example shows that the building obligation can be used by local planning authorities to increase the availability of building land. In Rothenbrunnen, the desired building and planning activities were performed without a deadline for structural development having actually been imposed, and the majority of the building land reserves has either been structurally developed or sold. This indirect effectiveness based on the mere existence of the building obligation and not its actual application shows that the instrument is highly effective. However, this does not mean that the attainment of the superordinate planning aims is guaranteed. In Rothenbrunnen, the pessimistic population prognosis of the canton turned out to be true, and the rural infrastructure could not be maintained.

Rothenbrunnen is a highly informative example for spatial planning. On the one hand, the building obligation is applicable to the existing building zone, according to the municipal building law and because it is subject to public law. On the other hand, a legal consequence – the right to take – that aims at the realisation of the planning aims is provided. According to public authorities, the risks involved are very restricted, even in case of the deadline for structural development actually being imposed and in case of an actual taking. The financial risk is low because of the aim of fast reselling, especially because an application in the event of a lack of demand is excluded, as in the model Rothenbrunnen. In the event of application, however, the high administrative effort (extensive obligations to provide proof and their likely judicial reviews) has to be taken into consideration, just like the temporal offset between imposing the regulation and it's becoming effective. This makes a land policy that focuses on the long-term even more important and the building obligation can therefore play an important, preventive role.

Legal concerns, in particular regarding a possible excessive invasion of the constitutional property guarantee, could not be proven in the case example, to which the well-rounded construction of the model Rothenbrunnen has definitely added. The two-level weighing of interests and the included consideration of the interests of the owners protect the fundamental private rights, whereby a confirmation of the federal court is still missing. At the same time, the interests of the public are satisfied as well. While so far there have hardly been any possibilities to guarantee the realisation of planning aims, now the dependence on the actions of the landowners is reduced and the planning system is becoming more balanced. The privileged position of the landowners to enjoy property rights is not excessively reduced, not even in extreme cases because of the possible full compensation. This is not only an important legal and political argument in the context of value guarantee. In planning terms, it also makes more sense to expropriate the land and to structurally develop it quickly rather than to de-zone it, which is the alternative, in which case compensation has to be paid as well and that leads to holes in the settlement structure. Additionally, focus on public interests has been significantly enhanced since the partial revision of the Spatial Planning Act and the therein included double consideration of both factual and explicit building obligation. The building obligation reflects a change of attitude concerning the property regime (Müller 1989: 180) and is a visible sign of a development away from passive land use planning towards active land policy.

Notes

1 For comparison, in Germany, 8–10.5 percent (in the urban context) or 12 percent (national average) of the building zone is structurally undeveloped (Lücke 1980: 1). In North-Rhine Westphalia alone, there is an available area of approximately 7,100 hectares (Lobeck et al. 2006: 5–7).

2 One remarkable exception is land readjustment (art. 20 SPA), which is hardly ever applied in Switzerland.

References

Antoniazza, Y. (2008) *Die Baupflicht*, Schulthess, Zürich.

ARE-GR (Regierungsbeschluss der Regierung des Kantons Graubünden) (2010) Protokoll Nr. 133 vom 23.2.2017. Online available via: https://www.gr.ch/_gemeindespiegel_docs/Rothenbrunnen_1_BD_Regierungsbeschluss.pdf

Bundesamt für Raumentwicklung (ARE) (2005) *Raumentwicklungsbericht 2005*, Bern.

Bundesamt für Statistik (BfS) (2013) *Die Bodennutzung in der Schweiz – Resultate der Arealstatistik*, Neuchâtel.

Bundesamt für Statistik (BfS) (2015) *Entwicklung der ständigen Wohnbevölkerung nach den 3 Grundszenarien*, Neuchâtel.

Davy, B. (2000) Das Bauland-Paradoxon: Wie planbar sind Bodenmärkte?, in: Einig, K. (ed.) *Regionale Koordination der Baulandausweisung*, VWF, Berlin, 61–78.

Davy, B. (2007) Mandatory happiness – Land readjustment and property in Germany, in: Yu-Hung, H. and Needham, B. (eds) *Analyzing land readjustment: Economics, law, and collective action*, Lincoln Institute of Land Policy, Cambridge, MA, 37–55.

Dieterich, H. (1983) Baugebot – ein Weg zur Bebauung erschlossener Baugrundstücke? *Städte- und Gemeindebund*, 2, 43–49.

Federal Council (2010) *Dispatch No. 10.019 from 19th January 2010 concerning the revision of the Spatial Planning Act*. BBl 2010 1049.

Hengstermann, A. and Gerber, J.-D. (2015) Aktive Bodenpolitik – Eine Auseinandersetzung vor dem Hintergrund der Revision des eidgenössischen Raumplanungsgesetzes, *Flächenmanagement und Bodenordnung (FuB)*, 2015(6), 241–250.

Hengstermann, A. and Gerber, J.-D. (2017) Die faktische und explizite Bauverpflichtung – eine Rezension des bodenpolitischen Instruments in Recht und Praxis, *Umwelt- und Planungsrecht (UPR)*, 37(1), 16–24.

Köhler, H. (1985) *Die Planverwirklichungsgebote als Instrument des Städtebaurechts*, Verlag Otto Schwartz, Göttingen.

Lobeck, M., Wiegandt, C. and Wiese-von Ofen, I. (2006) *Entwicklung von umsetzungsortientierten Handlungsschritten zur Mobilisierung von Baulücken und zur Erleichterung von Nutzungsänderungen im Bestand in Innenstädten NRWs*, Kurzfassung, Universität Bonn, Bonn.

Lücke, J. (1980) *Das Baugebot – Ein wirksames Instrument des Bodenrechts?* Verlag Franz Vahlen, Munich.

Menghini, O. (2012) Innovatives Modell zur Bekämpfung der Baulandhortung, *VLP-ASPAN InfoRaum*, 2012(3), 6–11.

Müller, G. (1989) Baupflicht und Eigentumsordnung, in: Haller, W., Müller, G., Kölz, A. and Thürer, D. (eds) *Festschrift für Ulrich Häfelin*, Schulthess Polygraphischer Verlag, Zürich, 167–181.

Nebel, R. (2014) *Siedlungsflächenmanagement Schweiz*, VDF, Zürich.

Rothe, K.-H. (1986) *Verwirklichung von Bebauungsplänen*, Bauverlag, Wiesbaden, Berlin.

Rothenbrunnen (2009) *Planungs- und Mitwirkungsbericht*, approved version, May 2009.

Rothenbrunnen (2010) *Zonenplan und Genereller Gestaltungsplan*, approved on 23 February 2010.

Schäfer, R. (1983) *Planverwicklichungsgebote in der kommunalen Praxis*, Deutsches Institut für Urbanistik.

Schlichter, O. (1993) Überlegungen zum Baugebot, in: Drieshaus, H.-J. and Birk, H.-J. (eds) *Festschrift für Felix Weyreuther*, Heymann Verlag, Köln Berlin, 349–375.

Stüer, B. (1988) Baugebot nach § 176 BauGB, *Die Öffentliche Verwaltung*, 8, 337–340.

A German perspective on building obligations: planning professionals try to remember

Michael Kolocek

This chapter is, one could say, about a land policy instrument that does not work – to solve a problem that does not exist. Of course, this is only half the truth, and in the following I will explain why.

Scarcity of land in Germany

Germany is a country of more than 357,000 square kilometers – 82 percent of it consists of farmland or woodland (Statistisches Bundesamt 2015: 7). In comparison to the size and topography of Switzerland, land seems to be anything but scarce in Germany. Land for urban uses and transport (*Siedlungs- und Verkehrsfläche*, in other words: developed land or building land) may, however, be scarce as it is in other countries, including Switzerland. This is particularly true with respect to affordable housing in growing cities such as Hamburg, Berlin, or Munich, and it has become a central issue in discourses on urban housing for the lower and middle income class.

The German Building Code (BauGB) states that land shall be used sparingly and with due consideration (§ 1a, par. 1, sentence 1, BauGB). The German government has devised several policies in order to reduce the conversion of open space. Probably the best-known German example is the 30-hectare goal, which was first mentioned in 1998 and has since been modified several times (Davy 2009: 283; see also Davy 2010), most recently in 2015 (Bundesregierung 2016: 158–159). The 30-hectare goal is aimed to slow down the conversion of open space such as farmland or woodland into developed land (i.e. for urban uses and transport). In 2030, no more than 30 hectares per day should be converted. Although several instruments have been mentioned in the context of the 30-hectare goal (Davy 2009: 283; Hagebölling 2013), the building obligation was not. Currently, the 30-hectare goal seems achievable; the rate of land conversion has been reduced from more than 120 hectares per day in the 1990s to 69 hectares per day in 2014 (Bundesregierung 2016: 159). Considering the preservation of open space, or what Davy (2009) calls 'land thrift', the government implemented laws to strengthen the inner urban development (Hagebölling 2013). The purpose was that stakeholders and others build on already developed land in inner cities instead of vacant land. As → *Hengstermann* mentioned for Switzerland, theoretically, the building obligation seems to be a suitable tool to strengthen inner urban development. In practice, however, it has not proven adequate, and private property rights seem to be more likely part of the problem than part of the solution.

The building obligation in the context of other instruments

However, I shall examine further how the German building obligation works – or, as the case may be, why it does not work. Despite its long history, which goes back to the medieval Building Law (Leisner 2009: 24–25), the instrument has been called a 'blunt sword' (Stüer 1988, see also → *Hengstermann*). The building obligation (*Baugebot*, also translated as 'building order') is described in two sections (§§ 175 and 176 BauGB) and is one of four urban enforcement orders (*Städtebauliche Gebote*). The others are modernisation and refurbishment order (*Modernisierungs- und Instandsetzungsgebot*, §177 BauGB), planting order (*Pflanzgebot*, § 178 BauGB), and development reduction and de-sealing order (*Rückbau und Entsiegelungsgebot*, §179 BauGB). A closer look at §§ 175 and 176 German Building Code might give an idea why this instrument does not play an important role in the daily work routine of German municipalities. Three main reasons shall be mentioned in the following.

The first reason deals with the stakeholders involved. Considering § 175, par. 1 German Building Code, the municipality is obligated to discuss the measure with all affected stakeholders. This includes owners, tenants, leaseholders, and any other parties. Such a requirement is not unusual in comparison to other instruments such as land readjustment, but it can be time-consuming, particularly if the specific piece of land under consideration comprises several properties or the property is in the hands of more than one owner. This makes the procedure rather inefficient.

Second, § 175 par. 2 German Building Code states that the ordering of measures under §§ 176 to 179 assumes that immediate implementation is required for urban development reasons. Leisner (2009: 68–73) mentions at least two main challenges here. Such urban development reasons must be formulated as precisely as possible. In the case of housing, for instance, it would not suffice to mention an urgent need for affordable housing (Leisner 2009: 72–73); the municipality would have to prove that the demand for affordable housing is considerably higher than the supply (Wallraven-Lindl and Strunz 2010: 67). From the perspective of necessity as a principle of proportionality (proportionality test), the building obligation must be the 'least restrictive measure' (*mildeste Mittel*) to achieve the aim. The building obligation is regarded as a provision defining the content and limits of property (*Inhalts- und Schrankenbestimmung*; art. 14, par. 2, German Basic Law; Leisner 2009: 120) and not as an expropriation. However, § 85, par. 5, German Building Code, which lists the purposes of expropriation, allows expropriating the owner if he or she does not meet the obligations under §§ 176, par. 1 and 2, German Building Code.

The third reason is an economic one and deals with the property owner. The municipality shall refrain from a building order where an owner cannot be expected to implement the project for economic reasons (§ 176, par. 3, BauG). In such a case the owner can require that the municipality take possession of the property (§ 176, par. 4, BauGB).

To sum up, the obligation to build might work if the number of affected parties is low (and all parties are willing to cooperate), the reasons for the proposed urban development orders are convincing (and pass the proportionality test), and the purpose is economically reasonable for the affected landowner(s).

Is the building obligation a suitable instrument for dealing with scarcity of land?

Picking up the main criteria presented in the introduction of the book, the German building obligation is neither effective nor efficient in dealing with the scarcity of land. The obligation to build would most likely be used to close building gaps (*Baulücken*) (Leisner 2009; Stüer 1988). Accordingly, even if policymakers used this instrument successfully, this would be time consuming and only affect a quantitatively small area. There are other land policy instruments that might be more effective and efficient in preventing the development of large areas: for example, fiscal instruments such as land taxation or the regulation on impacts on nature and landscape (*Eingriffsregelung*, § 1a BauGB; § 14 of the Federal Nature Conversation Act, BNatSchG). The instrument's practicability or legitimacy comes into question mostly in regards to the principle of proportionality because, in practice, it very often does not pass the proportionality test (Leisner 2009).

What Hengstermann describes in his case study for Rothenbrunnen in Switzerland might theoretically work in Germany as well. What I found most interesting (and most difficult to prove, of course) is the psychological effect. Sometimes, German municipalities, though illicitly, use the building obligation as a (empty) threat to motivate property owners to cooperate (Leisner 2009: 77, 78). German mayors occasionally mention the building obligation in interviews published in local newspaper articles. Of course, it is difficult to find out how successful such a threatening strategy is. However, about 30 years after Stüer (1988) called the building obligation a 'blunt sword', he might still be right. Taking Hengstermann's findings seriously and Stüer's metaphor literally, one could conclude that a sword might prove a suitable tool for threatening (if that is actually the intent), even if it is a blunt one.

The reader might allow a last short comment that looks at this instrument not only from a national but from a global point of view. The main idea of the building obligation is to force private property owners to build on land that is designated for building. In many countries worldwide, however, people are hardly likely to build because they are obligated to do so by a planning authority. Neither do they build on land that was designated for building; they frequently build without permission. Across the world, about 1 billion people live in housing units built on land that they occupied informally or illegally, often in slums or other spaces of inadequate housing (Kolocek 2017). Here, the 'obligation to build' does not derive from a planning authority but from the need to have a roof over one's head. In this light, the idea to oblige wealthy private property owners to build because land is considered a scarce resource sounds like a bad joke.

References

Bundesregierung (2016) *Deutsche Nachhaltigkeitsstrategie, die Bundesregierung*, Berlin.

Davy, B. (2009) Land thrift as sustainable development – The case of Germany's 30 hectares goal, in: van der Valk, A. and van Dijk, T. (eds) *Regional planning for open space*, Routledge, London, 279–300.

Davy, B. (2010) Freiraumsicherung durch Bodenpolitik – was passieren müßte, wenn wir das Ziel-30-ha ernst nähmen, in: Klemme, M. and Selle, K. (eds) *Siedlungsflächen entwickeln. Akteure. Interdependenzen. Optionen*, Rohn Verlag, Detmold, 258–271.

Hagebölling, C. (2013) Das Gesetz zur Stärkung der Innenentwicklung in den Städten und Gemeinden und weiteren Fortentwicklung des Städtebaurechts. Eine erneute BauGB-Novelle tritt in Kraft, *Natur und Recht*, 35(2), 99–105.

Kolocek, M. (2017) *The human right to housing in the face of land policy and social citizenship. A global discourse analysis*, Palgrave Macmillan, Basingstoke, New York.

Leisner, R. (2009) *Baugebot und Baufreiheit: Das Spannungsverhältnis zwischen dem einfach-gesetzlichen ausgestalteten Baugebot und der verfassungsrechtlichen Garantie des Eigentums*, Duncker & Humblot, Berlin.

Statistisches Bundesamt (2015) *Land- und Forstwirtschaft, Fischerei. Bodenfläche nach Art der tatsächlichen Nutzung*, Statistisches Bundesamt, Wiesbaden.

Stüer, B. (1988) Baugebot nach § 176 BauGB. Ein 'Stumpfes Schwert?', *Die öffentliche Verwaltung*, 8, April, 337–340.

Wallraven-Lindl, M.-L. and Strunz, A. (2010) *Städtebauliche Gebote nach dem Baugesetzbuch*, Deutsches Institut für Urbanistik, Berlin.

A U.S. perspective on obligations to build: planning professionals would be shocked

Harvey M. Jacobs

American applicability?

Most American landowners, land developers, and planning professionals would be shocked to read about the Swiss land policy tool of building obligation. In the limited space available to me for this commentary I will do two things – explain why Americans in general would be shocked, and reflect on how such a land policy approach fits into an ongoing dialogue about the core concept of what private property actually means.

Essentially nothing like the concept of building obligation exists in the U.S. What there is instead is a basically bi-modal basis for land use. Where land is privately owned, the landowner holds the land use decision. He can decide to under-use it or to use it to the limit allowed by zoning and other land policy tools. Zoning and related land policy tools provide a frame for land use, but they do not force a landowner to take advantage of the maximum limits available. Alternately, government can acquire the land (by free market sale or by expropriation) to facilitate more intensive land use.

Why is this the situation? American law and culture draw upon a notion of private property in which property functions as a bundle of rights. Regularly these rights include air rights, use rights, and the right to sell or lease (among others). A part of the use right is the right not to use and the right for the owner to select the timing for land use change. While other components of the bundle of rights have been modified over time (such as the air right), the use right – except as it has been shaped by zoning – has not been modified. So in the American context, government can incentivize and persuade towards land use change, especially land intensification, but it cannot actually control the timing or outcome of this change process.

What is interesting, though, is that the issue at the core of the building obligation as land policy has been an active component of American land policy debate for over a century, though almost always at the fringes of the debate. In the late 1800s, Henry George proposed a form of land taxation intended to force land intensification. His focus was on concentrated land holdings in cities; what he wanted was to provide for broader access to land for the working class. His work was very popular in the U.S. and throughout the British colonies, and found root, in modified form, in a few American cities and in places such as New Zealand. George himself ran for the mayor of New York City in 1886 on a land reform platform; he lost (though whether legitimately or not is contested). So-called Georgist taxation continues to have adherents globally.

But for Americans, there is a skepticism about the appropriateness of government involving itself in land intensification decisions. This skepticism is rooted in the experience with urban renewal in the decades of the 1950s–1970s and continuing into the present. Urban renewal appeared to demonstrate that government ideas for land use were not always accurate or correct, and that governmental actions in this regard were often at the expense of politically weaker communities and communities of color.

This debate was renewed in the early 2000s with the internationally renowned U.S. Supreme Court case of *Kelo v. New London, Connecticut.* In this instance, the city of New London sought to acquire 115 privately owned properties for land consolidation and subsequent redevelopment by a private developer. The well-known, though not officially acknowledged, intent of this process was to provide the property to Pfizer Pharmaceutical for development as a research facility. As an economic development strategy the city was foreseeing jobs, increased land tax revenues, and thus increased funds for local services. One hundred owners agreed to sell, while 15 resisted. The city proposed to expropriate the properties of these 15 owners. Susette Kelo became the spokesperson for the group of 15. Arguments against the proposed action were multiple. Ultimately the U.S. Supreme Court sided with the city, allowing the expropriation to proceed. But the controversy over the acquisition became so intense that in the end Pfizer declined to participate in the project. Today the project site sits vacant. To its opponents, the vacant site and the displacement of former residents is a testimonial to ill-informed government decision-making for land intensification.

Property rights in evolution

The core issue embedded in the land policy tool of building obligation is how the right to build is (or should be) shared between the private owner and the public. What is most interesting to me is understanding the Swiss policy approach in the context of a global discussion about property.

Private property, even in the U.S., has always been a social and legal institution undergoing change. That change has most often been prompted by changes in technology or social values. So, for example, in the early twentieth century, after the invention and commercialization of the airplane, private owners lost their air right 'to the heavens above' so as to accommodate the design and implementation of air highways. Owners maintained an air right, but now it is truncated, and not to the heavens above. In the latter part of the twentieth century commercial property owners lost their right to exclude customers, which they had done previously on racial, ethnic and religious grounds. Following the civil rights protests of the period, this right was removed from the commercial private property owners' bundle (though it remains in the bundle of noncommercial private owners). In each case there was resistance to the change, but ultimately it prevailed.

Similarly, the allowable scope of public regulation of privately owned land through policy tools such as zoning has expanded over the century. So certain spatial planning goals such as protection of agricultural land in the peri-urban area or the conservation of unique ecological lands are now possible in ways that would have been unimaginable to policy designers of earlier eras. These changes also elicited (and can still elicit) pointed resistance but have, overall, been grudgingly accepted. But the widespread implementation of these approaches is more limited than one might expect because of Americans' general skepticism about governmental action and their general adherence to an idea of strong private property.

Globally, including within the U.S., a debate has been reinvigorated about the very construct of property in a private property system. The form of private property dominant globally emerged out of eighteenth-century political-economic discourse and social change embodied in the American and French revolutions. The world of the eighteenth century was primarily rural, in decided contrast to today's world. How appropriate is an eighteenth-century model of property for an urban world with changing global climate conditions? How appropriate is this model for addressing new ideas about land use and land scarcity? To many scholars and activists the answer is: not very appropriate. Just as ideas about air rights and the right to exclude changed with changing technology and social values in the twentieth century, so too could ideas about the shared right to build. Property rights scholars and activists highlight how changing technology (e.g. drones) and changing social values (e.g. same-sex marriage) continue to reshape the property bundle.

The idea embedded in the Swiss policy of building obligation is one that acknowledges both the present structure of property and the ability to use that structure to change it in the realization of new ends. It is creative, and it has potential to address an important land issue.

Will the Swiss policy of building obligation find any potential for implementation in the U.S.? Not soon, but maybe in the future. In theory, in law and policy there is nothing that would prevent such an approach. But social-cultural values and institutional arrangements need to change first. While that may seem like a large precondition, it should be kept in mind how far land policy has come in a century. If change in that period is judged to be significant, it can be believed that further and future change is also possible.

The global community of land policy researchers and practitioners need to continue to hear about this innovation. While its success in Switzerland will not guarantee adaptive-replication, its failure to achieve expected results could warn off those who might try to address urban land scarcity similarly. Property rights systems and land policy structures are multifacted and highly adaptable. The Swiss approach to building obligation demonstrates this and encourages us.

Part IV

Redefining property rights to steer land uses

11 Pre-emption rights in France

Disputes over pre-emptions and the 'land scarcity'

Romain Melot

Introduction: broad description of the instrument's rationale

Land acquisition tools are in nature key subjects for the understanding of the relations between planning processes and property rights. Local governments involved in the land market have a dual role: they may act both as a '*passive* referee' (by issuing regulations and exercising control) and as an '*active* player' (by purchasing land assets) (van Dijk and van der Vlist 2015). The capacity of local authorities to combine land interventions that are both *passive* and *active* can be considered an important factor in achieving successful planning policies.

Expropriation and pre-emption are the most current mechanisms for prescriptive land acquisitions, but both instruments did not give rise to empirical studies to the same extent. Expropriation procedures have been studied by planners and sociologists as an empirical field for the observation of socio-legal strategies relating to social perceptions of fairness (Holtslag-Broekhof et al. 2014), compensation instruments (van Straalen and Korthals Altes 2014), and judicial practices (Melot 2013). As a less widespread acquisition tool, pre-emption only triggered scant case studies by social scientists, especially in France (Renard 2009). The inquiry presented here is based on the assumption that the peculiarities of pre-emption offer a particularly relevant vantage point to adress the issue of land scarcity. Pre-emption in French planning policies has indeed evolved significantly from an instrument implemented for large greenfield urbanisation to a legal tool used for more focused planning projects in tight land markets.

The organisation of this study is as follows. First, we outline the major points of pre-emption rights in the French legal system and the specific characteristics of pre-emption in land planning. We then expose the governance of this instrument within the peculiarities of the French political institutions by retracing the history of its implementation in local planning policies. Finally, we present two case studies in the Paris region that illustrate local debates regarding the use of pre-emption in a context of land scarcity, and we conclude on the general lessons drawn from the French situation.

Pre-emption in the French legal system: general provisions

Pre-emption may be generally defined as the right, entitled by law or contract, to acquire in first position a property planned by the owner to be offered for sale (Struillou and Hostiou 2011). Among the countries that have established pre-emption rights, the use of this instrument is rather uneven. In the Netherlands, for example, pre-emption plays an important role in local land policies and serves both the achievement of a planning project and the strenghtening of rent capture mechanisms (van Dijk and van der Vlist 2015). This instrument has long been a powerful lever for the implementation of active public strategies put in place by Dutch local governments (van der Krabben and Jacobs 2013). By contrast, the mere existence of pre-emption tools in the legislation does not mean necessarily that they are frequently implemented: in Japan, municipalities remain reluctant to use pre-emption and prefer to negotiate friendly acquisitions with landowners (Aveline 1995). Furthermore, when pre-emption is currently used at the local level, it may be bypassed by landowners through various legal techniques (self-realisation of a public project with the help of a developer) as shown in local Dutch case studies (Louw 2008).

Pre-emption rights are very common in the French legal system. In private contractual relations, the legislation has endowed tenants of pre-emption rights, as a way to rebalance asymmetries in property lease contracts and to ensure stable situations for tenants. Housing and farm tenants are thus entitled to acquire built or land properties in first position (whatever the nature of the property rented), if the owner has planned a sale project.

Aside from private law regulations, the types of pre-emption rights are very diverse in the French legislation of planning and land use policies. Public bodies (and certain private bodies bestowed with a public function by law) may be entitled by public law regulations of the right to acquire a real estate asset in first position, for reasons of public interest. Regarding agricultural issues, for example, private companies in charge of farmland management (*Sociétés d'Aménagement Foncier et d'Equipement Rural*) are given prerogatives of pre-emption by the Rural Code in order to foster agricultural projects and the setting up of new farmers. They may intervene to control speculation within the farmland market, when the prices negotiated in the sale projects appear to exceed the usual standards of local farmland values. Pre-emption may also be used by local governments at the level of departments (*départements*, which correspond to the NUTS 3 level) to acquire 'sensitive natural sites' or to protect 'periurban farmland and natural spaces'. But the main implementation of pre-emption rights concerns the field of urban planning, which is the focus of this contribution.

These various public law mechanisms of pre-emption are subject to general procedures they share in common. Pre-emption rights must first be instituted either by law (for farmland) or, most of the time, by a local decision, in accordance to legal provisions (vote of a municipal or department council, for instance). The local decision usually determines the criteria according to which pre-emption shall be enforced and may delimit through a specific zoning the spatial scope of future pre-emptions. Planned sales need to be notified by the landlord or his notary to the authority entitled to pre-emption rights with the mandatory indication of the property value estimated by the landowner. The local authority then has to make successively two kinds of decisions. First, shall the use of the pre-emption right be implemented or not, and second, shall the initial purchase price offer, i.e. the price valuated by the landowner, be revised or not? The decision to implement pre-emption may be challenged in *administrative* court by the owner or the aggrieved initial buyer. The choice to revise the price offer may be contested in *civil* court (cases of that kind are adjudicated by a special jurisdiction that is also in charge of disputes over compensation after expropriations). According to a report issued in 2007 by the State Council (highest administrative court in France), about 40 percent of the pre-emptions challenged in administrative courts are cancelled. Statistical data on civil litigation about the revision of sales prices are not available. If the local authority withdraws a decision of pre-emption, the transaction planned initially may be completed and the court may allocate compensation to the owner for the financial damage induced by the pre-emption procedure (Struillou and Hostiou 2011).

Various pre-emption procedures are available in urban planning for development or regeneration projects. Some are dedicated to specific real estate markets, like commercial buildings (for instance, pre-emption may be implemented to diversify commercial businesses within a neighbourhood and limit mono-activity). Apart from these specific cases, the most commonly used procedures are pre-emption in 'Future Development Zones' (*Zone d'Aménagement Différé*) and 'Urban Pre-emption Right' (*Droit de Préemption Urbain*).

Whereas Future Development Zones were designed in the 1960s for wide-ranging projects on large areas, through massive acquisitions of farmland for land reserves, pre-emption has become a local instrument for municipal planning policies after the decentralisation reforms and the institution of Urban Pre-emption Rights. This second procedure has then been frequently implemented for focused acquisitions of expansive urban properties. Urban Pre-emption Right is a mechanism used in complex tenure structures of entangled property rights and public law regulations, especially in a densely urbanised context.

Governance of the instrument

Historically, pre-emption as a legal instrument for planning policies was first instituted in the late 1950s to develop social housing in new neighbourhoods close to downtown and immediate suburb areas. France was still subjected to dramatic housing needs linked to the destructions caused by the war, the increasing rural exodus, and the demographic boom. The precarious living conditions of homeless or poorly housed people, the informal extension of slum areas in the Parisian suburbs, were important areas of concern.

Huge efforts for the massive output of affordable dwellings were undertaken in a few years in 'Priority Urbanisation Zones'. These areas were subjected to pre-emption rights and created in 1958, at the beginning of the De Gaulle presidency, as a symbol of political resoluteness. But the importance of housing crisis and the size of the projects planned (250 hectares in average in the Parisian region) challenged the government to scale up the system. Indeed, the political debates related to land use planning were guided by concerns about the availability of land resources at a low price for urban development. An ambitious project of nine 'New Cities' (*Villes nouvelles*) was scheduled by the state[1] in the Parisian region in the 1960s. It was economically based on pre-emption as a mechanism of rent capture (Renard and Comby 1990).

The 1962 'Pre-emption and Expropriation' Act provided to the state administration the power to delimitate, outside of urbanised or development zones, large areas belonging to 'Future Development Zones'. The new system was characterised by the leading role of the state in the procedure. The rationale of these legal regulations was to prevent speculations on farmland and to facilitate future acquisitions by public authorities at a low price for development projects. Public authorities were thus allowed to capture the land rent of private owners.

The legal mechanism of valuation of properties set up by the 1962 Act is common to pre-emption and expropriation procedures. It is based on the principle of 'blocked value': properties acquired must be valuated in relation to the building rights existing at the time when the area subjected to pre-emption or expropriation was established. For example, when pre-emption is finally implemented, farmland properties integrated in development zones in the meantime has still to be valuated in comparison to sales observed within the farmland market (and not within the market of developable land properties). Although some of the initial regulations have been relaxed (the duration of pre-emption zones, originally 14 years, was converted to five years in 2011, renewable once), the system of Future Development Zones is still in force and is often used for important projects.

From the 1960s onward, the paradox is that the use of pre-emption has been both massive and limited. *Institution* and *implementation* of pre-emption rights (in other words, the *potential* and the *actual* use of pre-emption) must be distinguished. The areas subjected to pre-emption have rapidly increased, to the point where it concerned large surfaces at the end of the 1960s (240,000 hectares of Future Development Zones established just for the year 1969). At the same time, the actual decisions of pre-emption remained focused on few properties (only 5 percent of the declared sale projects in the same year) (Topalov 1974).

The reason for this apparent paradox is that pre-emption in planning was not designed to be a *direct* tool for large public acquisitions, but an *indirect* one, an instrument to facilitate future acquisitions through the control of land prices. In itself, the French system of pre-emption has not been designed for the systematical purchase of properties in a defined area, but as a way of monitoring prices during a certain period preceding comprehensive acquisitions. This is the reason why a focused recourse to price control by means of pre-emption has proven to be sufficient to limit speculation without inducing significant public expenditures. According to the data issued by the French sociologist Christian Topalov, the prices of property planned for sale in pre-emption zones was 2.5 times higher compared to the valuations of the state administration in the early 1960s. At the end of the decade, the ratio was reduced to 1.5. This is clear evidence that targeted pre-emptions have actually succeeded in curbing speculative anticipations (Topalov 1974)

In official reports issued for the government in the 1960s, it appears obviously that pre-emption was considered as an efficient 'low cost' planning policy. This mechanism was seen as a way to compensate the shortcomings of the French institutions: the absence of a large public land portfolio in local communities (as opposed to the Netherlands), the limited public fundings available to fill the gap in this area within Northern Europe, and inadequate property taxation (owners of developable land are not financially put under pressure to sell) (Renard 2009).

The legislative regulations concerning pre-emption in the 1960s and 1970s have not been adopted without intense political debates. Repeatedly, the deputies and political parties representing the interest of farmers raised strong objections against the valuation mechanism unfavourable for landowners ('blocked value'). In parliamentary debates, they presented the reform as equivalent to an illegitimate taking of their property. Farmers were indeed the most impacted by the Future Development Zones, which were designed to monitor price anticipations in agricultural areas. As owners, they were partially deprived of the added value consecutive to land conversion, and as tenants, they have to face future expropriations. However, empirical researches lead in the Paris region suggested that the financial compensations received by farmers were for some of them an opportunity to reinvest in their farming businesses elsewhere (Bryant 1986).

Left-wing parties (political opposition in parliament during the 1960s and 1970s) agreed with the Gaullist majority on the necessity of rent capture, but were opposed to the leading place of the state in the pre-emption system. In 1982, under the Mitterrand presidency, the government initiated important decentralisation reforms (a long-standing demand of the socialist party, absent from government for more than 20 years). The most significant change was to transfer to municipalities new competences over planning issues (i.e. elaboration of development plans, allocation of building permits). As a consequence, the 1985 'Development Act' entitled municipalities to an 'Urban Pre-emption Right'. Although a specific vote of the municipal council was required to set up the area subjected to pre-emption rights, empirical research highlighted the success of the new legal instrument: in the

1990s, three-quarters of the municipalities adopted pre-emption regulations (Comby and Renard 1991). Furthermore, when urban pre-emption right is instituted, it is with a large scope most of the time, including all urbanised and development zones of the local plan (Morlet 2000). Pre-emption rights may also be transfered to larger local communities (public local authorities instituted by a cluster of municipalities). Lastly, municipalities have been endowed to institute 'Reinforced' Pre-emption Rights by resolution of the municipal council for transactions that are normally explicitly excluded from pre-emption by the law, i.e. lots of joint property and recently built properties.

Whereas the legislation in the 1960s instituted pre-emption areas controlled by the state (local communities could suggest, but not oppose this kind of mechanism), the evolution of pre-emption systems have turned out to be more and more decentralised. More recently, the 2014 Planning Act gave competence to intercommunal bodies to establish Future Development Zones, which was previously a prerogative of the state. In response to requests made by municipalities, the scope of pre-emption was also widened: in order to avoid circumventions of the law, pre-emption may now concern not only real property, but also shares owned in a company. These new regulations made it more difficult for landowners to escape from pre-emption by creating real estate companies in order to disguise a property transaction (Carpentier 2014).

The scope of pre-emption rights has extended dramatically over time (Pérignon 1991). According to the French Planning Code, pre-emption is enforceable in every 'development procedure', a concept that has itself become more and more flexible.

> The purposes of development procedures are to implement an urban project or a local housing policy; to sustain or extend economic activities; to foster leisure and tourism activities; to develop public facilities and research and education buildings; to take actions against substandard, unhealthy, or dangerous housing and manage urban regeneration; and to protect built or unbuilt heritage and natural spaces.
>
> (Planning Code art. L. 300–1)

The wide success of pre-emption at the local level can be explained by these flexible rationales. Pre-emption also offers clear advantages over other instruments. Expropriation is also legally flexible (it is based on the very open concept of 'public use', which is not clearly defined by legislation and was shaped by case law), but it is politically more sensitive. Moreover, expropriation has not been decentralised and remains a prerogative of the state. Even though municipalities are the most current initiators and beneficiaries of the projects based on public use and expropriation, they do not fully control the expropriation process and have to request the agreement of the state administration for its implementation. Pre-emption has the drawback of depending on isolated and occasional private sales, but in contrast to expropriation, this procedure only relies on the municipalities' initiative. These two instruments are often combined in practice, as pre-emption is often used for upstream acquisitions preceding systematical purchases through expropriation.

Another critical aspect of pre-emption tools is the setting up of a local price observatory. In areas subjected to pre-emption, the mandatory notification of sale projects is a very effective way of collecting market references. This permanent and inexpensive system provides a synthetic overview of the land market to local communities and helps them design planning projects that go far beyond the implementation of pre-emption rights.

Since the 1985 reform, pre-emption has become widely shaped by local initiatives and is now part of the everyday life in municipalities. The decentralisation process also changed the implementation level of this instrument: pre-emption as part of the local legal toolbox is used at the municipal scale, sometimes for small-size projects (Joye and Struillou 2012). This is the reason why we propose to focus our case study on the system of Urban Pre-emption Rights, which has become the most common use of pre-emption in planning policies.

Case study: empirical evidence; pre-emption practices and disputes in the Parisian suburbs (*Seine Saint-Denis* department)

In the precedent sections, we exposed the broad principles and historical backgrounds of pre-emption rights in French planning policies. In order to get a more detailed understanding of the effective use of pre-emption, the analysis was centered on the specific situation of Seine Saint-Denis department in the Paris region. A focus was placed on this department because local elected officials of this jurisdiction were particularly active in pre-emption policies. As a consequence, the department has concentrated a high rate of litigation in that matter during the past decade. Seine Saint-Denis is a densely populated department (1,150,000 inhabitants) and the poorest in France. Close to the city of Paris, it is attractive to middle-class households that can no longer afford dwellings in the capital city. Therefore, in some of the working-class towns of the department, housings and buildable land are subjected to tremendous price increases and rapid gentrification.

The case study analysis is based on various empirical data relating to local disputes in court, development plans, and public debates at the municipal level. In particular, the decisions adjudicated in favor of aggrieved owners (49 judgments) have been collected during a five-year period (2010–2015) by the administrative court of the department (Court of Montreuil). The urban projects mentioned in the attached decisions have been analysed. On the whole, projects of general interest at stake are mainly concerning housing programs. But it is worth noting that the most frequent category of

Table 11.1 Urban projects concerned in pre-emption disputes

Urban projects concerned in pre-emption disputes	*Number of cases*
Land reserves	9
Urban regeneration program	9
Social housing programs	6
Support for retail trade	5
Industrial and economic activities	5
Housing programs	3
Social facilities	2
Public roads	2
Substandard housing renovation	2
Other urban projects	6
Total	49

disputes relates to projects that are still undetermined, such as the establishment of land reserves. The motivation based on clearly scheduled urban design appears then to be problematic for the municipality (Table 11.1).

The geographical pattern of the sample shows that pre-emption disputes are concentrated on the immediate surroundings of Paris. The use of pre-emption rights and connected litigations thus mostly concern suburbs that are particularly attractive for gentrification because of their proximity to the capital. Certain municipalities are characterised by a high number of disputes that is linked to an active pre-emption policy. For that reason, we focused our inquiry on two municipalities (Montreuil and Saint-Ouen) that concentrate 21 out of the 49 cases filed in the department during the period studied.

Anticipating housing scarcity: conflicts over pre-emption for land reserves in Montreuil

As noted earlier, legal grounds for the justification of pre-emption are quite flexible. In addition, the French Planning Code provides that pre-emption does not necessarily have to be used for the *direct* implementation of the relevant project, but may also be used *indirectly* for the formation of 'land reserves'. 'Preemption rights are implemented to achieve (development procedures) in the general interest [. . .] or to establish a land reserve for the achievement of these procedures' (Planning Code art. L. 210–1). In the French legal system, a land reserve is a stock of built or unbuilt properties acquired by a public person for a future urban project and that may not be sold to private persons until the achievement of the project (knowing that the land may be developed either by private or public bodies thereafter).

The case law interpretation of pre-emption legislation may appear inconsistent with the notion of land reserve. In the *Lebouc v. Saint-Maur City* case, it has been stated that pre-emption should be justified by 'a precise project, that should have been discussed and taken into account, even though plans are not yet available' (Council of State, 25 July 1986). But land reserve acquisitions, on the contrary, are characterised in nature by haziness and undetermined designs that make any detailed argumentation difficult. The consequence of such contradictions is an important litigation in this matter and a legal uncertainty for local communities. More generally, these case law interpretations reflect the historical hesitations of French planning policies between prescriptive instruments and a restrictive framing for public acquisitions (Struillou and Hostiou 2011).

The city of Montreuil (100,000 inhabitants) is a clear example of these contradictions arising from the use of pre-emption rights for land reserves in a dense urban context. In 2012, the local administrative court reached a judgment concerning a pre-emption concerning a land plot. Eventually, the owner accepted to settle with the municipality. But in the meantime the initial purchaser filed a claim in court to challenge the pre-emption (a claim that was received by the court as the public decision has not been formally withdrawn). The pre-emption was motivated by the 'establishment of a land reserve for the development of an urban project combining dwellings and commercial activities in view of the forthcoming new tramway line in the neighbourhood' (Administrative Court of Montreuil, 20 December 2012). In 2013, another judgment was delivered in the same neighbourhood. The municipality argued that pre-emption was justified 'in order to keep with the existing land reserve policy regarding the housing shortage at the municipal level'. In its defence, the city hall mentioned that actions against scarcity of affordable housing was the object of a covenant with the state and that regeneration projects beneficiated of public support in the city blocks concerned by pre-emptions (Administrative Court of Montreuil, 30 May 2013).

The two files concern complex properties combining urban land and buildings. The 2013 case, for example, is located in a dense city block of small, irregular plots, typical of the old suburbs of Paris. The example underscores that land reserves established by Urban Pre-emption Rights are quite far from the postwar model of urbanisation management on a large scale.

In both cases, the municipal decision was cancelled because the judges consider that 'indications concerning an ongoing operation (were) insufficient to know about the nature of the urban project planned in the disputed properties.' These judicial disputes, although not representative of all pre-emption procedures, illustrate a planning paradox: pre-emption turns out to be very common at the municipal level for small-scale projects, but at the same time, the definition of the underpinning projects tends to be more general or fuzzy. In densely built areas, pre-emptions for land reserve are designed to safeguard potentialities for general interest projects (social housing, public facilities) in a context were developable plots are scarce and isolated. Scarcity and the difference of timescales between the individual sales scheduled on the short term and the urban project planned on the long term make it difficult for the municipalities to design a coherent and fine-scale schedule of acquisitions.

Housing scarcity and the fight against speculation in the city of Saint-Ouen

Paradoxically, the struggle against speculation is not included in the patchwork list of legal reasons admitted by the law (which is actually the case, as seen previously, for agricultural pre-emptions in the Rural Code), even though it was historically a central rationale for the adoption of the legislation. If the legal grounds that may be invoked to give reasons for pre-emption seem rather flexible, the mere reference to the necessity of land price monitoring is not in itself a valid reason according to the law, but is subordinated to the proof of a real planning project. However, case law decisions showed hesitations on this thorny legal issue. A decision of the Council of State acknowledged that pre-emption might be justified by the control of land prices, because it was the legislator's intention (as underlined by excerpts of parliamentary debates) (Council of State, 8 June 1994). But this decision referred to pre-emption in large areas (Future Development Zones) and did not include the case of Urban Pre-emption Rights (Struillou and Hostiou 2011).

The case of the city of Saint-Ouen (47,000 inhabitants), a northern suburb of Paris, illustrates the contradictions induced by these legal ambiguities. Like Montreuil, Saint-Ouen is a former working-class town that experienced rapid social changes due to its attractive proximity to Paris. To hamper the gentrification process and maintain a population of low-income inhabitants, the municipality became involved in a two-pronged, strong-will planning policy. First of all, the mayor negotiated a global 'development covenant' with private developers. The agreement stipulated fixed exit prices of the new housings produced. The prices negotiated were 10 percent below the values recorded in the new housing market of Saint-Ouen before the covenant. Moreover, the covenant also stipulated that 80 percent of the housings should be allocated for owner-occupied dwellings. Despite these constraints, 27 developers estimated that the developments remained profitable and agreed to sign the covenant.

Second, the municipality committed in a resolute and unreserved pre-emption policy. The City Hall systematically asked the tax administration of the state to valuate the properties according to standard criteria (comfort, works to be carried, etc.). However, the official reports issued by the municipality that we reviewed showed that only 8 percent of the planned sales were actually subjected to pre-emption. These data indicate that pre-emption is first and foremost used as a threat in the negotiation with the seller, to persuade him to review his offer if the price turned out to be above the market references.

This policy triggered several contentious appeals at the level of the municipality (in average, 10 percent of the pre-emption decisions were challenged in court). In the local administrative court of Montreuil, we collected ten cases of successful appeals filed in Saint-Ouen by aggrieved owners for the sole 2010–2015 period. Like the previous example in Montreuil, disputed pre-emptions in Saint-Ouen are all situated in the dense urbanised zones of the municipality. Consequently, the strategy of the municipality appears to be twofold: the covenant negotiated with developers applies to new developable zones, and pre-emption rights are used in already built areas.

The minutes of the town council meetings that we consulted provide numerous examples of the heated debates on this topic. In response to criticism from the opposition, the city councillor in charge of planning issues advocated the recourse to pre-emption by referring explicitly to the scarcity of low-cost dwellings for young households and the necessity of price monitoring:

> The practices of the speculators are inflating prices artificially and make affordable housing increasingly difficult to find. Moreover, local communities face massive cuttings in the financial state support for housing policies. In that context, municipalities are called in to the rescue to help developers to cover their cost. In that context, our pre-emption initiatives may be contested, but it seems to me much less offensive that the attitude of municipalities which do not comply with their legal duties to build social housing and are therefore subjected to financial sanctions.
>
> (Town Council meeting of Saint-Ouen, 27 September 2010)

In the same Council meeting, the councillor also indirectly argued that this strategy on the fringes of legality proved to be financially cost effective: according to figures quoted by the municipality, the compensations adjudicated by the court to the owners in cancelled pre-emption decisions (for the damage consecutive to the differed sale) represent only 13 percent of the savings obtained after revision of the sale price in pre-emption procedures. Implicitly, the city councillor thus admitted that price monitoring was the first rationale of pre-emption, and not a precise urban development. This strategy, as it was said, is technically illegal with regard to legislative and case law regulations.

This legal loophole is perfectly identified by the aggrieved owners who filed the pre-emption decisions in court. In an appeal adjudicated in 2011, the co-owners of an apartment submitted that

> the attacked decision was vitiated by an error of law because the municipality of Saint-Ouen pursued an objective of fight against land speculation which is not included among the legally admitted grounds.

> Furthermore, the decision was not based on any real project and it reveals a misuse of power as the sole purpose of the municipality was the reduction of the sale price.

The plaintiffs provide a detailed statement of the pressure put by the municipality in the negotiation process by the mere reference to the potential use of pre-emption.

For the court, the virtual use of pre-emption right as a threat in a negotiation amounts to a misuse of power – all the more so as the municipality proposed a valuation of the property that is less favourable than the price valuated by the state administration.

> The plaintiffs allege that they received a letter from the municipality inviting them to contact the land service 'to get more information about the sale of their housing'. They claim that they were then informed that the municipal services would waive the preemption right in case of reduction of the sale price. The preemption occurred following these contacts, after Mr and Mrs F. refused to revise the price. Furthermore, the preemption was set up by the municipality at a sale price significantly lower (160,000 euros) than the valuation made by the tax administration of the State (179,000 euros). [. . .] All these elements together constitute a body of consistent evidence that the allegations of the plaintiffs are substantiated.
>
> (Administrative Court of Montreuil, 20 October 2011)

The case of Saint-Ouen highlights that the use of pre-emption is often guided by a hidden agenda in local communities. As the legislation hesitated to authorise pre-emption for price monitoring, local elected officials set up alternative strategies consisting in motivating their decisions on an apparent project, whereas their prime objective is to limit the pace of price increases.

Contribution of the instrument in a situation of land scarcity

Pre-emption tools have long been regarded as a supplement to expropriation. The land price regulation system was dedicated to the upstream preparation of expropriation (containing price increases in order to reduce the cost of future purchases), or, more generally, to the preparation of negotiation under the threat of expropriation. As mentioned previously, disputes over the valuation of properties are regulated by rules common to pre-emption and expropriation and adjudicated by the same court. Historically, the prevalence of expropriation over pre-emption is symbolically underlined by the official name of this civil jurisdiction, simply known as 'expropriation court'. Nevertheless, the 'popularity' of pre-emption among local elected officials made it gradually much more than an additional tool in planning policies. It turned out to be politically less risky (pre-emption is less infringing to property rights), legally more flexible, and financially cost-effective.

In the 1960s and the 1970s, pre-emption was principally used for the establishment of large-scale land reserves for important urbanisation projects or the creation of new towns. The main challenges at that time were to capture the land rent and to stock farmland, which was considered as a plentiful resource for urbanisation. The decentralisation of planning policies at the municipal level (generalisation of development plans, institution of local pre-emption rights) radically changed the makeup of pre-emption mechanisms. Price monitoring is undoubtedly still at stake, but land scarcity turned out to be a core issue of public acquisitions. Local authorities mobilise pre-emption tools in densely urbanised neighbourhoods where properties available for affordable or social housing are a rare and expensive product.

The review of the French experience of pre-emption finally appears to be ambivalent. Pre-emption proved to address the land scarcity issue. It has been an efficient tool in limiting speculation and allocating land plots for housing programs in tight land markets, without incurring large public expenditures at the local level. That being said, there still remains some debate about legal uncertainty for public authorities and infringement to property rights for landowners. For example, unilateral price revision by public authorities, on the one hand, and unilateral waiver of sale by the owner (as a strategy to counter pre-emption), on the other hand, are powers that could be limited in order to improve the mechanism (Comby and Renard 1991). On this basis of detailed procedural safeguards for property rights, the political legitimacy of price monitoring in a context of land scarcity could be translated as efficient pre-emption tools for a fair planning policy.

More generally, the specific role played by pre-emption instruments in France illustrates the complementarity between regulation and acquisition tools. Development projects that are successful in mobilising pre-emption rights without judicial invalidation are those closely tied to explicit provisions of the local planning regulations. Conversely, the achievement of planning strategies scheduled in development plans is facilitated by acquisition tools like pre-emption. In this regard, the lesson drawn from the French experience may be the following: the use of pre-emption prerogatives appears to be a legal strategy adapted to local governments addressing heavy pressure on housing markets with constrained financial resources and a limited public land portfolio.

Note

1 By the term 'state', we refer to the national government (France is a unitary republic, not a federal one), whether it be its central or local services.

References

Aveline, N. (1995) *La Bulle foncière au Japon*, ADEF Editions, Paris, 142.

Bryant, C. (1986) Farmland conservation and farming landscapes in urban-centred regions: The case of the Ile-de-France region, *Landscape and Urban Planning*, 13, 251–276.

Carpentier, E. (2014) La loi ALUR et les droits de préemption publics, *Revue de Droit Immobilier*, 2014, 240–251.

Comby, J. and Renard, V. (1991) *Evaluation du droit de préemption*, Official report n° 1942 for the French National Assembly.

Holtslag-Broekhof, S., Beunen, R., van Marwijk, R. and Wiskerke, J. (2014) 'Let's try to get the best out of it' understanding land transactions during land use change, *Land Use Policy*, 41, 561–570.

Joye, J.-F. and Struillou, J.-F. (2012) *Les communautés et le droit de préemption. Report for the French Association of local communities* (online) available at: www.adcf.org/files/Note-AdCF-Droit-de-preemption.pdf (accessed 14 June 2017).

Louw, E. (2008) Land assembly for urban transformation: The case of s'Hertogenbosh in the Netherlands, *Land Use Policy*, 25, 69–80.

Melot, R. (2013) *La valeur en procès: Expropriation et stratégies judiciaires*, Adef Editions, Paris.

Morlet, O. (2000) Les pratiques locales de la préemption, *Etudes Foncières*, 33–39.

Pérignon, S. (1991) Pathologie du droit de préemption urbain, *Défrenois*, March, 341–352.

Renard, V. (2009) Property rights protection and spatial planning in Europe, in: Ingram, G. and Hong, Y. (eds) *Property rights and land policies*, Lincoln Institute of Land Policy, Cambridge, 216–229.

Renard, V. and Comby, J. (1990) *Land policy in France. 1945–1990*, Adef Editions, Paris.

Struillou, J.-F. and Hostiou, R. (2011) *Expropriation et préemption: aménagement, urbanisme, environnement*, Litec, Paris.

Topalov, C. (1974) *Expropriation et préemption publique en France, 1950–1973: Documents pour l'étude comparative des politiques foncières urbaines*, Centre de sociologie urbaine, Paris.

van der Krabben, E. and Jacobs, H. (2013) Public land development as a strategic tool for redevelopment: Reflections on the Dutch experience, *Land Use Policy*, 30, 774–783.

van Dijk, T. and Kopeva, D. (2006) Land banking and central Europe: Future relevance, current initiatives, Western European past experience, *Land Use Policy*, 23, 286–301.

van Dijk, T. and van der Vlist, A. (2015) On the interaction between landownership and regional designs for land development, *Urban Studies*, 52, 1899–1914.

van Straalen, F. and Korthals Altes, W. (2014) Compulsory purchase for biodiversity conservation in the Netherlands, *Land Use Policy*, 38, 223–232.

A Swiss perspective on pre-emption rights: impact without application

Stéphane Nahrath

How is pre-emption implemented in Switzerland?

Unlike France (→ *Melot*), the Netherlands, Germany, or Austria, the implementation of an unlimited state pre-emption right on building land is, in Switzerland, very limited. There is no explicit mention of this instrument in the federal legislation, and only two cantons – Vaud and Geneva, both located in western Switzerland – have introduced such an instrument in their current legislation. The canton of Geneva introduced a pre-emption right in favour of the state and the municipalities in 1993. Pre-emption can potentially be applied on all land plots located within existing – as well as future – building zones that are likely to be used for the construction of housing stocks, industrial development, the implementation of public facilities and airport infrastructures, or the protection of heritage buildings. It aims at providing state authorities with the capacity, first, to set up land reserves and, second, to prevent speculation leading to overprized land transactions, which could hamper public interest within planning processes. Pre-emption has proven to be quite efficient in Geneva as it helped both state and local authorities create favourable land property conditions for the implementation of land use policy objectives. It is, however, worth noticing that the full potential of pre-emption is rarely used by public authorities; the latter being, for example, very reluctant to use pre-emption in the case of building zone extension as allowed by law (Prélaz-Droux et al. 2009). The canton of Vaud has, for its part, very recently (12 February 2017) introduced in its cantonal Housing Act a limited pre-emption right on buildings and building land in favour of municipalities. It aims to promote the renovation of old housing stocks as well as the construction of new ones.

Although there exists, to our knowledge, no systematic survey on the implementation of a pre-emption right at the local (i.e. municipal) level in Switzerland,[1] one can claim, with very limited risk of error, that this type of land property instrument is absent from the policy instruments toolbox of most Swiss municipalities.

This reluctance to provide public authorities with policy instruments limiting private property rights may be explained by the persistence of a 'communitarian' ideology as well as the historic significance of (neo-)liberal ideas in Swiss political culture (Knoepfel and Schweizer 2015). Both phenomena have contributed to the development of a popular feeling of mistrust about (increasing) state power and have led political parties to fight for a limited and controlled transfer of decision-making powers to public authorities. The central political role played by civil society organisations and non-governmental organisations (NGOs) in solving public problems, as well as the very central importance of the 'subsidiarity principle' in Swiss polity (Linder 2010), both illustrate this kind of 'anti-state' ideology. It is, however, interesting to notice that there are significant differences between cantons regarding the role (to be) conferred to the state and public authorities. Whereas the cantons of Central and East Switzerland are good examples of this 'liberal', and, to a certain extent, 'anti-state' conception, cantons of western Switzerland (including Bern) have proven to be less reluctant to develop more interventionist public policies. It is thus not surprising to find the more interventionist land use policy instruments in this part of the country, such as taxes on added-value in Bern and pre-emption rights in Geneva and Vaud.

Effectiveness, efficiency, legitimacy, and practicability of pre-emption right

Empirical evidence from France (cf. *Melot*) and to a certain extent from Switzerland (Bellanger 2013; Prélaz-Droux et al. 2009; Tanquerel and Bellanger 2009) shows that the pre-emption right may be *effective* as well as *efficient* (notably in the case of indirect impacts: see developments below). However, as most interventionist instruments, *legitimacy* is a sensitive issue that tends to be tightly linked with *practicability*. These four criteria are further discussed in this section.

Effectiveness

A pre-emption right can impact landowners in *direct* and *indirect* terms. Direct impacts compel (private) landowners, willing to sell their plots, to cede them to state authorities (mostly local or regional). The main (positive) effects of such mandatory transfers of private land property titles to public ownership are twofold. Not only do public authorities gain access to strategic land plots that are crucial for implementing planning objectives of public interest, but the instrument also drastically limits speculative or hoarding behaviours of private landowners who seek to prevent the realisation of these objectives. In this regard, state pre-emption may also impede local (informal 'little') arrangements between private landowners, architects, and construction firms.

Indirect impacts consist mainly of pressure on landowners through the threat of pre-emption as well as an increase in the control of the local land market by public authorities, which is a resulting consequence of publicity and the transparency obligations imposed on landowners willing to sell their land plots.

Like many interventionist (property right oriented) instruments, the effectiveness of a pre-emption right results as much from its direct as from its indirect impacts: the public authorities' threat to use pre-emption is often a sufficiently strong signal to convince (private) landowners to use their property (land plots or buildings) in accordance with planning objectives. In the same way, the increased transparency of local land markets resulting from the obligation of publicity imposed on landowners provides public authorities with a substantial increase in their capacities to control these markets.

Efficiency

The efficiency of a pre-emption right varies significantly between direct and indirect impacts. Whereas direct impacts can be rather costly for public authorities depending on the size and the (market) value of the pre-empted plots, indirect impacts are very efficient, for the most part, as they are nearly free by-products.

It should, however, be noted that an interdependent relationship exists between the two types of impacts. Indeed, the strength of indirect impacts depends, to a certain extent, on the scope and frequency of the use of pre-emption by (local) public authorities: if never used, pre-emption will cease to be considered a threat by the landowners.

Legitimacy

Legitimacy depends first of all on the capacity of public authorities to enable the recognition and acceptance, by the citizens, the other political actors as well as civil society organisations, of public problems as sufficiently important to be solved through state intervention. Pre-emption's legitimacy will thus depend on the relationship – or the 'ratio' – between the type and importance of public interests at stake and the (perceived) scope of limitations imposed to private property. The acceptability of which depends on the dominant view of private property protection within the society.

Legitimacy also strongly depends on the power relationships between the actors negatively affected by pre-emption (first the landowners) and the beneficiaries of its implementation (municipalities, citizens, tenants, etc.). The broader the group of beneficiaries, the more legitimate the instrument. Conversely, the more powerful the negatively affected actors are (landowners, architects, construction firm, investors, etc.), the less legitimate the instrument. In particular, the strength of landowners' opposition will depend on the (real or imaginary) loss in value of their property. Therefore, legitimacy of pre-emption could probably be substantially increased through the integration of the developers, investors, and construction firms in the group of pre-emption beneficiaries.

But legitimacy of pre-emption also depends, on a more practical level, on its efficiency as well as on its concrete impact on public finances: if too expensive for the taxpayers, the instrument could also be contested by a part of its supposed beneficiaries.

Finally, it is worth noting that pre-emption contributes to the strengthening of the executive to the detriment of the legislative: municipal executives are given the power to drastically intervene on the land market with only loose control by the parliament.

Practicability

The implementation of an unlimited state pre-emption right usually requires at a minimum the following four steps: (1) zoning of the planning area concerned with pre-emption, (2) provision of funds for the acquisition of pre-empted land, (3) assessment of property value by an independent land commission, and (4) completion of land purchase by public authorities.

The main conditions for achieving these steps are the following:

- Existence of a clear legal basis;
- Strong political support from citizens, other political actors (notably legislative body), as well as civil society organisations;
- Availability of public funds;
- High reactivity and processing speed of the executive authorities.

Concluding remark

The Swiss example shows, by contrast, the rather high intervention capacity of French public authorities on land markets, in particular through the use of pre-emption. The latter is one of the main instruments allowing land acquisition, which can then be used for strengthening land use policy implementation. Whereas Swiss public authorities are most of the time obliged to negotiate, sometimes bitterly, with a number of more or less cooperative individual and/or collective landowners in order to implement their planning objectives and development projects, French authorities can rely, when interacting with private landowners, on the convincing power provided by the threat of pre-emption.

Notwithstanding this significant difference between the two countries regarding the power configuration in between private and public actors, as well as the intervention capacity of public authorities, it is uncertain if French land use regime can guarantee a better way of dealing with land scarcity. If it is likely that the intervention capacity of French authorities is allowing them to implement rather quickly planning decisions and projects, numerous examples have proven that (centralised) state planning processes with limited local and/or private counter-powers do not automatically lead to optimal decisions when dealing with land scarcity issues.

Thus, as the Swiss case shows, the obligation for public authorities – owing to the very limited public ownership on land – to negotiate with private landowners or investors (and, what's more, under the control of direct democracy) can sometimes lead to similar if not more optimal planning decisions with regard to a careful land use; the major problem being the huge amount of time necessary for the realisation of such development projects.

Note

1 On 1 January 2017, Switzerland had 2,255 communes/municipalities (Source: www.bfs.admin.ch/bfs/fr/home/bases-statistiques/agvch.html), which render such a survey rather hard to realise.

References

Bellanger, F. (2013) Déclassement et autres mesures de planification dans le canton de Genève, in: Foëx, B. (ed.) *Planification territoriale. Droit fédéral et spécificités cantonales*, Bâle Schulthess Verlag, Genève, Zürich, 85–112.

Knoepfel, P. and Schweizer, R. (2015) Le local et le global: quatre défis de la codification du droit foncier dans le cadre du processus de rédaction du Code civil suisse de 1907, in: Travési, C. and Ponsonnet, M. (eds) *Les conceptions de la propriété foncière à l'épreuve des revendications autochtones: possession, propriété et leurs avatars*, Pacific-Credo Publications, Marseille, 79–93.

Linder, W. (2010) *Swiss democracy: Possible solutions to conflicts in multicultural societies*, Palgrave Macmillan, Basingstoke.

Prélaz-Droux, R., Maunoir, A. and Tranda-Pittion, M. (2009) Politique foncière et aménagement du territoire dans les cantons de Genève et Vaud, *Projet d'agglo franco-valdo-genevois*, 10(3), Genève.

Tanquerel, T. and Bellanger, F. (eds) (2009) *La maîtrise publique du sol: expropriation formelle et matérielle, préemption, contrôle du prix*, Schulthess Verlag, Zürich.

A Serbian perspective on pre-emption rights: change that was necessary?

Sofija Nikolić

History: right of pre-emption in Serbia and former Yugoslavia

It is important to have an insight into the historical development of the right of pre-emption in Serbia and the former Yugoslavia in order to understand its main characteristics and purpose, which changed due to the different political and ideological circumstances in the country. Throughout the whole historical period and up to today, the right of pre-emption in Serbia is mainly used for acquiring agricultural land, whereas in France the instrument is primarily used for urban purposes. Scarcity of agricultural land and public interest were some of the main reasons that kept right of pre-emption dominant in that field. Looking through the history it is possible to find some similarities between the French and Serbian systems. Namely, in one period in Serbia pre-emption right was also used for urban purposes. That allowed municipalities to acquire land necessary for residential areas, public schools, hospitals, and other urban purposes without expropriation.

The right of pre-emption had existed in Serbia as early as the Middle Ages. This is evidenced by the Prizren Deed of Title, which originated during the reign of Emperor Dušan of the Nemanjić dynasty (1336–1366), and by articles 10 and 11 of the Codex Justinianus, which prescribed that cousins of sellers and residents of sellers' municipalities have the right to purchase the land in question before other interested parties. This rule has, as part of customary law, remained in force in later times during the Ottoman occupation that lasted from the fourteenth to the nineteenth century. In said period, Serbs lived in large family cooperatives (Kadlec 1924), which represented, similar to the old Roman familia, a community of people and goods. All goods, with the exception of personal items, were the ownership of the community and were part of the collective property. If one of the cooperatives was forced to dispose of some of its property, pre-emption right were established to the benefit of other cooperatives. During those times, the primary purpose of the right of pre-emption was to keep the land in the hands of the people who lived in that area and to prevent it from being transferred into the hands of foreigners. Circumstances have changed significantly with the enactment of the Serbian Civil Code of 1844. Family cooperatives have ceased to exist. Collective property was divided among former cooperative members and, from that time forward, individual property became dominant. However, the feeling of community, mutual solidarity, and support has remained. It is common knowledge that the majority of Slavic peoples are (were) traditionally closer to the idea of collectivism than the idea of individualism, and were prepared to accept the position that the public interest is above private (individual) interests. Thanks to this, the legal system in Serbia, as well as the legal system of the common state of South-Slavic peoples (Yugoslavia), incorporated different modalities of the right of pre-emption to the benefit of the (social) community.

Laws on Settlement, enacted during the Kingdom of Serbs, Croats, and Slovenians (1922) and the Kingdom of Yugoslavia (1931) prescribed that in case of the sale of land awarded to the settler by the state, rights of pre-emption were granted to other settlers in the municipality, agricultural cooperatives, and unions of agricultural cooperatives. These laws were of a special character (*lex specialis*) and derogated general rules prescribed in the Civil Code that established rights of pre-emption only to the benefit of co-owners and owners of neighbouring plots (Serbian Civil Code of 1844 art. 670, 672). Special rules were prescribed to ensure social peace and to prevent former large landowners from retaking the land that was nationalized and awarded to poor settlers from other parts of the country.

After World War II in Yugoslavia (and Serbia, which was part of Yugoslavia), construction of a new social order based on socialist ideology began. All legislation enacted by the former kingdom was removed, including that which prescribed the right of pre-emption. However, unlike the countries in the Eastern-European (Soviet) bloc, Socialist Yugoslavia preserved traditional legal institutions such as private property, contracts arranging the transfer of property, the possibility of inheritance, and others (Nikolić 2010). Restrictions were in place only with respect to the scope. Thus, for example, an agricultural household could have up to 10 hectares of arable land in private ownership in lowlands and up to 15 hectares in mountainous regions. This was the so-called maximum. Households of such size enabled a decent living to agricultural producers and ensured the stability of the entire social community. The majority of the total arable land was owned privately by individuals, while the rest was in ownership of agricultural cooperatives and self-governing agricultural companies (Gams 1961) founded by the state. The right of pre-emption was also developed in these ideological and normative frameworks.

The right of pre-emption could be established by law, contract, and will. Statutory right of pre-emption was by far the most common in practice and was set widely, both with respect to the goods on which it was established and the persons who could be its beneficiaries (holders). Statutory right of pre-emption with respect to agricultural land was granted to (1) agricultural companies or cooperatives, (2) municipalities, and (3) owners of neighbouring land plots (Law on Sale of Immovable Property art. 22) (Cvetić 2002). This normative decision was conceived to enable public interest to be met. First, agricultural companies enlarged their property by purchasing land owned by the state. Second, municipalities could, without expropriation and based on contracts, acquire lands that were necessary for construction of schools, hospitals, sports facilities, and entire residential blocks, all in accordance with zoning plans. Third, owners of neighbouring plots could enlarge their possessions and make more efficient use of their resources, which was also in the interest of the social community. Municipalities had pre-emption rights with respect to office space and land in the city development area (Law on Sale of Immovable Property art. 23, 25). When selling development land, owners were mandated to first offer to sell to the municipality in which the land is situated. If the municipality did not accept the offer within the prescribed deadline, the owner was free to sell the development land to third parties.

Statutory pre-emption right was widely applied in practice and contributed to an effective pursuit of public interest, without frequent resources to other legal institutes such as expropriation, which would imply a more direct interference of the state in property relations.

Following the change of social order in the 1990s, the right of pre-emption was significantly narrowed under the influence of neoliberal ideas.

Right of pre-emption with respect to agricultural land in Serbia

Today, right of preemption with respect to agricultural land is granted to owners of neighbouring agricultural plots. Owners of agricultural land are mandated to submit an offer to all holders of pre-emption rights at the same time before selling the land. The offer has to be made in writing via a registered letter and should contain all information on the immovable property, price, and other conditions for sale. It is necessary for the holder of pre-emption rights to declare, also in writing, whether he/she accepts the offer or declines it, within 15 days. If the offer is declined or the answer is not provided within the prescribed deadline the seller is free to sell the land in question to any third party (Law on Sale of Immovable Property arts. 7, 8). A holder of the right of pre-emption who did not receive the offer can file a lawsuit contesting the validity of the contract on sale and request to buy the land in question under the same conditions. (Law on Sale of Immovable Property art. 10).

When there are more neighbouring agricultural plots whose owners have the right of pre-emption, advantage is granted to the person whose land has a longer borderline with the property being sold. If the borderlines are equal in length, the advantage is given to the owner of a larger plot (Law on Sale of Immovable Property art. 6). Although it may seem, at first glance, that the right of pre-emption was established exclusively in the interest of owners of neighbouring plots, the legislator was guided by public interests as well when enacting this provision. As previously stated, pre-emption rights enabled enlargement of plots and thus better and more efficient use of available agricultural lands.

Provisions of the law regulating the right of pre-emption with respect to agricultural land are applied in practice. A significant role in the controlling the implementation of the right of pre-emption is given to notaries public. Namely, in order for a contract on sale of immovable property to be valid, it is necessary for it to be certified before a notary public. During the certification procedure, the notary public is mandated, among other things, to ensure that the right of pre-emption was not violated. If no offer was made to holders of the right of pre-emption, the notary in question will decline to certify the contract, thereby preventing the sale of agricultural land in question.

Although significantly narrower in comparison with the previous period, the right of pre-emption with respect to agricultural land is an effective means for furthering public and individual interests.

Right of pre-emption with respect to waterfront land in Serbia

Historical and political changes had a significant influence on pre-emption right. After the change of the social order pre-emption right was no longer used to meet a variety of public interests as in the period after World War II. Statutory pre-emption right maintained only for areas where the land is particularly scarce, as previously mentioned, for agricultural land (in a narrower scope) and for polders.

With the aim of protection from flooding, the right of pre-emption was established to the benefit of the Republic or the Autonomous Province with respect to sale of waterfront land. According to the Water Act, waterfront land is defined as land that contains water permanently or intermittently, including riverbeds, lake beds, and waterside areas. The coastal area that belongs to the waterfront land is between 10 meters and 50 meters wide, depending on the size of the watercourse and flood protection in certain areas. In accordance with the provisions of the Water Act, owners of waterfront land are mandated, when selling said land, to first offer it to the competent state body or body of the autonomous province. If the offer is declined, or the answer is not provided within 30 days, the owner is free to sell the land in question to any third party (Water Act art. 12). Introduction of pre-emptive rights creates the possibility for the state to exercise more control over land that contains water permanently or intermittently. This enables easier management of potential flood risks and creates possibilities for easier control over the manner and appropriateness of use of waterfront lands.

Right of pre-emption in Serbia was not mainly used for urban purposes as in France, except from the period after World War II until the 1990s when it was significantly narrowed under the influence of neoliberal ideas and it was no longer used as an instrument for urban planning. The right of pre-emption regarding agricultural land was the one that, with some modifications, remained from the previous period. As agricultural land is a scarce resource, pre-emption rights are used in order to provide better and more efficient land use, which is both in the private and public interest. Another field where pre-emption right is used in public interest is for managing potential flood risk by buying waterfront land. We can conclude that right of pre-emption in Serbia is also used as an instrument for achieving public interest, especially with regard to land as a scarce resource, but in almost completely different fields and for different purposes comparing to France. Nowadays, expropriation is an instrument used more frequently to satisfy public interests in the field of spatial planning in Serbia.

References

Cvetić, R. (2002) *Pravo preče kupovine*, Novi Sad, SCI.

Gams, A. (1961) *Osnovi stvarnog prava*, Belgrade, 122.

Kadlec, K. (1924) *Prvobitno slovensko pravo pre X veka*, translated and supplemented by F. Taranovski), Belgrade.

Nikolić, D. (2010) Legal culture and legal transplants – Serbian report, in: Sánchez Cordero, J. A. (ed.) *Legal culture and legal transplants, reports to the XVIII international congress of comparative law*, Washington, DC, 35–37 (online) available at: http://isaidat.di.unito.it/index.php/isaidat/ article/viewFile/62/71 (accessed 16 June 2017).

12 Tradable development rights in the U.S.

Making zoning flexible through market mechanisms

Thomas Skuzinski and Evangeline R. Linkous

Introduction

In 1972, New York City amended its zoning ordinance to create a 'Special Park District' bounded by 60th Street, Third Avenue, 38th Street, and Eighth Avenue (French 1976: 592), an area that included two private parks in the expansive Tudor City complex. The parks – which lie at opposite ends of a bridge spanning a major thoroughfare and that were viewable by most of the residences in the 12-building Tudor City complex – were 'surrounded by tall apartment buildings (and formed) a key spot of greenery, light and air in one of the most densely built, and worst polluted, parts of Manhattan' (Marcus 1974: 79). About 40 years after the completion of Tudor City in late 1970, Fred F. French Investing Company, the property's owner and manager, sold the complex to a real estate developer, Ramsgate Properties. The sale included two mortgages covering both of the parks (French 1976: 594).

Ramsgate planned redevelopment of the area around the 42nd Street overpass that would either build atop or overshadow the parks to accommodate new office buildings (French 1976: 591). In response, the city established the Special Park District, placing the parks in an overlay where only incidental recreational facilities could be built, and making the two parks 'granting lots', from which the owner could allocate or sell the lost building rights to 'receiving lots' (owned by itself or a third party) in the district. By purchasing the development rights, a receiving lot owner could gain a 'by right' increase in floor area ratio (FAR) of 10 percent, or up to 20 percent with a special permit approval (French 1976: 592). Before completion of a transfer, the city planning commission chairman would be required to certify a plan for continued maintenance of the park at the owner's expense (French 1976: 592, 593). Shortly after the regulation passed, payment on the park mortgages ceased because the parks – now public and undevelopable – could no longer serve as viable security. French brought a suit challenging the constitutionality of the rezoning and seeking compensation for the taking (i.e. expropriation) of his land, and ultimately prevailed.

Around the same time New York City designated the Special Park District, New Jersey created the Pinelands Environmental Council to help manage preservation of the state's Pine Barrens, a forest area containing an aquifer critical to the water system of the northeastern U.S. In 1979, Congress established more than 1 million acres of the Pinelands as the first resource to be protected in its National Reserve program, which targeted places of 'ecological sensitivity, natural beauty, and cultural importance' (Gardner 1991: 198–199). In partnership with the federal government, the New Jersey Pinelands Commission would oversee a program to limit development and protect Pinelands resources by awarding Pinelands Development Credits (PDCs) to landowners who recorded permanent deed restrictions on their property in accord with a Comprehensive Management Plan (CMP). The Pinelands Development Credits would be sold through market exchanges to owners of land in designated Regional Growth Areas or to a public Pinelands Development Credit bank (Gardner 1991: 201).

Hobart Gardner owned a 217-acre (ca. 88-hectare) farm in the Uplands Agricultural Production Area in the Pinelands, an area in which the original Comprehensive Management Plan permitted one accessory agricultural dwelling unit per 10 acres (4 hectares). In 1987, Gardner was considering subdividing his property into several 10-acre 'farmettes', but a Comprehensive Management Plan revision that year – made because of concerns about overdevelopment of agricultural areas – significantly restricted Gardner's options, allowing only one residential unit for every 40-acre (16-hectare) tract (Gardner 1991: 205). Hobart Gardner – like the French Investment Company – claimed that these actions were an expropriation of his property without compensation and challenged the Pinelands program in state court, but lost. Near the end of this chapter, after we arm the reader with essential background knowledge, we revisit the divergent outcomes in these two cases.

These stories describe two transfer of development rights (TDR) programs, and together illustrate how rights transfers can be used to preserve land that is scarce or at risk of becoming scarce. They also show how the public interest in land preservation can come into conflict with private rights, and how the legal system resolves this tension. The scarcity in both New York City and New Jersey arose because of the existing or potential gap between the post-development value of land and its preserved value, an economic dynamic that – under pure market conditions – would promote the transformation of urban parks into massive skyscrapers, and the incremental degradation of a major natural resource that included wildlife habitat, prime agricultural land, and a massive freshwater aquifer.

The conditions that give rise to scarcity are not just present in the East Coast megalopolis. The more than 200 TDR programs in the U.S. – which span diverse institutional, socioeconomic, and geographic settings – reveal the need to manage scarce land and community resources as an omnipresent issue, even in a country that seems to have vast reserves of land (Nelson et al. 2012). TDR originated in the U.S., where the tool was initially used to permit the sale of unused air rights to adjacent lots under the original 1916

New York City zoning ordinance (Giordano 1987). Since then, multitudinous TDR transactions have protected hundreds of thousands of acres of land from more intense development, with millions more acres eligible for protection. Although in use for more than a century, TDR gained momentum as a leading tool of the Smart Growth movement and growth management more generally. Some of the more well-known and successful programs are found in cities and counties within states that have or had some type of growth management (e.g. Maryland, Washington, and Florida).

The chapter proceeds in six sections. First, we review the basic features of TDR programs and discuss the rationale underlying the use of this tool. Second, we describe the governance and implementation of TDR programs. Third, we address TDR effectiveness, highlighting some limitations in the tool and existing research about its efficacy. Fourth, we consider the issue of legitimacy. In the conclusion, we briefly discuss policy implications and future research directions. As suggested by our discussion so far, we focus on the U.S. TDR has been studied in other contexts, and we recommend the reader supplement our discussion with other sources for a comparative perspective (e.g. China (Wang et al. 2009); France (Renard 2007); Italy (Renard 2007; Micelli 2002); Germany (Henger and Bizer 2010); the Netherlands (Janssen-Jansen 2008); and Taiwan (Shih and Chang 2015)).

TDR: basic features and rationale

A TDR program creates a market system for the re-allocation of development rights, shifting entitlements from a sending lot (or parcel) to a receiving lot (or parcel). In a typical TDR program, a local government designates a sending area of land targeted for protection, and allows sending area landowners to sever and sell their development rights to landowners in designated receiving areas planned for growth. As Costonis (1973: 85, 86) notes,

> development rights transfer breaks the linkage between particular land and its development potential. . . (avoiding) the either/or dilemma because it both protects the threatened resource and enables the owner of the restricted site to recoup the economic value represented by the site's frozen potential.

The transfer of development rights can be voluntary (i.e. sending lot landowners have the option to use their right to develop or sell it for compensation) or mandatory (i.e. regulations such as zoning limit or prevent further development of a parcel such that economic benefit can only be realized through a transfer). Once removed, usually permanently through a conservation easement recorded with the property title (Juergensmeyer et al. 1998: 446, 447), development rights can be sold for eventual use on other land, to a third-party landowner or a public TDR bank that brokers transfers among private landowners. Rights can also be shifted among properties under the same ownership, as was permitted in the Tudor City program. When attached to a receiving lot, the rights (which may be known as credits) can accord any of a wide array of benefits customizable to community interests: density and floor area ratio bonuses, increased setbacks, additional residential units, exemption from building permit quotas, or – most simply – the basic right to develop at all in a location where it has been otherwise restricted. TDR programs usually integrate with zoning provisions, with variation in use and bulk classifications often serving as a way to delineate sending and receiving areas and as a generator of supply and demand (Chiodelli and Moroni 2016). For example, a community may designate all agriculturally zoned lands as sending areas, and all high-density residential zones as receiving areas.

The underlying rationale common to all TDR programs is preservation of a scarce resource in the face of existing or anticipated growth (Pfeffer and Lapping 1994), and it is one among many tools available to governments in pursuit of that goal. Other approaches include purchase of development rights (PDR), where governments directly acquire land or development rights, or condemnation in exchange for compensation to the landowner under local governments' expropriation authority. A government could also use its regulatory power over land use to incentivize preservation (e.g. with a property tax abatement) or mandate it (e.g. by downzoning to decrease the allowable baseline use and bulk in an area).

What distinguishes TDR from traditional approaches is its market-based mechanism (Buitelaar and Needham 2007; Chapin 2012). If functioning properly, it should shift the costs of preservation to private actors, rather than require compensation because of expropriation (the direct purchase of property targeted for preservation) or a successful regulatory taking claim (the 'inverse condemnation' that occurs when property is devalued due to a regulation, such as TDR) (Juergensmeyer et al. 1998: 444, 445). Because of the reliance on formal, recorded deed restrictions rather than zoning designations or direct purchase, TDR preservation may be less susceptible to crumbling in the face of development pressure compared to more malleable planning policies. TDR uses compensation to balance inequities that can result from the differential limitations imposed by land use regulations. The well-known pattern of 'windfalls' and 'wipeouts' – a pattern in which some properties' values are substantially augmented at the expense of diminution in the value of others – is a redistributive injustice unlikely to be addressed fully by legal requirements of compensation owed to landowners due to expropriation, particularly when a regulation leaves enough of the original economic use of a property intact that a successful expropriation claim cannot be made.

TDR's shift away from traditional command-and-control regulation and towards a more market-driven approach can also assuage concerns about property rights infringement that often arise with regulatory diminution of property values. Many commentators have noted the long-standing emphasis on property rights in the U.S., an ideology that traces to the country's colonial heritage and the rights philosophy of John Stuart Mill (e.g. Jacobs 2008; Norton and Bieri 2014). This has resulted in a legal system in which the social or communal dimension of property ownership is severely diminished, and in which the public good and private rights are often antagonistically positioned. Against this backdrop, TDR functions as a tool that, in theory, should be able to advance the public interest in preservation while still acknowledging the value inherent in private development rights. Not surprisingly, TDR programs have fared well in states, such as Florida, that grapple with both strong growth pressures and powerful property rights constituencies.

TDR, then, is a tool that has remarkable potential for managing scarce resources through an efficient allocative mechanism driven by private exchange. It is a tool that, in theory, can balance strong property rights advocacy with countervailing interests in preservation and growth management. However, the move from theory to practice can be a difficult one and we discuss this in the next section.

Governing and implementing TDR

Land use control in the U.S. – from planning to zoning to the subdivision of land, along with myriad other regulatory tools – is extremely fragmented among tens of thousands of local governments, including cities, towns, counties, and a variety of other jurisdictional types. This institutional landscape exists because states – which have constitutional authority over a broad array of public health, safety, and welfare regulation through their reserved police powers – have delegated much of their land use planning and zoning power to local jurisdictions, either through broad grants of authority or piecemeal-enabling statutes. As with any land use regulation, the adoption and implementation of TDR programs is shaped directly by the system of initiative, immunity, and capacity that each state establishes for its local units.

The majority of TDR programs in the U.S. are administered by a single local government, often a county, or by a grouping of local units through an interlocal agreement. For example, the Boulder County, Colorado, program involves intergovernmental agreements between the county as a sending area and nine communities that serve as receiving areas (Pruetz and Standridge 2008: 82). State and local context drives distinct approaches to TDR in different places. For example, Pennsylvania TDR programs are typically organized as partnerships between urban townships (as receiving areas) and agricultural counties (as sending areas). In Florida, where counties absorb a large share of population growth and deliver many of the local services typically associated with municipalities, TDR is widely used at the county level as a way to rationalize growth. Just as regional governance structures – those that exist at a scale matching the economic unity of a metropolitan area or the ecological unity of a watershed, for example – are rare for even basic land use regulatory tools, so too are they atypical for TDR programs. The Pinelands program, described in the introduction, was able to function at a very large scale because it was backed by state enabling legislation and federal policy that specifically contemplated the possibility of TDR as a regional land use tool.

In the U.S., land use regulatory fragmentation and reliance on local governments creates an institutional geography that is often at odds with the geographies of real estate markets and resources in need of preservation. This can create myriad problems for local TDR administration. For programs targeting natural resource protection, local boundaries may not fully contain the resource targeted for preservation, potentially resulting in heightened development pressure on nearby unprotected areas. A local government may also not have an appropriately heterogeneous mix of potential sending and receiving parcels, and the redistribution of density may be suboptimal compared to what could occur across a larger region. For example, a community may have to over-designate receiving lots by including parcels without supportive infrastructure to ensure demand balances an oversupply of sending lots (or vice versa).

Governments whose boundaries do not coincide with the broader economic geography may also face a power imbalance with developers who function within a regional market. The latter will often have the capital liquidity necessary to be mobile within the entire region – they can build in any jurisdiction. The former, meanwhile, are pushed often into a competitive interlocal game in which the equilibrium strategy is to pursue growth relentlessly and, as a result, defer to developer demands that undermine TDR effectiveness (Peterson 1981; Logan and Molotch 1987). The public officials operating in many local jurisdictions are, at least in the U.S., faced with increasing demands on service provision and production, devolution of policy responsibility from higher levels of government, and reliance on property tax revenues that are often stagnant or shrinking. A TDR program might be attractive because it does not require direct payment for preservation from the public fisc, but many local governments are unfortunately not even in a position in which preservation is on the policy agenda.

A TDR program may have the appropriate geographic scale and the necessary grant of autonomy from a higher level of government, but the governing unit may lack the requisite technical and fiscal capacity needed to support the administrative expertise TDR requires. At first blush, TDR program administration seems fairly straightforward. In most programs, parcels or lots are typically located in separate areas that track underlying zoning classifications, leading many authors to regard TDR programs as a direct extension of zoning regulations (e.g. Renard 2007; Pruetz and Pruetz 2007). Indeed, when designating separate areas for a range of densities and intensities, a community is engaging in the same type of use-based and areal planning and zoning practices with which it is already familiar (Stinson 1996).

But even in this most traditional and most common type of TDR program – that is a 'zoning integrative' program with categorical or geographical distinctions among separate sending and receiving areas (Chiodelli and Moroni 2016: 423, 424) – officials must address an array of implementation questions while dealing with market dynamics and the local political economy. First, what should be the baseline densities in the sending and receiving areas, and what should each development right or credit award in the receiving area? Developers may be able to achieve their desired density through rezonings, special exceptions, or other provisions, undermining demand for additional density that must be purchased. In many communities, underlying zoning allows as much density as the market can absorb, rendering additional development rights through TDR valueless. Second, should the incentive offered in the receiving area be by right or by discretionary permit? The presence of a permitting process can promote legitimacy and perhaps even democratic anchorage of TDR, but it can also create too much uncertainty about the value of the development rights – a problem that ultimately led to the judgment against the TDR program at issue in *French*, as we detail later. Third, to what extent should other forms of zoning relief for receiving lots be limited to ensure other regulations are not competing with TDR? Should the program be mandatory or voluntary from the perspective of sending and receiving area landowners? Is a public bank necessary, and if so how much should it pay for development rights? A governing body might even consider breaking from tradition and establishing a TDR program that functions through a cap-and-trade exchange, as is common in other regulatory permit markets. Several authors have outlined this possibility (see Chiodelli and Moroni 2016; Walls and McConnell 2007; Thorsnes and Simon 1999). However, we are unaware of any extant example of this approach in the U.S.

When we consider the breadth of knowledge necessary for establishing a TDR program, it becomes clear that planners may not have – indeed, may probably lack – sufficient information or capacity, particularly when considering their impact on the land market. Although TDR programs build on the cap-and-trade framework used in the air and water pollution context, land markets differ because they lack interchangeable commodities and a large, robust marketplace. In land markets we find imperfect information about highly individuated goods (i.e. each parcel is inherently unique), strong sensitivity to timing, a limited number of buyers and sellers, and the possibility of temporary 'bubbles' (Fulton et al. 2004; Linkous 2016; Nelson et al. 2012).

This section demonstrates that no one 'right' answer exists to the question of optimal TDR governance and implementation strategies. Consider, for example, the opening narratives in this chapter. The New York City program was administered over a densely populated, multi-block urban area by one very large local government. It was a single-zone program, with strict sending lot regulations that prevented all development and a system of receiving area density bonuses that were in part by right and in part discretionary. By contrast, the Pinelands program covered a vast, mostly rural expanse of land directly involving dozens of local jurisdictions plus state and federal government oversight. It used a dual-zone approach, with categorical distinction among multiple types of sending areas that varied in their allowable density and intensity of use and a complex system of benefits accessible through purchase of development rights. The programs also varied in the additional layers of administration necessary for planning and implementation. The Special Park District in New York City, and other special districts like it established since then, have largely been an extension of the existing regulatory framework, while the Pinelands effort involved a separate statewide commission, an extra comprehensive management plan, extensive revision and monitoring of constituent local plans, and both a statewide development rights bank and another one for an individual county.

Evaluating TDR effectiveness

Assessment of the effectiveness of TDR remains rare and the evidence is mixed. Studies of TDR exhibit some consistent research design features. Most studies focus on highly successful TDR programs (e.g. Pruetz and Standridge 2008; Walls and McConnell 2007; Machemer and Kaplowitz 2002). Such research excludes the majority of programs, which have protected only a limited number of acres and have generated few transfers. Eight of the top TDR programs in the U.S., measured by number of acres preserved, have protected fewer than 5,000 acres each (Pruetz and Standridge 2008). Programs that have failed to generate any transfer activity are overlooked despite the valuable information they might provide.

Also, research tends to privilege *number of acres preserved* or *number of transactions* as the key outcomes. At a minimum, this approach fails to normalize by program goals (an internal measure of effectiveness) or by an objective appraisal of the number of preserved acres or transactions appropriate or feasible in a given context (an external effectiveness measure). The perspective also ignores the regulatory landscape. TDR programs exist, in every instance, alongside other land use tools, and may appear deficient as a preservation policy because other tools help carry this burden. For example, the TDR program in Monroe County, Florida, is one of a suite of stringent regulatory tools designed to protect the county's coastal resources, which include the Florida Keys and parts of the Everglades. These regulations strictly limit developable land in the county. TDR serves an important role in mitigating property rights impacts associated with these regulations, but the scale of TDR-facilitated preservation is small as a result. At a more fundamental level, the privileging of raw acreage or counts of transactions treats every acre or exchange of development rights as equally effective. Linkous and Chapin (2014) find evidence that TDR programs that protect large numbers of acres can still lead to fragmented development and sprawl in rural areas while failing to support compact community goals.

TDR research often uses descriptive single- or multiple-case studies. As a result, 'best practices' are typically lists of features that are functionally essential to any development rights market (and that the leading programs, not surprisingly, share) or are accounts of what has worked in a specific setting over a limited time frame. For example, Johnston and Madison (1997), in a review of four large and well-known programs, discuss at length the importance of consensus-building and education in eliciting community support for programs built from the ground up (i.e. those not mandated by state or federal legislation). Pruetz and Standridge (2008), in a meta-review of TDR articles about the largest U.S. programs, found that many shared common features, but these included readily apparent necessities such as a demand for bonus development in the receiving area, the need for receiving areas customized to local circumstances, and the importance of strict sending area regulations. Machemer and Kaplowitz (2002) examined three programs through an iterative case study approach, and found that successful programs featured, among many other characteristics, a strong political foundation and simple, cost-efficient administration.

The extant TDR research has produced evidence that has value and is foundational to an understanding of program function. However, many underexplored opportunities to better understand the efficacy of the tool remain. First, TDR could be studied through quantitative analysis. Given the many ways in which TDR programs can be structured and the fairly large population of programs, transactions, and parcels from which to draw data, TDR is well-suited to large sample quantitative evaluation. Unfortunately, such work – which could complement the findings from qualitative work – is rare.

Second, TDR has not been examined as a tool whose efficacy and impacts might vary with changes in the political economy in which the tool is implemented. Although the literature on growth management explores the roles of community socio-demographic attributes and development interests in influencing outcomes, this work does not specifically theorize or empirically test how TDR as a specific policy tool interacts with local, regional, and global capital flows or with the institutional setting. Such work could incorporate both spatial heterogeneity (differences across jurisdictions) and temporal heterogeneity (changes in contexts over time).

Finally, we observe that TDR researchers have yet to tackle the most pressing question for planners and policymakers: how does the tool perform compared to viable policy alternatives, including both traditional zoning mechanisms (such as variances or downzoning) as well as tools specifically targeted at preservation (such as purchase of development rights)? For readers of this book, the question is undoubtedly of considerable interest. To answer such a question, researchers would need not only a comprehensive TDR program database but also a comprehensive land use policy database. This would allow direct comparison of outcomes in places that are similar across multiple, theoretically meaningful dimensions with variation only in their suite of land use tools. While such work would be challenging, it would help practitioners gain insight into which tools will be most effective in managing and preserving scarce resources.

The legitimacy of TDR

Lastly, we consider the legitimacy of TDR programs. At the outset, we note that the functional legitimacy of TDR depends on a legal system with a few basic features. First, development rights should be distinct and severable from property ownership. A long-standing concept in U.S. property law, and one intrinsic to the function of TDR programs, is that of property as a bundle of rights that includes the rights to possess, exclude, transfer, and develop. This notion is present in legal systems that follow an Anglo-Saxon property tradition, while those following a Roman tradition favor a holistic conceptualization of property ownership (Renard 2007). Second, if a TDR program is governed by a unit that lacks its own land use regulatory authority, then the ability to engage in TDR must be enabled by the requisite higher level of government. Third, at a minimum, TDR must serve the public interest. In terms drawn from U.S. constitutional substantive due process jurisprudence, it must be rationally related to a legitimate state interest, which includes protection of the public health, safety, morals, or general welfare. Similar provisions are present in many legal systems. So long as TDR programs articulate preservation of scarce resources as a goal, they are likely to meet such requirements. A clear link to an existing public interest may also help secure the support needed to sustain TDR exchange. Montgomery County, Maryland, for example, has a deep history of pioneering land use policy and a large share of productive family farms, creating a strong interest in agriculture preservation through TDR. Similarly, TDR has fared well in communities with long-standing commitments to natural resource preservation (such as Boulder, Colorado, and the Lake Tahoe region) or places where farming has high cultural and economic value (such as Calvert County, Maryland, and Manheim Township, Pennsylvania; Fulton et al. 2004; Machemer and Kaplowitz 2002; Lane 1998).

After moving past these basic functional requirements, TDR legitimacy can be viewed through three lenses. First, do such programs garner public support? The officials who adopt and administer TDR programs are either elected or function within a bureaucracy that is not always well insulated from public pressures. We have already noted TDR's ability to appeal to property rights advocates who might otherwise oppose land use policy interventions, and this may be critical to overcoming a political economy that is strongly resistant to growth restrictions. Of course, some communities are resistant to growth and increased density and favor preserving community character. In these locales, TDR programs – which require higher density in the receiving area – may struggle for public legitimacy.

Second, TDR legitimacy may be undermined if the programs are perceived as captured by developers. Machemer and Kaplowitz (2002) identified a new generation of TDR programs in the 1990s and 2000s that responds to demand by developers for added density in rural and fringe locations. These programs, in contrast to the paradigmatic TDR examples, designate *receiving* areas in easier-to-develop greenfields where landownership is less fragmented and not-in-my-backyard (NIMBY) sentiment less likely. Linkous (2016) describes contemporary programs that provide vast new development entitlements on large, rural landholdings, suggesting an appropriation of the tool by development interests. In a non-U.S. setting, Shih and Chang (2015) show that TDR program outcomes in Taiwan are influenced by the monopoly power of well-connected investors.

Lastly, and related directly to the etymological roots of the word legitimacy, we must consider the constitutionality of TDR programs. The economic value of development rights has, in repeated cases, been the linchpin on which turned the legal validity of TDR programs. The stories from the opening of this chapter are illustrative. In the opinion in *French*, the Tudor City parks case, Judge Breitel recognized development rights as 'an essential component of the value of the underlying property' and noted that the challenged zoning amendment had rendered the rights once attached to the parks as

> utterly unusable until they could be attached to some accommodating real property, available by happenstance of prior ownership, or by grant, purchase, or devise, and subject to the contingent approvals of administrative agencies . . . events that may never happen because of the exigencies of the market and the contingencies and exigencies of administrative action.
>
> (1976: 597, 598)

In ruling the zoning amendment a violation of constitutional requirements, Breitel commented that 'the loose-ended transferable development rights in this case fall short of achieving a fair allocation of economic burden' (*French* 1976: 598). The court emphasized that the flaw was not in the notion of development rights transfer per se, but in the execution of the program. Any economic benefits from using the transferred rights were rendered, at best, uncertain and contingent because of the additional approval processes needed for their use at a receiving lot. The designation of the parks as undevelopable granting lots had – from the perspective of the developer-landowner – removed all reasonable economic value, forcing the developer to shoulder the entire burden of retaining the public value that remained from their use solely as parks.

By contrast, in *Gardner* (1991: 215) Judge Handler noted that the plaintiff

> retains several viable, economically beneficial uses of his land under the revised CMP. That those uses do not equal the former maximum value of the land in a less- or un-regulated state is not dispositive, for there exists no constitutional right to the most profitable use of property.

The two cases, each from a different state and a different era, hinged on the question of *how much deprivation of value is too much*? One could generalize that a complete ban on further development in a sending area coupled with a non-functional market with no buyers (including no ability for the government to serve as a buyer) would be definitively a regulatory taking requiring compensation. But beyond this extreme is a vast gray area within which most TDR programs operate.

Two U.S. Supreme Court cases – *Penn Central* (1978) and *Suitum* (1997) – provide a little more guidance but still leave TDR's status somewhat unsettled. The cases were not decided directly on the issue of TDR constitutionality, but each contained dicta that has been and will undoubtedly continue to be influential in shaping the judicial consideration of TDR programs.[1] In *Penn Central*, the Supreme Court remarked that

> [w]hile (development) rights may well not have constituted 'just compensation' if a 'taking' had occurred, the rights nevertheless undoubtedly mitigate whatever financial burdens the law has imposed on appellants and, for that reason, are to be taken into account in considering the impact of regulation.
>
> (*Penn Central* 1978: 33)

Similarly, a concurrence in *Suitum* by Justice Scalia reads in part that compensation provided via a TDR program can

> mitigat(e) the economic loss suffered by an individual whose property use is restricted, and property value diminished, but not so substantially as to produce a compensable taking. They may also form a proper part, or indeed the entirety, of the full compensation accorded a landowner when his property is taken.
>
> (*Suitum* 1997: 749, 750)

What all four cases emphasize is that the economic impact is at the heart of legitimacy, and must be evaluated to answer the constitutional question of whether regulatory expropriation has occurred. The value of the development rights, therefore, may be part of a legally required, just compensation scheme, or they may simply exist to more fairly distribute the benefits and burdens of scarce resource preservation. For those who view property ownership as containing inherent development rights and who hew closely to a strong property rights ethos, TDR – unlike traditional land use tools – acknowledges that what is being given up has value and that a private market (or at least a quasi-private market) is a reliable mechanism for advancing the public good. For those who view development value as bestowed by the government through its investment and regulations and, therefore, as part of the community's economic property, TDR can be framed as a way to mitigate distributive injustice. As noted earlier, regulations can produce windfalls and wipeouts – they can enhance the value of some properties at the expense of others. Constitutional guarantees may provide some limitation, but availing them requires the expense and delay of the judicial process. TDR programs create a transparent compensation mechanism. Thus, whether property rights are interpreted as individualistic or communitarian, development rights transfer can be a legitimacy-enhancing land use tool.

Conclusion

Undeveloped or underdeveloped land often has a dual identity as a scarce resource. To some, its greatest value lies in its present character as open space, farmland, a landmark, and the like, and it is this character as a diminishing resource that warrants preservation. To others, its greatest value lies in what it could become through development, and land that is suitable for development – that is not publicly held, that is not unbuildable due to natural features, and that exists in a market in which demand may arise – is itself a quite limited resource. TDR helps to reconcile the tension between these competing visions by allowing landowners to partake in the benefits of development while sharing the costs of preserving scarce resource lands. An optimal TDR program creates an efficient system of exchange in which the value of development rights transferred from preserved land (plus any retained rights) meets or exceeds the value of the land if developed, and in which the economic value of development elsewhere in the TDR jurisdiction offsets any tax base diminution from preservation. Unfortunately, the potential of TDR to achieve this balance often remains unfulfilled, and research needs to take a strong evaluative turn to better discern how TDR can achieve its promised outcomes. The question at the heart of this book – *can a given tool serve as an effective, practicable, and legitimate pathway to the preservation of a scarce resource?* – remains open with regard to TDR. What we do know is that TDR is a remarkably flexible tool, and that it has been able to preserve a diverse mix of scarce land and other community resources in the U.S. and internationally.

Note

1 Several authors have treated these cases at length, and we refer the reader to their work (e.g. Juergensmeyer et al. 1998: 461–467; Radford 1999; Lazarus 1997).

References

Buitelaar, E. and Needham, B. (2007) Property rights and private initiatives: An introduction, *Town Planning Review*, 78(1), 1–8.

Chapin, T. (2012) Introduction. From growth controls, to comprehensive planning, to smart growth: planning's emerging fourth wave. *Journal of the American Planning Association*, 78(1), 5–15.

Chiodelli, F. and Moroni, S. (2016) Zoning-integrative and zoning-alternative transferable development rights: Compensation, equity, efficiency, *Land Use Policy*, 52, 422–429.

Costonis, J.J. (1973) Development rights transfer: An exploratory essay, *The Yale Law Journal*, 83(1), 75–128.

French Inv. Co. v. City of NY, 1976. 39 N.Y.2d 587.

Fulton, W., Mazurek, J., Pruetz, R. and Williamson, C. (2004) *TDRs and other market-based land mechanisms: how they work and their role in shaping metropolitan growth*, The Brookings Institution, Washington, DC.

Gardner v. New Jersey Pinelands Com'n, 1991. 593 A.2d 251.

Giordano, M. (1987) Over-stuffing the envelope: The problems with creative transfer of development rights, *Fordham Urban Law Journak*, 16, 43.

Henger, R. and Bizer, K. (2010) Tradable planning permits for land use control in Germany, *Land Use Policy*, 27(3), 843–852.

Jacobs, H.M. (2008) The future of the regulatory takings issue in the United States and Europe: Divergence or convergence? *The Urban Lawyer*, 51–72.

Janssen-Jansen, L.B. (2008) Space for Space, a transferable development rights initiative for changing the Dutch landscape, *Landscape and Urban Planning*, 87(3), 192–200.

Johnston, R.A. and Madison, M.E. (1997) From land marks to landscapes: A review of current practices in the transfer of development rights, *Journal of the American Planning Association*, 63(3), 365–378.

Juergensmeyer, J.C., Nicholas, J.C. and Leebrick, B.D. (1998) Transferable development rights and alternatives after suitum, *The Urban Lawyer*, 441–475.

Lane, R. (1998) Transfer of development rights for balanced development, *Land Lines*, 10(2), 6–7.

Lazarus, R.J. (1997) Litigating Suitum v. Tahoe Regional Planning Agency in the United States Supreme Court, *Journal of Land Use & Environmental Law*, 12, 179.

Linkous, E.R. (2016) Transfer of development rights in theory and practice: The restructuring of TDR to incentivize development, *Land Use Policy*, 51, 162–171.

Linkous, E.R. and Chapin, T.S. (2014) TDR program performance in Florida, *Journal of the American Planning Association*, 80(3), 253–267.

Logan, J. and Molotch, H.L. (1987) *Urban fortunes: The political economy of place*, University of California, Berkeley.

Machemer, P.L. and Kaplowitz, M.D. (2002) A framework for evaluating transferable development rights programmes, *Journal of Environmental Planning and Management*, 45(6), 773–795.

Marcus, N. (1974) Mandatory development rights transfer and the taking clause: The case of Manhattan's Tudor City Parks, *Buffalo Law Review*, 24, 77.

Micelli, E. (2002) Development rights markets to manage urban plans in Italy, *Urban Studies*, 39(1), 141–154.

Nelson, A.C., Pruetz, R., Woodruff, D., Nicholas, J.C., Juergensmeyer, J.C. and Witten, J. (2012) The TDR handbook, in: *Designing and implementing transfer of development rights programs*, Island Press, Washington, DC.

Norton, R. and Bieri, D. (2014) Planning, law, and property rights: A US-European cross-national contemplation, *International Planning Studies*, 19, 3–4.

Penn Central Transp. Co. v. New York City, 1978. 438 U.S. 104.

Peterson, P.E. (1981) *City limits*, University of Chicago Press, Chicago.

Pfeffer, M. and Lapping, M. (1994) Farmland preservation, development rights, and the theory of the growth machine: The review of planners, *Journal of Rural Studies*, 10(3), 233–248.

Pruetz, R. and Pruetz, E. (2007) Transfer of development rights turns 40, *Planning & Environmental Law*, 59(6), 3–11.

Pruetz, R. and Standridge, N. (2008) What makes transfer of development rights work? Success factors from research and practice, *Journal of the American Planning Association*, 75(1), 78–87.

Radford, R.S. (1999) Takings and transferable development rights in the Supreme Court: The constitutional status of TDRs in the aftermath of suitum, *Stetson Law Review*, 28, 685.

Renard, V. (2007) Property rights and the 'transfer of development rights': Questions of efficiency and equity, *Town Planning Review*, 78(1), 41–60.

Shih, H. and Chang, H.B. (2015) Transfer of development rights and public-facility planning in Taiwan: An examination of local adaptation and spatial impact, *Urban Studies*, 53(2), 1244–1260.

Stinson, J.D. (1996) Transferring development rights: Purpose, problems, and prospects in New York, *Pace Law Review*, 17, 319.

Suitum v. Tahoe Regional Planning Agency (1997) 520 U.S. 725.

Thorsnes, P. and Simons, G.P. (1999) Letting the market preserve land: The case for a market-driven transfer of development rights program, *Contemporary Economic Policy*, 17(2), 256–266.

Walls, M.A. and McConnell, V.D. (2007) *Transfer of development rights in US communities: Evaluating program design, implementation, and outcomes*, Resources for the Future, Washington, DC.

Wang, H., Tao, R. and Tong, J. (2009) Trading land development rights under a planned land use system: The Zhejiang model, *China & World Economy*, 17(1), 66–82.

An Israeli perspective on TDR: trading for protecting

Nir Mualam

The idea of TDR sprouted in Israel in the early 1990s, when Tel Aviv's City Planning Department devised the first TDR scheme, using it to preserve modern and eclectic architecture in the historic urban core of the city (Bar Or 2013). This soon became a model for other local planning authorities who had sought to preserve their built heritage.

Israeli TDR policies have been promoted to secure public goods but they were also put in place to counteract potential 'takings' claims by landowners. Specifically, Tel Aviv-Jaffa's planning commission approved a local plan that nowadays enables the transfer of development rights, and at the same time grants owners additional incentives in the form of extra building rights. This package of incentives was intended to offset the costs of renovations of the historic building. In exchange, the owners of the receiving lot often sign an agreement with the granting lots in which they commit themselves to undertake certain preservation works. The result is often high-rise development (in receiving lots) alongside much smaller heritage structures in their vicinity. These 'planning deals' (Margalit 2013) are sometimes safeguarded by a site-specific statutory plan that removes rights from the granting lot and consequently upzones the receiving lot.

The Tel Avivian TDR program is the first and most significant program in Israel (Kimhi 2014: 91). It includes approximately 1,000 heritage buildings out of which 187 are earmarked for 'extra careful' protection. This means that the unused rights of those buildings must be transferred elsewhere (Marx 2014).

As a whole, however, Israeli planning has not managed to create the institutional and legal infrastructure to support TDR initiatives in other Israeli cities (Santo 2008). In recent years, several other cities such as Rishon-Le-Zion or Hertzliya looked to Tel Aviv in an attempt to learn how to put together local preservation schemes involving TDRs (Kimhi 2014), but so far these initiatives have not come to fruition. The reason behind this implementation gap is lack of expertise and local commitment to heritage protection in many localities. In addition, TDR is often introduced as part of a larger heritage plan. In turn, this might lead to arguments (and lawsuits) for the taking of property. Thus, introduction of TDR programs has been stalled. Despite these difficulties it is important to note that Israeli planners have increasingly become aware of TDR as a possible tool to protect natural environments (Gutthalf 2008) or to manage growth in densely populated areas that undergo urban regeneration (Klempert 2014).

Governing TDR programs in Israel

When a local planning authority wishes to introduce a TDR mechanism, it would normally have to be supported by regional planning bodies (Mualam 2015). This was the case for Tel Aviv, whose TDR policy had to gain state approval before its adoption. While the central government had approved local planning tools such as this, in general it stayed rather idle in devising national policies pertaining to TDR (Israel's State Comptroller 2005). This is certainly unlike the U.S. where state-enabling legislation can help in the transfer of development rights in certain jurisdictions.

Since TDR is not a mature practice in Israel, administrative expertise is rare. Except in Tel Aviv, municipalities have little or no experience in TDR (State Comptroller 2005). On a grander scale, the Israeli system has no TDR bank, and management plans are not in place either (Bar-Eli 2007).

Similar to the U.S., implementation issues abound; economists, the courts, and real estate appraisers often struggle with the issue of whether enough rights are granted to offset conservation costs. Moreover, it is not always easy to tie together several owners in a TDR deal. Thus, the municipal authority has had to act as a matchmaker, helping owners of heritage buildings initiate a transfer and look for a 'receiving' lot. Another challenge includes the taxation of the TDR deal by the Israeli Ministry of Finance who, for the first time, has had to determine whether or not to tax those transfers and whether to allow tax exemptions. This question mandates a careful assessment of the value of the air rights being transferred. Moreover, since the value of granting and receiving lots may be different depending on their location, the entire process entails a 'translation' of building rights, i.e. an evaluation of how many square meters can be transferred to the new location (Manoach 2014). This adds to the challenges of implementation because the entire process in ruled by appraisers, appeal tribunals, and the courts, and demands a certain degree of expertise to manage it (Mualam 2012).

Evaluating the efficacy of TDR programs

As in the U.S., in the Israeli arena an evaluation of TDR's efficiency ought to be carried out in light of its policy objectives. First, planners need to examine whether scarce resources were indeed protected and in what way. Second, they need to evaluate whether property rights were reasonably secured. These two poles mirror the two anchoring principles of TDR, namely to protect the public interest in land while securing private property rights.

It remains unclear whether Tel Aviv's TDR heritage program has been successful in devising a system that protects property rights. On the face of it, the program was not very successful in blocking lawsuits brought against the actions of the local planning commission. To the contrary, the evidence suggests that TDRs did not prevent owners of heritage properties from suing Tel Aviv city for an alleged diminution in their property value (Smolsky 2011). In fact there are hundreds of lawsuits for compensation, amounting to over 2 billion shekels (USD 500 million). These lawsuits, however, do not necessarily point to a distinct lack of efficiency of Tel Aviv's TDR program. Instead, they can imply a highly litigious environment.

An evaluation of the first five years of the Tel Aviv's heritage program indicates that the new program resulted in 20 detailed plans, involving 18 heritage buildings and 22 receiving lots (Marx 2014). The total amount of rights transferred was 12,000 square meters, which were eventually converted to 24,000 square meters in the receiving lots. Of the approximately 140,000 square meters in need of transfer due to the preservation scheme, less than 10 percent of those air rights have been transferred to another location. There is still an ongoing debate whether the program equips landowners with enough incentives to cover their costs.

Legitimating TDR

While the inception of TDR in the U.S. garnered a certain degree of public support, in Israel a relatively high level of institutional and public legitimacy was quickly replaced by a more careful and critical disposition, mostly expressed by planning experts and a group of academicians.

Before the first TDR program was introduced in Tel Aviv, Israeli courts had debated this policy (Santo 2008; Mualam 2012). Eventually, both the District and the Supreme Courts acknowledged the importance of adopting a market-driven and allocative policy, as long as it is in the public interest and does not impinge on private property rights (Administrative Petition 2003, 2001). This approach is very similar to that adopted by U.S. courts. Policymakers were also quick to adopt this novel tool. If it works in America, they argued, why not in the Middle East? This somewhat provincial approach was not unwarranted; as local governments faced an ever increasing threat of takings claims (Alterman 2007), the adoption of TDR was an essential lifebuoy. The public followed suit and supported the initiative, fuelled by numerous newspaper and media reporting about the importance of heritage protection.

However, it soon became evident that heritage protection and TDR expedited gentrification and resulted in socially regressive outcomes (Amit-Cohen 2005). Scholars exposed it as a market-driven mechanism that benefits developmental interests (Margalit 2014). This was supported by studies that showed that most transactions were carried out by incorporated bodies, not by the individuals who used to live in heritage properties in Tel Aviv.

Conclusion

The emerging Israeli model of TDR appears to follow the American prototype; it depends on free-market initiatives and the actions of private developers who buy and sell development rights. In addition, like the predominantly local impetus in the U.S., the Israeli mechanism of TDR is anchored in local (city-wide) legislation. However, few municipalities experimented with it. Moreover, national legislation does not play a major role, nor does it create proper institutional and financial settings for TDR or for cross-local transfers of development rights.

Urban regime scholars would certainly have a field day with the emerging Israeli TDR policy; although the policy is in its infancy, it faces increasing scrutiny. In Tel Aviv, TDR opened the hatch for multi-spot zoning where high-rises sprout in the existing low-rise fabric. The mechanism may be efficient, save government coffers, and espouse private and public partnership. However, criticism has been levied against its underlying ultra-liberal foundations and its warm ideological embrace of developmentalism that ignores thorny social and urban issues.

References

Administrative Petition (2001) 1361/01 (District Court of Tel Aviv) *Sarah Shiff v. The Local Planning Authority of Tel Aviv* (28 July 2002), Nevo Legal Database (by subscription).

Administrative Petition (2003) 3030/03 *Avraham Lev v. the District Planning Comm'n of Be'er Sheba* (2004) IsrSC 59(1) 851 (Isr.)

Alterman, R. (2007) When the right to compensation for 'regulatory takings' goes to the extreme: The case of Israel, *Washington University Global Studies Law Review*, 6(12), 121–153.

Amit-Cohen, I. (2005) Synergy between urban planning, conservation of the cultural built heritage and functional changes in the old urban center – the case of Tel Aviv, *Land Use Policy*, 22(4), 291–300.

Bar Or, A. (2013) *A time for conservation*, Bavel Publishing, Tel Aviv (Hebrew).

Bar-Eli, A. (2007) Transfer of development rights: Virtual real estate and the real money, *The Marker*.

Gutthalf, T. (2008) *Purchasing land or rights in land for conservation of open spaces*, Tel Aviv.

Israel's State Comptroller (2005) *Report on localities in Israel: Heritage protection by municipal authorities*, Jerusalem.

Kimhi, I. (2014) *Old versus new in Jerusalem: Issues in heritage protection policies*, Jerusalem.

Klempert, G. (2014) *Examination of economic and financial aspects of urban renewal projects: An initiative to empower older neighborhoods*, Jerusalem.

Manoach, R. (2014) On the legality of agreements between developers and local public authorities, *Mekarkein*, 13(3), 1–25.

Margalit, T. (2013) Land, politics and high-rise planning: Ongoing development practices in Tel Aviv – Yafo, *Planning Perspectives*, 28(3), 373–397.

Margalit, T. (2014) Multi-spot zoning : A chain of public – private development ventures in Tel Aviv, *Cities*, 37(1), 73–81.
Marx, B.-C. (2014) *Analysis of detailed statutory heritage plans inclusive of TDR mechanisms in Tel Aviv*, Haifa.
Mualam, N. Y. (2012) *Conflicts over preservation of the built heritage: A cross-national comparative analysis of the decisions of appeal tribunals*, The Technion – Israel Institute of Technology.
Mualam, N. Y. (2015) New trajectories in historic preservation: The rise of built-heritage protection in Israel, *Journal of Urban Affairs*, 37(5), 620–642.
Santo, Z. (2008) Transfer of development rights as a tool for heritage protection in Israel, *Mekarkein*, 7(5), 39–51.
Smolsky, R. (2011) Homeowners sue for devaluation, *The Marker*.

A Canadian perspective on TDR: you call that a 'market'?

Eran S. Kaplinsky

TDR schemes in Canada

Transferable development rights are a complex instrument of land use planning and conservation. A TDR scheme is created by imposing development restrictions on some lands and, in exchange, granting the affected landowners special license to engage in otherwise prohibited development of other lands. The scheme typically aims to preserve environmental, agricultural, aesthetic, or historical values (broadly defined in this volume as 'scarce resources'), or to cluster development in prescribed areas while minimizing it elsewhere. The details of each scheme vary: For example, the restrictions can be voluntary or compulsory, the development rights granted can be traded privately, or sold to the government to be banked, and so forth.

There are a few examples of TDR schemes in Canada, particularly in urban areas facing strong development pressures and rural areas of environmental or agricultural significance (Greenaway and Good 2008). The cities of Calgary and Vancouver implement a TDR scheme to protect heritage buildings in designated districts. Vancouver's program operates in accordance with the Vancouver Charter (SBC 1953, c 55), which requires the city to compensate owners of designated heritage buildings for the reduction in market value. Compensation can take the form of a density transfer bonus that may be sold on the open market and applied with permission of planning authorities to sites specifically identified in a zoning bylaw. Vancouver's program is extensive and well established, but in recent years, developers have complained that their investment in heritage conservation has not been suitably rewarded due to a surplus of density bonuses and shortage of suitable sites to apply them to (Urban Development Institute – Pacific Region 2003). The City of Calgary employs a more limited TDR scheme for heritage conservation allowing a bonus density transfer from designated buildings to other sites within a defined area in the downtown core. The program is not specifically authorized in the enabling legislation, but is implemented through the city's zoning bylaw. Outside Vancouver and Calgary, the use of TDRs for heritage preservation is uncommon. Other Canadian cities (notably, Toronto) secure heritage preservation through other non-monetary incentives such as density bonuses and relaxation of parking requirements and on-site regulations.

Rural communities have experimented with TDR schemes to protect farmland, rural landscapes, and environmental amenities (Greenaway and Good 2008). Some of these programs have not borne fruit for reasons that include lack of local support, weak economic drivers, and concerns over jurisdictional, administrative, and technical capacity (Driedzic 2016). Several programs yielded some success, but these have not yet been documented extensively or assessed in the literature. The Municipal District of Bighorn and Wheatland County, two rural municipalities in Alberta, have implemented local schemes for the transfer of permission to subdivide land. Wheatland County's program was adopted in 2006 to minimize fragmentation of farmland. Under the scheme, credit in lieu of the standard permission to subdivide one parcel out of every quarter-section of land may be applied to designated adjacent lands. The credits are recorded by the county, and where the sending and receiving lands are owned by different landowners, the values are negotiated privately. In contrast, Bighorn's scheme was adopted in response to a private developer's proposal to increase the subdivision and development potential in one of his holdings in exchange for registering a conservation easement against part of his other holdings. The proposed density transfer was viewed by local officials as a means to curtail rural sprawl and improve municipal efficiencies, and the municipal district enacted the necessary bylaws (*Keller v. Municipal District of Bighorn No. 8* 2010).

To promote the use of TDRs as an instrument of conservation and planning in Alberta, the provincial government enacted express provisions to authorize 'transfer of development credit schemes' in the Alberta Land Stewardship Act of 2009.[1] A TDC scheme may be established by a regional plan or by one or more local authorities with the approval of the provincial cabinet. A TDC scheme consists of a conservation area delineated for a prescribed purpose, a designated development area, a system of stewardship units (i.e. credits), and the necessary plan and zoning amendments. Following recent legislative practice, the precise details are left to secondary legislation (which has yet to be promulgated). An appetite for transferable development rights in Alberta remains, and several municipalities are awaiting further provincial guidance. In the meantime, other tools are implemented for these and allied purposes, including land use regulations, conservation easements, and so forth.

Assessment

That the American invention of TDRs has captured the imaginations of Canadian policymakers and experts is no surprise. After all, the American system of zoning has been wholly embraced north of the 49th parallel, along with the legal and other fictions that support it, and with hardly a regard to the differences in the constitutional setting and legal tradition between the two countries. Nevertheless, these differences have practical and legal implications for the reception and prospects for success of TDRs in Canada. Most important, in Canada, 'extensive and restrictive land use regulation is the norm' (*Mariner Real Estate Ltd. v. Nova Scotia* (*Attorney General*) 1999). Although the starting point of Canadian property law is that landowners are entitled to use and develop their property in any manner they choose, unless such an action would amount to a nuisance or a breach of contract or a restrictive covenant, common law property rights are not constitutionally protected in Canada and can be overridden by duly authorized regulations. Moreover, in contrast with the American jurisprudence (*Lucas v. South Carolina Coastal Council* 1992), in Canada, even the most restrictive and oppressive land use regulations have been held not to constitute a taking of property requiring compensation (*Canadian Pacific Railway v. Vancouver* (*City*) 2006). In recognition of this distinct Canadian legal position, the term 'Transferable Development Credits' was proposed and accepted as an appropriate replacement for the American term 'Transferable Development Rights' (Kwasniak 2004; Alberta Land Stewardship Act 2009). At any rate, the legal power of Canadian planning authorities to strip away the development potential of land with impunity (subject to political acceptance) reduces the impetus for the use of TDRs in Canada.

For example, in 2005, the government of Ontario established by legislation a green belt to protect 1.8 million acres of agricultural or ecologically sensitive land from development (Ontario Greenbelt Act 2005).[2] Had there been a legal obligation to compensate for the restrictions, the government might have contemplated granting affected landowners development rights that could be applied within the growth boundaries enshrined by the legislation. However, no such obligation exists, and the development potential of the land protected was extinguished rather than transferred.

In contrast, the Alberta Land Stewardship Act creates a statutory right to compensation – the only one of its kind in Canada (Kaplinsky 2012) – for property owners whose lands are designated for conservation in a regional plan. To protect land without paying monetary compensation, planning authorities may take advantage of the ability to establish a TDR scheme under the act.

In addition to the legal acceptance of uncompensated development restrictions in Canada, there are several conceptual challenges to the use of TDRs in Canada. The manipulation of development rights by government rests on the notion that development potential is 'a community asset that government may allocate to enhance the general welfare' (Costonis 1973: 85). But it is far from clear that land use controls enhance welfare overall, as opposed to the welfare of well-represented interests (Fischel 2015). A supposed advantage of TDRs over direct regulation is that they are a 'market-based' instrument, but that is as much a fiction as the legal fiction that 'development rights' are 'transferred' from one parcel to another. In a true market, economic values perform an allocative function by determining land use outcomes; in the case of TDRs, the outcomes are predetermined by the regulators, and economic values perform a distributive function by shifting the cost of conservation from one group of landowners to another. The difficulty planning authorities experience in valuing development rights and structuring a market has been one of the challenges to the implementation of successful TDR programs.

In fact, in three regards TDRs may be inferior to the more direct action of expropriating the right to develop and compensating the landowners. First, the creation of bonus development rights as compensation creates a currency for conservation but shields the real cost of conservation from the public. Second, the power to offer landowners in designated areas the option of buying their way out of planning restrictions (with the funds going to compensate owners of protected land) creates a powerful incentive for planning authorities to overregulate. The total effect of the scheme may be suboptimal level of development. Finally, the relaxation of land use restrictions such as height and density undermines the traditional health, safety, and welfare justification for regulation.

TDRs have rarely been studied in Canada, and the evidence is mixed. A common criterion is the number of transfer transactions, or the size of the area preserved, but there is little research, if any, comparing TDRs to alternative instruments for preserving scarce resources. It is easy to point out the murky policy objectives and conceptual problems surrounding the design and implementation of TDRs, but while the jury is still out, there is some evidence of success. What other planning instrument can claim a better record?

Notes

1 Alberta Land Stewardship Act, SA 2009, c A-26.8.
2 Greenbelt Act, 2005, SO 2005, c 1.

References

Costonis, J.J. (1973) Development rights transfer: An exploratory essay, *Yale Law Journal*, 83(1), 75–128.

Driedzic, A. (2016) Transfer of development credits under the Alberta Land Stewardship Act, in: *Buying a better environment? Market-based instruments & the Alberta Land Stewardship Act*, 2, Environmental Law Centre, Alberta.

Fischel, W.A. (2015) *Zoning rules! The economics of land use regulation*, Lincoln Institute of Land Policy, Cambridge.

Greenaway, G. and Good, K. (2008) *Canadian experience with transfer of development credits and their potential application to agri-environmental policy*, Miistakis Institute.

Kaplinsky, E. (2012) Property rights, politics, and community in Canada, and the Alberta Land Stewardship Act, *Housei Riron Niigata Journal Law and Policy*, 45(1), 78–111.

Kwasniak, A. (2004) The Potential for Municipal Transfer of Development Credits Programs in Canada, *Journal of Environmental Law and Practice*, 15(2), 47–70.
Urban Development Institute – Pacific Region (2013) letter to Mayor and Council of the City of Vancouver, 24 September (on file with author).

Court cases

Canadian Pacific Railway Co. v. Vancouver (City), (2006) 1 SCR 227, 2006 SCC 5 (CanLII)
Mariner Real Estate Ltd. v. Nova Scotia (Attorney General), 1999 CanLII 7241 (NS CA)
Keller v. Municipal District of Bighorn No. 8, 2010 ABQB 362 (CanLII)
Lucas v. South Carolina Coastal Council, 505 U.S. 1003 (1992)

13 Long-term land leases in France

An instrument to address scarcity of social housing

Sonia Guelton and Vincent Le Rouzic

Introduction

Long-term land leases[1] have been developed by both public and private entities for a long time in France with different purposes. While they were intended as a public policy instrument for supporting agricultural or rental affordable housing policies, long-term land leases also appear to be a means for public actors to support planning efforts. For the landowner, they are a way to hold title to the land and preserve some related social position or legal content. Today, a renewed interest for this instrument is observed. In the context of housing market pressures in the center of largest cities, public authorities promote land leases in order to develop lasting solutions for affordable homeownership and to fight the lack of available space for residential use or for business use, especially for small- and medium-sized enterprises (SMEs).

The goal of this research is to understand how this instrument can contribute to planning policy in a situation of land scarcity, and the key conditions to ensure its success. Section 1 reviews existing French public actors' practices. Section 2 gives information on the incentive conditions for private actors to operate under such circumstances, and the reason why it has not been largely developed in France until now. Section 3 describes and analyses French examples. Section 4 discusses the opportunity of developing new housing policy instruments. The increase of residential real estate values since the end of the 1990s and the resulting growing need of affordable housing have led to a new generation of long-term land leases.

The rationale of long-term leasing

In French law, the owner of a land may transfer to another the right to use that land while retaining legal ownership, under certain conditions as those proposed by a land lease. Long-term land lease is a contract (from 18 to 99 years in duration) under which the leaseholder can build (ground lease) or is obliged to build (building lease) according to the contract clauses. The leaseholder pays a ground rent to the landowner and keeps the property rights of the construction during the duration of the lease. These rights are heritable and transferable to another owner. At the end of the lease, the building property rights generally revert to the landowner without payment. Actually, the terms of the contract dictate what happens to the buildings or any kind of improvements at the end of the lease, which might give the landowner rights to the buildings, allow the leaseholder to remove the improvements, or give the landowner the option to purchase the improvements.

A long-term lease is generally concluded between a private owner who wishes to capitalise on his property rights over the long term, and a private developer who wants to benefit from the use of the land. In theory, long-term leases are used to deal with a lack of interest from the landowners in using their properties, in particular for real estate development. At the same time, public authorities are tempted to use the lease to reduce the occupation costs by renting land previously bought at a reasonable price. In both cases, the long-term leasing contributes to allowing a more efficient use of resources.

The discussion on the opportunity to implement long-term land leases refers to two major issues:

- Prices: The question here is to reduce the cost of land for a dwelling or for an industrial facility setting.
- Duration: This issue involves giving enough time to the leaseholder to recover the costs of his investment, as the buildings or the facilities will return to the landlord at the end of the lease.

Land lease conditions offer potential economic and legal benefits, which are often put forward to justify public or private strategies. The French experience enables identification of how these can be achieved in practice, and may differ depending on people and place. From an economic point of view, a long-term land lease allows the leaseholder to concentrate funding on building costs, and to defer payment of land, generally at a low cost. The developer can manage the land in order to optimise building profits while the landowner takes the risk of land price change. Infrequently in France, the landowner has some interest in receiving revenue from the lease in the long term, just as an investor could do. He is more often interested in getting his land back at the end of the lease, with an infrastructure he has not paid for. Typically, public authorities find it advantageous to improve local housing or business premises through such an agreement. Using this mechanism, it might become possible for young families to afford housing in an urban area, or for SMEs or craftsmen to locate in central urban areas.

Long-term leases should secure housing production and offer alternative sources of financing for private and semi-public housing production, when the market is risky and tight. At times when the market was depressed, in order to encourage initiative and to strengthen supply, local authorities became involved in the delivery of public services, for instance.

From a legal point of view, a long-term land lease is a way to overcome a rigid property right system or some legal constraint. Some examples are illustrative but remain rare. In the case of complex development projects, when floor surfaces are above public roads or public property, for example, a land lease is a way to preserve the public interest. It is a way to overcome the constraints of timeshare units, when co-owners do not agree to sell a site. In France, a land lease is often used as an instrument to bypass competition rules, when these state that a public entity cannot sell or lease a property at below the 'market price'. With a land lease, it is not easy to evaluate a 'market price' for rent, given the uncertainty of price changes for the duration of the lease. For the benefit of housing associations,[2] instead of referring to the value of the land market price, rent is based on the ability to pay and the 'cash value' of leaseholder revenues. The corresponding land price is rarely established or discussed. A land lease then appears as a legal arrangement that enables the land cost for affordable housing production to be lowered.

Additionally, a land lease is generally seen as a means of controlling land development in the short and long term. The contract may stipulate an obligation to build and include conditions, such as technical conditions for buildings or requirements concerning occupation, like tenants' maximum income levels or maximum rent levels. Public authorities will keep an eye on the public interest in projects developed on the land leased. At the end of the lease, the landowner recovers the land and can develop his own project. In the context of a long-established trend in urbanisation, leasing serves the redevelopment of cities. Retaining the ownership of the land in the long term can avoid high purchasing costs developers have to face in case of urban renewal processes, linked to the extra costs of expropriation and eviction.

Long-term lease contracts are being implemented in several contexts. Originally in France they applied to empty lands devoted to agriculture or natural purposes. A survey made in the north of the Greater Paris region (IUP 2013) points out that two-thirds of the lands connected to long-term leases remain empty (Table 13.1): 41 percent out of 3,400 sites still were agricultural land in 2013, and 23 percent were natural land. It was, in fact, the initial purpose of the contract to enable farmers to clear and plant on land without purchasing it, while landowners could keep the land as part of their family estates.

Over time, land leases also became contracts for other uses. The same survey identifies 6,500 contracts relating to construction, 80 percent of them for

Table 13.1 The distribution of land occupation, 2013, France (Data from cadastral information, 2013)

Land area	*Agricultural land*	*Natural land*	*Land for building*	*Land for leisure*	*Built land*
100%	41%	23%	3%	7%	27%

Table 13.2 The distribution of building types according to contracts, 2013, France (Data from cadastral information, 2013)

Number of building contracts	*Individual houses*	*Apartments*	*Commerce*	*Outbuildings*	*Offices*
100%	25%	54%	10%	10%	0%

housing and apartments, and 20 percent for commercial and outbuildings. It is to be noted that few contracts relate to office construction (Table 13.2).

In several cases, the implementation of a land lease occurred as a historical opportunity, more than as a strategy by the landowner. France has a long tradition of property accumulation, especially in the public sector where asset management has not been a priority until recently. Similarly, private owners tend to retain their land, even though they do not feel much interest in property, given that ownership costs, and in particular tax burdens, are very low. In this case, the purpose of a lease is to provide minimal occupation of a site, and to avoid any legal claim or limitation of property rights.[3] When the owner is a public institution, the purpose may be to avoid land remaining vacant or derelict. In other cases, several public administrations or agencies have had the objective of retaining ownership of some land in order to keep control over land use. In very special situations, when a site has special characteristics, such as ready access to the sea or to a river, public agencies, like port authorities or a railway company, will not sell it in order to enable their own strategic, company projects.

Taking into consideration these potential perceived benefits of lease contracts, the opportunity for implementing a land lease has been put on the government agenda in the 2000s in order to meet two specific, although antagonist strategies. First, the observation that numerous public properties were being left unoccupied pointed to the financial opportunity of leasing land in order to increase public revenue. The Ministry of Finance generally promotes the sale of land, and land is sold whenever possible. But this may be complex and long when the market is tight, or when there are financial difficulties and project developers are lacking. In such circumstances, public institutions have been encouraged to resort to the lease option as a way of optimising public land management.[4] Second, when land prices and costs are increasing rapidly, using ground leases can be a way of diminishing market prices, or stabilising price increases. A widening gap between the rapid growth of land prices and low increases of household incomes leads to a fall in building activity that cannot meet demand levels. During the past few years, several incentives have been launched by the French government to promote long-term land leases, especially for housing development. In 2013, a law gave the possibility to sell, or rent land at a significant discount, in order to develop social housing projects. These changes have opened the door for an increase of land lease contracts in order to fight land scarcity.

However, this situation has effectively been double-binding of local authorities, leading to split behavior on their part. In its search for new solutions, the government has created two new policy instruments based on long-term land leases to boost the real estate market and intermediate housing tenure.

Poor market responses

Currently, there is not a strong willingness to sign land lease contracts in France. Neither landowners nor leaseholders have reasons to do so. A third group of actors – building contractors – generally act as go-betweens that may help or hinder the process. The banks are not included in our analysis although they can play a key role in projects. Even if a land lease transfers property rights that can guarantee a loan (mortgage), banks still need to secure the risk of such a financial arrangement.

Statistics are scarce and we only can rely on specific situations (covering the north of the Greater Paris region; IUP 2013), and a national survey conducted in 1996 on social housing with a ground lease (Attard 2012). For each actor category, motivations to sign a ground lease will be underlined.

Looking at the landowners, these include a large number of public institutions (state or local authorities and public agencies), of which 43 percent are housing associations. A number of private companies are also landowners. Several of them are private or semi-public institutions,[5] mandated by a public institution to hold the land for the duration of a public interest project: an infrastructure project, housing for low-income households, offices for young businesses, and so forth. Contrary to what can be found abroad (as in London; Vorms 2011), very few are large, private, individual landowners. Indeed, large landowners are very few in France and their property mainly consists of forests or agricultural land (Table 13.3).

The importance of financial funds could increase within the system, although they are still emerging.

At the end of the process, the leaseholder appears to be a private institution or a housing association, again. Land lease is economically attractive for the lessee if he pays a very low ground rent. Some private leaseholders

Table 13.3 Landowners and leaseholders in a land lease contract: an example in the north of the Greater Paris Region, 2013 (Data from cadastral information, 2013)

	Landowner	*Leaseholder*
Public institution	10%	19%
Social corporation	43%	41%
Private corporation	33%	30%
Natural person	13%	9%
Other	1%	1%
Total	100%	100%

are indeed individual persons, due to the special legal arrangements in favor of home ownership that came into force from 2007 to the end of 2010.[6] These arrangements appeared to be costly for the public sector that finances the land. Finally, housing associations find it profitable to build their housing without paying the full costs of land. They can optimise their investment costs with the rental revenues over the lifetime of the buildings, and pass on the advantages of ground rent to the low-income tenants.

According to a national survey conducted in 1996 (Attard 2012), 54,000 affordable housing units were built under long-term land leases between 1990 and 1996, which accounted for a quarter of total affordable housing construction. The survey identified landowners: 75 percent were public institutions, among them municipalities account for 60 percent (Table 13.4). It is then clear that land leases are used as a means to support the public interest.

A small number of leases are signed with private corporations for the development of economic zones (in Strasbourg) or holiday and leisure residences (in the mountains or along the seaside). This activity is quite specific and, in this case, very profitable for the landowner as the ground rent can be high. These situations are greatly influenced by international practices. They do not correspond to the French tradition of retaining full ownership rights.

Some intermediary institutions operate the land under land lease contract and contribute to the system. The focus is on building contractors who provide housing or offices to final tenants. A distinction should be made between housing associations who rent the housing to households, and some experiments by the private developers who sell houses. As most housing associations work hand in hand with the public sector in France, they are generally in favor of land leases. Low ground rent has to be seen as a subsidy to develop projects in tight housing markets. Private developers only act as an intermediary between the landowner and the final occupier of the building. If such schemes are successful for commerce and tourism projects, commercialisation for residential projects face some difficulties in France, while there is a strong reluctance by households to buy what is considered to be an incomplete property. Finally in these experiments, private developers resell projects to housing associations.

Table 13.4 Long-term land leases in social housing, 1990–1996, France (National survey of buildings on free-hold land, CREPAH, 1996, in Attard, 2012)

Social housing constructions (number)			
Total	Built under land leases		
200,000	54,000		
	Among them land is owned by		
	Municipalities	Other public institutions	Private landowners
	60%	15%	25%

The case studies

Recently in France, there have been important changes in the use of land leases. Precisely in a context of scarcity of land, the government has considered long-term land leases as a 'new' tool to manage the land and to develop projects. It has raised a lot of expectations by municipalities facing tensions on the real estate market: Could it help to free up space for construction? To ease market pressures and bring the prices down? In order to shed light on these changes and discuss their supposed impacts, we focus here on different experiences in Paris and Lyon. Paris is the most expensive city in France, with social housing accounting for 18.5 percent of units. Lyon is France's third largest city after Paris and Marseille, and the second largest metropolitan area. In terms of real estate market, Lyon is one of the most expensive cities in France, after Paris, and more than 16 percent of housing units are in the social sector. These two major French cities are recognised as the places where land leases have been implemented on a large scale for a long time. Experiments focus on land leases for rental housing and for homeownership programs.

Affordable rental housing in Paris

In Paris, the city has signed land leases with housing associations such as *Paris Habitat* in order to provide housing to public sector employees. These leases have been commonly signed for a period of 55 years with a ground rent that could be valued at up to 30 percent value of the current value of the land. Today, considering the rising level of scarcity of land in the Greater Paris Region, it is an opportunity for the city of Paris to be able to provide housing to middle-class households under this arrangement. In addition, the policy appears to reflect a strategy of tax optimisation by the city, since the city's expenditures via leases are deducted from the fines it has to pay because social housing only makes up 18.5 percent of Paris's total housing supply, meaning the city does not meet the legal requirement of 20 percent: in 2015, the fines ran to 31 million euros.[7] There are, however, a few issues pending. In fact, the city has some financial interest acquiring lease revenues given its tight budget. These revenues were estimates at up to 37 million euros in 2012, or about 2 percent of the investment budget and 18.5 percent of the repayment of the debt. But the leaseholders are required to purchase the land at the end of the lease period, or when they decide to renew the buildings. This enables funding of the necessary renovations and securing a return on investment. It also needs to be pointed out that some building projects on ground leases cannot receive government grants.

Homeownership in Lyon

In Lyon, an autonomous but public entity, the *Hospices civils de Lyon* (HCL), has a long tradition of land leasing in the city center. In 1760, they owned almost 480 hectares of land. In 2013, they still accounted for 558 current contracts on about 67 hectares. The purpose of these contracts is to respect the willingness of land donors to allocate land revenues to the institution's activity. The HCL doesn't intend to offer affordable homeownerships. Traditionally, the leases were signed with private households for a period of 99 years, and were often renewed at the end of the lease for a further 30 years. Given the uncertainty regarding landownership, households did not pay much attention to the buildings and the maintenance of the housing. This illustrates a difficulty with the arrangement, as occupants of dwellings do not take care of properties unless they have complete ownership rights. For a long time, this contributed to the poor quality of housing in some areas of the city center, and the relative rigidity of the real estate market. In 2009, the HCL decided to rationalise their assets and raise revenues in order to renovate and extend their rather old hospitals and to reduce their debt. They began to sell some properties at the end of leases, when possible, or contract out new leases under better financial conditions. It is clear that HCL has selected properties in order to profit from land value surpluses. As a consequence, in this scheme, the HCL real estate price follows the market price, even if the owner does not have the full ownership rights.

Affordable homeownership in Paris

In the 1990s, a project of affordable homeownership was experimented with in the center of Paris: the city of Paris was the landowner and *Paris Habitat* developed a program of 19 affordable housing units with land leases lasting 99 years. Households would buy the ownership of buildings and pay rent for land. The initial price of 1,550 euros per square meter was attractive in comparison with the median market price of more than 4,000 euros per square meter.[8] Also the ground rent was set at a very low level (initially between 140 euros per year for a one-room apartment, 340 euros per year for a two-bedroom apartment, rising to 400 euros per year and 900 euros per year by 2007, respectively). At the end of the land lease, the landowner will recover the entire property (land and the buildings).

This experimental program underlines some limits of land lease for affordable homeownership without the control of a public administration. An audit published in 2007 (*Inspection Générale de la Mairie de Paris* 2007) identifies three major problems:

- The lack of transparency in the selection process: among the 19 households, six financed their acquisition with a down payment of more than 50 percent of the price of the flat.
- Due to a lack of administrative control, rent was unpaid for more than 15 years (100,000 euros unpaid, with a definite loss of 65,000 euros for the city of Paris).
- Without a resale formula, some households resold quickly (after fewer than five years), so that their capital gains from ownership ranged from 45 percent to 100 percent, even at a time when the real estate market was facing difficulties in the 1990s.

These examples underline various issues to be considered in the long-term lease decision. It is clear that financial conditions are central in the landowners' decisions, be they private parties or public institutions. Leases appear to be one source of revenue to be compared with others. But the long-term commitment gives other perspectives to the landowner who will compare it to the risk of short-term decisions. In the meantime, local authorities, whether they are landowners or not, have an interest in the instrument as long as it can help with their planning strategies in the long term: keeping the property of the land facilitates negotiation over the decisions made for the future of the site, and can help housing policies. It has to be said that in France, public policies have developed over decades to sustain affordable homeownership without a long-term vision: low income households can benefit from public subsidies, low taxes, and/or personal loans without interest. Currently, the possible drawbacks for public administrations are limited because the application of a nonspeculative clause cannot last more than ten years. Long-term leases offer a new possibility to stimulate affordable building, especially when land is scarce.

When public authorities are landowners, some conflicts of interest can be raised with the revenue objective. But public authorities can negotiate immediate payments of all (or a great part of) the leasing rentals for the duration of the leasing period. The short-term advantage meets their budget needs. As a counterpoint, the example illustrates the difficulty for public authorities of managing leases. Public administrations have generally low competences in fixing prices and collecting rents, and limited capacity to follow-up contracts. It is true that lease conditions seem rather complex to assess and control, and public administrations frequently look to simplify solutions.

Finally, in the specific case of affordable homeownership, the relevance of a local authority for the management of the land lease is at stake: monthly rent payments, the application of ground lease conditions, and so forth could best be managed by dedicated institutions. At the end of the day, French people are generally not enthusiastic about buying a long-term land lease. As a result, building companies or even housing associations will try to benefit from cheap purchase conditions granted by the landowner, especially the public landowner, and will push to recover full property rights as soon as possible. The goal of the instrument is then diverted.

New perspectives in a situation of land scarcity

The increase of residential real estate values since the end of the 1990s and the growing need of affordable housing have led public administrations to create a new generation of ground leases. Yet, new affordable homeownership models are really difficult to implement in France because of the way property rights are protected in the French legislation. In order to boost the real estate market and intermediate housing tenure, the French government has implemented new instruments inspired by the American community land trust (CLT). Community land trust is a nonprofit corporation devoted to developing and managing affordable housing for low-income households. It was initially experimented with in the U.S. 40 years ago, and the community land trust movement today has 250 organisations in the U.S., 170 in the UK, and some experiments in Belgium. The principle of community land trust is to separate the perpetual ownership of land and buildings. On one hand, the community land trust buys land and takes it definitively out of the market; on the other hand, households buy their dwellings as their primary residence and accept to pay a rent on the ground and to relinquish ownership following a specific resale formula. The perpetuity of the dual ownership is important to prevent the expropriation of households that buy the building when the ground lease ends.

This kind of affordable homeownership model is difficult to implement in France because ground leases cannot last more than 99 years or be tacitly renewable, and households lose property rights without any possibility of compensation. This explains why ground leases have not developed massively in France for housing. In order to create perpetual dual ownership, the community land trust model was introduced in France by the creation of a new nonprofit organisation (*organisme de foncier solidaire*, ALUR law 2014), and a new ground lease (*bail réel solidaire*, Macron Law 2015) designed solely for use to this end. This new land lease introduces two innovations: a resale formula and a land lease topped up at each cessation, in order to create land leases that last 99 years in writing, but are de facto perpetual. The main problem is that house prices are rising faster than incomes, which creates a growing affordability gap between what people earn and what they have to pay for housing.

The concept of community land trust seems to be promising in France. Even if community land trusts have not yet received the national government's authorisation decree, two metropolises (Lille and Rennes) have launched prefeasibility studies to create the first community land trusts in France. Their strategy has two steps: the first is to experiment with the model with a few operations; the second, in case of success, is to generalise the system to all policies of affordable homeownership. These two metropolises share the fact that they have developed strong land policies and a proactive approach to affordable homeownership policy for decades. In this context, the issue at stake is not to make homeownership more affordable, but to promote more lasting solutions in affordable homeownership. In order to prevent long-term re-subsidisation, the common characteristic of these new ground leases is to promote a new kind of tenure in which homeownership remains affordable, thanks to the application of a resale formula until the end of the lease.

Community land trust schemes present several advantages for public authorities and households: on the one hand, a community land trust is a nonprofit organisation dedicated to the stewardship of land (managing monthly rental payments, application of ground lease conditions, selection of households using financial criteria), and the community land trust guarantees the efficiency and the purpose of the project; on the other hand, the households have better guarantees of keeping the value of their investment because the *bail réel solidaire* is topped up at each cessation, in order to create ground lease that lasts 99 years in writing, but is de facto perpetual.

Conclusion

Long-term land leases were experimented with long ago in France in different situations, previously for agricultural land to assure farming and later in urban land in order to stimulate construction. Nowadays the opportunity of land leases is being looked at again, given the scarcity of land in large cities. French experiments underline a wide variety of objectives for the landowners, operators and the tenants, and several objectives have little connection with the scarcity of land. These objectives are still to be considered.

It is clear that long-term land leases remain an instrument to obtain revenues from the land without any effort needed in production. They allow owners to benefit from the sole property title. Some landowners also use the ground land leases in order to recover some assets in the long term. In addition, the building operator benefits from financial conditions that are considered as facilitating development, either for the financing or for the total cost of the land use. These are viewed as key enabling factors for the development of land. The French cases underline the ambiguous position of the tenant, be he a renter or an owner, as long as he has no guarantee to benefit from this arrangement. The tenant may benefit from a low rent or a low purchase price, but there is a high risk that the landowner or the operator ultimately gets the main benefit of the arrangement.

Looking at long-term land leases as an instrument of public policy, difficulties arise when the public purposes are not clear or are contradictory. French examples clearly show that local authorities pursue two objectives: to receive revenue from their own properties and to facilitate affordable housing or business settlements. Obviously, the introduction of ground lease contracts can have a distortive impact on the housing market. When building operations are subject to private market conditions and acceptability without any control, this can lead to carelessness and poor economic use of land. Or it may lead to the opposite, exacerbating speculative positions. This has been the case in most situations of ground leases used in France. By contrast, when the land is kept under the responsibility of a public, or a collective stakeholder, long-term land leases can be a powerful instrument to fight against scarcity of land. French experiments have proven to be the more efficient to offer rented housing at a lower price than the market prices. But they suffer from a lack of administrative support and control from the public sector. Different formulas could improve the use of leases, providing some renewal guarantees or resale possibilities, and giving the responsibility of the management to a collective nonprofit institution. Notwithstanding these practical matters, the main contribution of the instrument to combat the scarcity of land is to change the value of the property. The use value of the land becomes more important than the financial price. Such a reversal could help rebalancing the functioning of the land market.

Notes

1 'The ground landlord, or landowner, signs a long ground lease or a building lease with a developer. He keeps the freehold. The developer lays out the land and resells the leasehold to lessees or leaseholders who will build on the site. Very often a building contractor builds the building. The leaseholder can rent the house to tenants. The leaseholder pays a ground rent. The building contractor who sells the house for himself is called a speculative contractor' (Higgins 2002: 59, 60).
2 Housing associations are commonly defined as public or private nonprofit organizations that aim at building and stewarding affordable rental housing for low-income households.
3 According to the property rights legislation, land being unoccupied and ownerless can legally come within the sphere of communal ownership.
4 Established in the updated general Code on Public Property in 2006.
5 Called public local bodies, including the famous 'Mixed Economy Companies' whose capital is controlled by local authorities (which hold a 51 percent minimum of the share capital).
6 From 1 January 2007 to 31 December 2010, 'PASS Foncier' as a legal home ownership scheme was in operation in order to facilitate private house building or purchasing for modest-income households. Such households could benefit from a building lease, in order to defer land purchase for up to 25 years.
7 Under the Article 55 of the law called *SRU*, of 13 December 2000, social housing is defined as rented social housing (not affordable homeownership), which benefits from a public financial scheme.
8 *Chambre des notaires de Paris*, median square meter price of old apartments, by city quarters.

References

Attard, J.-P. (2012) *Dissociation de la propriété du sol et du logement, transposition des pratiques des Community Land Trust aux activités de l'établissement public foncier d'Ile de France*, rapport pour l'EPFIF, 133.

Higgins, J. (2002) La croissance de Londres: une description par le vocabulaire des formes urbaines (XVIe–XIX e siècle), in: Topalov, C. (ed.) *Les divisions de la ville*, UNESCO, Maison des sciences de l'homme, 47–79.

Inspection Générale de la Mairie de Paris (2007) *Rapport Enquête sur un programme immobilier expérimental de l'OPAC d'accession à la propriété.*

IUP (Institut d'urbanisme de Paris) (2013) *Le bail de longue durée pour le développement de l'habitat?* Mémoire pour l'obtention du Master 'Urbanisme et aménagement' parcours Maitrise d'Ouvrage des Projets Urbains, Université Paris-Est Créteil, 52.

Vorms Bernard (2011) *Le bail emphytéotique: une voie pour aider l'accession dans les zones les plus chères?* Études et Éclairages for Agence Nationale pour l'Information sur le Logement [online] Mai 2011, 15. Available at: www.anil.org (accessed 5 July 2017).

A Swiss perspective on time-limited property rights: strategic use for active land policy

Jean-David Gerber

In Switzerland, long-term ground leases (GLs) have a long history in the management of farm land. In recent years, the instrument has been increasingly discussed in the context of active land policies and strategic urban planning. The few cities that are using this instrument actively have gained renewed scientific attention (Gerber et al. 2017).[1]

Long-term ground leases in Switzerland

Ground leasing is defined in the Swiss Civil Code. The general principles are shared with other legal systems based on civil law, including France. Under this system the landowner may, while retaining legal ownership, transfer to a third party the right to use his/her land under the conditions defined in the initial contract (Needham 2003). Ground leases make it legally and economically possible to erect, use, and sell a permanent building on the land. In Switzerland, ground leases are granted for up to 100 years. Like farmland leases, ground leases are material rights, or rights in rem, which means that they exist independently of who the leaseholder is. Therefore, a ground lease is a right that can be traded and has a monetary value.

Ground leases are private law instruments but, as the example of France shows, they can be used by municipalities to reinforce the implementation of plans. The use of ground leases as an instrument to steer spatial development implies a close collaboration between landowners and planners; this condition is most easily met when ground leases are granted on municipal land.[2] Allocating ground leases on municipal land can be considered a form of 'planning by contract'.

Swiss land use planning is orchestrated by the Federal Land Use Planning Law of 1979 that introduced a hierarchical structure of plans regulating land uses (Knoepfel and Nahrath 2007). In Switzerland, only local zoning plans are binding on landowners (Bühlmann et al. 2011). However, their implementation is mostly reactive: municipalities await private development proposals – expressed in applications for building permits. Indeed, the designation of land in a land use plan does not automatically lead to the realization of the foreseen land uses, because owners of the plots of land cannot (with few exceptions) be forced to implement the plan. So there can be a gap between the real supply of developable parcels (depending on the willingness of landowners to sell or to develop) and the potential supply (depending on land use plans) (Davy 2000).

The strategic use of ground leases in land use planning

Municipalities in Switzerland develop strategies to address this gap. These strategies are deliberate and goal-oriented applications of certain instruments such as expropriation, land readjustment, amicable purchase, and so on. Among these different instruments, ground leases play a central role in cities such as Zurich or Bienne. The land policy strategy of these cities allows a more effective implementation of land use plans than planning instruments alone (e.g. zoning) without bearing the financial risk involved in directly participating in land development. However, a strategy based on ground leases is conditional on the existence of a municipal real estate portfolio.

Ground leases granted by municipalities on public land lead to a division of the bundle of rights between the municipality and a private ground lease holder. Development rights are private, but limited in time. They are also more restricted than those resulting from pure private property, because they can only be used in a way that is compatible with the goals defined in the initial contract. As the French example (→ *Guelton and Le Rouzic*) shows, ground leases are traditionally used by public actors to support affordable housing or nonprofits. They can also be used to provide affordable land to private companies (e.g. start-ups) or to benefit from a stable source of income over time through lease revenue (financial dimension) (Haila 2000; VLP/ASPAN 2011). The role of ground leases in urban planning has largely remained unexplored (but see Bourassa et al. 1996; Needham 2003).

Differences and similarities with France

Like in France, a Swiss ground lease is a time-limited property title whereby the landowner, whether public or private, transfers the development rights of a parcel to the owner of the building for a given period of time (up to 100 years) in exchange for annual rent payments. In this sense, a ground lease creates a time-limited exception to the accession principle. According to the accession principle, landowners are also the owners of immovable objects, such as buildings that are attached to the land. By tightening the bundle of rights in favor of the landowner, the accession principle plays a fundamental role in making property more exclusive and rigid. Ground leases reintroduce some flexibility in this system, but at the end of the lease period, all improvements made to the land by the owner of the building revert back to the landowner, according to the terms of agreement stipulated in the initial contract. As in France, ground leases are registered as property in the land registry as distinct and permanent rights. An earlier termination of a ground lease amounts to an expropriation.

Swiss law specifies that the landowner must pay the holder of the expired right adequate compensation for the buildings that have reverted to his/her ownership. Additional clauses concerning reversion can be stipulated in the initial contract (e.g. obligation to restore the plot of land to its original condition). Ambiguous formulation of the contractual stipulations concerning reversion often lead to conflictual situations.

Contrary to France, Swiss law governs the content of the ground leases in a very general way (art. 779 of the Swiss Civil Code, CC). Details must be agreed upon in the ground lease contract, and parties have considerable latitude in this regard. Swiss ground leases are much more flexible than French ground leases that need to belong to specific types defined in the law (*bail réel immobilier* and *bail réel solidaire*). In the ground lease contract, the parties may also specify additional clauses, such as the destination and the architectural treatment of buildings, the allocation of undeveloped land, or the prohibition of activities or provisions relating to green spaces.

Connection between planning and property rights

Empirical evidence from Switzerland shows five main advantages of time-limited property rights in connection with land use planning.

1 *Long-term management of a stock of public real assets.* Ground leases are an alternative to the outright sale of land. The planning literature shows that public ownership has many well-known advantages for a municipality (facilitation of land exchanges, reduction of hoarding or speculation, capture of the betterment value resulting from planning). Due to new performance standards imposed upon public administrations (Gerber 2016), many municipalities are pressured to implement a short-term austerity policy. Contrary to municipalities that are selling their land to repay debts, some cities are not willing to abandon their economic power for a mere regulatory power. Ground leases play a central role in this context: they are the instrument that allows public actors to manage a large stock of land over the long term, by bringing part of it temporarily back into the land market. Ground leases make it possible for public authorities to become (or remain) landowners without becoming developers.
2 *Including urban planning objectives in the definition of land titles.* As a landowner granting ground leases, a municipality can formulate lease contracts in such a way that they closely adhere to planning goals (e.g. to support specific companies or housing cooperatives). Ground leases go even further than zoning, because they specify – in the definition of

the ground lease – the rights and duties of individual target actors in connection with urban planning goals.

3 *Opportunity to reallocate parcels at the end of the time-limited property right.* Once a company does not need its real estate anymore – due to moving abroad, reorienting its strategy, merging with another company, and so on – it is often used in a suboptimal way, from a planning perspective. Ground leases allow the city to reshuffle the cards and avoid potential lock-in situations. Land can then be used for other development priorities.
4 *Better control of land prices.* In the twentieth century, one of the main rationales for cities to acquire land was to keep speculation under control. In other words, they were expecting to prevent the price of land (exchange value) from being disconnected from its use value. Landowning municipalities can rely on ground leases to promote the use value of land. Ground leases can be granted to noncommercial housing cooperatives leading to a partial decommodification of land (Gerber and Gerber 2016). Wherever the municipality is the landowner, it can decide to whom it grants a ground lease. Through contract terms and lease rates, it can influence the rent price in the dwellings built on its parcels.
5 *Continuous source of income.* Lease revenue can be a source of revenue for the municipality. Since the value of the location depends on the results of land use planning, lease revenue can be considered a form of public value capture.

Conclusion

Land use planning takes place at the interface between property rights and public policy, the two major sources of formal legal constraints (Gerber et al. 2009). However, as the numerous lock-in situations demonstrate (e.g. hoarding), the translation process between these two logics of constraint can easily seize up. Landowners have a de facto veto right. In many situations, especially in complex property-right constellations, when land becomes scarce, the inertia of landownership might be too strong. This is where a strategy relying on municipal ownership and time-limited property rights has the greatest potential: such a strategy reinforces the translation process between publicly defined development goals and the property-right order because the expiration date put on property rights allows planners to reshuffle the cards and because the terms of the contract can include planning-relevant clauses.

Notes

1 The present commentary takes up the main arguments of this publication.
2 Technically ground leases can also be granted by private or semi-public landowners. In urban environments, these actors rarely strategically follow goals linked with spatial planning.

References

Bourassa, S. C., Neutze, M. and Strong, A. L. (1996) Managing publicly owned land in Canberra, *Land Use Policy*, 13(4), 273–288.

Bühlmann, L., Haag, H., Jud, B., et al. (2011) *Einführung in die Raumplanung*, VLP, Bern.

Davy, B. (2000) Das Bauland-Paradoxon: Wie planbar sind Bodenmärkte?, in: Einig, K. (ed.) *Regionale Koordination der Baulandausweisung*, VWF, Berlin, 61–78.

Gerber, J. D. (2016) The managerial turn of municipal spatial planning in Switzerland, *Planning Theory & Practice*, 17(2), 192–209.

Gerber, J. D. and Gerber, J. F. (2016) Decommodification as a foundation for ecological economics, *Ecological economics*, 131, 551–556.

Gerber, J. D., Knoepfel, P., Nahrath, S. and Varone, F. (2009) Institutional resource regimes: Toward sustainability through combining property rights theory and policy analysis, *Ecological Economics*, 68, 798–809.

Gerber, J. D., Nahrath, S. and Hartmann, T. (2017) The strategic use of time-limited property rights in land-use planning: Evidence from Switzerland, *Environment and Planning A*, 49(7), 1684–1703.

Haila, A. (2000) Real estate in global cities: Singapore and Hong Kong as property states, *Urban Studies*, 37(12), 2241–2256.

Knoepfel, P. and Nahrath, S. (2007) Environmental and spatial development policy, in: Klöti, U., Knoepfel, P., Kriesi, H., et al. (eds) *Handbook of Swiss politics*, NZZ Verlag, Zürich, 705–733.

Needham, B. (2003) One hundred years of public land-leasing in the Netherlands, in: Bourassa, S. C. and Hong, Y. (eds) *Leasing public land: Policy debates and international experiences*, Lincoln Institute, Cambridge, MA, 61–82.

VLP/ASPAN (2011) Le droit de superficie, *Territoire & Environnement*, June 2011.

An Australian perspective on heritable building rights: paramount property rights

Rebecca Leshinsky

Dealing with scarcity in Australia – the context of affordable housing

Australia is a large continent, and with most cities located around the coast, demand for housing is greatest in these locations. This pressure is experienced particularly in state capitals, and has made the scarcity of affordable housing a much greater concern than scarcity of land. As in France, property rights and the ownership of land are paramount. Land tenure is understood in the context of freehold and leasehold interests with ownership and leaseholds able to be held by natural or legal persons in commercial and residential capacities. Australian residential occupancies have traditionally not been held via long leases, with the exception of the Australian Capital Territory (Canberra; Bourassa et al. 1996).

Long-term leasing, as per the French model, is certainly of relevance to housing concerns in Australia, particularly for not for profit community housing providers (CHPs), who now play a significant role in housing low(er)-income households. Addressing housing scarcity has been on the Australian federal government's agenda for many years and is becoming even more urgent since the major Australian cities are constantly growing. Melbourne is growing at a rate of 100,000 persons per year (ABS 2016), which explains the current expansion of the role of the community housing sector. This stems from a 2009 Council of Australian Government Housing Ministers Conference commitment that the community housing sector would include up to 35 percent of low-cost social housing. This target has not been reached, but the sector did achieve about 16 percent of all social housing by 2014 (Hulse 2014).

Land use planning and development in Australia has an important role to play in providing for more affordable housing. Municipalities can mandate that a number of social and affordable homes be included in private developments as a condition of planning approval. The number of potential affordable homes developers are obliged to build is determined by either negotiated agreements made between a developer and the planning authority during the planning assessment process, or fixed requirements specified as a proportion of housing or development value, often described as 'inclusionary zoning'. A voluntary incentive model could be encouraged to further reduce costs for developers. Types of planning incentives include the following: modifying planning standards based on performance criteria – for example, increasing site yield to encourage low cost housing like boarding houses, student accommodation, and retirement villages in designated areas; bonus systems that relax specified development controls, typically height, density, setback, or parking controls, in exchange for constructing dedicated affordable housing; and planning process incentives where projects that include affordable housing attract special treatment in the planning process, such as fast-track approvals, reduction, exemption, or refund of application fees, infrastructure charges, or rates. As in France, temporary property rights are also not favoured in Australia. Community land trusts have been touted in Australia, but to date these have had very limited take-up (Crabtree et al. 2013).

Trialing a novel model for social and affordable housing in Australia

As government spending on social housing is diminishing, some Australian states are trialling a model for the maintenance of existing aging government housing stock, and for the provision of additional low-cost housing (Pawson et al. 2016). This is through the use of long-term leases and associated contracts to assist with the operational side of these endeavours. It is a different model, with some similarities, to the ground leases described by Guelton and Le Rouzi. In Australia, ownership and control of social housing has traditionally been held in the hands of state government housing authorities or religious-oriented entities. With leasing and associated contractual arrangements for the management and redevelopment of parcels of properties to community housing providers (CHPs), Australian state and federal governments are attempting to address housing supply issues and increase the stock of social housing in a financially viable way. It is anticipated that the transfer model will enable community housing providers to leverage state-transferred assets and seek finance to build more stock, which is something that governments are unwilling to do. A further aim is to address the structural financial deficit that is a result of the growing gap between rental revenue and the costs of running the portfolio of housing authorities. Under this model, the Housing Authority (HA) retains an interest in parcel properties via caveats and associated encumbrances on the land, so that ultimate control and use of the land always rests with the HA, allowing for some input from the CHP. Then through the use of contracts, property and tenancy management is 'transferred' to community housing providers. Some vacant land, owned by the housing agencies, is also being 'transferred' to community housing providers for the development of new social and affordable housing stock, but again this is usually via the housing authority retaining its interest on the certificate of title. These agreements run for 10 to 20 years, with options for extensions. The intention is to wait and see what the future steps should be for the property assets and associated land, with no intention for community housing providers to become absolute fee simple owners of these parcels of land. The agreements are usually subject to an initial trial period of two years, at the end of which a review of the arrangement including finances is undertaken by the parties. The contractual obligations, however, are very onerous on community housing providers and can include provisions for termination of control of properties upon default of their contractual obligations. Compensation on termination is at the minister's discretion, suggesting that such compensation will be hard won.

Community housing providers are responsible for insurance and municipal rates and charges, often without any concessions. They are also liable for maintaining and repairing transferred properties, and this includes substantial backlog defects and maintenance. Some contracts require community housing providers to use, where possible, social enterprises and local organisations to carry out maintenance and repairs (Pawson et al. 2016: 38), but with very limited tax breaks for the use of these subcontractors. As the housing authority retains an interest in the properties, there are concurrent leases (housing agency and community housing provider) with social housing tenants. This allows community housing providers to leverage from the Commonwealth of Australia Rental Assistance (CRA)program, for maintenance and further development of parcel properties. The model being used by the various Australia states is providing for a mechanism for the maintenance of aging social stock and the creating of more affordable housing, and further states are adopting the model, in their own right. New South Wales, for instance, is in the process of launching an expanded social housing program where long-term leases will play a much greater role (NSW Government 2016). There are risks, such as too much reliance on leverage funding from the CRA program scheme. Private finance itself may shy away from loaning funds to community housing providers because of the ownership and control structure where housing agencies retain an interest on titles to parcel properties. Overall, long-term leases are being put to the test, and it will be interesting to gauge longer-term effectiveness of the model, which can be an asset for more social and affordable housing in Australia.

Concluding remarks

The recommendations put by Guelton and Le Rouzic offer opportunities for alternative processes for considering affordable housing. Ground leases, as the authors explain, control land development in the short and long term. The contract may stipulate an obligation to build and include conditions, such as technical ones for buildings or requirements for occupation (e.g. tenants' maximum income levels or maximum rentals). There are similarities and differences with the models used in Australia and France. The increase of residential real estate values in France since the end of the 1990s, and the growing need for affordable housing have led public administrations, in France and elsewhere, to contemplate new models for ground leases. The authors describe a model from Paris, where ground lease with housing associations (such as Paris Habitat) operate to provide more affordable housing. This would be of great benefit to low-income families as well as lower-income essential civil servants such as teachers, social workers, policy and municipal clerks, a group struggling to afford private urban housing in urban areas. There is much more still to be said about the use of long-term leases, ground leases, and other property and planning instrumentality and comparative best practice in both in France and Australia as to how they can offer new possibilities to stimulate affordable housing and commercial spaces, particularly for the growing demand from start-up businesses.

References

Australian Bureau of Statistics (ABS) (2016) (online) available at: www.abs.gov.au/ausstats/abs@.nsf/mf/3101.0 (accessed 27 January 2017).

Bourassa, S.C., Neutze, M. and Strong, A.L. (1996) Managing publically owned land in Canberra, *Land Use Policy*, 13(4), 273–288.

Crabtree, L., Blunden, H., Phibbs, P., Sappideen, C., Mortimer, D., Shahib-Blunden, A. and Chung, L. (2013) *The Australian community land trust manual* (online) available at: http://imap.vic.gov.au/uploads/Strategy%20Documents/The%20Australian%20CLT%20Manual%2020130409.pdf (accessed 27 January 2017).

Guelton, S. and Le Rouzic, V. (2016) *Long-term land leases, the French case in instruments of land policy: Dealing with scarcity of land.*

Hulse, K., Reynolds, M. and Yates, J. (2014) *Changes in the supply of affordable housing in the private rental sector for lower income households*, 2006–11, AHURI Final Report No.235, Australian Housing and Urban Research Institute, Melbourne (online) available at: www.ahuri.edu.au/__data/assets/pdf_file/0010/2035/AHURI_Final_Report_No235_Changes-in-the-supply-of-affordable-housing-in-the-private-rental-sector-for-lower-income-households,-2006–11.pdf (accessed 27 January 2017).

New South Wales Government (2016) *Government future directions for housing in New South Wales* (online) available at: www.socialhousing.nsw.gov.au/?a=348442 (accessed 16 June 2017).

Pawson, H., Martin, C., Flanagan, K. and Phillips, R. (2016) *Recent housing transfer experience in Australia: Implications for affordable housing industry development*, AHURI Final Report No. 273, Australian Housing and Urban Research Institute Limited, Melbourne.

Part V

Redistributing property rights to steer land uses

14 Strategic land banking in the Netherlands

Experiencing Dutch dilemmas

Tejo Spit

Introduction

Within a public perspective on land policies, *land banking of regional authorities* is a very special instrument, as it links spatial policymaking directly to its implementation. Therewith, it is greatly increasing the effectiveness of spatial policymaking. Yet, its effectiveness also depends upon its specific context. It will be made clear that the potential of land banking for the implementation of regional spatial policies is enormous, especially in the Netherlands, for it adds a powerful instrument, rooted in private law, to the regional spatial planning toolkit. Traditionally, the Dutch provinces played an important role in regional spatial developments, using instruments based on public law. Nowadays, however, they are also getting more and more involved as an active (private) player on regional land markets as well. Analytically, these two roles create many controversies as public and private interests of provinces tend to mix. This results in controversies in terms of effectiveness (including efficiency) and legitimacy. Both theoretically as well as empirically, the controversies can be reduced into three tension areas, concerning (1) rationales for regional land policies, (2) conflicts of interests with municipalities, and (3) inflation of land prices.

Empirically, provinces in the Netherlands use land banks for two purposes, resulting in different approaches: (1) specific large development projects for commercial purposes, mostly housing (e.g. *Zuidplaspolder* – Zuid Holland, *Blauwe Stad* – Groningen) or (2) developments for public purposes, mostly nature-, environmental-, or recreational developments. Both approaches encounter many problems, deeply rooted in the earlier mentioned controversies. Although most provinces have huge ambitions in the field of provincial land policies, these controversies are the main reason why they are reluctant to enforce the instrument of land banking on a large scale. Therewith, although the potential of provincial land banking is promising, until now its practical implication in the Netherlands is relatively restrained because of the limits set upon its use, especially in terms of efficiency (read: finances).

What is land banking?

A land bank is an institution, either public, semi-public, or privately owned, that purchases and sells real estate property (especially land) for public-oriented purposes. It can be considered a specific vehicle, complementary to the set of instruments of public authorities, that strives for improvement of urban and regional development. Although the legal construction of a land bank (public, semi-public, or private) is important, it is often the simple outcome of the occasion and circumstances. Land banks are primarily meant to be a pragmatic instrument to overcome either generally unwanted spatial developments or as an extra power, complementary to the existing public authority policy instruments. Especially in the latter case, land banks can be very powerful as public and private instruments are combined to serve the same goals. Land banking is a rather common phenomenon and can be used for many (spatial) goals (Harrison 2007). Ranging from the U.S. and Australia to Europe, land banks can be found everywhere. Yet, their goals (and their subsequent reputation) vary. Land banks can, for instance, also be founded for speculative reasons. Since the most important motive to establish a land bank lies in public-oriented goals (and not profit), in this contribution public goals are considered essential. This is important, because the public perspective creates two characteristics of land banks: first, a local (or regional) embeddedness; and second, both a short-term and a long-term strategy.

Therewith, land banks are often rooted (and funded by) local (or regional) communities and/or local (or regional) authorities. The combination of knowledge and money provides extra power to the instrument that supports local and/or regional development. This can be considered a basic explanation for its success in general. Consequently, one could say that the closer the relation with local or regional authorities is, the more powerful land banks can perform. Of course, this creates ethical dilemmas (Lefcoe 1977; Hoekveld and Spit 2008).

In most land banks, public authorities are prominently represented and we expect the ethical dilemmas to be well-known (Hartmann and Spit 2015). Practical experience from the U.S. (De Wit 2004) shows that land banks can be very successful, although their history is rather recent. The first land bank was believed to be created in St. Louis in 1971. Most of the American land banks were meant as instruments to fight declining urban and rural areas, and were mostly initiated by municipalities (Harrison 2007), therewith representing a public initiative. This is in sharp contrast to the UK, where land banks find their origins in the private sector: landed gentry and real estate developers (Levene 2009). Therefore, in the UK land banking serves more private (read: commercial) goals. This can lead to massive speculation as can be seen in Australia, where land banking is often also rooted in the private sector.

With reference to the earlier mentioned definition of land banks, in which the public objectives are dominant, we limit our contribution to land banking for public purposes. In this sense, land banks can be set up by public or by semi-public organizations. As our main goal is to identify controversies, we take the perspective of a regional public authority, because in this role the dilemmas of land banking show itself, both theoretically and empirically, in the sharpest way.

Land banking and the necessity of a regional direction in spatial planning

The wish for some sort of spatial coordination at a regional level can be observed everywhere (Albrechts et al. 2010) and regional land banking can be considered a complementary instrument to increase the effectiveness of regional spatial policymaking. Yet, the involvement of regional authorities in spatial planning is not self-evident. Not only did the former prime minister of the UK shut down the Greater London Council (1986), but similar fates can be observed since then to other regional authorities and not only in the UK. Due to (neo)liberal political thinking, a reduction of power in regional authorities can be found all over the world. At the same time the need for some sort of (especially spatial) regional direction is also called for, resulting in the re-emerging of similar regional authorities. In the London case, this resulted in the establishment of a new Greater London Authority in 2000, under the Blair regime (Atkinson and Wilks-Heeg 2001). The London case is only an example of the struggles that appear on a regional scale. On the one hand there is always the (neoliberal) wish to deregulate and on the other hand there is also the ever-present wish (and sometimes urgency) to regulate developments that are too large (either in scale or capacity) for local authorities to handle. Therewith, in spatial planning, the issue of regional direction is of everlasting concern (Spit and Zoete 2016: 137–143). The wish for a regional direction in spatial planning in the Netherlands is rooted in the (politically inspired) conviction that large differences between regions are not acceptable in a small country. Also, there is a widespread believe that this cannot be solved without public intervention. Similar considerations can be found all over the world. Especially in other small countries and countries with a socialist orientation, this wish is prominently visible. But, also in larger countries and countries with a more (neo)liberal background, different types of a regional direction in spatial planning can be observed. This type of steering, however, is not always systematically organized, but often consists of ad hoc arrangements fuelled by an urgent need to solve upcoming spatial problems that the local authorities cannot handle otherwise. Therewith, an effective regional planning needs to be tailored to both the actual regional situation, as well as the administrative wish for steering from a public perspective. In spatial planning the relevance of a regional direction in general is increasing because of a strong tendency towards spatial scale enlargements fuelled by economic arguments. Within this tendency, two developments can be distinguished, the first of which is a technical increase in scale that all firms and provisions face. They simply need more and more clients in order to provide their services in an efficient way (or make money). Second, spatial developments and administrative borders coincide less and less. This is due to the fact that societal developments with spatial consequences have become increasingly dynamic, whereas administrative structures remain rather stationary (Smallenbroek and Spit 1992). Therewith, it can be observed that the need for some sort of spatial coordination at a regional level is increasing everywhere.

As said before, the instrument of land banking can be considered complementary to public policy in spatial planning. Normally, in public policy documents the goals/objectives, including the corresponding conditions are defined and other societal actors can act and apply for building permits, which will be granted if the applications fit the spatial planning ambitions and the conditions attached to it. The problem that can occur in a 'normal' situation is that little or no societal actors are prepared to implement the ambitions that are formulated in the spatial plan. Therewith, public authorities depend heavily upon the willingness of other actors to implement their spatial plans. Capacity building is the key issue for a successful implementation of spatial plans (Hartmann and Spit 2014). In those situations, local or regional land banking can have an enormous added value. Not only can they start buying up land and start realizing the public ambitions, but they can also try to seduce other societal actors to combine forces in order to do so. They can even fuel up the development process by simply facilitating land swaps and so forth. Also, as there are direct links between the public authorities and the land banks, changes in development programs due to changing circumstances and/or ambitions can be achieved relatively easily. In short, land banks can be a tremendous asset in assisting the implementation of public spatial policymaking, both at a local as well as at a regional level. The latter is more difficult, however.

Controversies in regional land banking

Most land banks are organized at the local level (Levene 2009). At the local level, land banking links (spatial) policymaking directly to its implementation. This makes spatial policymaking not only very effective, because it does not need to involve (many) other actors with regard to its implementation, but it also increases (a 'vice versa effect') the importance of spatial policymaking itself. Other advantages are that the direct relation between policymaking and policy implementation increases the adaptiveness of spatial policy to changing needs and circumstances and it can improve a sense of community. Furthermore, profits of local land banking activities go to the involved local investors and are not dispersed all over the country. In contrast to local land banks, land banking at a regional level is much more complex. Yet, it is as desirable as at the local level for the same reasons, more or less.

The example of the Netherlands – where most provinces have adopted some sort of land banking to complement their spatial policymaking – is very interesting in this respect because it illustrates the controversies of land banking at the regional level most visibly. Analytically, two connected roles in this respect can be distinguished: land banking as a private activity and spatial planning as a public activity. These roles create many controversies as public and private interests of provinces tend to mix, especially concerning issues of effectiveness (including efficiency) and legitimacy. Both theoretically as well as empirically, the controversies can be reduced into three tension areas. These tension areas are in themselves not exclusive for regional land banking, but their persistency in land banking issues is. Also, one has to realize that these tension areas are interrelated, implying that choices in one tension area will have an effect on others. The tension areas of concern are identified in the next three sections.

Rationales for regional land policies

Principally, regional land policies (including land banking) are only justified when municipalities cannot cope with the problem themselves, for example, when the scale of the problem is too large for them to handle or if they do not have the (political, financial, or technical) capacity to deal with it. Legitimacy is at stake here. A simple example from practice in the Netherlands is a location for a large waste disposal plant. If a large area of land is already available in a land bank, it not only doesn't need to be acquired anymore (which is effective), but it also (because of its size) puts neighbors at some distance, thereby decreasing the level of resistance. In a densely populated land this represents not only a huge technical and financial issue for municipalities, but especially a complex environmental issue (pollution and traffic). An effective solution then often collides with legitimized interests of direct and indirect neighbors (the justice criterion). As regional land banking tends to increase the effectiveness of spatial solutions, the justice criterion may come under pressure. A dilemma then pops up, concentrating itself on the tension between the urgency of solving the problem in an effective and efficient way and at the same time honoring the direct and indirect interests of stakeholders involved.

Conflicts of interests with municipalities

When regional authorities are active in land banking, they are literally buying up land within municipal territories. This implies that municipalities are in control of the land use. Theoretically, a municipality can agree, disagree, or be indifferent towards this ownership of land. In practice, the relationship between regional authorities and local authorities is a multifaceted relationship, which is easily overshadowed by mistrust and doubts. Hence, a direct private involvement of regional authorities on municipal territory will most likely be met with local distrust and not-in-my-backyard (NIMBY) behavior. Following the example of the waste disposal plant, every municipality will immediately agree that this problem should be solved, yet not within their territory. Other examples for regional land banking (e.g. recreational use of nature development) will be met with similar municipal mistrust, because a municipality can either have other direct plans or consider this a thread for possible other future developments. Either way, the tension will be eminent.

Inflation of land prices

Since in the Netherlands all municipalities are also active on the land market, buying up land, servicing the land, and selling it again (Needham 2007), the involvement of regional authorities implies an important extra competitor. And thus the competition on local land markets will increase, possibly pushing land prices upward. The higher the ambition on regional land banking, the higher the competition will get, thus representing a third field of tension, because neither the regional authorities nor the municipalities will favor such a development. Only land sellers would profit from it. The issue at stake is that if governments want to be effective and efficient in the implementation of their spatial policies (local and/or regional), land banking could help immensely. The paradox that this tension field creates is that, a very active land banking scheme would increase the effectiveness of spatial policies immensely, while at the same time it would undermine its efficiency (because of the increasing costs due to rising land prices). Also, the issue of the stakeholders (who gets what and why?) remains unsolved. This can be considered an issue of justice.

These controversies mirror the difficult position of regional authorities: while municipalities are in the lead of directing spatial policies (in the Netherlands), the provinces also have to 'translate' national and European policies and guidelines into their own spatial policies that fit the regional needs. On top of that, land banking creates (and certainly at a regional level) its own tension fields. The combination of both should warn regional authorities not to use the strategy of land banking too lightly, while at the same time the promise of its effectiveness remains ultimately attractive for any ambitious tier of government.

Preliminary results from the Netherlands

Regional land banking policies

Many provinces in the Netherlands could not withstand the promise of effectiveness of regional land banking. Yet, at the same time the notion of its problems were also taken seriously (Spit and Zoete 2016: 196). The ambitions of regional land banking were furthermore fuelled by the spatial ambitions of the national government as formulated in the national memorandum on spatial planning in 2004 (Nota Ruimte 2004) and enhanced by the attitude of municipalities who embraced the concept of development planning (a very active form of land policy). Therefore, in order to facilitate their ambitions in terms of land banking most provinces (such as North Holland) have drawn up policy documents in which they formulated their goals, ambitions, rules, and procedures of their regional land banks. Often (again in the case of North Holland), this is also confirmed in the political program of the province. Although the financial crisis and the reduced spatial ambition of the national government (Ministerie IenM 2012) have somewhat softened up the ambitions of most provinces, the temptation of the advantages of this strategy prevailed.

What was regulated in those provincial policy documents? Well, apart from a number of procedural arrangements most provinces formulated a number of spatial priorities. Four types of priorities dominate these regional land banking strategies:

- Priority is given to buy land in order to assist in specific provincial obligations, such as broadening a provincial highway or the extension of a provincial nature area.
- Priority for the anticipating purchase of land for a specific provincial goal that has to be realized in time (say within 10 to 15 years).
- The purchase of land in order to realize buffers with the help of revolving funds is prioritized. This serves not only (indirectly) provincial goals, but is also without financial risks.
- By pursuing a specific price-setting policy with the sale of the land, each province is able to set (read: subsidize) their own specific goals.

Land banks are that attractive to regional authorities in the Netherlands that some provinces have already organized their land banking activities in a separate private organization (such as the Grondbank Laag Holland in the province of North Holland). And others are considering it.

A special problem occurs in this respect. As most provincial policies concern rural areas and provinces tend to avoid conflicts with municipalities (having different interests by definition), most provinces are actively engaged in land banking in the rural areas. In rural areas most of the land has an agricultural land use, which will not come as a surprise when one realizes that about 60 percent of all Dutch land use is agricultural (Spit and Zoete 2016: 239). The problem arises when these lands have been reassigned (either by municipalities or provinces) to another type of use, especially for infrastructure, nature, or a recreative land use. In those case, the value of the land decreases. Often the value of land that is bought for 5 euros per square meter (average price in the Netherlands for agricultural land) decreases to 2 euros per square meter for other uses. In other words, regional land banking for provincial purposes often needs to be heavily subsidised. Needless to say, most provincial ambitions have reduced their ambitions in this respect since the financial crisis. Regional land banks organise the implementation of their policies in (large) projects. Among the most risky ones are those in which the provinces try to realise housing objectives, such as the 'Zuidplaspolder project' in the province of South-Holland and the 'Blauwestad project' in the province of Groningen in the north of the Netherlands. Of course, in the Netherlands, most of these housing projects involve municipal commitment, but sometimes (such as in the case of Zuidplaspolder and Blauwestad) two provinces get deeply involved.

Regional land banking projects

In order to realize regional land banking policies, spatial projects are organized. Whether the projects are organized for commercial purposes (e.g. large housing programs) or for noncommercial goals (e.g. nature areas), all projects have two things in common: they are complicated and they are all dominated by financial risks (efficiency). Some examples will illustrate the type of complexity and how financial risks dominate these projects.

The example of the Zuidplaspolder project

The Zuidplaspolder is a mostly agricultural area that is located in the southeast part of the Randstad near Rotterdam. The aim is to develop this area in such a way that it truly functions as a transition area between the urbanized metropolitan area of Rotterdam and the traditional rural area of rest of the Randstad. The development program aims to provide a creative combination of functions, housing, as well as agricultural functions, that is greenhouses. The creativity focuses on the areas of energy, logistics, and housing. The province of South Holland fears that if the development of this area is carefully directed by the province it will get urbanized in the same way it did between 1989 and 1996. In that period more than 80 hectares per year got urbanized in a more or less chaotic way. The province feared that the Zuidplaspolder would be developed in a similar way, which they considered an undesired development.

In 2002 the province took the initiative and started working on a regional spatial development of the entire area of more than 10,000 hectares. The Zuidplaspolder was about half that area in size (4,902 hectares). It is one of the largest building sites in the Netherlands. Next to the dominant development (of housing) and agricultural industry (greenhouses) in this area, 350 hectares must be developed as industrial sites. As such a large area has to be developed in stages, six subareas and subprograms have been defined in 2008 and 2009 for which land use plans have been drawn up by the respective municipalities. In order to realize these plans in 2004 a regional land bank (Grondbank RZG Zuidplas) was established, in which three smaller municipalities (together for 20 percent), the municipality of Rotterdam (40 percent), and the province of South Holland (40 percent) participated. The Grondbank RZG Zuidplas immediately started buying up agricultural land in those areas meant for development. In 2011 the acquisition of land was stopped because of the financial crisis.

In 2016 the municipality of Rotterdam openly spoke about a 'failed development project' (Onnink 2016) and estimated that now the losses are building up. In discussion with the city council, the responsible alderman stated that the losses already had amounted to 9.2 million euros. On the question 'Why don't we step out of this land bank?,' he responded that 'one does not step out of a flying airplane,' indicating the huge costs (tens of millions euros) such a step would take (Onnink 2016).

As a regional land bank, the Grondbank RZG Zuidplasx operates as private firm. This implies that precise figures are hard to get by. But apart from technical problems (i.e. due to the fact that the Zuidplaspolder is the lowest point in the Netherlands, 6.76 meters below sea level), the development activities of this land bank mostly suffered from the changed market circumstances. Therewith, although there is little information at hand about it, one may expect that the relevance of the theoretical controversies as shown earlier are blown away by the effects of the collapse of the real estate market in the case of this regional land bank.

The example of Blauwestad

Since the 1980s in the north of the Netherlands, there has been a broad discussion going on about how to strengthen the declining economy in this part of the country. The first ideas about a major transition in land use were formulated as early as 1990 (Smink 2013: 61–73). It lasted until 2001 when an agreement was signed between the province of Groningen and three municipalities. Next, some project developers and societal partners were added to the consortium that was responsible for the initiation the land bank Blauwestad. The goals of Blauwestad were to convert agricultural land into:

- A new lake of more than 800 hectares;
- A new nature area of 350 hectares;
- Tourist and recreational provisions;
- The possibility to buy plots of land for housing purposes (1,500 dwellings in 10–15 years' time) next to the lake or in the midst of the new nature area.

The idea was that because of the decline in this particular area, agricultural land would be plentiful and relatively cheap. At the same time, the large number of commercial dwellings, which could be built rather flexibly (and thus expensively), would provide enough money to compensate expenses, or at least keep the losses at a minimum. In 1998 Blauwestad started with the land acquisition and in 2004 the digging of the lake started. In 2006 the first plots were sold and the building of houses started. Around 2010 the first disappointments were made public (Provincie Groningen 2010). Apparently, after five years no more than 186 plots were sold and the financial crisis had also hit this part of the Netherlands. The sale of plots stagnated. At the same time, the price for agricultural land had gone up. This implied that the budget for land acquisition was exceeded by 100 percent (gone up to 50 million euros). By 2016 most of the project developers had left the consortium, as they had little financial commitments to the land bank and considered the prospects not positive. At the same time the province of Groningen announced that they had already taken a loss of 70 million euros.

As a regional land bank, Blauwestad functioned more as a project bureau under public direction than as a real (more or less) independent land bank. Therefore, it was the public partners (especially the province of Groningen) that had to take the losses. In hindsight, one could say the spatial ambitions were far too high for this particular area. At the same time, the development of Blauwestad in Groningen confirmed the theoretical assumption that land prices (in this case, agricultural land) do go up, if more (ambitious) actors start buying up land.

Examples of regional land banks for recreational or nature purposes

Most of the 12 provinces in the Netherlands use regional land banks in order to promote recreational or natural purposes. Even one of the smallest provinces (Zeeland) has established a regional land bank. When the Grondbank Zeeland started in 2010, it got control of a 312-hectare parcel of land within the territory of the province, representing a value of 23 million euros (Blommaert et al. 2014: 10). The program of the Grondbank Zeeland is a good example of the diversity of activities of a regional land bank in the Netherlands. Most of the land is not directly used for provincial projects, but rather as medium for exchange or simply kept in reserve. As most provinces are actively engaged in the implementation of recreational and nature areas, the sum of the smaller (and ongoing) projects seems much more important than the few larger projects, such as the Wieringerrandmeer in the province of North Holland, for example. As both the direct costs as well as the financial risks are so high, larger projects are not a very attractive development strategy for regional land banks. In the case of the Wieringerrandmeer, the province of North Holland stopped the project, because the direct costs mounted up to 23 million euros, accompanied by an amount of 86 million euros in terms of direct risks and another staggering amount of 110 million euros for indirect risks (Smink 2013: 54).

Conclusion and discussion

Regional land banking as an instrument for the implementation of spatial goals is a powerful instrument as the Dutch experience shows. Although one can debate the physical effects in terms of spatial quality as well as the success, the implementation process is very effective. And sometimes efficient as well, as it prevents the need for other actors to get involved in order to implement the spatial plans and programs. Regional land banking, therefore, not only speeds up development processes, it is also very effective when dealing with speculative behavior of third parties. Yet, one cannot deny that it is also a very risky one, because of the financial risks involved. The Dutch examples show that two types of risks can be distinguished:

- *Institutional risks*, which are inherent to the character of the instrument in relation to the goals for which it is used. There are two types of institutional risks. The first is of an organizational nature and the second one is financial. As the governance structure of regional land banks is mostly (at least) at arm's length from the democratically chosen governments, one can argue that democracy can come under pressure. This is certainly the case in those regional land banks in which private parties are also involved. But even when only public authorities are represented in the governance structure of regional land banks, it is still a two-step election. It is easy to understand that this type of institutional risk increases with the importance with the issues the regional land bank has to deal with and vice versa. As for the other institutional risk, the financial one, it is important to understand that, at least in the Netherlands the land to be acquired by land banks is mostly agricultural land, for which the land bank has to pay the existing agricultural market value. In the example of the Netherlands the average price for agricultural land is about 5.5 euros per square meter (Kadaster 2015). This type of institutional risk becomes visible when one realizes that the value of land for nature and forests in the Netherlands is about 2 euros per square meter, while at the same time serviced land for housing purposes can be sold for 250–500 euros per square meter (Van Marwijk et al. 2015: 27). This example illustrates that when land banks are involved in regional projects for recreational or nature purposes, the immediate loss is at least 3.5 euros on every square meter they develop. On the other hand, regional land banks can gain a lot of money in the development of housing projects. Unless of course, there are other (market) risks involved.
- *Market risks* can also be divided in two types. One has to with the location and one is caused by economic developments. Commercial projects (e.g. housing) are especially vulnerable in this respect. In our Dutch cases, the last type of market risk was so overwhelmingly present

> that it overshadowed the advantages that came along with the institutional risks. In the case of Blauwestad, it was even worse, as this case suffered heavily from both types of market risks, for even when the economic tide was still running high, the sale of plots for houses was disappointing.

What can we learn from the Dutch case?

First, it must be noted that the Dutch provinces seem very aware of the controversies as sketched earlier. The delicate relations with Dutch municipalities are respected and the rationales for regional land banking are seemingly well rooted in regional responsibilities, as is shown in the list of priorities in regional land banking. Therefore, legitimacy seems to play an important role in shaping regional land banking in the Netherlands. However, inflation of acquisition prices could hardly be avoided in a small country with relatively many actors on regional land markets. This undermines an efficient use of the instrument.

Second, land banking seems such an attractive instrument, and the use of a regional land bank sets trains in motion that could hardly be stopped. Blauwestad and Zuidplaspolder are literal examples of this conclusion, while Wieringerandmeer could only be stopped at high costs.

Also, the Dutch practice suggests that the success of regional land banking as an instrument is unlikely to be successful if used in isolation. The use of complementary mechanisms, public either private, strengthen its efficiency and effectiveness. American and African examples point to similar findings (Harrison 2007: 22).

In the end we cannot but conclude that the promise of a more effective instrument was too tempting for most regional authorities in the Netherlands. As an instrument regional land banking was broadly embraced and embedded in regional policies. In terms of legitimacy the relations with other actors were in an administrative sense very well respected. Yet, in the end, the promise of a very effective instrument was nullified by the financial losses. Therefore, the practical implication of regional land banking in the Netherlands is relatively restrained because of the limits set upon its use in terms of efficiency.

References

Albrechts, L., Healey, P. and Kunzmann, K. (2010) Strategic spatial planning and regional governance in Europe, *Journal of the American Planning Association*, 69(2), 113–129.

Atkinson, H. and Wilks-Heeg, S. (2001) *Local government from Thatcher to Blair: The politics of creative autonomy*, Polity, Cambridge.

Blommaert, M., van Galen, A., Tillema, M.P. and Veenstra, E. (2014) *Inventarisatie vastgoed en gronden Provincie Zeeland*, Kadaster, Apeldoorn.

de Wit, J. (2004) *The multiple benefits of land banking and comprehensive land bank planning for Detroit*, Kirwin Institute for the Study of Race and Ethnicity, Ohio State University.

Harrison, K. (2007) *International land banking practices: Considerations for Gauteng province*, Gauteng Department of Housing, South Africa.

Hartmann, T. and Spit, T.J.M. (2014) Capacity building for the integration of climate adaptation into urban planning processes: The Dutch experience, *American Journal of Climate Change*, 3(3), 245–252.

Hartmann, T. and Spit, T.J.M. (2015) Dilemmas of involvement: Comparing active (Dutch) and passive (German) approaches to land management, *Land Use Policy*, 729–737.

Hoekveld, G. A. and Spit, T.J.M. (2008) Ethiek in de ruimtelijke ordening: op weg naar een nieuwe inbreng, *Bestuurswetenschappen*, 6, 68–87.

Kadaster (2015) *Agrarisch grondmarkt*, Kwartaalbericht LEI Wageningen UR/Kadaster.

Levene, T. (2009) Land banking – The plot thickens, *The Guardian*.

Marwijk, R. van, Brugman, L. and Pellenbarg, M. (2015) *Onderzoek naar nieuwbouwgrond transacties. Ontwikkeling volumes en prijzen in de periode 1993–2013*, Kadaster, Apeldoorn.

Ministerie van infrastructuur en Milieu (IenM) (2012) *Structuurvisie Infrastructuur en Ruimte. Nederland concurrerend, bereikbaar, leefbaar en veilig*, Ministerie IenM, Den Haag.

Needham, B. (2007) *Dutch land use planning. Planning and managing land use in the Netherlands, the principles and practice*, Sdu Uitgevers, Den Haag.

Nota Ruimte (2004) *Ruimte voor ontwikkeling*, Ministry of Housing, Spatial Planning and the Environment, The Hague.

Onnink, G. (2016) Exit Zuidplaspolder gaat tientallen miljoenen euro's kosten, *Algemeen Dagblad*, 26 May.

Provincie Groningen (2010) *Blauwe stad in het Oldambt: ontwikkelingsvisie*, gemeente Oldambt/provincie Groningen, Groningen.

Smallenbroek, A.J.H. and Spit, T.J.M. (1992) Regions and regionalization in the Netherlands, *Tijdschrift voor Economische en Sociale Geografie*, 1992(5), 234–240.

Smink, W. (2013) *Maatschappelijk draagvlak: tot op zekere hoogte?*, masterthesis, Utrecht University, Utrecht.

Spit, T. and Zoete, P. (2016) *PLANOLOGIE. Een wetenschappelijke inleiding in de ruimtelijke ordening in Nederland*, (Tweede druk) Groningen (in planning).

A British perspective on strategic land banking: critical voices on land banking

Deborah Peel

The strategic use of scarce environmental resources is clearly a matter of societal concern. Certain features of the land resource differentiate it from, say, air or water, since land is relatively fixed and finite in nature. Land also varies in terms of its inherent desirable qualities, such as its location, accessibility, productivity, or cultural meaning. Planning goals, and the means deemed to be appropriate and just by which to implement political or state objectives, likewise vary.

A fundamental factor for the production and distribution of goods, land provides a life-supporting role. How we value land varies, however – over time, space, and community, and considering identified needs and intended outcomes. Decisions about the use and development of land are differentiated in accordance with prevailing property rights, scales of activity, and governance regimes in which actions (can) take place. In developed capitalist mixed economies, land attracts potentially competing demands and private interests, raising questions about its instrumental and intrinsic value, and its use in the public interest at both site-specific and strategic scales.

This book contends that appropriate instruments are necessary to allocate, develop, and manage the land resource in effective (meeting intended objectives fairly), efficient (e.g. financial or other costs), practicable, and legitimate ways (in relation to both inputs and outputs). Using case studies, *Spit* explores these dilemmas at the regional level by examining strategic land banking by certain Dutch provinces. Designed to overcome the so-called implementation gap (Barrett and Fudge 1981), this instrument is intended to advance strategic planning goals and provide public goods that might not be provided by the market, or be underprovided by adjacent local government authorities not cooperating or otherwise lacking individual capacity.

Spit identifies four interrelated priorities underpinning regional land purchasing, land banking, and price-setting strategies, namely (1) meeting immediate provincial obligations; (2) anticipating future provincial goals; (3) creating financial buffers through revolving funds; and (4) pricing land to meet desired goals. He concludes that, while regional land banking by the state can coordinate land assembly for strategic projects and speed up development processes, there are (i) institutional and (ii) market hazards. First, in institutional terms, the use of arm's-length (private) regional land banks potentially raises questions of democratic legitimacy. Second, in land markets, the price of land reflects the use and potential use value of land. Financial losses may thus be incurred by the state if certain desired regional projects are to be secured through subsidisation, such as land conservation and public recreation over agricultural production. Notwithstanding these limitations, might this instrument be transferable to a British context?

Planning systems, cultures, and operating contexts vary considerably in terms of their national characteristics, political goals, administrative and legal arrangements, cross-scalar state interactions and influences, and the relative strength of different state, market, and civil interests and actors (Newman and Thornley 1996). This commentary reflects on this instrument's potential transferability, drawing on Rose's (1991) contingencies in relation to international lesson-drawing, including the degree of uniqueness of the constituent elements, complexity of the intended policy goals and associated policy interdependencies; similarity of the institutional and organisational arrangements, resourcing, and values; and the scale of change required to adopt the measure. An established culture and institutional experience of promoting an active land policy in the Netherlands has prompted provincial actors to emulate practice traditionally associated with land assembly and site preparation by municipal authorities. As Spit notes, regional level administration in England is relatively limited. Could such values, behaviours, and practices fit the UK context?

In contrast to zoning and codified planning systems, the UK tradition is discretionary, emphasising local decision-taking on a site-by-site basis (Sheppard et al. 2017). The British 'plan-led' approach means decisions are made on their individual merits and relevant material considerations. Primacy is given to the development plan and adopted policies. In contrast to Dutch active land policy, involving land purchase, land servicing (such as infrastructure provision), and land disposal, land assembly by state actors for development purposes is rare in the UK. Compulsory Purchase Orders are similarly an exception. At first glance, regional level land banking would not appear to have the necessary fit since the scale of change required would be too great, lacking the basic institutional arrangements and potential for organisational replicability with respect to capacity, resourcing, and statutory authority.

To British ears, the term 'land banking' (or 'land hoarding', to use emotive terminology) is somewhat problematic, particularly in debates around housing land supply. An analysis of undeveloped land with residential planning permission for England and Wales identified almost 500,000 extant permissions for homes, which nonetheless remained unbuilt, despite identified housing need (Local Government Association (LGA) 2016). One explanation was that certain volume housebuilders were using strategic land banking tactics for profit, since early assembly of land can accrue greater uplift, or betterment, as the land progresses through the planning process (Shelter 2016). The Housebuilders Federation (2016) challenged the Local Government Association's (2016) conclusions, arguing that nondelivery of housing is not due to land banking per se, but rather a consequence of other factors, such as lengthy planning processes, bureaucracy, and completion of the necessary implementation steps, ranging from the appointment of contractors to the discharging of planning conditions, financial considerations, or economic viability issues. In this context, the Royal Town Planning Institute (RTPI; 2014) made the case for greater transparency in the operation of land markets, commenting that 'The key is to ensure that these land banks are not excessive, and that developers are incentivized to build.' This prompts the question: how?

Spit focuses on the active role played by certain Dutch provinces in strategic land acquisition and banking. He shows how anticipatory land banking can be justified in terms of meeting the necessary land supply and feeding the development pipeline. Nonetheless, the desired goals (and motivations) of public and private actors may differ widely. Market and financial conditions are important, but so, too, are the legal parameters within which different actors can legitimately act. Questions must be raised as to the motives of any single body that owns or controls land and only releases or trades that land under certain conditions. In the UK context, de facto land banking by the state has attracted criticism. In assessing housing land availability, the Lyons Housing Review (2014) drew critical attention to the 'surplus' land held by local authorities and the use of financial institutional intermediaries, such as banks, which also hold land, and in which the UK government has an important stake. It recommended that '[i]ncreased transparency of landownership, options and transactions should apply to all landowners, not just private sector ones' (p. 64). Recommending establishing a 'single, comprehensive or transparent register of surplus public land', it suggested, would enable the government 'to undertake a comprehensive review to establish whether there is evidence of anti-competitive behaviour or destructive speculation and if necessary, take action to address it' (p. 64). This approach represents an attempt to address issues of legitimacy, through enhanced transparency; and manageability, through an enhanced role for coordinated land registration and knowledge, alongside associated initiatives to stimulate the timely release of land.

In tandem, the Lyons Housing Review (2014) advocated a more active leadership role by local authorities and creative partnerships, involving public-public and/or private-public actors, so that effective and efficient use could be made of public assets, including deploying tools such as the Essex Property Asset Map, an online mapping system for pooling public land knowledge. Similarly, the Royal Town Planning Institute (2014) pointed to the efforts of Joint Strategic Planning Committees in England to perform proactive roles in land assembly by bringing together landowners for a development site. Here, a critical consideration for public bodies is making the best use of public assets and not selling land below market value; indeed, strategic land assembly involving the public sector is subject to strict rules relating to procurement and compliance with the Official Journal of the European Union. Reiterating the need for public accountability, the Royal Town Planning Institute (2014) observed:

> As the largest landowner in the UK (although its holdings are rarely described as 'land banking'), the public sector needs to consider wider public benefits such as better quality housing, flexibility and access to job markets and growing local economies, when releasing land. The requirement imposed by HM Treasury for the public sector to maximise returns on the sale of the land is often the key determinant in whether land becomes available on the market.

The Dutch experiment of provincial strategic land banking raises institutional considerations around efficiency, effectiveness, and legitimacy, including matters relating to the exercise of due diligence and due process by public bodies and the potential transaction costs involved in auditing and oversight. Moreover, the (financial) burdens assumed by the state in furthering the public interest in this way are consistent with established arguments in relation to addressing market failure in advancing public goals. The strategic control offered by land banking, as understood in the Dutch context, can potentially better serve regional objectives. Yet, as Spit identifies, there are market risks in land banking since land value is susceptible to potentially adverse changing market conditions, including the macroeconomic context, and local behaviours. From this perspective, such state-authorised speculation is vulnerable to the same market risks as the private sector. Through acquiring and banking land to serve the public interest, the state is nevertheless removing land from the market, inducing a scarcity of its own, creating monopoly conditions and thereby distorting the operation of the land market. Practically, current UK debates emphasise due diligence and transparency in landownership data, improving public asset management, initiatives to incentivise implementation of planning permissions, and improvements to the planning process. There is a related exhortation for stronger municipal leadership and working in partnership.

Consideration of alternative strategic policy instruments, particularly in relation to housing land supply and mega-regeneration schemes, are being considered, including the Netherlands' active land policy (RTPI 2014). It is also recognised that new institutional and organisational approaches may be required to overcome the implementation gap. Interestingly, then, TAYplan (2015: 5), one of four Strategic Development Planning Authorities designated in 2008 to address regional issues in Scotland, has observed:

> Looking beyond land supply, infrastructure and available land is critical to support and unlock development potential. Planning authorities

and developers need help in this and there is a case for national agencies to support them to that end by front-funding infrastructure and land assembly. The current model where the private sector carries the risk for assembling land and providing infrastructure presents major challenges when infrastructure is needed ahead of the development and increased land values that pay for it.

References

Barrett, S. and Fudge, C. (1981) *Policy and action: Essays on the implementation of public policy*, Routledge, London, New York.

Home Builders Federation (2016) *Permissions to land: Busting the myths about housebuilders and 'land banking'*, HBF, May, London (online) available at:www.hbf.co.uk/fileadmin/documents/research/HBF_Report_-_Landbanking_May.pdf (accessed 15 December 2016).

Local Government Association (2016) *475,000 homes with planning permission still waiting to be built*, Media release issued 7 January (online) available at: www.local.gov.uk/web/guest/media-releases/-/journal_content/56/10180/7632945/NEWS (accessed 15 December 2016).

Lyons Review (2014) *Mobilising across the nation to build the homes our children need*, Digital Creative Industries, London (online) available at: www.policyforum.labour.org.uk/uploads/editor/files/The_Lyons_Housing_Review_2.pdf (accessed 15 December 2016).

Newman, P. and Thornley, A. (1996) *Urban planning in Europe: International competition, national systems, and planning projects*, Routledge, London, New York.

Rose, R. (1991) *Lesson-drawing in public policy: A guide to learning across time and space*, Chatham House Publishers, Chatham, NJ.

Royal Town Planning Institute (RTPI) (2014) *Lyons Housing Review*, submission by the Royal Town Planning Institute, February (online) available at: www.rtpi.org.uk/media/876525/lyons_review_rtpi_corrected.pdf (accessed 15 December 2016).

Shelter (2016) Land banking: What's the story? *Policy Blog* posted 14 December (online) available at: http://blog.shelter.org.uk/2016/12/land-banking-whats-the-story-part-1/ (accessed 15 December 2016).

Sheppard, A., Peel, D., Ritchie, H. and Berry, S. (2017) *The essential guide to planning law: Decision-making and practice in the UK*, Policy Press, Bristol.

TAYplan (2015) *TAYplan SDPA submission to independent review of Scottish planning* (online) available at: www.gov.scot/Resource/0049/00492795.pdf (accessed 15 December 2016).

A U.S. perspective on land banking: just not the American way

Richard K. Norton

'Land banking' in the U.S. resembles little what it appears to be in the Netherlands. Rather, land banking in the U.S. is much narrower in scope, and it is applied in different contexts to address different problems. Or, perhaps, some number of land-banking-like policy goals are promoted in the U.S. as in the Netherlands, but different terms are used to describe those approaches. One of the constant challenges in conducting a cross-national comparative assessments is discerning whether perceived differences are real or merely semantic, and whether perceived similarities are real or rather inaptly described (Norton and Bieri 2014).

Spit's survey of the Dutch context suggests that the concept of land banking is used fairly broadly in the Netherlands, encompassing – at least in concept – actions where the government assembles, holds, and then sometimes conveys back to private parties title interests to land for a fairly broad array of purposes. Even so, it primarily involves public assembly of land in order to coordinate and speed up private development projects that in turn advance regional or provincial urban planning and land development goals. With that understanding, I describe here some purposes for which land-banking-like activities might be engaged in the U.S., along with the narrower use of the concept of 'land banking' in the U.S. as that term and concept is typically employed.

The first thing to note is that public planning does not play as prominent a role in shaping land use patterns in the U.S. as it does in many European countries, including the Netherlands. The U.S. is not as close to being a planned economy, there is no coordinated federal planning system as such, and most states have delegated most of their land use planning and development management authorities down to their local governments (Berke et al. 2006). In that context, planning is engaged by localities as a way to analyze the community development issues of most concern to them and to justify the legally significant land use regulations (e.g. zoning) and infrastructure policies they adopt (Norton 2011), the latter activities often recognized as part of the formal planning system in Europe but not in the U.S. The connections between policy-oriented planning and legally significant land use management are often weak and hard to discern, however, and localities in the U.S. approach their interactions with land developers from a different starting point than do those in other countries.

With that background, there are generally four purposes in the U.S. for which the government, or a public-acting private entity, obtains and holds land in fee ownership or through a partial title interest, either perpetually or for subsequent conveyance to private developers, including for public ownership and use; in response to planning/market omissions; in response to planning/market failures; and as a means to facilitate private development that advances municipal or regional land development goals. Ironically, only the second and third of these purposes are sometimes given the label land 'banking' in the U.S. (although they do not appear to be the primary use of land banking in the Dutch context), while the fourth is not engaged in or thought of as land banking in the U.S. (while that is the primary purpose for which land banking is used in the Dutch context).

First, with regard to public ownership and use, federal, state, and local governments own a variety of public lands and facilities that shape private development in numerous ways (e.g. post offices, town halls, train stations), albeit those lands are often owned and developed with little regard to their potential effects on private development. Public ownership also occurs in the form of public parks and public resource lands (e.g. national forests), the latter often open to private resource development leases (e.g. ranching, mining). These land holdings represent or support various public goods, and while they might be conceived as land 'banked' by the government, they are not routinely thought of in that sense.

Second, I use the term 'planning/market omissions' here to describe situations where markets normally do not, and would not be expected, to provide land uses that yield public benefits because they are not readily profitable through private market transaction (i.e. the definition of a public good, not normally provided through private market exchange). They are not really market 'failures' because one would not expect those uses to be provided by the market in the first place. They also represent planning omissions, at least in the U.S. system, because planning has not traditionally encompassed the goal of providing for these land uses through analysis and regulation, at least not as aggressively as appears to be the case in the Netherlands. Two prominent examples here are natural resource lands that provide public benefits but are not as protected through direct governmental action as they might be: wetlands (and related natural lands) and farmland.

Vast wetland areas have been lost throughout the U.S. to development since settlement by European colonists (ELI and IWR 1994). One approach that might be taken to protect the wetlands that remain, and that is taken to some extent, is to regulate land use directly to prevent additional loss. This approach is highly problematic in the U.S. context, however, because of the fear of regulatory taking claims (Merriam and Frank 1999). Another approach that has become fairly prominent is 'wetland mitigation banking'. Wetland banking involves the identification of high value (or potentially restorable) wetlands in areas not under development pressure and the protection of those lands through public acquisition. Private developers contribute funds to defray the costs of acquisitions through payment of fees in lieu of setting aside wetlands on the project site they seek to develop (i.e. developers 'mitigate' the loss of the wetlands they are allowed to fill on site by paying for the perpetual protection of wetlands elsewhere).

A practice related to wetland banking is the acquisition of conservation easements on privately owned land. Generally, these easements are acquired by 'land trusts', nonprofit entities that obtain partial title interests in lands – specifically, the rights to develop them – and then essentially bank those interests perpetually to prevent urbanization of the land. Conservation easements are also typically used, if not more so, to protect high value conservation or resource lands in the U.S. context, including especially prime farmland (Brewer 2003). The acquisition of conservation easements is akin to 'wetland banking', but it is not conventionally thought of as a land-banking approach.

Third, I use the term 'planning/market failures' to refer to situations where interacting planning-market systems have provided urban development, infrastructure, and related amenities but those developments have declined over time through disinvestment, population emigration, and so on, for a whole host of reasons in the U.S. context (e.g. 'white flight', suburban expansion). A prominent result of this land pattern has been the accumulation of vacant properties in central urban settings held by government (typically counties) because of tax foreclosures. The typical response by these local governments has been to sell the properties as quickly as possible through auction in order to get them off the public role and back into private ownership as quickly as possible. The problem, however, has been speculation and continued disinvestment in these properties, perpetuating the pattern of decline.

A relatively recent response to this phenomenon has been the consolidation of parcels obtained through tax foreclosures by a specially created governmental entity to either hold the lands in public ownership for the benefits they provide (e.g. urban parks, open space) or to rationally consolidate them and then facilitate private development that will (hopefully) prompt urban revitalization. This is the governmental activity that is conventionally referred to as 'land banking' in the U.S. context, and the governmental entity created to conduct it is conventionally referred to as a county 'land bank' (Shah 2016). Unlike the Netherlands, however, this practice does not involve assembling land proactively for the purpose of promoting development that advances regional planning goals, but rather consolidating and conveying land already owned because of tax foreclosures to promote more rational and beneficial urban revitalization than would occur through the tax foreclosure and auction process otherwise.

As an aside, another related approach in the U.S., one used more commonly and somewhat more in line with land banking as employed by the Dutch, is the practice of tax increment financing (TIF). The use of tax increment financings involves spending public funds on infrastructure in a designated district that is intended to promote new urban development (or typically urban revitalization) within that district, and then recapturing the incremental increases in tax revenues occurring in that district because of new private development (Dye and Merriman 2006). This approach, however, is all about providing – or more precisely financing publicly the provision of – infrastructure in order to promote urban development or revitalization, not the assembly or conveyance of the land itself.

Fourth and finally, aside from tax increment financing districts and financing, governmental activities in the U.S. that seem to come the closest to land banking in the Dutch context include the governmental investment (and sometimes acquisition and subsequent conveyance of land) to promote the development of large-ticket facilities like convention centers or sports stadia; that is, facilitating large-scale developments that private investors are reticent to provide without public subsidy and that public officials perceive will incentivize larger urban economic development goals (see Rosentraub and Swindell 2009; Sanders 2014).

Again, however, these projects are typically more about the public financing and provision of infrastructure, rather than land assembly per se. More important, they are highly controversial and contested in terms of whether the public subsidies provided are really needed (or are the sports team owners and developers merely playing different localities off of one another), and whether they really succeed in providing the larger economic development benefits promised. Moreover, when pursued to the point of necessitating the expropriation of private land to ensure adequate assembly of land for feasible projects, they can prompt litigation under the federal 'takings' doctrine (e.g. *Kelo v. City of New London*, 545 U.S. 469 (2005), upholding the public condemnation of land for private development under the federal takings doctrine), and indeed may be prohibited altogether under corresponding state takings doctrines (e.g. *Wayne County v. Hathcock*, 471 Mich. 445 (2004), striking down the public condemnation of land for private development under Michigan's takings doctrine).

In sum, land banking in U.S. is a concept and term used more narrowly than in the Netherlands given the U.S. context. 'Wetland banking' is used as a means to mitigate the loss of viable wetlands to ongoing urban development, and 'land banking' is used as a fix to a dysfunctional tax foreclosure process, one designed to promote urban revitalization of those tax-foreclosed properties. There is little engagement in the U.S., however, of broader efforts to assemble land in order to coordinate and speed up private development projects that in turn advance municipal or regional planning goals; that's just not the American way.

References

Berke, P.R., Godschalk, D.R., Kaiser, E.J. and Rodriguez, D.A. (2006) *Urban land use planning*, University of Illinois Press, Urbana and Chicago.

Brewer, R. (2003) *Conservancy: The land trust movement in America*, University Press of New England, Lebanon, NH.

Dye, R.F. and Merriman, D.F. (2006) Tax increment financing: A tool for local economic development, *Land Lines*, January, 2–7.

Environmental Law Institute (ELI) and Institute for Water Resources (IWR) (1994) *National wetland mitigation banking study: Wetland mitigation banking: Resource document*, Institute for Water Resources, Water Resources Support Center U.S. Army Corps of Engineers, Alexandria, VA.

Merriam, D.H. and Frank, R.M. (1999) *The takings issue: Constitutional limits on land use control and environmental regulation*, Island Press, Washington, DC.

Norton, R.K. (2011) Who decides, how and why? Planning for the judicial review of local legislative zoning decisions, *Urban Lawyer*, 43(4), 1085–1105.

Norton, R.K. and Bieri, D.S. (2014) Planning, law, and property rights: A US-European cross-national contemplation, *International Planning Studies*, 19(3–4), 379–397.

Rosentraub, M. and Swindell, D. (2009) Of devils and details: Bargaining for successful public/private partnerships between cities and sports teams, *Public Administration Quarterly*, 33(1), 118–148.

Sanders, H.T. (2014) *Convention center follies: Politics, power, and public investment in American cities*, University of Pennsylvania Press, Philadelphia, PA.

Shah, S. (2016) Saving our cities: Land banking in Tennessee, *University of Memphis Law Review*, 46(4), 1080–8582.

15 Expropriation for urban development purposes in Germany

Consider very carefully before using it

Juliane Albrecht

The expropriation of land for urban development purposes is regulated in Germany in §§ 85 ff. Federal Building Code (*Baugesetzbuch* – BauGB *2004*). In the Federal Building Code (BauGB), expropriation is primarily an instrument for the implementation of land use plans such as the general right of pre-emption, land reallocation, or provision of local public infrastructure (Scheidler 2016: 510). Expropriation assists land management by supplying plots for well-ordered urban development (Battis 2006: 119), and hence can help to achieve governmental goals in land consumption and preservation.

Historical background

The historical background on the emergence of expropriation in Germany shows how scarcity of (building) land led to the development.

Historically, the expropriation of property for urban development purposes is rooted in nineteenth-century laws promulgated by the federal states in the wake of the Industrial Revolution aimed at removing from private ownership land required for public works such as rail or road construction (Runkel 2009: preliminary remarks to 85 ff., rn. 9). In the beginning of the twentieth century, the housing shortage after World War I necessitated uniform and more simplified expropriation regulations than in the existing state laws. As a consequence, on the level of the German Empire, the ordinance on the rectification of the most urgent housing shortage of 9 December 1919 (*Behebungsverordnung* 1919) was adopted, providing for a simplified acquisition of small- and medium-size flats.

After World War II, an urgent reform of existing urban planning provisions, especially the regulations on expropriation, was required to allow for reconstruction of destroyed towns and villages and the accommodation of millions of resettlers and refugees. In some states, the Behebungsverordnung was suspended, whereas other states questioned its validity and compatibility with the property right of art. 14 Basic Law (BT-Drs. 1/2281: 16). For similar reasons, the application of so-called Reconstruction Laws (*Aufbaugesetze*), which had been adopted by the states before the foundation of the

Federal Republic of Germany in 1949, were also problematic in terms of constitutional law. The *Aufbaugesetze* extended the possibilities for expropriation, including not only the procurement of building land but also for other purposes of urban development. Expropriation was regulated in these laws in different ways.

The Procurement of Building Land Act of 1953 (*Baulandbeschaffungsgesetz* 1953) was adopted to overcome this fragmentation of expropriation law at least for the purposes of housing construction. It intended to provide a workable regulation, which nevertheless conforms to the constitutional requirements for legal clarity and legal certainty. Due to the significance of expropriation measures for all involved parties, each element of uncertainty, which could give cause for doubts regarding the legal force of the decisions of the expropriation authority, should a priori be excluded for constitutional reasons (Federal Government 1951: 16f.). The *Baulandbeschaffungsgesetz* was primarily intended to supply land for housing by legislating for the compulsory sale of land to the state, which then sold such land to private individuals for the purpose of residential development. In the foreground was the intention of the legislator, to allow for immediate satisfaction of the momentary need for building land. However, it was also taken into account that the law should later be integrated in a future comprehensive regulation of the whole building and land law (Federal Government 1951: 17).

This comprehensive regulation was established by the Federal Building Act of 23 June 1960 (*Bundesbaugesetz* – BBauG 1960). In line with its general urban planning objectives, it allowed expropriation by the municipality not only for the purpose of procurement of building land but in general for building use in accordance with a municipal binding land use plan. Moreover, under certain conditions, expropriation of property can also be requested in favour of building use of private parties. This extension of the purpose of expropriation aims to enable the implementation of urban land use planning (Federal Government 1958: 86). Further expropriation purposes were supplemented by the amendment of the Federal Building Code in 1976, concerning the enforcement of building orders and the preservation of a building structure subject to a preservation statute. The amendment of the Federal Building Code in 2004 added the preservation or removal of building structures in urban redevelopment areas as further expropriation purpose.

Constitutional basis for expropriation

Under Germany's constitution, the expropriation of property is closely regulated by guarantees of property ownership laid out in art. 14 of the Basic Law (*Grundgesetz* – GG). The content of ownership is not stipulated by the constitution but is determined by the sub-constitutional legislator. This includes ownership according to civil law (§§ 903ff. Civil Code, *Bürgerliches Gesetzbuch* – BGB) as well as all asset-related rights such as heritable buildings rights and the general right of pre-emption but *not* expectations of future profits and likely financial gain. The prevailing opinion is that protection extends to established and operating businesses insofar as their existence is threatened. The rights of local residents are only protected in core areas such as the permanent right of access, whereas additional regulations can be specified by the sub-constitutional legislator.

The guarantee of ownership distinguishes between expropriation (art. 14 par. 3 GG), on the one hand, and the contents and limits of ownership, on the other (art. 14 par. 1 cl. 2). According to the jurisdiction of the Federal Constitutional Court (*Bundesverfassungsgericht* – BVerfG), expropriation is defined as the full or partial revocation of concrete, subjective legal positions (BVerfG, Ruling of 15.07.1981 – 1 BvL 77/78). In contrast, a determination on the contents and limits of property occurs when the legislator specifies rights and obligations in a general and abstract fashion. The Federal Constitutional Court bases its distinction between expropriation, on the one hand, and the contents and limitations of ownership, on the other, not on the gravity of the intrusion but qualitatively.

According to art. 14 par. 3 s. 2 Basic Law (GG), expropriation can be achieved in two ways: through the law as legal expropriation or pursuant to some law as administrative expropriation. Legal expropriation empowers the legislator to revoke specific ownership rights directly (art. 14 par. 3 s. 2 1. Alt.GG). In regard to administrative expropriation, on the other hand, the legislator empowers administrative bodies to revoke property ownership of individuals by means of administrative act (art. 14 par. 3 s. 2). Expropriation for the purpose of urban development according to §§ 85 ff. Federal Building Code is framed as administrative expropriation, that is the regulation of expropriation in the Federal Building Code (BauGB) in the form of an administrative act.

In regulating expropriation, the legislator has to observe relevant constitutional requirements. Therefore, according to art. 14 par. 3 s. 1 Basic Law, expropriation is only permissible for the general good. Furthermore, expropriation as well as all violations of property rights must obey the legal principle of proportionality, that is they must be suitable, necessary, and proportional to realise the pursued aim. Finally, the law conferring the power of expropriation must also regulate the form and extent of compensation (the so-called Junktim Clause, art. 14 par. 3 s. 2) (BVerfG, Ruling of 26.10.1977 – 1 BvL 9/72). Compensation is determined by an equitable balancing of the public interest as well as the interests of all affected parties (art. 14 par. 3 s. 3 GG).

Reflecting the constitutional empowerment of art. 14 par. 2 s. 2, the legislator has framed expropriation for the purpose of urban land use planning within §§ 85ff. Federal Building Code as an instrument to ensure well-ordered urban development. The individual conditions upon which expropriation is contingent will be described in the following.

The subject of expropriation, § 86 Federal Building Code

The subject of expropriation can be the ownership rights to land or individual plots including the appurtenances of a plot (§§ 93, 94, 95 BGB), which can either be fully expropriated or encumbered (§ 86 par. 1 BauGB). Expropriation of ownership means that the ownership rights of the affected party are entirely abolished and the beneficiary makes a standard purchase of property that has no ownership rights attached (Just 2004: 394). The encumbrance of ownership means creating a right in rem, which limits the absolute right of ownership in the use of land (Battis 2016: § 86 rn. 2).

In addition to ownership rights, § 86 par. 1 no. 2 Federal Building Code determines that other rights to land can be removed or encumbered, such as easements and heritable buildings rights (Just 2004: 395). Claims under the law of obligations can also be removed (§ 86 par. 1 nr. 3). These include, for instance, claims arising from a purchase agreement, the pre-emption right under § 463 civil law (BGB) as well as rental or leasing rights (Just 2004: 395).

Permissible purposes of expropriation, § 85 Federal Building Code

Section 85 par. 1 Federal Building Code specifies which purposes may be served by expropriation. It names in detail those conditions under which expropriation is admissible for the public good (art. 14 par. 3 s. 1 GG; Just 2004: 392).

Expropriation to assist urban planning

The first and most important reason for the public expropriation of property under § 85 para. 1 no. 1 Federal Building Code is the intention to use a plot or to prepare a plot for use according to the designations in the municipal binding land use plan (*Bebauungsplan*). The permissible designations of such a land use plan are laid out in detail in § 9 (e.g. designations on the type and degree of building and land use). The purpose of expropriation as specified in § 85 par. 1 no. 1 is to implement a municipal land use plan and its various designations. This is termed expropriation to assist urban planning (Just 2004: 392). The designations laid down by a municipality within a binding land use plan as permitted under § 9 Federal Building Code can thus serve as valid reasons for expropriation (Dolde 1991: 234).

However, property can only be expropriated for 'the strict purpose of urban development' and not simply 'to realise any measure related to urban development' (BVerfG, Ruling of 24.3.1987 – I BvR 1046/85, Boxberg Ruling). If, for example, expropriation pursues the general goal of creating employment, of improving the regional economic structure, or of establishing a university, these are not considered as meeting the conditions set out in § 85 par. 1 no. 1 Federal Building Code (Just 2004: 392). Such cases require a specially crafted law of expropriation (§ 85 par. 2 BauGB) that precisely defines the purposes and necessary conditions for expropriation (Stüer 2009: 620).

Use of undeveloped plots or those developed to a very low level

The second purpose of expropriation is to make use of unplanned plots within built-up areas (§ 85 par. 1 no. 2 BauGB). Accordingly, undeveloped plots or those developed to a very low level that do not lie within the area covered by a binding land use plan but that lie within a built-up area can be expropriated for use or can be supplied for some use, particularly for the purpose of infill development, in accordance with regulations under building law (§ 34). Infill development constitutes a particular public good as it serves to reduce land consumption (Halama 2009: § 85 rn. 44).

Expropriation for land compensation or to compensate revoked ownership rights

Other permissible purposes of expropriation are to procure plots as compensation for expropriation (§ 85 par. 1 no. 3 BauGB) or to replace rights abolished by the expropriation of property (§ 85 par. 1 no. 4). The background to the expropriation for compensation is the regulation in § 100 that, if ownership meets certain conditions, then the owner can apply for compensation against expropriation in the form of land. If these requirements are satisfied, then according to § 85 par. 1 no. 3, land can be expropriated to provide compensation. Expropriation to replace ownership rights (§ 85 par. 1 no. 4) is regulated by § 101. According to § 85 para. 1 nos. 3 and 4, these forms of expropriation are intended as kinds of 'assisting measures' to provide compensation in the form of land or to grant ownership rights to resolve other cases of expropriation (Runkel 2009: preliminary remarks to §§ 85ff., rn. 8).

Enforcement of building orders

According to § 85 par. 1 nr. 5, expropriation is also admissible in order to enforce a previously unsuccessful building order under § 176 by revoking ownership of a plot and offering this for sale to those willing to carry out the order (expropriation to fulfil a building order). The expropriation can also be demanded by the municipality in favour of a party willing to develop the land (§ 87 par. 3 s. 2). First, it is necessary that attempts are made to enforce the building order by means of an administrative act, for example threat of a fine. If this repeatedly fails, then the municipal authorities can investigate whether the intended development can instead be achieved through expropriation (BVerwG, Ruling of 15.2.1990 – 4 C 45.87). In this case, however, additional benefits to the public good must be named to justify expropriation (Scheidler 2016: 512).

Preservation of a building structure subject to a preservation statute

According to the case group specified in § 85 par. 1 no. 6 Federal Building Code, expropriation is also admitted for the purpose of preserving a building structure situated within an area covered by a preservation order. In such cases, the plot can be expropriated and sold to a new owner who agrees to preserve the building structure. Here the following aims must be pursued: preservation of the building for its own sake (protection of historical buildings and monuments) or maintenance of the constitution of the resident population (protection of social setting; Halama 2009: § 85 rn. 72ff.).

Preservation or removal of building structures in urban redevelopment areas

According to § 85 par. 1 no. 7 Federal Building Code, expropriation can also serve the purpose of preserving or removing building structures in a legally designated urban redevelopment area under § 171d par. 1 in order to secure redevelopment measures that reflect various developmental and social needs on the basis of a development concept devised by the municipality (§ 171b par. 2) or a social development plan (§ 180). Urban redevelopment areas are those afflicted by a considerable loss of essential urban functions (e.g. caused by high rates of long-term vacant housing) and where improvements are undertaken in order to create sustainable urban structures (§ 171a par. 2).

Requirements for the admissibility of expropriation, §§ 87ff. Federal Building Code

Reflecting the constitutional principle governing expropriation as laid out in art. 14 par. 3 s. 1, the requirements for expropriation are precisely formulated in §§ 87ff. Federal Building Code.

The general good

Corresponding with the requirements specified in art. 14 par. 3 s. 1 Basic Law as well as the legal principle of proportionality, expropriation is only admissible in individual cases where this serves 'the general good' and the purpose of expropriation cannot reasonably be achieved in any other way (art. 87 par. 1 BauGB). This regulation links the general good with the constitutional principle of necessity as applied to individual cases.

However, it is insufficient to say that the form of land use specified in the municipal land use plan and named as the purpose of expropriation necessarily serves the general good in the same way as every other planning measure. Rather, expropriation is only admissible if some *extraordinary* objective and concrete interest exists for the realisation of a specific development measure, one that goes beyond the standard public interest in a planned development and that necessitates the violation of ownership rights for the general good. In other words, there must be some 'particularly vital and urgent public interest' (BVerfG, Ruling of 24.3.1987 – I BvR 1046/85, *Boxberg Ruling*). Use of the term 'general good' implies a balancing of wider societal benefits against the legal protection of ownership (Just 2004: 395). In this way, expropriation is only admissible if it is found to be suitable, necessary, and proportional in some significant fashion (Breuer 2015: § 87 rn. 10).

Expropriation can also be used to enable the *private* purchase of land if the intended development serves *both* the general good and some private purpose. The requirement of serving the general good as well as the principle of proportionality limits but does not reject the admissibility of expropriation to favour private ownership (Battis 2006: 125). Clearly, many public services are performed by private companies rather than state agencies. For example, private operators are involved in energy provision; they establish and maintain schools, hospitals and retirement homes (Halama 2009: § 87 rn. 59, BVerfG, Ruling of 18.2.1999 – 1 BvR 1367/88 et al., *Waldorfschule Ruling*). If the purpose of a business lies in the supply of essential public goods and services or is legally secured as an essential public task, then private-law structures and the standard business aim of maximising profits become secondary considerations (BVerfG, Ruling of 20.3.1984 – 1 BvL 28/82).

However, if the general good does not directly benefit from the business purpose but is rather an indirect consequence of business activities, for example through the creation of new jobs in an area with weak economic structures, then the Federal Constitutional Court views expropriation as inadmissible (BVerfG, Ruling of 24.3.1987 – I BvR 1046/85). In the light of this ruling, it seems highly unlikely that plots of land designated in the municipal land use plan as serving private purposes could be expropriated for the benefit of private developers if the intended development serves the general good only to the extent that it satisfies local demand for housing and business premises (Halama 2004: § 87 rn. 60). Expropriation, for instance, is also inadmissible for the development of racecourses that favour private riding companies (BVerfG, Ruling of 4.7.2002 – 1 BvR 390/01).

In any case, expropriation is only admissible where its purpose cannot be reasonably achieved by any other means (§ 87 para. 1 s. 1 2nd Clause BauGB, see also Federal Court of Justice – *Bundesgerichtshof* – BGH, Ruling of 25.10.2001 – III ZR 76/01). In other words, it is first necessary to investigate whether the purpose to be served by expropriation cannot be realised by another approach that violates the rights of the affected party to a much lesser degree (Battis 2006: 125). Expropriation must always be the 'last resort' (Just 2004: 395). Clearly, this is not the case if, for example, similarly suitable public plots are available (BVerfG, Ruling of 19.12.2002 – 1 BvR 1402/01). Expropriation is also inadmissible for purely fiscal reasons, for example, to save the costs of leasehold payments on a plot (ban on fiscal expropriation) (BGH, Ruling of 19.2.1976 – III ZR 147/73; Scheidler 2016: 513).

Obligation to undertake purchase negotiations and evidence for realisation of expropriation purpose

Section 87 par. 2 s. 1 Federal Building Code also regulates to protect ownership rights against unreasonable expropriation by requiring that the applicant has made a serious but vain attempt to privately acquire the land subject to expropriation on acceptable terms. Private purchase therefore takes precedence over expropriation (Halama 2004: § 87 rn. 63). Negotiations must be conducted with serious intent and with the aim of achieving a resolution acceptable to all parties (BVerwG, Ruling of 19.10.1966 – 4 C 57.65). The owner must be granted a reasonable period for deliberation (Halama 2004: § 87 rn. 67).

The applicant must provide evidence that the land will be used for the designated purpose within a suitable term (§ 87 par. 2 s. 2 BauGB). In particular, the applicant must clearly announce the intended use of the land to be expropriated and must show sufficient own funding or creditworthiness (Halama 2004: § 87 rn. 82). This requirement is aimed at preventing the hoarding of building land or other forms of misappropriated land use (Breuer 2015: § 87 rn. 40).

If, following legal expropriation, the intended purpose of expropriation cannot be achieved, § 102 Federal Building Code specifies that the former owner of the property can demand the reinstatement of ownership rights (re-expropriation). If the purpose of expropriation is removed, then the intrusion on private ownership as defined by art. 14 par. 3 Basic Law is no longer legitimate.

The party benefitting from expropriation

Expropriation with the aim of urban development can be granted to public-sector entities as well as private entities, provided they pursue a legitimate purpose of expropriation (§ 85 par. 1 BauGB; Halama 2004: § 87 rn. 87). Section 87 par. 3 s. 1 Federal Building Code violates this principle to the extent that expropriation of a plot with the purpose of preparing it for building use (§ 85 par. 1 no. 1) or to make it available for building use (§ 85 par. 1 no. 2) is only permitted in favour of a municipality or a public agency charged with public infrastructure provision (expropriation privilege).

While the privilege regarding expropriation in preparation for building use is intended to enable the provision of large contiguous areas to developers (Federal Government 1958: 89), the privilege regarding expropriation to make land available for building use can free private users from the dangers of an expropriation procedure (Halama 2004: § 87 rn. 90).

For the municipality, this expropriation privilege corresponds with the duty of disposal according to § 89 par. 1 s. 1 no. 2, par. 2 Federal Building Code. Under this duty, land that has been expropriated by the municipality in order to be prepared for building use or made available for building use must be disposed of as soon as it is possible to achieve the purpose that lays behind the acquisition, or this purpose is no longer applicable (Halama 2004: § 87 rn. 87). Thus the municipality is legally obliged to ensure that the land is developed in line with the designated use by disposing of it to a third party under agreement of corresponding conditions (Runkel 2011: § 87 rn. 118). The duty of disposal under § 89 Federal Building Code is aimed at preventing municipalities from permanently retaining plots intended for private use and 'thereby establishing a policy of excessive land hoarding' (Halama 2015: § 89 rn. 65).

Scope of expropriation

According to § 92 par. 1 s. 1 Federal Building Code, expropriation may only be granted to the extent that the plot is required to achieve the purpose of expropriation. Where the purpose being pursued by expropriation can be achieved by encumbering the plot with a right, expropriation is to be restricted to encumberment (§ 92 par. 1 s. 2). This reflects the legal principle of necessity or the smallest possible violation of rights (Scheidler 2016: 514).

Under § 92 pars. 2–4 Federal Building Code, expropriation may also be extended to favour the owner. Under certain conditions, the owner can, for example, demand expropriation of the property rather than some form of encumberment (par. 2), complete expropriation rather than partial expropriation of property (par. 3) as well as the extension of expropriation to the appurtenances of a plot (par. 4). The aim is to ensure economic continuity, that is to prevent the dispersal of economically cohesive property (Halama 2010: § 92 par. 10).

Legal consequences: compensation for expropriation

According to § 93 par. 1 no. 1 Federal Building Code and corresponding to the requirements of art. 14 par. 3 Basic Law, compensation is due for expropriation. This is intended to provide the affected party with a suitable indemnity for the loss incurred by the revocation of ownership rights (Just 2004: 399). Compensation may be demanded by any person whose rights are adversely affected by expropriation, resulting in some financial detriment (§ 94 par. 1 BauGB). The beneficiary of expropriation is legally obligated to make compensation (§ 94 par. 2 BauGB).

According to § 93 par. 2, compensation is provided first, for rights forfeited as a result of expropriation (§ 95), and second, for property loss of other kinds arising through expropriation (§ 96). Examples of such financial detriment are a reduction in the market value of remaining plots or costs arising in connection with removal activities as a result of expropriation. Compensation is normally provided in the form of money (§ 99). However, under certain conditions specified in §§ 100, 101 Federal Building Code, the owner may apply for compensation in the form of land or the granting of other rights.

The amount of compensation is determined by considering an equitable balance of the interests of the general good and the affected parties (art. 14 par. 3 GG). It should enable the affected parties to acquire an object of equal value. Other disadvantages that may arise (e.g. forgone profits) do not have to be fully compensated. In this regard, the law on expropriation specifically uses the term *compensation* 'rather than *damages*'. Under § 95 par. 1 Federal Building Code, the amount of compensation is assessed on the basis of the current market value of the plot to be expropriated or of any other subject of expropriation. The market value is set at the time when the expropriation authority adjudicates on an application for expropriation.

Under § 194 Federal Building Code, the market value is defined as the price that would be obtained in ordinary transaction at the time when the assessment is made, taking into account the existing legal circumstances and the actual characteristics, general condition, and location of the property or other object of assessment, without consideration being given to any extraordinary or personal circumstances. Independent committees of valuation experts are charged with determining property values (§§ 192, 193). These regularly compile purchasing price data for property and use this data to determine standard ground values. The intention of the legislator in establishing the committees of valuation experts and their purchasing price data was to provide an instrument to ensure market transparency. The details of how to determine standard market values are regulated by the ordinance on guidelines to determine the market values of property (ImmoWertV 2010).

The expropriation procedure

The expropriation procedure is regulated by the provisions laid down in §§ 104–122 Federal Building Code. These reflect the procedural requirements relating to ownership rights as laid out in art. 14 Basic Law (Battis 2016, preliminary remarks to §§ 85ff., rn. 13). Application for an expropriation procedure to the expropriation authority is always the last means that the benefitting party can resort to when all other efforts to secure an agreement satisfactory to all parties have failed.

The preliminary expropriation procedure begins with the submission of an application for expropriation to the municipality within whose territory the land subject to expropriation is situated (§ 105 BauGB). The intention of this provision is to ensure that the special knowledge that a municipality possess of local circumstances can be introduced at this preliminary stage to the actual expropriation procedure. The municipality is required to present the application for expropriation with its comment to the expropriation authority (normally the higher administrative authority of a state) within one month (§ 105 s. 2).

The expropriation authority is required to grant the property owner, the applicant and those authorities affected by the expropriation to be given the opportunity to make representations (§ 107 par. 1 s. 3). In cases where ownership is to be withdrawn or a building lease established, the expropriation authority is required to obtain an opinion on property values from an independent committee of experts in order to determine the amount of compensation (§ 107 par. 1 s. 4). All questions relating to expropriation and compensation are discussed at the hearing. The expropriation authority must act as an intermediary between all parties involved in the expropriation procedure and strive to achieve some form of agreement (§ 110 par. 1).

If the parties involved cannot reach agreement, the expropriation authority passes an expropriation resolution (§ 112 par. 1). This resolution determines the amount of compensation and the interest to be paid. The expropriation authority bases its decisions on the land values calculated by the committee of experts. The resolution on expropriation is an administrative act that can be contested by the parties involved by lodging a motion for a court ruling (§§ 217ff.).

Once the resolution on expropriation ceases to be defeasible, the beneficiary of expropriation must render or deposit the financial compensation. Thereafter, any of the parties involved can request that the expropriation authority execute the resolution on expropriation (§ 117 par. 1). This order of execution affects the legal changes determined in the resolution on expropriation (§ 117 par. 5). The order of execution includes the putting in possession of the expropriated land on the designated day (§ 117 par. 6).

Expropriation of property as a strategic instrument to achieve land use goals?

Expropriation of property has a wide field of application: The provisions in § 85 par. 1 no. 1 Federal Building Code determine that, in principle, every form of use listed in § 9 can justify expropriation if these are specifically named in a binding land use plan. For example, expropriation by the municipality to prepare land for development can enable the creation of large cohesive areas of building land. Additional aims of expropriation can be to exploit undeveloped plots in built-up areas or to implement urban development goals of preservation and renovation. At the same time, the law provides safety mechanisms to ensure that expropriation does not merely serve an excessive policy of land hoarding.

Expropriation is clearly an effective instrument to obtain ownership of land. Sections 104 ff. regulate for a strict procedure to be carried out by specially constituted agencies that investigate all conditions, legal and otherwise, regarding an expropriation application, gather necessary information, and initiate safety measures with the land registry. The resolution on expropriation is an administrative act with immediate external legal consequences. The ensuring execution order effects the transferral of ownership and encompasses legal possession of expropriated property. The expropriation of property enjoys a high degree of legitimacy in view of the clearly regulated procedure with the right to a hearing, the involvement of valuation experts, the neutral position of the expropriation authority, the obligation of the beneficiary to provide compensation, transparency in the process in determining property values, as well as a comprehensive range of legal protections.

At the same time, expropriation is not a suitable strategic instrument to realise policy goals in urban land use. This is due to the strict focus on the public good as well as the requirement that each case of expropriation be considered individually. Clearly, the legal guarantee of ownership rights presents a major hurdle for the admissibility of expropriation. It is not sufficient that the conditions for expropriation be identified in the abstract; they must be clearly established in each individual case. In order to prove reasonable grounds for the expropriation of a property, it is necessary to consider the particular interests of the owner. This prevents the strategic application of expropriation as an instrument to steer urban development. The group of potential beneficiaries is also considerably restricted by the fact that expropriation in favour of private ownership is only admissible in the case of a particularly urgent and vital public interest. This constitutes a major barrier to the strategic application of this instrument.

Moreover, expropriation must always be the last resort after all other means of achieving a generally acceptable solution by noncompulsory sale have been explored or the required land for development cannot be supplied from public stock. This is reflected in the design of the expropriation procedure, which is such as to encourage an amicable solution between the involved parties and hence to avoid expropriation wherever possible. In this way, expropriation functions somewhat in the background to motivate all those involved to seek agreement rather than as a strategic instrument for the implementation of goals in land use and consumption.

In addition to these various procedural and legal barriers to the admissibility of expropriation, the applicant also faces various risks of litigation as well as potential costs in time and money that limit the efficiency and workability of this instrument. The entire procedure from the preliminary steps up to the passing of the expropriation resolution and its execution can take a considerable period of time. Clearly, this can impede implementation of the intended purpose of expropriation. If the application for expropriation is rejected or withdrawn, the applicant bears the procedural costs for the administrative work of the expropriation authority, the drawing up of the expert evaluation as well as all lawyers' fees (§ 121 par. 1 BauGB). To this is added the risk that the expropriated party may contest a resolution on expropriation or on compensation, which clearly will lengthen the entire procedure. If the expropriated party wins this case, the beneficiary of expropriation is also required to pay court costs. In view of these potential risks, any potential beneficiary will consider very carefully before resorting to the instrument of expropriation.

References

Battis, U. (2006) *Öffentliches Baurecht und Raumordnungsrecht*, 5th ed., W. Kohlhammer Publishing, Stuttgart.

Battis, U. (2016) Preliminary remarks to §§ 85ff., in: Battis, U., Krautzberger, M. and Löhr, R.-P. (eds) *Baugesetzbuch*, 13th ed., C.H. Beck Publishing, Munich.

Battis, U., § 86, *ibidem*.

BauGB – *Baugesetzbuch*, in the version promulgated on 23 September 2004 (Federal Law Gazette I p. 2414).

Baulandbeschaffungsgesetz of 3 August 1953 (Federal Law Gazette I p. 720).

BBauG – *Bundesbaugesetz*, of 23 June 1960 (Federal Law Gazette I p. 341)

Behebungsverordnung – Verordnung zur Behebung der dringendsten Wohnungsnot of 9 December 1919 (Law Gazette of the German Empire p. 1968).

Breuer, R. (2015) § 87, in: Schrödter, W. (ed.) *Baugesetzbuch*, 8th ed., Nomos Publishing, Baden-Baden.

Dolde, K.-P. (1991) Städtebauliche Enteignung und planerische Abwägung, in: Franßen, E., et al. (eds) *Bürger – Richter – Staat*, Festschrift für Horst Sendler, C.H. Beck Publishing, Munich, 225–239.

Federal Government, *Explanatory memorandum to the draft of the Procurement of Building Land Act of 28 May 1951*, BT-Drs. 1/2281 (Bundestag printed paper).

Federal Government, *Explanatory memorandum to the draft of the Federal Building Code of 16 April 1958*, BT-Drs. 3/336 (Bundestag printed paper).

Halama, G., § 85, in: Driehaus, H.-J., et al. (eds) *Berliner Kommentar zum Baugesetzbuch*, Vol. 2, Carl Heymanns Publishing, 16th update October 2009.

Halama, G., § 87, *ibidem*, 3rd update July 2004.

Halama, G., § 89, *ibidem*, 31st update October 2015.

Halama, G., § 92, *ibidem*, 16th update April 2010.

ImmoWertV – Immobilienwertermittlungsverordnung of 19 May 2010 (BGBl. I S. 639).

Just, J.-D. (2004) Förmliche Enteignung, in: Hoppe, W., Bönker, C. and Grotefels, S. (eds) *Öffentliches Baurecht*, 3rd ed., C.H. Beck Publishing, Munich.

Runkel, P., Preliminary remarks to §§ 85ff., in: Ernst, Zinkahn, Bielenberg, Krautzberger, *Baugesetzbuch*, 93rd update, October 2009.

Runkel, P., § 87, *ibidem*, 98th update, January 2011.

Scheidler, A. (2016) Die Voraussetzungen der städtebaulichen Enteignung, *Zeitschrift für Umwelt- und Planungsrecht*, 36(11+12), 510–516.

Stüer, B. (2009) *Handbuch des Bau- und Fachplanungsrechts*, 4. Aufl., C.H. Beck Publishing, Munich.

A Dutch perspective on expropriation: the pragmatic way

Barrie Needham

The rules

The legal rules in the Netherlands for expropriation for urban development are in many ways similar to those in Germany, as described by Albrecht. The main differences seem to be in the purposes for which it can be applied (more widely in the Netherlands), the way in which compensation is calculated, and the pragmatic and non-ideological way in which it is viewed.

Expropriation (*onteigening*, expropriation of *all* the rights on a piece of landed property) is regulated in the Law on expropriation (*Onteigeningswet*), which still has the form and content of the law of 1851, although modified many times since then. This law sets down the rules both in general, and for urban development in particular (and also for other purposes, such as for military purposes, water defence, roads, canals, flooding). In all cases, the process is in two parts: First, the decision about the application to expropriate the property, and second, the decision about the amount of compensation. But the two parts overlap. The application has to be accompanied by a statement of the amount of compensation being offered. The amount actually paid is determined by the court, but the owner needs to have an idea of the amount he/she will receive, in order to decide whether or not to resist the expropriation. And if the application to expropriate has been granted, it is possible to pay the defendant (*de verweerder*) an advance on the compensation, because the second process can take a long time.

Title 4 of the law regulates expropriation 'in the interest of land use development, housing, public order and upholding the law on drugs'. The applicant can be a public body or a recognised housing association (which is an independent organisation subject to public rules and light public supervision). The application is made to the relevant minister, and the decision about granting it is a decree of the national government. The landowner who objects to the expropriation can appeal against this decision, and the appeal is settled by an independent administrative court. If the application is granted, the court appoints a number of independent experts to advise the court about the amount of compensation. It is not possible to appeal against the judgment of this court.

Under Title 4, expropriation can be granted for a large number of reasons, among which are:

- Realising a legal land use plan or maintaining the existing land uses designated in that plan;
- Improving bad housing;
- Maintaining the public order.

The application is not granted lightly: expropriation is the 'ultimum remedium', the way of last resort. It has to meet all of the following three conditions: Is the required change in the public interest? Does the required change need to be realised quickly? Can the required change be brought about in any other way? How these conditions are applied can be illustrated by taking the case when expropriation is used for realising a land use plan.

Suppose there is a binding land use plan that has been legally established and includes specific locations designated for a park, and other locations designated for a shopping centre. The legal processes for formally approving the land use plan require that the plan be 'in the public interest'. It is, therefore, 'in the public interest' that the park and the shopping centre be realised on those locations. If the owner of the land for the park does not want to provide it, neither does he/she want to sell the land to someone who will, the court will support an application for expropriation. If the owner of the land for the shopping centre does not want to provide that, nor sell the land to someone who will, the court will support expropriation. If that owner says: 'I will provide the shopping centre,' but delays doing that 'unreasonably', then too will the court support expropriation.

How the owner reacts to the possibilities offered by the land use plan and to the threat of expropriation depends on the rules for granting compensation for expropriation. These rules are not simple. It is the value that the property would have in a free market transaction (and, therefore, not the subjective value to the owner if that would be higher). No account should be taken of the effects on that value of any public works (such as drainage or roads) carried out in order to realise the desired change. But account must be taken of the effects of the land use designation for which the land is to be expropriated. But note: account must be taken of *all* the new land uses in the *whole complex* for which the particular property is being expropriated (the 'complex value'). The boundaries of the land use plan that legitimates 'the public interest' can affect, therefore, the amount of compensation.

How does this work out in practice? We restrict ourselves to the application for urban development.

The practice (effectiveness, efficiency, legitimacy, practicability)

The principle of expropriation is not contested socially or politically. It is widely accepted that private ownership of land can stand in the way of realising 'the public good'. The legal rules are applied pragmatically, which takes the sting out of ideological differences. The legal processes can take a long time: but the provision that an advance can be paid on the compensation makes long delays less painful.

There have been political disputes. Until 1988, appeals against an expropriation order were determined by a court that was *not* independent of the national government. It took an appeal to the European Commission for Human Rights to get that changed (Benthem-arrest). And in 1977, differences of opinion within the ruling coalition about the compensation for expropriation were the occasion for the national government to fall. It was the old political question: compensation at existing value, or at new value? The argument for existing value is that if the plan had not been made, the land would have kept its existing value. So why should the owner gain financially because of a new plan? The counter-argument is that the old plan prevented more profitable uses of the land, and the new plan lifts some of those restrictions. The present law follows the counterargument, but says that the new value is that of the land without any infrastructural improvements and is the 'complex value'.

The pragmatic way in which expropriation is viewed and applied is apparent in practice. If the relevant public body wants to acquire land, it first tries to reach an amicable agreement with the owners. That is legally required before the public body may apply for expropriation. If the owner does not want to sell, the public body will tell the owner,

> Then we can start an expropriation procedure. But that takes a long time. And costs a lot in legal fees. If you want, you can resist. You will probably lose the case. Then you will receive compensation around X. If you agree to sell amicably, we will offer you X plus 10 percent. You get more that you probably would by fighting the case, and you get it more quickly.

Given that practice, it is no surprise that expropriation is not common.

The other evidence of pragmatism (in contrast to an ideological approach) is that most appeals are motivated financially. To understand this, it is necessary to refer to the compensation ruling, especially the effect of the 'complex value'. Suppose that the complex is a housing estate with houses, schools, parks, road, and so forth. The market value of the land (per unit area) is the *average for the whole complex*. If the owner has land that is designated for a park, he/she will probably not want to provide that. If he/she is prepared to sell it amicably to the public body, the price might be the (low) value of park land. So the owner will negotiate hard, if necessary alluding to the possibility of expropriation (although knowing that he/she would lose the process), with the aim of getting the higher price of the complex value. If the owner has land designated for a shopping centre, he/she knows that the value in that new use is higher than the average complex value. It is for that reason that he/she might want to contest the expropriation. And the grounds would be: 'I can realise that shopping centre myself, thank you.' The applicant, fearing delays, might then say, 'It is not realistic that the defendant could develop the shopping centre himself. For he is a farmer, or a householder, or has riding stables, or a few run-down industrial premises, or some such.' At which the defendant says, 'I have a legal contract with a big commercial property developer in which he and I agree jointly to develop my land for a shopping centre on the lines of that specified in the plan.' In other words, the defendant says: expropriation is not necessary for realising the desired land use change. If the court is convinced, the expropriation is not allowed.

It will be seen that the law allows expropriation in order to allow land to be used for commercial purposes (such as private housing, shopping, offices, industry), whereby the expropriating body itself does not realise those uses, but sells the land to developers who will. There are two main reasons why this is not politically contested. One is that expropriation is not granted if the first landowner can and will, directly or indirectly, realise the new uses (without too much delay). The other is that commercial developers are often all too happy that a public body helps them (if necessary by expropriation) to amass developable building sites.

Land scarcity

In one sense, expropriation is always about scarcity. There is a desire to realise a particular land use, for which land in a particular location is necessary. The owner of that land does not want to sell it. There is scarcity in the supply of land in that precise place. Expropriation forces the owner to supply the land.

One might think that the Dutch with such a high population density (about 450 people per square kilometers of dry land) would be very concerned about the scarcity of land in the wider sense. However, their concern is expressed more in terms of the *efficiency* with which land is used. And efficiency is achieved by not having parcels of land unnecessarily unused or vacant, and by having complementary land uses near to each other. It is with those aims that expropriation is used. It makes urban redevelopment easier, and in that way relieves pressure on greenfield sites. But it makes greenfield development also easier, for the Dutch practice is that such development should take place within large integrated sites, and expropriation has been widely used (or threatened) by municipalities in order to assemble the separate landownerships necessary for such integrated development.

A U.S. perspective on expropriation: a radically different view

Dan Tarlock

Expropriation in Germany, condemnation in the U.S.

Both Germany and the U.S. permit government bodies and sometimes private entities to force property owners to sell full or partial title to the government or authorized private entity. All countries distinguish between the power to regulate the use of land to minimize the imposition of external costs on neighbors and the acquisition of land for projects that provide widespread public benefits. There are, however, important differences between the two countries that reflect the attitudes towards private property and government action. The differences start with the terminology used to describe government power.

In the U.S., the authority of all levels of government to force a sale of property starts from Article V of the federal constitution: 'Nor shall private property be taken for public use, without just compensation.' The federal states are free to impose additional restrictions on governments. The U.S. does not use the term expropriation to characterize government power. With minor exceptions in federal state constitutions, the term is reserved for foreign, often revolutionary, governments that seize property without first offering compensation. When governments acquire property, they exercise the power of 'eminent domain' or *dominium eminens*, Latin for supreme lordship. The U.S. Supreme Court has described eminent domain as an inherent attribute of sovereignty 'whenever it is necessary or appropriate to use the land in the execution of any of the powers granted to it by the constitution' (*Boom Co. v. Patterson*, 98 U.S. 403 (1879)). When the power is exercised, governments condemn rather than expropriate land. Article V requires that compensation be paid or shortly after title is transferred to the government or authorized entities.

Article V permits two types of challenges to a condemnation action. The first challenges the authority of the government to acquire the property for the designated use. The second allows the property owner to challenge the amount of the compensation as inadequate and thus unjust.

The public purpose challenge: U.S. and Germany compared

Article V limits the condemnation of property to 'public use'. Initially, the federal government did not need to acquire much land because it owned so much. Thus, the law of eminent domain developed at the state level. Starting in the early nineteenth century, state courts expanded the meaning of public use, and in four major decisions between 1896 and 2005, the U.S. Supreme Court has validated this expansion.

At first blush, the U.S. and German laws of expropriation appear quite similar. The legal standards, public purpose and general good, both serve to limit the use of expropriation. The chief difference is that the German law has always been defined by statute whereas the U.S. law developed through judicial decisions; legislative restrictions have always existed but they have only accelerated in recent years. However, on closer examination, a paradox appears. One would expect that German courts would not seek to impose limits on expropriation for two reasons. First, since the founding of the modern nation in 1870, Germany has had a strong but benevolent Hobbesian state (1933–1945 aside). Second, the federal states have strong land use planning and regulation. In contrast, the U.S. can be described as a limited Lockian state, in which the concern is with limiting the exercise of power, and the country has a weak land use planning tradition.

Both countries limit the power of the government to acquire property through a compulsory title transfer through legislation and judicial decisions, but the German law now appears stricter than the U.S. law because the expropriation of land to satisfy local demand for housing and business premises is forbidden. In contrast, the U.S. Supreme Court has sanctioned the use of eminent domain for economic development to a greater extent than has Germany, but the federal states have cut back the court's liberal definition of public use.

The evolution of public use in the U.S.: from a liberal to strict test

There are now at least five separate definitions of public use that roughly represent the expansion of the power by Supreme Court and federal high court decisions from the early nineteenth century to the present.

- The earliest definition was use by the public through government use, such as a military facility;
- As states began to build public roads and canals, public use was defined as actual use by the public;
- The development of railroads and the generation of electricity by public utilities, private corporations regulation, led to the delegation of the power of eminent domain to private parties for actual use by the public;

- Post–World War II urban renewal led to a break with a traditional state function such as defense or actual use by the public to a definition of public use as the transfer of land that has a direct public benefit or purpose;
- Finally, the rise of intergovernmental competition for economic development led to a break with the previous tests and the adoption of an indirect public benefit or purpose.

The Supreme Court extended the power from classic public goods such as roads to allow the condemnation of land to create the Gettysburg National Military to commemorate the Civil War battle that stopped the advance of the Confederate Army into the northern Union States (*United States v. Gettysburg Electric Ry.*, 160 U.S. 668, 679 (1896)). Modern jurisprudence rests on three cases. The first arose as the use of eminent domain increased after World War II. Many cities wanted to rebuild blighted or marginally valuable areas. Large blocks of urban land had become scarce; small owners who refused to sell had a bilateral monopoly and could substantially increase the cost of large-scale urban renewal projects. In the landmark case of *Berman v. Parker* (348 U.S. 26 (1954)), the Court approved the condemnation of a non-blighted department store as part of a larger redevelopment plan for Washington, DC, in a sweeping endorsement of the transfer of property from one private owner to promote the efficient use of scarce land. However, by the 1970s, large-scale urban renewal projects were criticized on multiple equity and economic grounds. States and cities also became more aggressive in trying to attract development to increase their tax base, and abuses such as the condemnation of land to eliminate a competitor of a business began to be litigated. Academic and popular calls for limit on the exercise of eminent domain increased.

Thirty years later, the court sanctioned the condemnation of a leasehold interest in Hawaii to transfer the land to home buyers in fee simple. Five families, descendants of early missionaries, created an artificial scarcity of land available for housing. In its opinion, the court emphasized the state's unique situation justified the correction of a 'land oligopoly' (*Hawaii Housing Authority v. Midkiff*, 467 U.S. 229 (1984)). The final and most controversial decision is *Kelo v. City of New London* (545 U.S. 469 (2005)). By a 5–4 vote, the Court approved the condemnation of property in a declining industrial city in Connecticut for a housing and office complex to support a major pharmaceutical company that promised to locate its headquarters nearby. The Court held that property could be taken for another private use if there was a public benefit, but imposed a planning-based limitation. Though the city could not take petitioners' land simply to confer a private benefit on a particular private party, "the takings at issue here would be executed pursuant to a carefully considered development plan", which "was not adopted 'to benefit a particular class of identifiable individuals" (467 U.S.: 476–477).

The decision set off a fierce, effective, and continuing hostile reaction in many states, especially as the project litigated in Kelo fell through after the pharmaceutical company did not relocate in the city. Mrs. Kelo's small pink house became a symbol of resistance to government power, and as of 2016 the property remains vacant (Ilya Somin (2015): 235).

Kelo was denounced by name in the 2016 Republican Party platform, but the decision had already been eroded. Forty-two of the 50 federal states have passed legislation to limit *Kelo*. The majority flatly prohibited the use of eminent domain for economic development purposes, including prohibitions against eminent domain for purely tax revenue purposes or the transfer of someone property to another private entity. Connecticut now prohibits condemnation if the primary purpose is economic development (Conn. Gen. Stat. § 8–193(b)(1)). Others limited condemnation only to 'blighted areas' or demanded greater public involvement in the decision to counter 'expert' planners. A few states such as New York continue to allow the condemnation of non-blighted land for public purposes such as sports arenas. (*Goldstein v. New York State Urban Development Corp.*, 921 N.E.2d 16 (N.Y. Ct. App. 2009)).

Conclusion

In the end, the U.S. and Germany have radically different views of eminent domain. In both countries, the instrument started out as a way to prevent a property owner from preventing the construction of a vital public good, such as a highway. In the U.S., it became more difficult for private developers to assemble large tracts of land for redevelopment because of holdouts. The Supreme Court consistently endorsed the use of eminent domain for urban renewal. However, starting in the 1970s, large-scale urban renewal projects fell out of favor and criticism of the use of eminent domain to redistribute land between private owners mounted. Germany curbed the use of condemnation for this purpose but continues to allow its use for well-planned public-private projects. When the U.S. Supreme Court did not significantly curb the use of the power, the federal states did. Today, eminent domain is seen as an attack on private property no matter how much the public might benefit from a project. Thus, the myriad of current limits on condemnation may create an artificial scarcity of land for pipelines, transmission lines, and a wide range of needed infrastructure investment that clearly meet the traditional public purpose standard.

Reference

Ilya Somin (2015) *The Grasping Hand: Kelo v. City of New London and the Limits of Eminent Domain, University Of Chicago Press*, Chicago.

16 Nationalization of land in Scotland

Private property and the public interest

Greg Lloyd

In modern capitalist market economies, the ideological primacy of private property rights is held to be essential to the efficient and effective allocation of resources, effective operation of labour and capital markets, and wealth creation and accumulation of profit. In the context of land, however, there is an additional complexity: in reality there is a relatively confused basket of property rights – common rights, public rights – which co-exist alongside private property. This creates constantly shifting sets of relations and tensions that then have implications for the efficiencies and effectiveness of the market economies. Notwithstanding this dynamic context – within the layered, competitive, and diverse bundle of rights, responsibilities and interests – the principal ideological imperative remains that of private property. The power of the private property narrative is brought wonderfully to life in the historical novel *Harvest* (Crace 2013), which imagines a week in an English medieval village in which the enclosure of common land is being executed. The protagonist of the privatisation of the common land or the public interest asserts that this will transform 'a village of Enough, [to] a settlement of More' (Crace 2013: 186). The advocated or perceived social, economic, and environmental benefits of private property effects are justified on the advocacy of stewardship, but this is socially constructed through a private property rights prism.

This chapter seeks to contribute to a broader understanding of the role of property rights in society and to consider how these may be rebalanced in the public interest by examining some historical insights and contemporary actions. To better understand the challenging nature of the land question, it draws on the broad logics of new institutionalism (Williamson 2000). It then references the importance of considering historical experiences in establishing private property as the conventional, accepted, and normal customs and conventions, the nature of the formal rules of the game that establish and sustain the perceived legitimacy of private property, the dynamic and complex ways in which land and development interests – the principal agents of deliberation, including landowners, financiers, developers, and consumers – work to create profit and wealth and establish power, and the social consequences or public space outcomes – the public interest.

Obtaining the public interest in land can be secured through landownership, including the nationalization or municipalisation of land, design and implementation of land use planning regulations and policies and financial-fiscal arrangements. These tend to be perceived, in a wider private property rights discourse, in contested ways. Thus, land nationalization is rejected as being counter to civil liberties, planning is resisted, and taxation provisions viewed as politically problematic (Andrew et al. 2007). There is a need, then, to devise a more nuanced approach to articulating the public interest in the defined context of private property. This chapter explores the ongoing land reforms in Scotland that seek the sage use of land for the collective well-being of Scotland. Land reform is defined in a Scottish context as measures that modify or change the arrangements governing the possession and use of land in Scotland in the broader public interest (Reid 2015). Such a reform agenda is not anti-private property but seeks a more inclusive notion of the public interest so that it is given greater legitimacy and respect in societal and political affairs. In effect, it seeks to challenge the linear and mechanistic assumptions of the private property position as something that is organic and normal.

Towards an alternative prism?

Today, the dynamic medium through which such property rights are defined, exchanged, and enforced is that of private land and property development markets. While these do not operate in an absolute way – being stewarded through public policy, planning regulations, and fiscal arrangements – such interventions are continuously contested and challenged. In effect, private property trumps the public interest. The conditions determined by private property rights and property interests create powerful distributional narratives – raising questions about natural justice, social equity, and the concept of the public interest. In such terms fundamental questions arise concerning the possibility of alternatives to private property in serving both efficiency and equity considerations. This mirrors, reflects, and is a consequence also of the powerful normalisation of neoliberal economic and political ideas (Mirowski 2013). These very particular ideological conditions have established private property at centre stage. The implications for the public interest are profoundly challenged by such individualistic and libertarian metrics.

Reflecting the contested intellectual and legal miasma, debates and conversations about land use and development, its ownership and tenure, the associated relations of power, privilege, and influence, and the perceived performance of regulation and planning tends to the vexatious. Land discourses are riddled and layered with contradictions and tensions. Rarely are these explored in any reasoned or progressive manner. At once, for example, land is both a basic factor of production in the capitalist mode of production and a human right with respect to social accessibility to property ownership. At the same time, land is highly visible, a material consideration for economies and communities, which involves the physical concept of terra firma and includes its broader ecological resource base; and yet land can be invisible with respect to its intrinsic narratives of ownership, control, and influence (Massey and Catalano 1978). Power relations associated with landownership and property development tend to be hidden and yet are highly political in determining the allocation of resources and the opportunities in societies. Again, land is a social asset with powerful community values, relating also to histories, customs and traditions, cultures, and identities that combine to form an essential bedrock of social capital; and at the same time, land and property are important economic commodities, offering the potential for development to benefit communities and neighbourhoods, to create wealth and income. Yet here, land can become commodified and misused in conventional market processes leading to speculation and inflation. Similarly, the land and its attendant eco-systemic resources are both material – the bedrock of societal well-being and productivity – and highly vulnerable to pollution, flooding, and overuse (Hetherington 2015). Yet, the concept of the public interest remains elusive in this world of private property.

Concepts of property rights in land are also highly charged and vexed matters, involving bundles of private, common, and public rights in an uneven fashion over time and space. Relations between legislative and institutional structures may also be differentiated according to specific groupings of agents and interests in a land and development matter. This highlights the complexities of the underlying social and power relations in land matters – the relationship between private interests including owners, developers, builders, financiers, and occupiers and what might be described as a broader community-based concept of the public interest. This creates a set of changing relationships that carry powerful emotional arguments, confrontational political positioning and posturing, and is embedded in an unbalanced priority for private property. Reference to the advocacy of private think tanks railing against the effects of planning controls over private property makes the case well (for an example, see Morton 2012). This particular hegemonic social construction is all pervasive and is bound up with the requirements of advanced market capitalist economies. As a consequence, the public interest or the idea of a broader societal or community well-being has been eroded.

The pernicious effects of private property are very evident. The exercise of monopoly interests in land holdings and the effects of speculation in property that may result in land banking serve to ensure a dysfunctional land supply and inflated land prices. Market pressures and the exploitation of land on greenfield areas for private development purposes can concomitantly result in redundant brownfield sites being ignored and unable to contribute to relieving pressures for development (Taylor and Walker 2015). The turn to capture or enclose public spaces and community parks for private purposes is a consequence of this imbalance in political priorities (Minton 2009). In particular, greenbelts – a long established planning nostrum drawn from an earlier social democratic ideology – have come under direct attack from a neoliberal perspective. It has been argued, for example, that greenbelts should be made more accessible for private sector house building with appropriate compensation for those private interests that may be affected together with local arrangements for communities to increase the housing supply. In effect, the public interest in the greenbelt is being made vulnerable to its monetisation. This has drawn critical opprobrium – even from the traditional supporters of the government's policy agenda – an editorial in *The Daily Telegraph* (2015), for example, stated

> it is extremely disappointing that ministers are now attempting to water down planning rules to allow thousands of houses to be built on Green Belt land. It is all the more disappointing that their proposed rules were published without fanfare or public ministerial comment. That low key approach does not engender confidence in the Government to act in good faith.

The radical transformation of economic ideas over time (Fine and Milonakis 2008) that serve to distort our current social constructions of change are important. This sets the context to understanding the changing morphology of the land question. Notwithstanding the fundamental importance of land to society – in terms of contributing community well-being, enhancing place identity, promoting economic and political actions – the intellectual basis of understanding land has been eroded. Narratives around land have been increasingly de-conceptualised, de-contextualised, and de-intellectualised. In effect, a political economy of land and property has been replaced by the economics of construction and development. The central arguments here are that private rights have become hegemonic, private ownership and tenure rest on private arrangements, the public interest in land use and development has been devalued, neoliberal ideology has bolstered this bias and indeed has served to normalise private metrics, and established concepts have been recast. Essentially, private property has become normalised and the public interest vilified. In this process, ideas and understandings have been transformed around the private model.

A case in point is that of the role of infrastructure in land use and development. To facilitate property development, infrastructure in the form of energy, water and waste, and other utilities are required. Flying in the face of its internal neoclassical economic logic (the public goods aspects of infrastructure to support land development) that can lead to an inefficient provision of supporting services, a neoliberal ideology has opened up the case for its private provision. This has led to issues around the strategic, site-specific, and integrated provision of infrastructure for development, inhibiting, for example, the supply of housing and other development and ongoing debates around its appropriate funding. This represents another aspect of the land use planning system that has been challenged and exposed to ideological manipulation. The private interest has asserted the private sector ideology and fiefdom over the public interest with respect to the land question.

Scarcity of land, for example, has also been reconfigured under the private property right domain – despite being the basic economic and societal challenge of reconciling needs, wants, and available resources – it is not only a complex and contested concept but is socially constructed in a very specific way (Mullainathan and Shafir 2013). Conventionally cast in neoclassical economic terms, scarcity is socially constructed in terms of a mismatch between supply and demand. Yet the emphasis on its understanding and prescription tends to fall on the supply side – scarcity being constructed as a shortfall in the provision or availability of a good or service. This interpretation makes it of immediate importance for understanding the operation of (capitalist) land markets. Land supply is assumed to be fixed in absolute (or quantitative) terms and limited further through land use planning regulations in relative (and qualitative) terms. The focus on the problems of the supply side has become normalised – and attention then tends not to fall on the specifics of the demand side.

The housing position in London is a topical example. The consideration of demand is eschewed in favour of a supply side focus (London Housing Commission 2015). There is no real countervailing regional industrial policy framework to positively divert excess demand away from London and the southeast of England to the wider national and devolved economy (Martin et al. 2015). Instead the focus turns on the limited supply side of the equation in London itself. The emphasis falls on the reasons for the restricted housing construction (and beyond that) the relative paucity of building land being made available by planning authorities. In these feverish circumstances – as private interests proliferate and become the norm and public or social interests are marginalised or ignored – it is difficult to assert the contrary. It is not only ideas that have been transformed but society has created an intellectual deficit around land. North (2011: ii), for example, observed that

> the tools we use to translate understanding into a framework are institutions composed of formal rules, informal norms, and enforcement characteristics. Institutions are very blunt instruments to deal with very complex issues. Perhaps because the norms of behaviour and the formal rules do not work or because enforcement is imperfect, the problems are still unresolved. Underlying the economic and social institutions must be a political framework. In order to understand that framework and how societies work, we need a theory of politics, that does not exist.

Is there a case for the public interest? If so, how can it be regained?

The land question is more than the nature of the relations, regulations, and performances involved in planning and development. In the context of private property rights and interests, defining the public interest is fraught with definitional and operational problems. It is more than reforming planning arrangements or devising new fiscal provisions to address the perceived supply side agenda. It is about understanding the hidden power of landownership, the efficiency and effectiveness of legal and tenurial arrangements, the nature of the associated political contestation, and the inherited historical and cultural dimensions and experiences around land. It is about societal well-being and future agendas of social justice, resilience, and sustainability. Here some insights may be drawn from the institutional and organisational dimensions of land reform in Scotland.

Land reforms in Scotland

Land matters have played a critical role in the maturation of Scotland's political and cultural heritage (McCrone 2001). Land – its ownership, tenure, use, development, and regulation – is iconic in Scotland. It reflects a highly complex and contested history of ideas and experiences. The eighteenth and nineteenth centuries witnessed the enforced dispossession of people in the Highlands of northern Scotland by landowners to enable the land to be used for more profitable activities, such as sheep and deer. The infamous Highland Clearances resulted in a mass displacement of Scots, the creation of a global diaspora and, for those who were able to remain, the establishment of crofting communities (Hunter 1976). Crofting comprised small-scale agrarian activities, including fishing and common grazing on the poorer quality land. It was a specific form of feudal land tenure and an identity that rested on communal ways of agricultural working representing an adaptation to the availability of the land and quality of the soil (Busby and MacLeod 2010). It involved the common holding and use of land – run rig – that provided for a more economically effective way of addressing scarcity and securing relatively more socially just outcomes. Run rig allowed for efficiency and equity in agricultural (subsistence) production and engendered a common understanding of the public interest in the crofting communities. Indeed, crofting was acknowledged as having created a number of advantages for the sparsely populated, peripheral region including population retention and rural development (Sutherland et al. 2014). It is argued here that the common holding allowed for an assertion of a public interest working within the confines of the consequences and realities of private landownership, tenure, and the assertion of private property rights.

Such circumstances precipitated debates around the relationship of private property and understandings of a threatened public interest. In Scotland, in the late eighteenth century, for example, a moral philosopher, William Ogilvie – who was from the minor landed classes – published an anonymous tract (Land Reform Scotland 1997). Described as 'a pastoral prose poem' (MacDonald 1997: 29), it decried the monopoly power of private landownership and advocated a public interest on the grounds of natural justice.

In terms of historical provenance, this contrarian reasoning reflected the emerging ideas of the time – the broad period of intellectual change known as the Enlightenment (Gay 1996). The Enlightenment represented the beginnings of logic and reason in public discourse, and the questioning of established and authoritarian institutions such as the nobility and the Church (Heilbroner 1961). It led to a number of fundamental changes in government thinking and had profound political effects on power and politics in following years. Important ideas promoted reason and rationality, natural justice, and the need for empirical evidence to legitimise public policy and action. The nature of rights was explored and it was held that would facilitate enhanced economic development through the promotion of markets (Roll 1961). Ogilvie was observing, reflecting, and writing at a time of great change in intellectual ideas, and he was able to draw on earlier thinking about economic matters and the role of land and property. The point being is that there is an established tradition of concern with the effects of private property rights on the broader public interest in Scotland.

With the subsequent industrialisation and modernisation of the Scottish economy there has remained an enduring concern with the various facets of land – including critically its concentrated ownership and its associated political and economic attributes (Wightman 1996). Attention principally turned on the protection of agricultural tenants. Various land reforms were put into effect in the nineteenth century to promote greater security of tenure and fair rents. Notwithstanding these measures, the land question remained unresolved in Scotland.

Devolution in 1999 allowed for another perspective – an opportunity to address the legal and administrative inconsistencies, the economic disincentives of the inherited feudal tenurial arrangements (Macmillan 2000). In essence this may be seen as seeking to secure greater efficiency and effectiveness in Scotland's land and property markets and promote a broader based construct of the public interest. This reflects the wider human rights dimension in the land question. Land reform is defined in a Scottish context as 'measures that modify or change the arrangements governing the possession and use of land in Scotland in the public interest'. It is important to note that the land reform apparatus was being put into place alongside the modernisation of the land use planning system and the preparation of a land use strategy (Lloyd and Peel 2010).

In Scotland in the late 1990s, and following the turn to devolution, more deliberate attention was paid to a land reform process. This was intended to set out the objectives of land use and land reform; the basis for public sector involvement in land matters; and bring together a comprehensive range of measures for removing barriers and promoting positive action (Lloyd and Danson 2000). The devolved political landscape in Scotland prompted a growing interest in land reform driven in part by a powerful human rights dimension. This articulated the case for a broader public interest in the land question in Scotland.

Following devolution, and based on a number of studies and consultations, a first phase of land reform was executed. A number of legislative measures were introduced: The Abolition of Feudal Tenure etc. (Scotland) Act 2000, the Land Reform (Scotland) Act 2003, and the Agricultural Holdings (Scotland) Act 2003. In particular, the 2003 Land Reform Act introduced a public right of responsible access to land, a Community Right to Buy rural land when it was put on the market, and a Crofting Community Right to Buy regardless of whether it was for sale (Sellar and David 2006). These measures were intended to promote the public interest in different ways – the community right to buy in particular sought to enable opportunities for rural stability in localities of highly concentrated private landownership.

Subsequent scrutiny of the 2003 Land Reform Act highlighted a range of problems with the Community Right to Buy and Crofting Community Right to Buy provisions. These included concerns about administrative complexity and unwieldiness. As a consequence, in 2012 the Scottish government established the Land Reform Review Group, which was asked to identify how land reform might (1) enable more people in rural and urban Scotland to have a stake in the ownership, governance, management, and use of land; (2) assist with the acquisition and management of land and assets by communities; and (3) generate support, promote, and deliver new relationships between land, people, economy, and environment in Scotland. The group reported in 2014 with over 60 recommendations. It asserted that there was no single measure that would modernise landownership patterns in Scotland and deliver land reform measures that would better serve the public interest (Land Reform Policy Group 2014). This heralded a second phase of land reform to better secure the public interest. In November 2014, the First Minister, as part of the Programme for Government, set out the Scottish government's vision that Scotland's land must be an asset that benefits the many, not the few. Political priorities became more evident and the Scottish government published a consultation paper that advocated a Land Rights and Responsibilities Policy, transparency of landownership, the establishment of a Scottish Land Reform Commission, and a new Land Reform (Scotland) Bill (Scottish Government 2014).

The Land Reform (Scotland) Bill was introduced to the Scottish Parliament in June 2015. This set out ten recommendations around land rights and responsibilities; the creation of a Scottish Land Commission (which would, for example, review the impacts and effectiveness of land law or policy); a right of access to information about persons in control of land for interested parties; guidance about engaging communities in decisions relating to land that may affect communities; a right to buy land to further sustainable development for eligible Community Bodies; provision for stronger access rights and rights of way; and a raft of substantial amendments to both the Agricultural Holdings (Scotland) Act 1991 and the Agricultural Holdings (Scotland) Act 2003 (Edwards et al. 2015). In effect the proposed land reforms have continued in the subsequent period with the purpose of increasing community ownership of land. This rests on the perceived advantages of collective engagement with the land resource. It allows for a broader articulation of a public interest. Resting on the benefits of social access to land in the interests of justice and equity is contrasted with the perceived injustices perpetrated by private property rights in Scotland (Wightman 2015). Run rig is a product of land and a driver for an alternative way of working. Not surprisingly, the ideology behind the bill is focused on ensuring land in Scotland is used in the public interest and to the benefit of the people of Scotland. But some landowners have argued that it is this very ideologically driven agenda that will jeopardise the rural economy. This is unsurprising as the hegemony of private property is essentially being exposed but not challenged. In tandem, the Scottish government requested the Registers of Scotland to complete the Land Register by 2024, setting a target of 1 million acres in community ownership by 2020.

The Land Reform (Scotland) Act 2016 subsequently requires the Scottish government to publish a statement on land rights and responsibilities and review this position every five years. The statement will contain a set of principles to guide the development of public policy on the nature and character of land rights in Scotland, to ensure that the full public benefits from land in Scotland are realised. A Scottish Land Commission will seek to ensure that land reform is an ongoing process of change to secure the public interest. Among other things, the legislation seeks to promote greater transparency in land matters and better engagement between landowners and local communities. A right to buy land to further sustainable development puts Scottish communities at the heart of land reform by empowering communities to buy land where this is necessary to further sustainable development and where certain conditions are met. The Community Empowerment (Scotland) Act 2015 further extends the Community Right to Buy to urban Scotland, amends and simplifies the 2003 Land Reform Act, and introduces a right to buy 'abandoned or neglected' land in certain circumstances without a willing seller.

The land reforms being devised and implemented in Scotland seek to promote and enable a more inclusive public interest in the land question. The different measures reflect to a large extent the historical provenance of land reforms and agendas in Scotland. Concerns over the concentrated pattern of ownership and the implications for community well-being extend across rural and urban areas. The principal narrative of the reforms is to promote greater transparency and due diligence with respect to land use and development decisions. Yet, arguably, the innovative dimension to the reforms is that they retain the bedrock of private property.

Conclusions

This chapter started from the premise that the establishment of private property rights has had considerable implications for planning and the public interest. This is presented in terms of the unbalanced power of private property that has destabilised the political and power relations associated with landownership, its use, and development. This bias was and remains evident in a dysfunctional state-market-civil framework, which has brought planning into popular disrepute. It has also created a screed of ongoing issues in land and development markets. This is evident in the context of an infrastructure deficit to support land and property development, the enclosure of public spaces, unbalanced local and regional housing markets, redundant and vacant land, and the inability for society to address key matters, such as affordable housing. The private property rights template is the starting point, and the chapter has argued that the maturation and normalisation of neoliberal ideology has further exacerbated the position by perpetuating the attendant conflicts and challenges. Further, the primacy of the private property rights hegemony is incapable of resolving them and, it is argued, throws into question the very essence of democracy within capitalism (Streeck 2014). Under these normative narratives, new social constructions of the land question are required based on deeper and respected notions of the public interest, collective well-being, the common weal, and the longer term. A conventional alternative might be a radical alternative, but such is the turn to neoliberal metrics in society and polity that a more nuanced way is needed. Here the land reform in Scotland reflecting historical experience, present-day conditions, and incorporating ambitions for a more resilient future is seen as more appropriate. It seeks to rebalance to public interest while not threatening the private property rights base – perhaps creating a new lexicon in contemporary land economy.

References

Andrew, A., Pitt, M. and Tucker, M. (2007) The evolution of betterment in the United Kingdom, *Journal of Retail and Leisure Property*, 6, 273–280.

Busby, N. and Macleod, C. (2010) Rural identity in the twenty-first century: A community of crofters or crofting communities? *Journal of Law and Society*, 37(4), 592–619.

Crace, J. (2013) *Harvest*, Picador, London.

The Daily Telegraph (2015) A stealthy and sly attack on Green Belt, Editorial, 9 December.

Edwards, T., Kenyon, W., Pollock, S. and Reid, A. (2015) *Land reform (Scotland) bill*, SPICE Briefing 15/49, The Scottish Parliament, August, Edinburgh.

Fine, B. and Milonakis, D. (2008) *From political economy to economics: Method, the social and the historical in the evolution of economic theory*, Routledge, London.

Gay, P. (1996) *The enlightenment: The science of freedom*, Norton, London.

Heilbroner, R.L. (1961) *The worldly philosopher*, Simon & Schuster, New York.

Hetherington, P. (2015) *Whose land is our land? The use and abuse of Britain's forgotten acres*, Policy Press, Bristol.

Hunter, J. (1976) *The making of the crofting community*, John Donald, Edinburgh.

Land Reform Review Group (2014) *The land of Scotland and the common good*, May, Edinburgh.

Land Reform Scotland (1997) *William Ogilvie's birthright in land*, Othila Press, London.
Lloyd, M.G. and Danson, M.W. (2000) The land reform policy group in Scotland, *Local Economy*, 15(3), 214–224.
Lloyd, M.G. and Peel, D. (2010) Land matters: Towards a land use strategy in Scotland, *Town & Country Planning*, 80(10), 497–500.
London Housing Commission (2015) *Capital failure: Understanding the roots of London's housing crisis*, ippr, December, London.
MacDonald, D.C. (1997) in Land Reform Scotland (1997) *William Ogilvie's birthright in land*, Othila Press, London.
Macmillan, D.C. (2000) An economic case for land reform, *Land Use Policy*, 17(1), 49–57.
Martin, R., Pike, A., Tyler, P. and Gardiner, B. (2015) *Spatially rebalancing the UK economy: The need for a new policy model*, Regional Studies Association, London.
Massey, D.B. and Catalano, A. (1978) *Capital and land: Landownership by capital in Great Britain*, Edward Arnold, London.
McCrone, D. (2001) *Understanding Scotland: The sociology of a stateless nation*, Routledge, London.
Minton, A. (2009) *Ground control: Fear and happiness in the twenty-first century city*, Penguin Books, London.
Mirowski, P. (2013) *Never let a serious crisis go to waste*, Verso, London.
Morton, A. (2012) *Why aren't we building enough attractive homes? Myths, misunderstandings and solutions*, Policy Exchange, London.
Mullainathan, S. and Shafir, E. (2013) *Scarcity the true cost of not having enough*, Penguin, London.
North, D.C. (2011) Foreword, in: Cole, D. and Ostrom, E. (eds) *Property in land and other resources*, Lincoln Institute, Boston, MA.
Reid, A. (2015) *Land reform in Scotland*, SPICE Briefing 15/28, The Scottish Parliament, June, Edinburgh.
Roll, E. (1961) *A history of economic thought*, Prentice Hall, New York.
Scottish Government (2014) *The future of land reform in Scotland*, A Consultation paper, Edinburgh.
Sellar, W. and David, H. (2006) The great land debate and the Land Reform (Scotland) Act 2003, *Norwegian Journal of Geography*, 60(1), 100–109.
Streeck, W. (2014) *Buying time: The delayed crisis of democratic capitalism*, Verso, London.
Sutherland, L., Matthews, K., Buchan, K. and Miller, D. (2014) Beyond crofting: Assessing change on Scotland's small-scale holdings, *Scottish Geographical Journal*, 130(4), 223–242.
Taylor, M. and Walker, C. (2015) *Garden villages: Empowering localism to solve the housing crisis*, Policy Exchange, London.
Wightman, A. (1996) *Who owns Scotland?* Canongate, Edinburgh.
Wightman, A. (2015) *The poor had no lawyers: Who owns Scotland and how they got Edinburgh*, Birlinn Limited, Edinburgh.
Williamson, E. (2000) The new institutional economics: Taking stock, looking ahead, *Journal of Economic Literature*, 38(3), 595–613.

A Czech perspective on nationalization of land: the post-socialist view

Jirina Jilkova

Land nationalization as described by → *Greg Lloyd* for the Scottish case is motivated by the concept that private property trumps the public interest connected with questions about natural justice and social equity. Greg Lloyd is confronted with conflicts in spatial planning. His inspiration for the idea of land nationalization as 'medicine' and a regulating instrument is inspired by the Scottish Land Reform. The idea of land nationalization by Greg Lloyd is rooted in the historical conflicts of landownership in the UK (e.g. Wallace 1892), and in this context may be understood as a realistic proposal for restructuring land property rights and strengthening public interest in land use planning.

In the article, two conflicts related to land use are reflected and sometimes mixed up in the presentation of roots and impacts: (1) the land mostly in urban areas being the subject of competition among different use modes, e.g. the transformation of green parks to development land – called by Lloyd 'economics of construction and development'; and (2) the historical experience of Scotland with the Highland Clearance connected with a mass displacement of Scots in the eighteenth and nineteenth centuries, which has (perceived as negatively) influenced the socioeconomic development of Scotland. For the elimination of these 'inherited feudal tenurial arrangements' (in the article referred to by Macmillan 2000) a new model of property rights to land – the Land Reform (Scotland) Bill is presented as an instrument for broader articulation of public interest. The Land Reform (Scotland) Act 2016 requires setting principles for guiding the development of public policy on the nature of land rights in Scotland. The focus is on public benefits from land in Scotland – and this is a politically driven agenda implemented in a democratic decision process, as the act requires the review of the position of Scottish government every five years. A target of 1 million acres of community ownership by 2020 was set.

The author calls this concept a form of 'nationalization of land'. It is important to say that this is not the nationalization of land comparable to the nationalization of land in Eastern and Central Europe in the twentieth century. In those countries, a large-scale expropriation of land in rural and urban areas occurred. However, in the further development of Scottish land property rights legislation, there might be some idealistic visions of benefits coming from real land nationalization in terms of equity and effectiveness. In his chapter, Greg Lloyd draws an interesting picture about the effective solution of conflicts in land property rights. It provides inspiration for reflecting and discussing the risks as well as the potential social conflicts and negative long-term impacts of land nationalization.

The author of the comments wants to characterize the unintended long-term effects of the large-scale nationalization of land using the case of land collectivization and land nationalization in some countries of Central and Eastern Europe. The critical description relates to the agricultural land that provides a strong inspiration for the critical comments on the idea of land nationalization.

The communist ideology, which was politically dominant in Russia in 1917 with its general opposition to individual property rights, was inspired by Karl Marx's theory.

The Bolshevik regime, on the day after seizing power from the Provisional Government in October 1917, issued a decree 'On Land' that abolished private ownership of land and implemented a large-scale nationalization of land. The farmers were forced to enter so-called collective farms and act as paid workers. Their status was independent from the share of land in the cooperative, as is the model in Western Europe. The original land property rights of former landowners working in cooperatives did not play any role.

The Soviet model of agricultural land use spread around Central Europe after 1945 following the way of the Soviet army fighting against the German army. The political changes in Central Europe (the so-called socialist revolutions) were followed by changes and even the elimination of property rights for industrial assets and agricultural land.

The process of land nationalization and land collectivization did not have the same intensity in all countries (see e.g. Swain 1998). In Poland, the small private farms with an area of some hectares continued to exist. The case of Czechoslovakia was the introduction of the almost total expropriation of agricultural land with the abrupt restructuring of property rights followed by the social transformation of rural areas. In most socialist countries, even small farmers were forced by the local political actors to give up their individual rights to agricultural land. It has to be mentioned that the formal property rights were lost only by the large owners; the owners of smaller areas of land (the size of up to 100 hectares) kept their formal rights but with no disposition rights to their land. Therefore, this process might be referred to as a de facto expropriation of land.

The acceptance of this process by the rural population and farmers was very low as most farmers were opposing it. They were forced to enter the cooperatives (legal entities in which they usually collectively managed the agriculture of the whole village, but later established larger joined entities) by different means: the prescription of delivery obligations of agricultural products they were not able to fulfil, social pressure including regular police control, financial penalties, court processes that resulted in prison, and even the resettlement of whole families from prospering agricultural farms into housing with poor equipment. The family of the author of these comments experienced this painful process. They managed a farm the size of 20 hectares (which was in the beginning of the 'socialist time' considered middle size). They were not resettled, but they were treated by different legal and illegal means including prison. They perceived their social status as being that of slaves or serfs.

After the political change in 1989, only a small number of landowners demanded to get their land back. Currently, more than 90 percent of the agriculture land in the Czech Republic is not managed by its original owners, but by tenants (mostly by legal successors of the socialist collective farms).

The whole process of collectivization and expropriation resulted in abrupt social and cultural changes in rural areas. The social group of farmers (landowners) cultivating their land personally, relying on long-term intergenerational experience, with strong individual bonds to their property, has quickly and almost completely disappeared. For Czech agriculture, the model of manager (principal) and employees is dominant. The average size of agricultural plots is still significantly larger than in neighbouring countries such as Poland, Germany, and Austria. The formal property rights (landownership displayed in the cadastre) are rather split. Typically, in post-socialist countries the land parcels have multiple owners because of the 50-year break from the natural process of heritage (the land was passed to all heirs in equal shares). More important and more significant are the long-term effects of changes in effective property rights (who the manager and the user of the land is). The interrupted process of the intergenerational transfer of land resulted in farmland ownership fragmentation (small landownership parcels). The owners of small-size parcels rent the land to tenants, who continue the format of large agricultural farms. There is strong empirical evidence of land degradation connected with the post-socialist model of agriculture that even influences the flood protection and water regime of the landscape. Sklenička (2014) calls this 'The Farmland Rental Paradox': the fragmentation of land restricts the free decision of owners on land use; an economically highly effective agriculture is forced but is followed by the loss of identification of landowners with their land and its social functions. Most owners of agricultural and forest land live outside the rural areas. Their efforts to actively contribute to the management of their land are connected with the quite high transaction cost – they live in places a great distance from the community of their original family. They have to negotiate the management of their land and the price of rent with monopolistic structures of large companies. The social changes in rural areas followed – the historical structures of rural communities were destroyed and after the political change in Czechoslovakia in 1980, there was an intensive process supported by public subsidies necessary to restore the rural communities. There is a clear causal link between land nationalization in the socialist time and two negative effects: the nonsustainable management of agricultural land with the especially negative environmental effects and the abrupt changes in addition to the ruined social life in rural areas, which has slowly recovered in the past few years, but really very slowly.

Conclusion

The idea of land nationalization might promise an effective instrument for the management of conflicts concerning land use planning and the assurance of public interest. We have to distinguish between the two scales of nationalizations. The historical experiment in socialist countries with the large-scale expropriation of agricultural land and the collectivization of farmers was driven by political demand (with declaratory accent on equity), not by an idea of effectiveness. However, the historical experience of the Soviet and post-Soviet era warns us against this concept implemented on large scale. The destructive social changes in rural communities and the negative impacts on non-market services of land as well as the sustainable management of the landscape are a very high price for the predominance of an equity paradigm in agricultural land use.

The debate about the expropriation of rather small land parcels is becoming quite intensive in Central Europe in the context of infrastructure development and specific public interventions like flood protection, for example the comparison of the German and Czech expropriation procedures for the purposes of spatial planning indicates stricter rules in the Czech Republic, so they often block effective measures in the current planning practice in Central Europe. The nationalization or expropriation of land cannot be implemented as a recurrence to the totalitarian idea; an effective scheme of public deliberative process about property rights for specific pieces of land including a compensation scheme has to be established.

References

Macmillan, D.C. (2000) An economic case for land reform, *Land Use Policy*, 17(1), 49–57.

Sklenička, D. (2014) The farmland Rental paradox: Extreme landownership fragmentation as a new form of land degradation, *Land Use Policy*, 38, 587–593.

Swain, N. (2008) Typologie východoevropských podob kolektivizace (Typology of collectivization forms in Eastern Europe), in: Blazek, P. and Kubalek, M. (eds) *Kolektivizace venkova v Československu 1948–1960 a středoevropské souvislosti* (Collectivization of countryside in Czechoslovakia 1948–1960 and the context of Central Europe), Dokořán, Praha.

Wallace, A.R. (1892) *Land nationalisation its necessity and its aims being a comparison of the system of landlord and tenant with that of occupying ownership in their Influence on the well-being of the people*, Swan Sonnenschein & Co, London, New York.

A Greek perspective on nationalization of land: kilt and fustanella[1] – same principle, different colours

Konstantinos Lalenis

Greg Lloyd provides a general framework of analysis, concerning property rights in modern market economies, and their implications for public interest. It is argued that that the neoliberal ideology and its reflection in the handling and management of private property rights in land has created a destabilization of the political and power relations associated with landownership and its management. He then focuses on Scotland, describing the land reform there, which seeks to secure a more resilient future, and protect and promote the public interest, while at the same time not threatening the private property rights.

Giving commentary to the topic of nationalization of land in Scotland from the perspective of the national setting of Greece is both difficult and challenging. To start with, a short review of the Greek history of land development is essential. When the new Greek state was established in the 1830s, it inherited the official property of Sultan land and distributed part of it to local farmers in the form of low price mortgages. Since then, small land properties were further solidified by popular revolts imposing land redistribution to farmers, and distribution of urban and agricultural land to refugees from Asia Minor and Eastern Thrace in 1923. Small properties in land became – and still are – the dominant characteristic of land in Greece (Lalenis 2001).

Since then, the establishment of full-fledged capitalism was never seriously attempted and instead, a peculiar type of statism was enforced, characterized by populism, excessive centralization, and political clientelism (Lagopoulos 1984). Property of land was characterized by two, often contrasting, phenomena: private property was excessively protected against any effort for socialization, collectivization, or concession of it to the public good; and small property was encouraged and protected against any invasion of big capital that would result in types of land agglomeration and would upset the traditional pattern of political influence (Tsoulouvis 1987).

From the 1950s on, intensity of land exploitation, widespread illegal construction, increases in urban population and high building densities in cities caused severe scarcity of urban public space. Although private property was still 'sacred' in the attitudes of the average person, there was popular consensus for the necessity to improve urban sustainability by restricting private property rights.

At the beginning of the twenty-first century, the global dominance of free market economics diverted Greek politics from the socialist orbit of the 1980s and turned it towards neoliberalism. The private sector was encouraged to intervene in the land market and invest, and big land property was perceived as essential for much-needed development. Eurocrises, and in particular the International Monetary Fund (IMF) instructions for handling the Greek economic deb, led to a critical revision of the up to then 'untouchable' public character of public land and various categories of 'commons'. Airports and ports were sold or leased to private companies (the port of Piraeus was sold to the Chinese shipping company COSCO, and nine regional airports to FRAPORT); seashores, beaches, and valuable pockets of public land were made available for private developments and exploitation; while public goods as energy and communications were also set as objects for privatization. Privatization of uses of public land was further encouraged after 2010, as a means to overcome the economic crisis, and as part of the obligations of the Greek government to its European and IMF lenders. This took the form of various instruments and processes, provided by laws 3894/10 and 4146/13 'in order to encourage strategic investments' (Lalenis 2015).

Scarcity of public space in the urban environment has been considered of prime importance for the land issue in Greece. In addition to the globally familiar methods of acquiring public land (free market purchases and expropriation), a variety of instruments of land policy have been used. The planning legislation of 1923 provided for 'Acts of Analogism' in which properties 'giving' part of them in the Urban Plan as public space (roads, squares, etc.), were offering this part without reimbursement up to a maximum zone of 15 meters wide. Later, laws 947/1979, 1337/1983 and 2508/1997 specified general obligations of every private land property in the form of contributions in land and money. Contributions were escalating, according to the area of each plot, in such a way as to protect and encourage small property of land. Protection of small land property was also obvious in building regulations, where smaller plots of land had higher building ratios. Finally, instruments for obtaining and securing public space also include (1) rights of preference -where the local municipality has the right to intervene in all transactions concerning land in a specific area and buy in pre-agreed prices-, (2) 'social' building ratio -where the municipality allows extra building ratio as a bonus to land owners/developers in an area specified by the Master Plan, and retains part of it to be used for amenities- and (3) transfer of building ratio -where the owner of a plot of land and/or building designated for public space or considered as part of architectural heritage, can transfer his building rights to other areas, specifically designated by the Master Plan (Lalenis, 2001).

After the historical review of land issues in Greece, it is essential to underline that the political approach adopted in Lloyd's article, regarding property rights in modern capitalist, market economies, and their implications for public interest, is also shared in this commentary. The fact that 'the conditions determined by private property rights and property interests create powerful distributional narratives' is the same for Greece at least as much as in Scotland.

An interesting point in Lloyd's chapter is that the main focus is on the theoretical framework of landownership and reforms and on the aims of the related policies. The sequence of acts, bills, committees, and recommendations signifies a rational development on policymaking. At the same time, there is no particular insistence on possible implementation problems. This is completely different from the Greek reality, where the implementation gap is the most significant factor of success or failure of policies (Mare Nostrum project, CBC MED 2016), and it dominates the related research.

Regarding land policy instruments in Scotland and Greece, one can observe that while in Scotland they are fewer, of a more abstract nature, embodying sociopolitical dimensions (recommendations, acts); in Greece they are much more precise, quantitative, numerous, and in the form of laws. In Scotland, the acquisition of public land by local communities seems to be through obtaining legal powers to buy land in free market transactions. In Greece, private properties of land have the legal obligation to contribute in land and money for public spaces and amenities, through a variety of alternative land policy instruments. Heavy bureaucratic procedures and political clientelism may delay and discourage the related implementations, however.

Another significant point of diversion between the Scottish and the Greek case of the land issue is the size of land properties and its political implications. In Scotland, big land properties are mostly the case. They are favoured by the neoliberal approach for land management, and they tend to dominate the power game between them and the local communities in an institutionalized framework. Small properties in land are the dominant characteristic in Greece. They are politically influential, but on a local level. On a central level of administration, the current neoliberal approaches favour the formation of big properties by new economic agents, attractive to big investments. The power game in Greece, between traditional landowners, new economic agents, and local communities, is quite complex, unpredictable, and often out of institutionalized frameworks.

In concluding the above comparative commentary, one could say that in land issues, tradition is quite different in Scotland and in Greece – expectedly so, since the two countries belong to very different legal and planning traditions. Scotland is a legal hybrid of the British and the Napoleonic families (Newman and Thornley 1996: 30; Lalenis and Tosics, 2008), and a member of the Land Use Management planning tradition (EU Compendium 1997), while Greece is a hybrid of the Napoleonic and the Germanic legal families, and a typical member of the 'urbanism' tradition. The new conditions, though, of globalization, and neoliberal approaches in planning and development (accelerated, in the case of Greece, by the economic crisis and the hastily imposed memorandums with the international lenders) have led to conversions. So, both countries nowadays are moving towards two other approaches, the comprehensive integrated approach, and the regional economic approach (ESPON 2.3.2).

So, contrary to the title of the commentary, could one claim that both kilt and fustanella may turn pink in a neoliberal laundry?

Note

1 A *kilt* is a knee-length, non-bifurcated, skirt-type garment with pleats at the rear, originating in the traditional dress of men and boys in the Scottish Highlands. A *fustanella* is a traditional pleated skirt-like garment, which is also referred to as a kilt, worn by men of many nations in the Balkans (Southeast Europe). In Greece, fustanella is considered a national costume.

References

European Commission (1997) *Compendium of European spatial planning systems.*

European Spatial Planning Observatory Network (ESPON) (2005) *ESPON Project 2.3.2*, Governance of Territorial and Urban Policies from EU to Local Level.

Lagopoulos, P. (1984) Urban and regional planning in Greece, in: Williams, R.H. (ed.) *Planning in Europe: Urban and regional planning in the EEC*, George Allen & Unwin, London.

Lalenis, K. (2001) *'Planning by Decree': Incompatibilities of planning laws and planning policies in Greece, during the 20th century. Analysis, perspectives*, Planning at the Turn of the Century, WPSC 2001, Shanghai.

Lalenis, K. (2015) *Coastline preservation in Greece: Introduction to the legal and institutional framework*, Mare Nostrum Project, CBC MED.

Lalenis, K., De Jong, M. and Mamadouh, V. (2002) Families of nations and institutional transplantation, in: De Jong, M., Lalenis, K. and Mamadouh, V. (eds) *Institutional transplantation*, Kluwer Academic Publishers, Dordrecht.

Lalenis, K. and Tosics, I. (2008) *Typologies of EU national governance and spatial planning systems*, PLUREL WP2.2.

Newman, P. and Thornley, A. (1996) *Urban planning in Europe; international competition, national systems and planning projects*, Routledge, London.

Tsoulouvis, L. (1987) Aspects of statism and planning in Greece, *International Journal of Urban and Regional Research*, 2(4).

Part VI

Conclusion

17 Planning with or against property rights

Jean-David Gerber, Thomas Hartmann, and Andreas Hengstermann

Planning and scarcity

Sceptics could argue that scarcity is inherent to our (mainly) materialist approach to the environment and to natural resources. Indeed, a specific scientific discipline has evolved to deal with scarcity – economics, 'the study of scarcity, of how societies make choices concerning how to use their limited resources' (Stiglitz 1988: 10). Therefore, a new book on scarcity could only be redundant. But this book has a particular take on the scarcity of land. It does not focus on land markets and their ability to allocate scare resource units. Markets play a surprisingly limited role in the different contributions of this book, because land is not a typical good. Rather this book seeks to question how planners and other actors deal with the scarcity of land in their everyday practice.

This book builds on the observation that land use planning, through zoning, is the main public policy in charge of coordinating land uses, and therefore continuously creates and releases situations of scarcity. Yet urban sprawl remains a worldwide concern. It seems that planners, reflecting the choices of their political leaders, avoid directly dealing with building land scarcity – or land unavailability – within existing building zones and choose to expand city boundaries towards the countryside, where political resistance is smaller. As noted in the introduction, planning instruments have evolved in a context of resource profusion and have inherent difficulties dealing with changing uses within the already built environment (for instance, to densify and to fill building gaps). The different contributions of this book confirm the observation that renouncing greenfield development is never an easy task. It seems that, indeed, planners do have an issue with scarcity.

The main question addressed in this book specifies the link between planning and scarcity as follows: how can public intervention strategically manage the scarcity of buildable land, either increasing or decreasing it, in order to promote a more sparing use of resources overall? This way to formulate the problem purposefully puts the institutions, the rules of the game, at the centre of the analysis. It is the presence of complex interests rooted in well-established institutions, such as property titles, easements, or concessions that make planning difficult in the built environment. We had three main objectives in mind as we answered this main question.

1. We focused on land policy instruments and analyzed the *mechanisms* impacting scarcity, with a particular emphasis on their ability to release lock-in situations that make land unavailable for development or other purposes formulated in land use plans.
2. We highlighted how a given instrument could *strategically* be used by actors, insisting on the fact that the *effectiveness* of an instrument depends on many parameters. Actors do not follow homogenous goals, but are constantly trying to shape implementation processes for their own advantage. The political acceptance of more proactive forms of planning might not always be given either because thwarting the plans of landowners may be a risky business for politicians.
3. We provided examples from different national contexts. Historical and social-political specificities of local situations make it impossible to identify generally valid action strategies and even less one-size-fits-all instruments, but the confrontation with international experiences is often a *source of inspiration*.

These three objectives are interrelated and led to the discursive structure of the book, where the main chapters expose the working mechanisms of the instruments, and the commentaries provide information on different national contexts. The comparison of the main chapters and commentaries reveal the strategic use of instruments in different contexts.

Scarcity at the meeting point of planning and landownership

Following our constructivist approach to scarcity, elements of the environment become resources when they interact with and become integrated in a system of production that reveals a potential use for the element of the environment in question. The system of production defines the elements of the environment that are desirable in a given society. In most cases, sooner or later, resources uses become competitive due to the restricted amount of resource units available. This limitation is often (partly) physical. For instance, only a limited amount of plots of land are suitable to grow vineyards. Similarly, the total number of plots of land located on the shore of a given lake is limited.

However, even in these two examples, the phenomenon of scarcity is politically constructed. Urban growth boundaries in Oregon (see → *Sullivan*) or reference land values in Germany (→ *Voß and Bannert*) are largely designed to affect scarcity of land – in the former case the resource that ought to be protected is the greenbelt around a city, whereas in the latter it is the efficient use of inner-urban building land.

In practice, the uses of the resource land are determined by two main formal institutions. First, the land use plans define the intended uses of a given area. Land use plans are the result of political debates, which reflect a social and political compromise among the concerned actors at a given moment of time and crystallize power relationships. Land use plans define a development goal but are not able to guarantee subsequent implementation. Second, property rights protect the landowners against the action of the state through land use plans and other planning instruments. They can only develop their plots of land according to the prescriptions of the land use plans, but in most cases they cannot be forced to undertake any development ('negative planning').

The contributions of this book highlight the fact that scarcity of land results from the combined interaction of land use plans (public policy) and property rights. Land use plans define the spatial and temporal boundaries of a given resource use (e.g. agriculture, high-density housing, nature conservation), but landowners decide whether their parcels are available for the intended use. Therefore, scarcity is something that needs to be managed by planners *and* landowners, although the latter usually feel less indebted to the community in which they live than public administrations that are under the direct control of elected officials.

The influence of planners on scarcity is twofold. On one side, planners create scarcity through their planning activity because they ban specific activities from specific zones. On the other side, because planners are often reluctant to confront powerful landowners, they too often expand the zones where too much scarcity occurs. Typically, this leads to greenfield development and sprawling cities. Expansion usually does not take place because of a physical lack of suitable parcels but because those parcels are not available for sale and development.

Scarcity is therefore a daily challenge for planners. Tackling scarcity issues implies a need to confront landowners. Often, when spatial planning and policy faces new challenges, there is a claim that new instruments are needed (i.e. in the Netherlands the introduction of land readjustment is discussed; see commentary by → *Holtslag-Broekhof*). The general proposition in this book is that dealing with scarcity of land does not necessarily require new instruments. The point of departure for this book is to elaborate on how instruments of land policy are used strategically by municipalities and other public bodies to manage land as a scarce resource. It is essential to understand not only how instruments function, but moreover how they can be used strategically.

In this book, we presented four ways to influence the uses of the land and therefore scarcity. This allowed us to classify the different instruments in four categories:

1 Regulating land uses without impacting property rights. This embraces policy instruments with no impact on the content of use or disposal

rights, such as information campaigns and economic incentives such as taxes or subsidies.

2 Steering land uses through regulation impacting property rights. Such policy instruments have an impact on the scope and content of use or disposal rights (i.e. restrictions on use rights or restrictions on disposal rights).
3 Redefining property rights to steer land uses. Such legal redefinition has an impact on the scope and content of use or disposal rights.
4 Redistributing property rights to steer land uses. This implies changing the structure of the distribution of property rights.

The different instruments of land policy have different effects on scarcity of land. Some effects are intended, others are indirect. The contributions of this book reveal that the instruments' effects on scarcity of land are very different. The following sections elaborate on those effects along the four main categories of instruments of land policy.

Regulating land uses without impacting property rights

The instruments belonging in this category are not designed to restrict use rights to resources. They are therefore weaker than the other instruments discussed in this book. However, as the different contributions of this book show, information is a source of power and *reference land values* impact the landscape in which land transactions take place. Taxes that are designed to provide an incentive to landowners, such as *land taxation*, are effective as well, but empirical evidence shows that the rate of the tax is a much-contested issue. Other kinds of taxes are collected to finance public intervention. *Betterment taxes* allow municipalities to capture the added value resulting from planning measures (zoning) and to reinvest this money into planning-related interventions elsewhere.

Intended impact on scarcity

One of the underlying assumptions of *reference land values* is that land markets can only lead to efficient land uses if all market actors have full information on land value. Differential access to information creates distortions and prevents an effective functioning of the market. In other words, intransparent land markets support large players on the market. This leads to uneven competition and speculative behaviours, which can ultimately aggravate scarcity of land. Reference land values address this market failure and reduce information asymmetries on the land market. The German case indicates that the public information on land reference values may lead to a delay of price increases; however, evidence for permanent price dampening effects is lacking.

The *land value tax* is based on the financial value of the publicly desired land use, not the actual land use by the landowner. Therefore, the land value tax is a market instrument that sets incentives for landowners to comply with the planned land use. If land value tax is properly implemented, then the level of resulting scarcity corresponds to the politically defined goals of the land use plan.

The price of land results for the most part from factors independent of the landowner – such as the location, the infrastructure, and the legal situation. The legislator can establish instruments for *capturing the added value* (planning gain). The gain of this instrument can be used to finance planning measures and to compensate landowners who are suffering from planning restrictions. In this sense, the instrument addresses scarcity resulting from suboptimal allocation of building rights. Without sufficient financial resources, planning often ends up in lock-in situations because any reconsideration of previously decided land uses – in particular downzoning – implies high costs for compensating land users for the loss of land value. A betterment tax is an elegant way to compensate planning losses with planning gains.

The rationale of the *land value taxes* and also *added value capture* is not mainly to address scarcity, but to address the injustice issue of planning gain. The rationale of reference land values is to prevent speculation with land. This is also related to social justice as the objective is to prevent inflated land prices. Ultimately, all three are indirect instruments for influencing scarcity of land.

Strategic use and political acceptance

The contributions of this book show that, even if these three instruments have many theoretical advantages, their transposition in applicable laws is very tricky. *Reference land values* lead to transparency on information that is considered sensitive by some market actors, in particular those who benefit from the lack of information. In many countries, these powerful actors are able to prevent open information on land value.

A condition for *land value tax* to address scarcity issues is the availability of reliable information on the tax basis, that is the land values based on the development rights granted by the plans. As mentioned, this proves to be politically very tricky to achieve in many countries. The instrument essentially requires a much elaborated system of land valuation. In practice, it seems that landowners, investors, and speculators are not willing to abandon their liberty to postpone the developments intended by the planning documents.

The legitimacy of *betterment taxes*, too, is highly contested because of the underlying interests and ideological orientations concerning the scope of private property. Three aspects impacting successful implementation are particularly debated: the tax level, the timing of tax collection, and the definition of the tax basis.

Paradoxically, in the three instruments – reference land values, land value taxes, and betterment taxes – it is not the instrument itself that is contested in terms of effectivity, but rather their strong redistributive effects. They are only inconsistently and fragmentarily implemented, which reduces their effectivity and therefore harms their legitimacy.

Source of inspiration

The contributions and discussions about these types of instruments reveal that due to their large-scale applicability, the effect on scarcity of land is potentially high in all three instruments. Mostly indirect contributions would be shown through better functioning land markets or improved conditions for planning. To address scarcity issues, these instruments need to be complemented with instruments from the other types.

Steering land uses through regulation impacting property rights

The instruments of this category include the more traditional instruments of spatial planning – such as binding *land use plans, urban growth boundaries*, as a form of regional planning, or *land readjustment* – but also less common instruments such as *building obligations*. Such instruments aim to restrict (or expand) use rights to resources in the name of general planning objectives. They are potentially powerful instruments to deal with scarcity. However, as the contributions of this book show, their command-and-control character requires a strong legal basis, which is not always given to intervene against scarcity.

Intended impact on scarcity

Land use plans are not designed for tackling scarcity issues in particular – rather they are used to balance the different interests in land and to manage them in a context of limited land. But *land use plans* inherently create scarcity through the designation of more or less exclusive uses in dedicated areas. Scarcity is the by-product of exclusivity. Within a given zone, the effectiveness of measures against scarcity of building land (e.g. higher density) crucially depends on the willingness of the target groups – landowners – to realize the desired land uses. Contrary to the UK for instance, where collaboration of public and private actors is done outside of formal land use plans, Dutch municipalities use *negotiated land use plans* to increase the effectiveness of land use planning by actively involving the landowners in the realization of the plans.

Urban growth boundaries protect the land outside of the boundaries from development – the inherent rationale of this instrument is land thrift. Reducing scarcity of undeveloped land increases scarcity inside the growth boundary. This can result in raising prices within the built-up area, which reinforces exclusivity and scarcity even more (gentrification). *Urban growth boundaries* can therefore promote sprawl further away because of leapfrog development. The effectiveness of the instrument depends on the compliance of municipalities with the urban growth boundary. *Urban growth boundaries* can therefore be considered a form of regional planning (as illustrated in the German case) and thus do not directly impact landowners, but rather municipalities which enforce building restrictions through their own planning documents.

The effect of *land readjustment* on scarcity is less obvious than land use plans or urban growth boundaries. The instrument essentially helps implementing planning objectives in situations where landownership is fragmented. Land readjustment makes it possible to rearrange the shape and size of parcels that are not suitable for the desired land use. Without such an instrument, developers need to acquire the land through other ways. Because acquisition on the land market takes time, pressure builds up on the municipality to extent the building zone elsewhere. Therefore, by providing solutions to lock-in situations, land readjustment prevents unnecessary extensions of building zones. *Building obligation* is an even more extreme way to close the gap between actual and intended land uses. By setting a deadline for filling the potential development right, the implementation of the land use plan can be guaranteed. Because building obligation is a far-reaching intervention in the way landowners can use their plot of land, an overruling public interest is essential to legitimate this intervention. As the contributions of this book show, whether scarcity is yet considered a problem important enough is open to discussion.

Strategic use and political acceptance

In many national contexts, urban development is the main source of revenue for municipalities (through sales tax, income tax, etc.). Even in countries where municipalities have a less vital incentive to expand, the belief that growth will increase their tax basis is nevertheless very strong. Under these circumstances, *land use plans* are often a headlong rush towards urban sprawl. Wherever target groups are closely integrated in the planning process or if municipalities have a direct interest in cooperating with large private actors, such as in the Netherlands, the efficiency of plan implementation might increase, but at the expense of too restrictive stipulations. The municipalities need to find a balance between the necessity to negotiate with landowners and the defence of public interests. Tackling scarcity is certainly a major public interest, but without the backing of higher-tier authorities or other political support, municipalities might feel alone in confronting such a challenge.

The *urban growth boundary* of Portland, Oregon, has gained worldwide attention because it is a restrictive planning measure that was able to stand in front of more immediate financial interests. Obtaining a majority in favour of such restrictions is always a challenge. More than any other instruments, the urban growth boundary gains support from landowners and inhabitants right on the edge of it because of the amenity values it is able to secure. Urban growth boundaries or other forms of regional land use plans (such as in Germany) are rare in practice. It requires an institutionalization of the collaboration between different municipalities or the development of supralocal authorities. This is not easy to achieve in a context where municipal self-administration is considered an asset.

Land readjustments and *building obligations* are powerful instruments, perhaps even too powerful for many planning contexts. However, as building land gets scarcer, they might be (re)discovered. The effectivity of land readjustments depends on the enforcement mechanisms, in particular on the possibility of constraining landowners to participate. A delicate balance needs to be found between the protection of individual rights, in particular those of small landowners under pressure by large developers to give way, and the public objectives to provide less resource-intensive planning. The different models of land readjustments, from voluntary to mandatory, need to be appraised from this perspective. The effectiveness of building obligations depends on determining the conditions of possible application and of legal consequences in case of noncompliance. Often, threatening to engage into a land readjustment or building obligation procedure is enough to unlock a particularly tangled-up situation.

Source of inspiration

Most of the instruments in this category need to address more than one planning goal. Spatial planners need to balance many different interests. The fight against land scarcity is only one among many issues, including economic growth, a socially just distribution of land, healthy urban living, flood-resilient cities, and so forth. A strong public interest is needed to legitimate public intervention in property rights. Scarcity is certainly a central issue, but an emerging one. A strong restriction of property rights is difficult to impose in the name of scarcity, but things are changing as resources are getting scarcer.

Redefining property rights to steer land uses

Instruments of this third type resulted from the redefinition of the scope and content of property rights. Such modifications or adaptations of the definition of the underlying institution of our economic system are rather rare, even if small changes can occur every now and then. The rationale behind such changes is that they will streamline the relationships among users of the resource ideally without the intervention of the state using its authoritative power. It is therefore not surprising that, of all discussed instruments, *transferable development rights, pre-emption rights*, and *long-term leases* are among the most market oriented.

Intended impact on scarcity

Transferable development rights are based on the conviction that the market is able to solve scarcity issues alone, as long as the framework conditions are properly defined. Locations where the demand is high will automatically find a balance with locations with lower demand through price mechanisms. However, experts disagree on the way to formulate the framework in which building rights should be transferred.

Like transferable development rights, *long-term leases* granted on public land rely on the conviction that private actors – or public actors acting as private landowners – are in a better position to decide about individual plot uses than planners. Long-term leases open many options to address issues of scarcity through a periodic reallocation of uses. To achieve the desired outcome, the parameters of the lease contract need to be properly adjusted. Such variables are, for example, the duration of the leasehold, the amount and conditions of lease-payments (annuity or single payment), and the return policies.

Pre-emption rights can always be agreed upon on a case-by-case basis with the consent of the landowner but, when the instrument is implemented by law in a spatially comprehensive manner, it can be used to facilitate access to land for public purposes. A useful side effect is its positive effect on land price inflation because the landowner cannot sell the land above market prices lest the municipality steps in. In this respect, it is more an instrument of market control. But both ways of using the instrument help address issues of scarcity.

Strategic use and political acceptance

The evaluation of the strategic use of *transferable development rights* is difficult because cases where this system has been implemented are scarce. Empirical evidence tends to show that the incentives might not always be high enough to obtain the desired effects. The organization of a system of transferable development rights can soon become very complicated. It is interesting to note that the buzz created by this instrument might also be the result of politicians or planners who want to show that they are 'with it', considering that this instrument, as a prototype for a market instrument, is very much in line with so-called new public management reforms. However the system often seems to grapple with the fact that land is not a standard market commodity.

Long-term land leases on public land are a useful instrument to introduce a long-term perspective in planning. When a public authority grants a lease for 60 years, it needs to think about the future in a very concrete way when it drafts the lease contract: plans are frequently changed, but lease contracts remain. When the lease expires, the question arises of the potential new affectation of the plot. This complexity – which is the essence of planning – scares many public actors who prefer to sell the land and collect the cash, rather than to think in the long term.

Pre-emption rights only address scarcity issues indirectly. The problem is that the effectiveness of this instrument depends on the willingness (or necessity) of the landowners to sell their plot of land. Although pre-emption rights have no impact on actual use rights, the restriction in the disposal rights that they introduce has a deep impact on the collective imagination regarding property rights. The case of Serbia shows that – although the instrument is unpopular – it has survived so far because it is considered to be of such importance for specific planning purposes (flood risk management, protection of agricultural land, and specific neighbour's constellations).

Source of inspiration

International experience concerning these types of instruments reveals that planners should not construct their actions taking into consideration only the public policy side. The use of property rights instruments, such as long-term development leases, usefully complement more standard planning instruments. Property-right instruments are more robust and long term than plans. They can therefore introduce long-term considerations in policy implementation processes that are otherwise structured by the deadlines imposed by political legislatures.

Re-distributing property rights to steer land uses

Instruments of the fourth type target the distribution of property rights: they aim to take rights from targeted landowners and transfer them to others. In this sense, they are even more interventionist than the other instruments. If backed up by powerful legitimation mechanisms and if following clearly defined objectives, these instruments are very effective in dealing with issues of land scarcity. *Expropriation* is extensively used for the development of specific (mostly transport) infrastructures. The debate is open whether it should be used for other planning purposes as well. *Land banking* can be a solution to manage land as a resource, that is as a given stock of plots of land that are (temporarily) allocated according to specific needs. Finally a discussion on *nationalization* is needed because it asks the fundamental question whether our legal order, following the French Revolution and its alacrity to turn the page on the ancient regime, might not have gone too far in securing exclusive rights to land. New forms of more inclusive ownership might have to be invented in a world where resources, including land, become scarce.

Intended impact on scarcity

When available land is lacking for the spatial implementation of a public task, it is one of the prerogatives of the state to remedy this situation through *expropriation*. Often the threat of expropriation is enough to convince landowners to negotiate. Expropriation is a standard procedure for the construction of roads or railways because it is not possible to acquire contiguous plots through other means. As discussed in the contribution by → *Norton*, expropriation could theoretically also be used to target other forms of scarcity.

Land banking also directly impacts scarcity by fluidizing the interaction between supply and demand. Land banks also allow public actors to reinforce plan implementation through the allocation of the plots available through the land bank according to the objectives of the plans.

Like expropriation, (partial) *nationalization* of land is a possible answer to the mismatches between planning objectives and landownership distribution.

Strategic use and political acceptance

The contributions of the book show that *expropriation* plays a different role in the three national settings. This has to do with the different definitions of public interest, the need for compensation and its appraisal, and the cases where it can be applied. In redevelopment projects, developers often put pressure on public actors to use their power of expropriation to eliminate the resistance of individual small landowners. This is where a democratic debate on the use of expropriation is needed: is expropriation legitimate to redevelop brown fields, to fight against housing scarcity, or to make land more readily available for new development?

In *land banking* too, the role of the state needs to be clearly defined, because it remains open to discussion whether a public authority should manage land for profit. In some cities in the U.S., land banks were used to rescue the land market that collapsed after the economic crisis. In the Netherlands, land banks play an important role on the land market with corresponding risks if the economy slows down. In any case, whether land banking is carried out by a public or semi-public structure, the responsibility for losses or the allocation of profits needs to be clearly defined.

The discussion on nationalization is interesting in a context where new public management puts pressure on public authorities – for example through new public accounting standards leading to the activation of property assets – to sell the land that is not directly linked to the implementation of a public task. Similarly, global discourses push many countries in the Global South to privatize state or customary land, especially in larger cities. The contribution of this book can be understood as an appeal to caution: once sold, land cannot be acquired so easily anymore and land has much more than just a monetary value. Contrary to privatized land, public land can be managed according to objectives which have been democratically decided upon.

Source of inspiration

The three instruments discussed in this section rely on the conviction that the identity of the landowner has an impact on the way land is managed. Following this rationale, changing landowners can help solve scarcity issues. Depending on the national traditions, such profound interventions might have difficulty finding public acceptance. However, this debate should remind us that forms of ownership are more plentiful than the simple dichotomy between private and public ownership. Foundations, trusts, or other nonprofit organizations can provide interesting long-term alternatives. Common property or other forms of multiple ownerships can also contribute to providing solutions in a context of scarcity.

Concluding remarks

Scarcity is a challenge for planners. So far, greenfield development has allowed planners to postpone the moment when they would have to tackle the management of scarcity (although urban sprawl creates other forms of scarcity, involving such things as natural resources, scenic landscape, or the environment). Many powerful interests have been taking advantage of this model based on spatial expansion, in particular those who take advantage of scarcity to speculate or those who benefit from the high land prices resulting from scarcity. The politics of scarcity often call for keeping the status quo leading to incremental spatial expansion, instead of changing development priorities.

Scarcity therefore is often seen as a risk, the risk to see planners gain more importance over other actors in development. But scarcity can also be seen as a chance, a chance for a discipline to become more proactive. Planners need to find ways to reinforce their position in front of other powerful interests grounded in robust property rights. To do so, municipalities can also become landowners and use property rights as an instrument. This strategy is currently explored by public authorities who also own land and aim to acquire more. Planning is often perceived to take place against property rights, but planning can also work with property rights. However, this strategy also contains risks, in particular if public actors acquire land with profit objectives in mind and if democratic control is malfunctioning. The recent economic crises showed how municipalities who played a very active role in land policy can struggle (e.g. in the Netherlands).

The end of greenfield development is a challenge. Scarcity issues and redevelopment of built areas necessitate another way to use policy instruments than with greenfield development. Creativity is needed. This book is an attempt to illustrate this new way of using policy instruments strategically for better handling of scarcity of land. In this vein, planners need to prove Bernoulli wrong when he stated in the opening of his book in 1946: 'It is the one, who owns the land, who decides the development of our cities.'

Reference

Stiglitz, J.E. (1988) *Economics of the public sector*, 2nd ed., W.W. Norton, New York, London.

Contributor biographies

Juliane Albrecht is a senior scientist and project manager at the Institute of Ecological Urban and Regional Development (IOER) in Dresden, Germany. She holds a PhD in Law and has extensive research experience in environmental law and planning law. Dr. Albrecht's research impact is evidenced by more than 70 national and international publications.

Joana Almeida is Assistant Professor at Instituto Superior Técnico, Lisbon University. She teaches spatial planning, urban planning, decision theory, and real estate development. Her research focuses on urban conflict management, urban governance, tourism impacts, and urban regeneration.

Rachelle Alterman is Professor of Urban Planning and Law at the Technion – Israel Institute of Technology. She is the founding president and honorary fellow of the International Academic Association on Planning, Law, and Property Rights (PLPR) and an Honorary Member of the Association of European Schools of Planning.

Janet Askew was President of the Royal Town Planning Institute in 2015. She is Visiting Professor in Planning Law at Ulster University and a member of the International Platform of Planning Law Experts. She is the UK's representative on the European Council of Spatial Planners. She researches planning law in relation to regulatory regimes and land value capture.

Jörn Bannert is a research employee at the Geodetic Institute at Leibniz University Hannover. He teaches and researches in real estate valuation.

Tzuyuan Stessa Chao is an associate professor at National Cheng Kung University, Taiwan. Her research interests include the legal and institutional regime of spatial planning and healthy cities and well-being studies. She is currently one of the Regional Planning Committee board members in Taiwan and acts as an expert consultant in enacting the new National Spatial Planning Law system in Taiwan.

Beatriz Condessa is Assistant Professor at Instituto Superior Técnico, Lisbon University. She teaches and researches in urban management, focused on the integration of urban planning, law and urban economics, and she has special expertise on application of equity in land use planning.

José Antunes Ferreira is Associate Professor at Instituto Superior Técnico, Lisbon University. He teaches and researches in spatial and urban planning. He is Vice President of the Portuguese Association of Urban Planners and he was the chair of the Local Organizing Committee of the 17th AESOP Annual Congress in Lisbon. He has coordinated a wide range of urban projects and studies on urban policies during the last 25 years.

Jean-David Gerber is an associate professor at the Institute of Geography of the University of Bern. His research interests lie in urban planning, property rights, and the connections between the two, as well as in housing, landscape, large-scale land acquisitions, and processes of decommodification.

Sonia Guelton is Full Professor at Paris School of Planning in University of Paris Est. Her research focuses on land economics, urban economics, and socio-economics issues, and she has special expertise on land and planning management. She is President of Association Fonciers en débat which supports la revue foncière (www.revue-fonciere.com/).

Thomas Hartmann is Associate Professor at Wageningen University & Research. He teaches and researches on justice and the city, land and water governance, and he has a special expertise in land policies and planning instruments. He is the vice president of the international academic association on Planning, Law and Property Rights (www.plpr-association.org).

Andreas Hengstermann is a teaching and research assistant at the Institute of Geography of the University of Bern, Switzerland. He teaches and researches in planning system, instruments, and law with special focus on mechanisms explaining the gap between policy goals and actual local implementation. He is an elected member of the Executive Committee of the International Academic Association of Planning, Law, and Property Rights (PLPR).

Sanne Holtslag-Broekhof is Process Manager of Spatial Planning at the Dutch Kadaster. She regularly publishes on land policy and land management. She studied spatial planning at Wageningen University, where she successfully completed her PhD (2016) titled *Dealing with Private Property for Public Purposes*.

Alois Humer is a researcher at the Austrian Academy of Sciences. He teaches and researches spatial planning systems and cultures mainly from a European comparative perspective. From 2017 to 2019, he is a visiting fellow at Aalto University in Finland (FWF-Erwin-Schrödinger-Programme no. J-3993-G29).

Harvey M. Jacobs is on the faculty at the University of Wisconsin–Madison, U.S. and is Visiting Professor at Radboud University Nijmegen, the

Netherlands. He is especially interested in how societies define property, the institutions they develop to manage the relationship between private and public rights in property, and the social conflict that emerges around these issues.

Leonie Janssen-Jansen is Professor of Land Use Planning, Environmental Sciences Group at Wageningen University in the Netherlands. Her current teaching, research, and publications focus on the relation between planning and urban development, landscapes, metropolitan challenges, real estate (office vacancy), and planning and law. Understanding institutional change in relation to innovation for raising the quality of the urban environment is an important focus on her research agenda.

Jirina Jilkova is Full Professor at J. E. Purkyne University in Usti nad Labem (Czech Republic). She studied agriculture in Germany. Her research focuses on regulation, regulatory instruments, and their evaluation. She is Chair of the Regulatory Impact Assessment Board of the government of the Czech Republic.

Thomas Kalbro is Professor at the Royal Institute of Technology (KTH) in Stockholm. His teaching and research area is law and economics related to land development. He is President of the European Academy of Land Use and Development (www.landuseacademy.org).

Eran S. Kaplinsky is Associate Professor at the Faculty of Law, University of Alberta. He researches and teaches in the areas of municipal and planning law, property law, and economic analysis of law. His published work focuses on property rights, expropriation, and compensation, and the economics of land use regulations.

Michael Kolocek is Research Assistant at the Chair of Land Policy, Land Management, and Municipal Geoinformation, School of Spatial Planning, TU Dortmund University, Germany. He teaches land policy, property evaluation, land mangement, and discourse analysis. His key research interests are discourse analysis, housing, property rights, informality, de-commodification, and dignity.

Theo Kötter is Professor of City Planning and Land Management at the University of Bonn since 2003. Before starting his scientific career, he had extensive experience in all fields of urban development in practice. His current research is focused on planning theory and land policy addressing sustainable land use. He now draws upon all this experience to teach his students.

Konstantinos Lalenis, MEng, PhD, is Associate Professor in the Department of Planning and Regional Development, University of Thessaly, Volos, Greece. His specialization is in Urban Planning and Urban Governance. He was awarded for Excellence in Teaching by AESOP, and for Academic Excellence by the Greek Ministry of Education. Current research interests include participation and governance issues, planning law and institutional frameworks, strategic planning, and planning practices.

Antonia Layard is a professor in law at the University of Bristol. She teaches and researches in property, planning and urban law, with special expertise in law and policy relating to housing, regeneration, and public space.

Vincent Le Rouzic is a PhD candidate at Paris 1 Panthéon-Sorbonne University (C.R.I.A.). His research specializations are on land policy, social housing, and shared ownership schemes. He is also president of the association Community Land Trust France.

Rebecca Leshinsky is a barrister with many years of experience in the areas of property law and land use planning. She has worked for the Department of Planning in planning law reform and teaches at RMIT University (Melbourne) in the school of Property, Construction and Project Management (PCPM). Rebecca's research is focused in property and land use planning instrumentality, and of late, the impact of Blockchain on the property market.

Evangeline R. Linkous is Assistant Professor at the University of South Florida. Her research focuses on land use policy and law, growth management, agriculture and food systems planning, and rural and exurban area planning.

Greg Lloyd is Professor Emeritus in Urban Planning at Ulster University and Visiting Professor at the Land Use Planning Group, Wageningen University. He is a fellow of the Academy of Social Sciences and sits on the editorial board of Scottish Planning and Environment Law. He continues to research land questions and matters in these challenging and dysfunctional times.

Dirk Löhr, MBA 1964, is Professor of Taxation and Ecological Economics at the Trier University of Applied Sciences (Environmental-Campus Birkenfeld), Germany. Moreover, he works as tax adviser and is also a member of the supreme public real estate assessment board of the state of Rhineland-Palatinate (Germany). Löhr is one of the initiators of the campaign 'Grundsteuer: Zeitgemäß!', which lobbies for the introduction of a land value tax in Germany.

Marko Marskamp is a PhD researcher at the ETH Zürich and the University of Lausanne in Switzerland. Currently, he is a visiting scholar at the Simon Fraser University in Burnaby, Canada. He is researching and blogging on the re-thinking of zoning.

Romain Melot is Research Fellow at Université Paris-Saclay and Assistant Director of the Research Unit INRA-Sadapt. His research is conducted in the field of legal sociology and explores various issues on land use conflicts and the social uses of law in rural and urban areas. Relying on statistical inquiries and case studies, the methodology of his works copes with empirical objects like contractual negotiations, legal consciousness, legal expertise, production, and interpretation of rules at the local level. His studies particularly focus on the way local actors resort to courts. He is a co-editor-in-chief of the journal *Economie rurale*.

Ana Morais de Sá is Assistant Professor at Instituto Superior Técnico, Lisbon University where she teaches in spatial planning and urban management. Her research interests focuses on the relationship between land policies, land economics, land and property taxation, and the planning practice.

Nir Mualam is Assistant Professor in the faculty of Architecture and Town Planning, the Technion – Israel Institute of Technology. He litigated land use law cases for over a decade while working in local government. He specializes in municipal taxation, land use regulation, urban policy, and property law. His research interests include urban design, housing, heritage conservation, planning processes, and institutions.

Stéphane Nahrath is Full Professor of Political Science at the Swiss Graduate School of Public Administration (IDHEAP) of the University of Lausanne (Switzerland). His teaching, research, and publications relate to the analysis of environmental and land use planning policies, to urban politics and governance, as well as to the analysis of institutional resource regimes.

Barrie Needham holds a degree in economics from Cambridge University, England, and a PhD from the University of Nijmegen in the Netherlands. He moved to the Netherlands in 1978 and became a Professor of Spatial Planning at Nijmegen in 1994. Main research interests and publications are about the relationship between land and real estate on the one hand, and spatial planning on the other.

Sofija Nikolić is a PhD student at the Faculty of Law, University of Belgrade (Serbia), and she was teaching associate at the same faculty. She is a research assistant at the Faculty of Law, University of Bremen (Germany). Her research focuses on property law, agricultural law, housing law, and spatial planning.

Leif Norell is an expert on real estate valuation and law and economics. He was previously employed by the National Land Survey of Sweden and is currently working as a consultant.

Richard K. Norton is Professor in the Urban and Regional Planning Program and Professor in the Program in the Environment at the University of Michigan, U.S. He teaches and conducts research in the areas of planning law, sustainable development, and coastal area management. He currently serves as President of the International Academic Association on Planning, Law, and Property Rights.

Deborah Peel is Emeritus Professor of Planning at the University of Dundee and a Visiting Professor at Wageningen University. She is a co-author of *The Essential Guide to Planning Law: Decision-Making and Practice in the UK*, published by Policy Press.

Thomas Skuzinski, JD, PhD, is Assistant Professor of Urban Affairs and Planning in Virginia Tech's School of Public and International Affairs and a fellow with the Global Forum for Urban and Regional Resilience. He uses a sociological institutionalist lens to study the preferences and behaviors of local government political and administrative actors, especially about land use and resilience policies.

Tejo Spit is Full Professor in Urban and Regional Planning at Utrecht University, but also holds a position in the Land Use Planning Group of Wageningen University and Research. He specializes in land policy, planning methodology, infrastructure planning, and administrative aspects of spatial planning.

Edward J. Sullivan is a retired planning law attorney with 45 years of experience in the field. He teaches planning law at Portland State University, Lewis and Clark Law School, and Willamette University College of Law, and is the author of numerous articles on planning law in general and planning law in Oregon in general.

Wendy Tan is currently Assistant Professor of Infrastructure and Transportation Planning at the Department of Spatial Planning and Environment at the University of Groningen in the Netherlands. Her academic work combines her interest as an architect, urban designer, and planner by focusing on the implementation of land use and institutional perspective in planning processes.

Dan Tarlock is University Distinguished Professor Emeritus, Illinois Institute of Technology Chicago-Kent College of Law. His teaching and scholarship has concentrated on environmental, land use planning, and water resources management law.

Joost Tennekes is a scientific researcher at PBL Netherlands Environmental Assessment. His research interest is in institutional analysis of planning processes regarding urban development, publicly funded real estate, infrastructure, and climate adaptation.

Fabian Thiel is Interim Professor for construction law, real estate and property valuation at Frankfurt University of Applied Sciences and Associate Professor for geography at the Justus-Liebig-University in Giessen. He holds a MSc in Law, and BSc, MSc, PhD and habilitation in Geography. His main teaching and research interests include land and constitutional law, investment law, property valuation, land management, and geosystem analysis.

Erwin van der Krabben is Professor of Planning and Property Development at Radboud University (NL) and (part-time) Professor of Real Estate at the University of Ulster (NI). His research and publications focus on land policies, municipal finance, the interaction between planning and land and real estate markets, and property rights, while his work covers topics in these fields both in Europe and in Asia.

François-Xavier Viallon is a political scientist and research collaborator at the University of Lausanne. He teaches classes on public policies and land policy instruments in the technical university of Yverdon. His research interests are land use policy, natural resource management, property rights and public policies, and the commons.

Winrich Voß is Full Professor at Leibniz University Hannover (LUH) and holds the chair of Land and Real Estate Management. He teaches and researches in property valuation, property market issues in urban and rural development, international land policies, and sustainable land management. He is a board member of the European Academy of Land Use and Development (EALD) and Speaker of the LUH-Research Center Transdisciplinary Rural and Urban Spatial Transformation (TRUST).

Fabian Wenner, MSc, BSc, is a research and teaching associate at the Chair of Urban Development at Technical University of Munich's (TUM) Department of Architecture since 2014. He holds degrees kristin in Spatial Planning from TU Dortmund and Urban and Regional Planning Theory from LSE London. His research interests encompass urban economics, transport planning, as well as IT tools in planning.

Martin Wickel holds a professorship for Law and Administration at the HafenCity University Hamburg. His academic interests encompass planning law, building law, and environmental law including connections to administrative law, constitutional law, and the law of the European Union. He is Dean of the master's program Resource Efficiency in Architecture and Planning.

Index

For Product Safety Concerns and Information please contact our EU representative GPSR@taylorandfrancis.com Taylor & Francis Verlag GmbH, Kaufingerstraße 24, 80331 München, Germany